WILHELM REICH

Selected Writings

WILHELM REICH

SELECTED WRITINGS

AN INTRODUCTION TO ORGONOMY

New York

FARRAR, STRAUS AND CUDAHY

Published simultaneously in Canada by
Ambassador Books, Ltd., Toronto

Manufactured in the United States of America

Love, work and knowledge are the well-springs of our life. They should also govern it.

FOREWORD

This anthology of selected writings from the works of Wilhelm Reich was conceived as an introduction to Orgonomy, and it is presented without editorial comment or interpretation in the simple belief that those who seek knowledge must go to its source.

It has been difficult to make this selection. The vastness of Wilhelm Reich's scientific accomplishments has always created a problem of "too muchness." In this instance, the problem was principally one of what to omit—of how to satisfy the restrictions imposed by the limited space. It was hauntingly felt that to exclude any one piece of the material already published might deprive the reader of a rare opportunity to observe the historical development of the science of Orgonomy, and to follow this development as evidence of the consistent application of the functional method of thinking. Thus, the assumption of responsibility for making an adequate selection was not lightly undertaken. I would like to thank Chester M. Raphael, M.D. and Elsworth F. Baker, M.D. for their valuable help in the preparation of this volume.

Among the great wealth of excluded material is Wilhelm Reich's *Last Will and Testament*, signed three days before his imprisonment on March 11, 1957. The contents of this document are generally unknown, and this fact has helped to create confusion among those who wish to learn of his work, and anxiety in others who are concerned about its protection. Therefore, in order to clarify and to reassure, I wish to make public the basic tenets of this *Will*.

With the exception of a few specific bequests, Wilhelm Reich gave his entire estate to a Trust Fund to be held and administered under the name of the Wilhelm Reich Infant Trust Fund for the following uses and purposes.

1. To safeguard the truth about my life and work against distortion and slander after my death. . . .

In order to enable the future student of the PRIMORDIAL COSMIC ENERGY OCEAN, THE LIFE ENERGY discovered and developed by me, to obtain a true picture of my accomplishments, mistakes, wrong assumptions, pioneering basic trends, my private life, my childhood, etc., I hereby direct that under no circumstances and under no pretext whatsoever shall any of the documents, manuscripts or diaries, found in my library among the archives or anywhere else be altered, omitted, destroyed, added to or falsified in any other imaginable way. The tendency of man, born from fear, to 'get along with his fellow man' at any price, and to hide unpleasant matters is overpoweringly strong. To guard against this trend, disastrous to historical truth, my study including the library and archives shall be sealed right after my death by the proper legal authorities and no one shall be permitted to look into my papers until my Trustee, hereinafter named, is duly appointed and qualified and takes control and custody thereof.

These documents are of crucial importance to the future of newborn generations. There are many emotionally sick people who will try to damage my reputation regardless of what happens to infants, if only their personal lives would remain hidden in the darkness of a forsaken age of the Stalins and Hitlers.

I therefore direct my Trustee and his successors that nothing whatsoever must be changed in any of the documents and that they should be put away and stored for 50 years to secure their safety from destruction and falsification by anyone interested in the falsification and destruction of historical truth.

These directives are established by me solely for the *preservation of documented truth as I lived it during my lifetime.*

2. To operate and maintain the property at Orgonon under the name and style of the Wilhelm Reich Museum . . . in order to preserve some of the atmosphere in which the Discovery of the Life Energy has taken place over the decades.

3. I have throughout all of my lifetime loved infants and children and adolescents, and I also was always loved and understood by them. Infants used to smile at me because I had deep contact with them and children of two or three very often used to become thoughtful and serious when they looked at me. This was one of the great happy privileges of my life, and I want to express in some manner my thanks for that love bestowed upon me by my little friends. May Fate and the great Ocean of Living Energy, from whence they came and into which they must return sooner or later, bless them with happiness and contentment and freedom during their life times. I hope to have contributed my good share to their future happiness. . . .

. . . all income, profits or proceeds due me and the Trust from royalties on tools originating in my discoveries shall be devoted to the care of infants everywhere, towards legal security of infants, children and adolescents in emotional, social, parental, medical, legal, educational, professional or other distress. Part of the proceeds may be used for basic orgonomic research.

The Wilhelm Reich Infant Trust Fund shall be "mainly devoted and safely directed" to this end.

Mary Boyd Higgins, *Trustee*

New York, 1960

CONTENTS

WILHELM REICH

Selected Writings

BIOGRAPHICAL NOTE

Wilhelm Reich was born on March 24, 1897, in the German-Ukranian part of Austria, as the son of a well-to-do farmer. His mother-language was German, and until 1938 Wilhelm Reich (hereafter WR) was an Austrian citizen.

Although he was taught the Old Testament as well as the New from the standpoint of scientific interest, WR had no religious education and adhered to no religious creed or political party. His early education (1903-7) was as a private student. He passed his examinations at an Austro-German public school and attended a German high school between 1907 and 1915, preparing for natural sciences. He graduated in 1915 with *"Stimmeneinhelligkeit."*

WR's interest in biology and natural science was stimulated early by the life on the farm, close to agriculture and cattle-farming and breeding in which he took part every summer and during the harvest. Between his 8th and 12th years, he had his own collection and breeding laboratory of butterflies, insects and plants under the guidance of a private teacher. The natural life functions, including the sexual function, were familiar to him as far back as he could remember, and this may well have determined his later strong inclination, as a bio-psychiatrist, toward the biological foundation of the emotional life of man, and also his biophysical discoveries in the fields of medicine and biology, as well as education.

This Biographical Note, and the material on the succeeding pages, consisting of the Scientific Development of Wilhelm Reich, Glossary and Prefatory Note, are taken from *Bibliography on Orgonomy*, 1953. The Biographical Note has been slightly changed and brought up to date. Scientific Development has been brought up to date and the wording but not the meaning of the Prefatory Note has been changed slightly.

After the death of his father in 1914, WR, then 17, directed the farm work quite on his own, without interrupting his studies, until the war disaster put an end to this work and destroyed all property in 1915. He was in the Austrian Army from 1915 to 1918 (a lieutenant from 1916 to 1918) and was at the Italian front three times.

In 1918, WR entered the Medical School of the University of Vienna, earning his living and paying his way through school by tutoring fellow students in pre-medical subjects. As a war veteran, he was permitted to complete the 6 year course in 4 years, and he passed the 18 Rigorosa in 18 medical subjects and received "excellent" ("ausgezeichnet") in all the pre-medical subjects. He was graduated and obtained the M.D. degree in July, 1922.

During his last year of medical school, WR took postgraduate work in Internal Medicine at the University Clinics of Ortner and Chvostek at University Hospital, Vienna. He continued his postgraduate education in Neuro-Psychiatry for two years (1922-24) at the Neurological and Psychiatric University Clinic under Professor Wagner-Jauregg, and worked one year in the disturbed wards under Paul Schilder. His postgraduate study also included attendance at polyclinical work in hypnosis and suggestive therapy at the same University Clinic and special courses and lectures in biology at the University of Vienna. Also, while still in medical school, in October 1920, WR attained membership in the Vienna Psychoanalytic Society, then under Professor Sigmund Freud.

WR began psychoanalytic and psychiatric private practice in 1922. By 1933, the demands of work in orgone energy research required the termination of private practice.

WR was First Clinical Assistant at Freud's Psychoanalytic Polyclinic in Vienna (under the directorship of Dr. Edward Hitschmann) from its foundation in 1922 until 1928; Vice-Director of the Polyclinic, 1928-1930, and Director of the Seminar for Psychoanalytic Therapy at the same institution, 1924-1930. As a member of the faculty of the Psychoanalytic

Institute in Vienna, 1924-1930, WR gave lectures on clinical subjects and bio-psychiatric theory. He did research in the social causation of the neurosis at the Polyclinic from 1924, and at mental hygiene consultation centers in various districts in Vienna (*Sozialistische Gesellschaft fuer Sexualberatung und Sexualforschung*); centers which he founded and led from 1928 through 1930. He continued his mental hygiene work in Berlin, 1930-1933, as lecturer at the Psychoanalytic Clinic and at the Worker's College, and as head physician in mental hygiene centers of various cultural organizations in Berlin and other German cities. In the winter of 1933, Hitler assumed complete power and WR was forced to leave Germany.

Between 1934 and 1939, WR lectured and did research in *orgone biophysics* at the Psychological Institute of the University of Oslo, Norway.

In 1939, having received an invitation from the representative of American Psychosomatic Medicine, Theodore P. Wolfe, M.D., Wilhelm Reich came to the United States and transferred the Orgone Energy Laboratory to Forest Hills, N.Y. During the years from 1939 to 1941, he was Associate Professor of Medical Psychology at the New School for Social Research in New York City, giving lectures on orgone biophysics.

The *Orgone Institute* was founded by WR in 1942 in New York, and in the same year over 200 acres of land were acquired in Maine and called "*Orgonon,*" the future home of *Orgonomy,* the *Science of the Life Energy.* The Wilhelm Reich Foundation was founded in Maine, 1949, by students and friends, to preserve the Archives of WR and to secure the future of his discovery of the Cosmic Orgone Energy.

In 1954, the Federal Food and Drug Administration initiated a complaint for an injunction against Wilhelm Reich and the Wilhelm Reich Foundation, attacking specifically and clearly designed to discredit Wilhelm Reich's monumental discovery of the Cosmic Life Energy—Orgone Energy. WR refused to be forced into court as a "defendant" in matters of basic natural research, and he explained his position in a "Response" addressed to the United States District Judge for the District of Maine.

On March 19th, a Decree of Injunction was issued *on default.* *

Wilhelm Reich was subsequently accused of criminal contempt in disobeying this injunction and, following a jury trial in May, 1956 in which his plea was "not guilty," he was sentenced to two years imprisonment. The Foundation was fined $10,000, and an Orgonomic physician was sentenced to one year and a day in prison.

On November 3, 1957, Wilhelm Reich died in the Federal Penitentiary at Lewisburg, Pa.

---

* The Decree of Injunction and WR's "Response" to the Complaint for Injunction are reprinted in the Appendix of this volume.

SCIENTIFIC DEVELOPMENT OF WILHELM REICH

Wilhelm Reich's basic scientific discoveries include the following: Orgasm theory and technique of Character-Analysis (1923-34); Respiratory block and muscular armor (1928-34); Sex-economic self-regulation of *primary* natural drives in their distinction from *secondary, perverted* drives (1928-34); The role of irrationalism and human sex-economy in the origin of dictatorship of all political denominations (1930-34); The orgasm reflex (1934); The bio-electrical nature of sexuality and anxiety (1935-36); Orgone energy vesicles, BIONS, (1936-39); Origin of the cancer cell from bionously disintegrated animal tissue, and the organization of protozoa from bionously disintegrated moss and grass (1936-39); T-bacilli in sarcoma (1937); Discovery of the bioenergy (Orgone Energy) in SAPA Bions (1939), in the atmosphere (1940); Invention of the Orgone Energy Accumulator (1940); and the Orgone Energy Field Meter (1944); Experimental Orgone Therapy of the Cancer Biopathy (1940-45); Experimental investigation of primary biogenesis (Experiment XX, 1945); Method of Orgonomic Functionalism (1945); Emotional Plague of man as a disease of the bio-energetic equilibrium (1947); Orgonometric equations (1949-50); Hypothesis of cosmic superimposition of two orgone energy streams as the basis of hurricanes and galaxy formation (1951); Antinuclear radiation effects of Orgone Energy (The Oranur Experiment, First Report, 1947-51); Discovery of DOR (deadly orgone energy) and identification of its properties including a specific toxicity (DOR sickness) (1951-52); Identification of Melanor, Orite, Brownite and Orene and initial steps toward preatomic chemistry (1951-54); Use of "reversed" orgonomic potential in removing DOR from the atmosphere in cloudbusting and weather control (1952-55); Theory of desert formation in nature and in man (the emotional desert) and demonstration of reversibility (Orop Desert Ea and the Medical DOR-Buster) (1954-55); Theory of disease based on DOR accumulation in the tissues (1954-55); Equations of gravity and anti-gravity (1950-57); Development and practical application of Social Psychiatry (1951-57).

GLOSSARY

A new scientific discipline must employ new terms if old ones are inapplicable. Orgonomy introduced the following terms:

ANORGONIA. The condition of diminished or lacking orgonity (q.v.).

ARMOR. *See* character armor, muscular armor.

BIONS. Energy vesicles representing transitional stages between non-living and living substance. They constantly form in nature by a process of disintegration of inorganic and organic matter, which process it has been possible to reproduce experimentally. They are charged with orgone energy (q.v.), i.e., *Life Energy* and may develop into protozoa and bacteria.

CHARACTER. An individual's typical structure, his stereotype manner of acting and reacting. The orgonomic concept of character is functional and biological, and not a static, psychological or moralistic concept.

CHARACTER-ANALYSIS. Originally a modification of the customary psychoanalytic technique of symptom analysis, by the inclusion of the *character* and *character resistance* into the therapeutic process. However, the discovery of the *muscular armor* necessitated the development of a new technique, namely vegetotherapy. The later discovery of *organismic orgone energy* ("*bioenergy*") and the concentration of atmospheric orgone energy with an orgone energy accumulator necessitated the further development of character-analytic vegetotherapy into an inclusive, biophysical *orgone* therapy. (*See* physical and psychiatric orgone therapy.)

9

CHARACTER ARMOR. The sum total of typical character attitudes, which an individual develops as a blocking against his emotional excitations, resulting in rigidity of the body, lack of emotional contact, "deadness." Functionally identical with the muscular armor.

CHARACTER, GENITAL. The un-neurotic character structure, which does not suffer from sexual stasis and, therefore, is capable of natural self-regulation on the basis of orgastic potency.

CHARACTER, NEUROTIC. The character which, due to chronic bioenergetic stasis operates according to the principle of compulsive moral regulation.

EMOTIONAL PLAGUE. The neurotic character in destructive action on the social scene.

MUSCULAR ARMOR. The sum total of the muscular attitudes (chronic muscular spasms) which an individual develops as a block against the breakthrough of emotions and organ sensations, in particular anxiety, rage, and sexual excitation.

ORGASM. The unitary involuntary *convulsion of the total organism* at the acme of the genital embrace. This reflex, because of its *involuntary* character and the prevailing orgasm anxiety, is blocked in most humans of civilizations which suppress infantile and adolescent genitality.

ORGASTIC IMPOTENCE. The absence of orgastic potency. It is the most important characteristic of the average human of today, and—by damming up biological (orgone) energy in the organism—provides the source of energy for all kinds of biopathic symptoms and social irrationalism.

ORGASTIC POTENCY. Essentially, the *capacity for complete surrender to the involuntary convulsion* of the organism and *complete discharge* of the excitation at the acme of the genital embrace. It is always lacking in neurotic individuals. It presupposes the presence or establishment of the genital character, i.e. absence of a pathological character armor and muscular armor. Orgastic potency is usually not distinguished from erective and ejaculative potency, both of which are only prerequisites of orgastic potency.

ORGONE ENERGY. Primordial Cosmic Energy; universally present and demonstrable visually, thermically, electroscopically and by means of Geiger-Mueller counters. In the living organism: *Bio-energy, Life Energy.* Discovered by Wilhelm Reich between 1936 and 1940.

ORANUR denotes orgone energy in a state of excitation induced by nuclear energy. (DOR denotes *Deadly OR* energy.)

ORGONE THERAPY.

Physical Orgone Therapy: Application of physical orgone energy concentrated in an orgone energy accumulator to increase the natural bio-energetic resistance of the organism against disease.

Psychiatric Orgone Therapy: Mobilization of the orgone energy in the organism, i.e. the liberation of biophysical emotions from muscular and character armorings with the goal of establishing, if possible, orgastic potency.

ORGONITY. The condition of containing orgone energy; the quantity of orgone energy contained.

ORGONOMETRY. Quantitative orgonomic research.

ORGONOMIC ("ENERGETIC") FUNCTIONALISM. The functional thought technique which guides clinical and experimental orgone research. The guiding principle is that of the *identity of variations in their* common functioning principle (CFP). This thought technique grew in the course of the study of human character formation and led to the discovery of the *functional* organismic and cosmic orgone energy, thereby proving itself to be the correct mirroring of both living and non-living basic natural processes.

ORGONOMY. The natural science of the cosmic orgone energy.

ORGONOTIC. Qualities concerning the orgonity of a system or a condition.

SEX-ECONOMY. The body of knowledge within Orgonomy which deals with the economy of the biological (orgone) energy in the organism, with its *energy household.*

STASIS. The damming-up of Life Energy in the organism, thus the source of energy for biopathy and irrationalism.

STASIS ANXIETY. The anxiety caused by the stasis of sexual energy in the center of the organism when its peripheral orgastic discharge is inhibited.

STASIS NEUROSIS. All somatic disturbances which are the immediate result of the stasis of sexual energy, with stasis anxiety at its core.

WORK DEMOCRACY. The functioning of the natural and intrinsically rational work relationships between human beings. The concept of work democracy represents the established *reality* (not the ideology) of these relationships which, though usually distorted because of prevailing armoring and irrational political ideologies, are nevertheless at the basis of all social achievement.

PREFATORY NOTE

Since the appearance of the first works of Wilhelm Reich in 1921, the old, essentially sexological and psychologically oriented sex-economy has developed into the science of the *cosmic Orgone Energy, ORGONOMY.* This development was accompanied by a complicated branching-out and ramification of the science of the Living which today one can follow systematically only with difficulty. One of the reasons for this is the fact that the publications, brought out over a time span of more than thirty years, were not only printed in many different publishing houses and organs, but also, because of the social catastrophes, the original publications are scattered all over Europe and the United States, and are often difficult to obtain. Still, in spite of everything, the subject of the work of Wilhelm Reich has remained a functional and logical whole. Whoever compares the first endeavor toward a biophysical formulation of instinctual processes in "Zur Trieb-Energetik" (1923) with the latest orgonomic work, will easily discover the red thread which, in a work period of a third of a century, runs through all the clinical, experimental, and theoretical labors: *The theme of the bio-energetic function of excitability and motility of living substance.*

It has now been shown in many ways that the readers of the publications are not oriented about the so very important precursors in the development of orgonomy. This lack leads to many misunderstandings about the nature and function of this new and young science. It has further been shown that very many friends of orgonomy see in the transition of Wilhelm

Reich's work from psychiatry to the natural-scientific mastery
of the riddle of living substance a breach that seems illogical.
In reality there is no breach. On the contrary: Wilhelm Reich
came *from natural science* to psychiatry. His labors on the
problem of "instinctual energy" form from the very beginning
(1920) the core of his *natural-scientific* conception of psychic
phenomena, from which gradually the research method of
Orgonomic Functionalism resulted. This method has led to the
discovery of the Cosmic Orgone Energy, and in this way has
subsequently demonstrated the correctness of the first tendencies toward a natural-scientific, i.e., *bioenergetic* formulation
of the basic questions of psychiatry. In this connection, the
sociological works are not less important than the clinical ones.
The *social* existence of the human animal is indeed, seen bio-
energetically, a small summit on the gigantic mountain of his
biological existence. Only in the light of this disparity in significance between the social and biological existence of the
human animal does the knowledge of orgonomy clearly come
into focus, revealing that the human race has succumbed for
several thousands of years to a tragic development. Through
his bodily armoring, the human animal has separated himself
from his biological origin, and, with the biological also from
his cosmic origin, and has developed an instinctual structure
that functions in an essentially irrational way. The result is the
present chaos of our civilization, which man today can meet
only with anxiety and horror.

The key to the tragedy of the human animal lies *outside* his
social and psychological ways of thinking and being. For both
his ideas and social practices are themselves a result of his
biological "original sin," a term one can apply with good reason
to the biological deterioration of the human animal.

To the deadly character of the social catastrophes of the
human animal corresponds the deep earnestness of the orgonomic realm of problems, and the critical seriousness of the
biological revolution of our times.

The bibliography of publications appended to this volume

has as its goal the making accessible to students and workers in the realms of the science of man at large, the simple lines of Wilhelm Reich's research. This compilation is not complete. The bibliography does not contain the complicated and detailed discussions, with friend and foe, of the life function; nor does it contain books and articles in the fields of literature, psychiatry, psychoanalysis, education, sociology, natural philosophy and natural science which were clearly influenced by orgonomic thinking since the early 1920's, without mentioning specifically the source of orgonomic knowledge. Still, as a start this biblography will fulfill its purpose: It will transmit to the student the clear impression that through all the complexities of the social, psychological, and biological sciences on the human animal there runs a simple red thread. To grasp this thread is a crucial task of our age.

I. INTRODUCTION

What is the most difficult of all?
What seems the easiest to you:
To see with your eyes
What lies before your eyes.—GOETHE

THE WORKSHOP OF ORGONOMIC FUNCTIONALISM

The cosmic orgone energy was discovered through the consistent application of the functional method of thinking. We began with methodical, strictly controlled thought processes which led from one fact to another. Thus, over a period of about 25 years, seemingly unrelated facts knitted together to form a unitary picture of living functioning, which today, 1949, as the still incomplete scientific structure of orgonomy, is submitted to the judgment of the world. It is therefore necessary to describe the "functional thought technique."

It is advantageous to permit the earnest student of natural science not only to see the product, but also to initiate him into the *secrets of the workshop* where, through strenuous exertion, the product is formed. It is a mistake in scientific exchange to present only the beautifully polished and objection-free results, as in an art exhibit. Such a display of finished products alone presents many disadvantages as well as advantages for their creator as well as for their user. The creator will all too easily be inclined to show productions complete and without error,

From *Ether, God and Devil*, 1949. (A detailed bibliography appears in the Appendix.)

and to conceal gaps, uncertainties, and disharmonious contradictions in his scientific knowledge. In doing so, he does an
injustice to the feeling for the genuine process of scientific
research. The user of the product will have no realization of
the severity and intensity of the demands placed on the scientific researcher, if he is to reveal and describe riddles of nature
practically. He will never learn how to think and speak along
with the pioneer scientist. Only the rare automobile driver has
a correct perception of the human exertions, of the complexity
of intellectual and manual labor necessary for the production
of an automobile. Our world would look better if the consumers
of work knew more about the *process* of work and the life of
working people, if they did not pluck so carelessly the fruits
of others' labor.

In the case of orgonomy, the presentation of a part of the
laboratory work-method is especially called for. The greatest
difficulty in grasping the orgone theory lies in the fact that the
discovery of the orgone has solved *too many* and *too great*
problems all at once: the biological basis of psychic diseases,
biogenesis and with that the cancer biopathy, the ether, the
cosmic yearning of the human animal, a new physical energy,
etc. It was always *too much* that came up and presented itself
in my workshop: an overabundance in facts, new connections,
corrections of old and erroneous views, in the linkings of
separate, specialized branches of natural-scientific research. As
a consequence, I often had to defend myself against the reproach that I did not respect my proper scientific boundaries,
that I had undertaken *"Too Much At Once."* I had not undertaken too much, and I was not scientifically immodest. No one
has felt the TOO-MUCHNESS as painfully as myself. I have not
gone after the facts, but the facts and connections streamed to
me. I had to take pains to meet them attentively and to arrange
them systematically. In so doing, many, very many facts of
great significance were lost; others could not be comprehended.
Still the vital point and basic principle in the discovery of the
orgone energy seem firmly established and so arranged that

others can continue to work on the structure I could not complete. The plethora of new facts and connections, especially concerning the relationship of the human animal to his universe, can be explained by a very simple analogy:

Did Columbus discover New York, or Chicago, the fisheries in Maine, the plantations in the South, the great water works or the natural treasures on the West coast of America? He did not discover, did not build or work out all this in detail. He only discovered a part of a seacoast that up to that time was unknown to European man. The discovery of the barren coastal stretch on the Atlantic Ocean was the key to everything that in the course of a few centuries has become "North America." Columbus's accomplishment did not lie in the construction of America, but in the mastery of apparently insurmountable prejudices and difficulties which blocked his way in the preparation of his sea journey, in its execution, and in the landing on strange and dangerous shores.

The discovery of the cosmic energy succeeded in a similar fashion. I have in reality made only one SINGLE discovery: THE FUNCTION OF THE ORGASTIC PLASMA CONTRACTION. It represents the coastal stretch from which everything else has developed. The mastery of the human prejudice against concerning oneself with the biophysical emotion which moves man most deeply was far more difficult than the comparatively simple observation of the bion, or the equally simple and self-evident fact that the cancer biopathy is rooted in the general shrinking and disintegration of the life apparatus.

"What is the most difficult of all? What seems the easiest to you: To see with your eyes what lies before your eyes," said Goethe.

What has always astonished me was not that the orgone existed and functioned, but that man, in the course of 20 centuries, so thoroughly overlooked it or argued it away whenever it was observed and described by individual researchers who were close to life. In *one* respect only is the discovery of the orgone different from the discovery of America: orgone energy functions in all men and before everyone's eyes. America had first to be reached.

A very essential part of the work in my workshop now consisted in trying to understand why humanity in general and the natural scientist in particular were frightened away from so basic a phenomenon as the orgastic contraction. A further workshop task, one which was accompanied with much abuse and slander, lay in observing, tracing, understanding, and surviving the bitter hatred that was placed in the way of my orgasm research *by friend and enemy*. I firmly believe that biogenesis, the ether question, living functioning, and "human nature" would long since have been mastered by many scientific workers, if these basic problems of natural science had not had *one*, and *only one* avenue of approach: the problem of the orgastic plasma contraction.

When I succeeded, in spite of all hindrances and enmities, in concentrating on this one problem for three decades, in mastering it, in orienting myself in it as a *basic* natural function, I began to notice that I had stepped beyond the intellectual framework of the present-day human character structure and, with that, the civilization of the last 5,000 years. Without intending to, I found myself *outside* of its boundaries. I realized that for this reason the world would not understand me, even if I were to bring forth the simplest and most easily verified facts and connections. *I found myself in a new and different realm of thought* which I had to explore thoroughly before I could go further. This process of finding my orientation in the functional realm of thought, in contrast to the mechanistic-mystical thinking of patriarchal civilization, claimed some 14 years, from about 1932 to the writing of this treatise, 1946-47.

The reproach is often raised against my writings that they are much too concentrated, and therefore force the reader to the most intense reflection. One would like, so they say, to enjoy an important book in the same fashion as one enjoys a beautiful landscape riding along slowly in a comfortable car.

One would prefer not to hasten at a furious speed in a straight line toward a determined goal.

I admit that I could have presented *The Function of the Orgasm* in 1,000 instead of 300 pages, and the orgone therapy of the cancer biopathy in 500 instead of 100 pages. I admit further that I have never made the effort to familiarize the reader with the essence of my method of thinking and doing research which provides the soil for the harvest of orgonomy. That has undoubtedly caused much harm. I can advance as my apology the fact that I have opened up several scientific realms in the course of the past decades; these I had first of all to present in neat, synoptical form, in order to keep step with the development of my research. I know that I have built nothing more than foundations and scaffolding, that in many places the building lacks windows, doors and important fixtures, and that as yet it offers no comfortable armchairs.

I therefore plead to have the *pioneer* character of this basically *different kind* of research considered my justification. I had to gather my scientific treasures *quickly*, wherever and however I found them; this happened in the short periods between six changes of domicile which were imposed on me partly by "peaceful" and partly by the most tumultuous social conditions. I had to build up my means of livelihood again and again, first 1930 in Germany, then 1933 in Copenhagen, 1934 in Sweden and Norway, 1939 in America. Looking back, I wonder how it was possible that I succeeded in acquiring even the essentials. I lived and worked for almost two decades "on the run," so to speak. All this taken together made a comfortable atmosphere impossible; and without a comfortable and assured academic atmosphere it is not possible to give leisurely, broad presentations of discoveries. Another reproach, that I unnecessarily provoked the public through the use of the word "orgasm" in the title of a book, I must reject. There is not the slightest reason for being ashamed of this function. Whoever feels offended when it is mentioned certainly need not read any further. But the rest of us refuse to have any barriers dictated to us in our scientific work.

When I started to write the present manuscript, I undertook to make up for in breadth and leisureliness of presentation what I had to refrain from doing for so long a time. I hope I will now be spared the reproach that I have taken my research "too seriously" because I now give it "so much" space.

Since everything in nature knits together in one way or another, the theme of "orgonomic functionalism" is practically inexhaustible. My natural-scientific interests and studies blended the humanistic and scientific accomplishments of the 19th and early 20th century into the living tool that later, as "orgonomic functionalism," took on useful and applicable form. Although functional thinking is here described systematically for the first time, it was, nevertheless, applied by many researchers, more or less consciously, before, in the form of *orgonomy*, it finally overcame the rigid barriers in natural science. I would like now to mention a few of the most important names to whose bearers I am greatly indebted: De Coster, Dostoievski, Albert Lange, Friedrich Nietzsche, Lewis Morgan, Charles Darwin, Friedrich Engels, Semon, Bergson, Freud, Malinowski. If I said earlier that I had found myself in a new realm of thought, one must not take that to mean that orgonomic functionalism had been "finished" and had only been waiting for me; no more does it mean that I simply appropriated the methodology of Bergson or Engels and applied it smoothly to my own realm of work. The formulation of the thought technique was itself a work-accomplishment which *had* to be supplied in the struggle of my daily activities as physician and researcher against the mechanistic *and* the mystical explanations of the living. Thus, I have not created some kind of a new philosophy which, following or approximating other philosophies of life, would attempt to bring the living closer to human comprehension. *No, this is not a philosophy*, as many of my friends believe. *On the contrary, it is a tool of thinking that one must learn to use if one wishes to explore and deal with the living.* Orgonomic functionalism is no luxury item that one may use or discard as one pleases. It joins together the laws of thinking and the perceptual functions which one must master if one wants children and adolescents to grow up in a *life-affirmative manner* in this world, if one wishes to bring the human animal again into harmony with his natural biology and with surrounding nature. One may be against such a goal for philosophic or religious reasons. One may, of course, as a "pure philosopher" declare that the "unity of nature and culture" is impossible or harmful or unethical or unimportant. But no one may today come out and assert that the splitting up of the human animal into a cultural and a private, an official and a personal existence, into a "preserver of higher values" and "an orgonotic energy system," does *not* undermine his health in the truest sense of the word, does *not* cripple his intelligence, does *not* destroy his *joie de vivre*, does *not* paralyze his initiative, does *not* plunge his society again and again into chaos. The protection of the living demands functional thinking in opposition to mechanism and mysticism as surely as the protection of traffic demands good brakes and a faultlessly working signal-apparatus.

I would like to declare myself in favor of the most rigorous scientific *order of freedom.* It is not a question of philosophy or ethics, but of the protection of social functioning, e.g., whether a child of four experiences his first genital excitations with or without anxiety. A doctor, educator, or social administrator can have only *one* and not five explanations for the sadistic and pornographic phantasies which a boy or girl entering puberty develops under the pressure of pornographic moralism. It is not a question of philosophical possibilities, but of social and personal *necessities* to prevent, by all means, thousands of women from perishing from cancer of the uterus because they were brought up in abstinence, because thousands of cancer researchers either do not want to know this, or out of social anxiety do not express themselves. It is a murderous philosophy which again and again advocates the suppression of living functioning in children and adolescents.

If one searches for the origins and wide ramifications of the official ideology, especially as it refers to questions of the personal life of the masses, one arrives again and again at ancient, classical philosophies concerning life, the "state," "absolute values," the "world spirit," etc. These are taken over in an age which, as a consequence of these "harmless" philosophies, has degenerated chaotically, an age in which the human animal has lost his orientation and his self-esteem, and has senselessly thrown away his life. Thus, *it is not a question of philosophies, but of practical, decisive tools in the formation of human existence; it is a question of the choice between good and bad tools* in the reconstruction and reorganization of human society.

A tool alone cannot accomplish work. *Living* men are needed who utilize tools in order to master nature. Thus it is the *human character structure* which determines how the tool is to be shaped and what purpose it is to serve.

The armored, *mechanistically rigid human* thinks mechanistically, produces mechanistic tools, and forms a mechanistic concept of nature.

The armored human, who senses his orgonotic bodily excitations in spite of his biological armoring, but does not understand them, is the *mystical person*. He is not interested in "material," but in "spiritual" things. He forms a mystical, supernatural concept of nature.

And so the mechanistic, like the mystical human being, stands within the boundaries of his civilization which is ruled by a contradictory and murderous mixture of machines and gods. This civilization forms the mechanistic-mystical structures of men, and the mechanistic-mystical character structures reproduce the machine-mystical civilization. Mechanists as well as mystics find themselves *within* the given framework of mechanico-mystically conditioned civilization. They cannot grasp the basic problems of this civilization since their thinking and their world picture correspond exactly to that very condition which they reflect and perpetually reproduce. One need only think of the murderous civil war between the Hindus and Mohammedans following the division of India to realize the disastrous influence of mysticism. And one need only think of the "Age of the Atomic Bomb" to understand what mechanistic civilization is.

Orgonomic functionalism stands from the very start outside the framework of a mechanistic-mystical civilization. It did not arise, say, out of the need "to bury" this civilization. Thus it is not intentionally revolutionary. Orgonomic functionalism represents the way of thinking of the *living human who is unarmored* and therefore in contact with nature inside and outside himself. *The living human animal behaves like any animal, functionally; the armored human behaves mechanistically and mystically. Orgonomic functionalism is a living expression of the unarmored human being, his working tool with which he comprehends nature.* This method of thinking and working will be a progressive power of social development only because it OBSERVES and CRITICIZES MECHANISTIC-MYSTICAL CIVILIZATION FROM THE STANDPOINT OF THE NATURAL LAWS OF THE LIVING, and not from the narrow view of state, church, economy, culture, etc.

Since, today, within the intellectual framework of mechanistic-mystical character structures, the living is misunderstood, mishandled, feared, and often persecuted, it is clear that orgonomic functionalism finds itself outside the framework of mechanistic civilization. Where it finds itself within the framework, it must step out again if it wishes to function. And "to function" means here nothing else than *to investigate, understand, and protect the living as a natural power.* It was an important insight of orgone biophysics, from its very first beginnings, that the living simply functions, that living functioning is the essence of life and that it has no "purpose" or "meaning" beyond that. The search after a meaningful purpose of life grows out of the armoring of the human organism which obliterates living functioning and replaces it with rigid formulae. The living being who is unarmored does not seek a meaning or goal of his existence for the simple reason that he functions spontaneously—without a "thou must"—meaningfully and purposefully.

The connections between methods of thinking, character structures, and social order are simple and logical. They explain why it is that so far all men who comprehended and advocated the living in one form or another found themselves always *outside* the ways of thinking which have governed human society for thousands of years; for this reason, they have so often suffered and perished. And where they appear to have penetrated, it can be regularly shown that the armored bearers of mechanistic civilization, every time, robbed the living of the individual qualities of its teaching and, by watering it down or by "correcting" it, incorporated it again into the old framework of thought. Functional thinking finds itself outside the framework of our civilization because the living itself is outside of it, because it is not investigated but misunderstood and feared.

II. THE ORGASM THEORY

THE DEVELOPMENT OF THE ORGASM THEORY

FIRST EXPERIENCES

In December, 1920, Freud referred a young student to me who was suffering from compulsive rumination, compulsive counting, compulsive anal phantasies, excessive masturbation and severe neurasthenic symptoms, such as headaches and pains in the back, lack of concentration, and nausea. The compulsive rumination immediately turned into compulsive associating. It looked pretty hopeless. After some time, an incest phantasy broke through, and for the first time the patient masturbated *with satisfaction*. With that, all the symptoms disappeared suddenly. In the course of a week they gradually returned. When he masturbated a second time, the symptoms disappeared again, only to return again after a short time. This was repeated for several weeks. Finally it was possible to analyze his guilt feelings about masturbation and to correct some practices and attitudes which interfered with complete gratification. After that, his condition improved visibly. After nine months of treatment, he was discharged, considerably improved, and able to work. He kept in touch with me for over six years; he married and remained well.

At the same time, I treated a waiter who suffered from complete lack of erection. The treatment ran smoothly. In the

From *The Function of the Orgasm*, vol. I of *The Discovery of the Orgone*, 1948.

third year, the unequivocal reconstruction of the "primal scene" was possible. When he was about two years old, his mother had another child, and he was able to watch the delivery from the next room. He received the vivid impression of a big bloody hole between his mother's legs. All that remained in his consciousness of this impression was a feeling of *"emptiness"* in his own genitals. According to psychoanalytic knowledge of that time, I connected the lack of erection merely with the traumatic impression of the "castrated" female genital. That was doubtless correct. But not until a few years ago did I begin to give closer attention to and to understand the genital "feeling of emptiness" in my patients. It corresponds to the *withdrawal of biological energy from the genital.* At that time, I misjudged the general attitude of this patient. He was quiet, placid, "good," doing everything that was asked of him. He never got upset. In the course of three years' treatment, he *never* got angry or critical. That is, according to the concepts of that time, he was a "well integrated," thoroughly "adjusted" character, with only one serious symptom ("monosymptomatic neurosis"). I reported the case in the technical seminar, and earned praise for the correct elucidation of the traumatic primal scene. His symptom, lack of erection, was fully explained—theoretically. As the patient was industrious and "adjusted to reality," none of us was struck by the fact that just his lack of emotionality, his complete imperturbability, was *the* pathological characterological soil on which his erective impotence could persist. My older colleagues considered my analytic work complete and correct. But on leaving the meeting I felt dissatisfied. If everything was as it should be, why did the impotence fail to budge? Obviously, here was a gap that none of us understood. A few months later I discharged the patient, uncured. He took it as stoically as he had taken everything else all this time. The consideration of this patient impressed on me the important character-analytic concept of *"emotional block"* (*"Affektsperre"*). I had thus hit upon the highly important connection between the prevalent rigid character structure of today and genital "deadness."

This was the period when psychoanalytic treatment was beginning to take more and more time. When I started out, an analysis of six months was considered long. In 1923, a year was considered a matter of course. The view even gained ground that two or more years would not be bad, considering the fact that neuroses were very complicated and serious disturbances. Freud had written his famous "History of an infantile neurosis" on the basis of a case analyzed for five years; true, he had obtained from it the knowledge of a whole infantile world. But the psychoanalysts were making a virtue out of necessity. Abraham contended that for an understanding of a chronic depression years were needed; that the "passive technique" was the only correct one. Among themselves, colleagues joked about the temptation to sleep during analytic hours; if a patient did not produce any associations for hours on end, one had to smoke a lot to keep awake. Some analysts even derived high-sounding theories from this: If the patient kept silent, "perfect technique" required equal silence on the part of the analyst, for hours and weeks. I tried myself to follow this "technique." But nothing came of it; patients only developed a profound helplessness, a bad conscience, and thus became stubborn. Jokes, like that of the analyst who, in the course of a session, awoke out of a deep sleep and found the couch empty, did not improve matters; nor did profound explanations to the effect that there was no harm in the analyst falling asleep, inasmuch as his unconscious dutifully kept watch over the patient. In short, the situation was depressing and looked hopeless. On the other hand, Freud warned against therapeutic ambitiousness. Years later I understood what he meant. After having discovered the mechanisms of the unconscious, Freud himself originally had entertained the definite hope of being now on the way to a dependable causal therapy. He was wrong. His disillusionment must have been enormous. His conclusion, that one must, above all, keep investigating, was correct. Premature therapeutic ambitiousness is not conducive to the discovery of new facts. I had no more of an idea than anybody else as to the field into which this necessary research would lead. Neither did I know that it was the psychoanalysts' fear of the social consequences of psychoanalysis that made them arrive at such bizarre attitudes in the question of therapy. It boiled down to the following questions:

1. Is Freud's theory of the etiology of the neurosis complete?
2. Is a scientific theory of technique and theory possible?
3. Is Freud's theory of instinct correct and complete? If not, in what respects?
4. What makes sexual repression necessary, and with it, the neurosis?

These questions contained, in embryo, everything that later came to be called *sex-economy*. If these retrospective questions had been consciously formulated at that time, they would have kept me forever from any further investigation. It is my good fortune not to have had at that time any idea of the consequences of these questions, and thus to have been able to go on quite naively with my clinical work and my work toward the elaboration of the theoretical edifice of psychoanalysis. I did it with the conviction of working for Freud and *his* life work. In connection with my own life work, I do not regret for a moment the suffering which this not very self-confident attitude brought me later on. This attitude was the very prerequisite for my later discoveries.

SUPPLEMENTATION OF FREUD'S THEORY OF THE ANXIETY NEUROSIS

As mentioned before, I came to Freud through the field of sexology. It is thus not surprising that his theory of the *actual neuroses* (*Aktualneurosen*) which I later termed *stasis neuroses* (*Stauungsneurosen*) struck me as much more in keeping with natural science than the "interpretation" of the "meaning" of symptoms in the "psychoneuroses." Freud applied the name of actual neuroses to neuroses which resulted from present-day (*"aktuelle"*) disturbances of sex life. According to this concept, anxiety neurosis and neurasthenia were disturbances which lacked a "psychic etiology." Instead, they were the *immediate* result of dammed-up sexuality. They were like toxic disturbances. Freud assumed the existence of *"chemical sexual substances"* which, if not correctly "metabolized," caused such symptoms as palpitation, cardiac irregularity, acute anxiety attacks, sweating and other vegetative symptoms. He did not establish a connection between anxiety neurosis and the vegetative system. Anxiety neurosis, so his clinical experience showed, was caused by sexual abstinence or coitus interruptus. It had to be distinguished from neurasthenia, which, in contradistinction, was caused by "sexual abuse," such as excessive masturbation, and which was characterized by pain in the back, headaches, general irritability, disturbances of memory and concentration, etc. That is, Freud classified *according to their etiology* syndromes which official neurology and psychiatry did not understand. For this, he was attacked by the psychiatrist Löwenfeld, who, like hundreds of other psychiatrists, denied completely the sexual etiology of the neuroses. Freud was trying to adapt his concepts to clinical terminology. As he put it, the symptoms of the actual neuroses, in contrast to those of the *psychoneuroses*, especially hysteria and compulsion neurosis, betrayed no psychic content whatsoever. The symptoms of the latter always had a tangible content, *also always of a sexual nature*. Only, the concept of sexuality had to be taken in a broad sense. At the bottom of every psychoneurosis was the incest phantasy and the fear of injury to the genital. They were, indeed, *infantile* and *unconscious* sexual ideas which expressed themselves in the psychoneurotic symptom. Freud made a very sharp distinction between actual neuroses and psychoneuroses. The psychoneuroses, understandably, occupied the center of the clinical interest of the psychoanalyst. According to Freud, the treatment of the actual neuroses consisted in the elimination of the harmful sexual practices, such as sexual abstinence or coitus interruptus in anxiety neurosis, excessive masturbation in neurasthenia. The psychoneuroses, on the other hand, called for psychoanalytic treatment. In spite of this sharp distinction, Freud admitted a connection between the two. He thought it likely that every psychoneurosis centered around an "actual-neurotic core." This illuminating statement, which Freud never followed up, was the starting point of my own investigations of stasis anxiety.

In the actual neurosis in Freud's sense, biological energy is misdirected; it is blocked from access to consciousness and motility. The anxiety ("*Aktualangst*") and the immediate vege-tative symptoms are, as it were, malignant growths which are nourished by the undischarged sexual energy. But on the other hand, the peculiar psychic manifestations of hysterias and compulsion neuroses also looked like biologically meaningless malignant growths. Where did *they* derive their energy from? Undoubtedly from the "actual-neurotic core" of the dammed-up sexual energy. This, and nothing else, could be the *source of energy* in the psychoneurosis. No other interpretation would fit Freud's suggestion. However, the majority of psychoanalysts opposed Freud's theory of the actual neuroses. They contended *that actual neuroses did not exist at all;* that these disturbances, also, were "psychically determined"; that even in the so-called "free-floating anxiety" unconscious psychic contents could be demonstrated. The chief exponent of this view was Stekel. He, like others, failed to see the fundamental difference between psychosomatic affect and psychic content of a symptom. In other words, it was quite generally contended that every kind of anxiety and nervous disturbance was of *psychic* origin, and *not of somatic* origin, as Freud had assumed for the actual neu-roses. Freud never resolved this contradiction, but he continued to adhere to his distinction between the two groups of neu-roses. Notwithstanding the general assertions as to the non-existence of anxiety neurosis, I saw such cases in great numbers in the psychoanalytic clinic.* However, the symptoms of the actual neuroses had undeniably a psychic *superstructure*. *Pure* actual neuroses are rare. The distinction was not as sharp as Freud had assumed. Such specialized questions may seem unimportant to the layman. But it will be shown that they contained decisive problems of human health.

There could be no doubt: *The psychoneuroses had an actual-neurotic core and the actual neuroses had a psychoneurotic superstructure.* Was there any sense in making the distinction? Was it not just a matter of a quantitive difference?

While most analysts ascribed everything to the psychic content of the neurotic symptoms, leading psychopathologists, like Jaspers, contended that psychological interpretation of meaning, and thus, psychoanalysis, were not within the realm of natural science at all. The "meaning" of a psychic attitude or action, they said, could be comprehended only in terms of philosophy, and not of natural science. Natural science dealt

---

* *Translator's note:* The same situation still exists in this country. A leading American psychoanalyst wrote me some three years ago: "I personally don't believe that there is a word of truth in that notion that so-called actual neuroses have somatic symptoms which have no psychic meaning. . . . I think, as a matter of fact, that a good many analysts are in doubt about this, although with customary over-solicitude about the old man's feelings, don't argue about it very much in the open. . . . One sees intense anxiety so frequently in patients who have no orgastic impotence that I cannot believe in the reality of the whole notion. I think that Freud must have been over-impressed by a couple of early experiences, or possibly by some element in his own personal struggle with masturbation." Similarly, one of the most widely read psychoanalytic writers in America referred in a recent paper to Freud's theory of the actual neuroses as "the now generally discarded theory of anxiety."

From my own experience over some eight years here, I can confirm the fact that one does not see cases of actual neurosis in private psychoanalytic practice, or only extremely rarely. Due to their predominantly somatic—not psychic—symptomatology, anxiety-neurotic patients, as a rule, do not seek the help of the psychiatrist or psychoanalyst. They go to the cardiologist, gynecologist, gastroenterologist or other specialist, according to what their symptoms happen to be. In the psychiatric clinic of a general hospital, however, these patients are seen every day. They are referred there from the medical, surgical, gynecological and other clinics, usually after attempts of treatment without recognition of the real cause have failed. In a psychiatric clinic, the psychiatrist who is able to recognize an anxiety neurosis soon finds himself with an imposing record of patients who—after many years of futile treatment—improved rapidly and considerably once their condition was diagnosed correctly.

only with *quantities* and energies, philosophy with psychic *qualities;* and there was no bridge between the quantitative and the qualitative. It was plainly a matter of the question as to whether or not psychoanalysis and its method belonged to natural science. In other words: *Is a scientific psychology in the strict sense of the word at all possible?* Can psychoanalysis claim to be such a psychology? Or is it only one of the many philosophical schools? Freud himself paid no attention to these methodological questions and quietly continued to publish his clinical observations; he disliked philosophical discussions. But I had to fight such arguments on the part of un-understanding antagonists. They tried to classify us as mystics and thus to settle the question. But we knew that—for the first time in the history of psychology—we were engaging in *natural science.* We wanted to be taken seriously. It was only in the hard-fought controversies over these questions that the sharp weapons were forged with which I later was able to defend Freud's cause. If it were true that only experimental psychology in the sense of Wundt was "natural science," because it measured human reactions quantitatively, then, I thought, something was wrong with natural science. For, Wundt and his pupils knew nothing of the human in his living reality. They evaluated him according to the number of seconds he needed to react to the word "dog." They still do. We, on the other hand, evaluated a person according to the manner in which he handled his conflicts in life, and the motives which activated him. To me, there loomed behind this argument the more important question as to whether it might be possible to arrive at a concrete formulation of Freud's concept of "*psychic energy,*" or whether it might be possible even to subsume it under the general concept of energy.

Philosophical arguments cannot be countered with facts. The Viennese philosopher and physiologist Allers refused to enter upon the question of the existence of an unconscious psychic life, on the grounds that the assumption of an "unconscious" was "*a priori* erroneous from a philosophical point of view." I hear similar objections today. When I assert that highly sterilized substances produce life, it is argued that the slide was dirty, or that, if there seems to be life, it is "only a matter of Brownian movement." The fact that it is very easy to distinguish dirt on the slide from the bions, and equally easy to distinguish Brownian movement from vegetative movement, is not taken into consideration. In brief, "objective science" is a problem in itself.

In this confusion, I was unexpectedly aided by such everyday clinical observations as the ones provided by the two patients mentioned above. Gradually it became clear that *the intensity of an idea depends upon the quantity of the somatic excitation* with which it is connected. Emotions originate from the instincts, consequently from the *somatic* sphere. Ideas, on the other hand, certainly are a definitely "psychic," "non-somatic" thing. *What, then, is the connection between the "non-somatic" idea and the "somatic" excitation?* For example, the idea of sexual intercourse is vivid and forceful if one is in a state of full sexual excitation. For some time after sexual gratification, however, it cannot be vividly reproduced; it is dim, colorless and vague. Just here must the secret of the interrelation between the *"physiogenic"* anxiety neurosis and the "psychogenic" psychoneurosis be hidden. The first patient temporarily lost all his psychic compulsion symptoms after he had experienced sexual gratification; with the return of sexual excitation, they recurred and lasted until the next occasion of gratification. The second patient, on the other hand, had meticulously worked through everything in the psychic realm, but in him, sexual excitation remained absent; the unconscious ideas at the root of his erective impotence had not been touched by the treatment.

Things began to take shape. I began to understand that an idea, endowed with a very small amount of energy, was capable of provoking an *increase* of excitation. The excitation thus provoked, in turn made the idea vivid and forceful. If the excitation subsided, the idea would collapse also. If, as is the case in the stasis neurosis, the idea of sexual intercourse does not arise in consciousness, due to moral inhibition, the excitation attaches itself to other ideas which are less subject to censorship. From this, I concluded: the stasis neurosis is a *somatic* disturbance, caused by sexual excitation which is misdirected because it is frustrated. However, *without a psychic inhibition, sexual energy can never become misdirected.* I was surprised that Freud had overlooked this fact. Once an inhibition has created the sexual stasis, this in turn may easily increase the inhibition and reactivate infantile ideas which then take the place of normal ones. That is, infantile experiences which in themselves are in no way pathological, may, due to a present-day inhibition, become endowed with an excess of sexual energy. Once that has happened, they become urgent; being in conflict with adult psychic organization, they have to be kept down by repression. Thus, the chronic psychoneurosis with its infantile sexual content, develops on the basis of a sexual inhibition which is conditioned by present-day circumstances and is apparently "harmless" at the outset. This is the nature of Freud's "regression to infantile mechanisms." All cases that I have treated showed this mechanism. If the neurosis had developed not in childhood, but at a later age, it was shown regularly that some "normal" inhibition or difficulty of the sexual life had created a stasis, and this in turn had reactivated infantile incestuous desires and sexual anxieties.

The next question was: Are the customary antisexual attitude and sexual inhibition which initiate every chronic neurosis "neurotic" or "normal"? Nobody discussed this question. The sexual inhibition, e.g., of a well-brought-up middle-class girl seemed to be considered as entirely a matter-of-course. I thought so myself, or rather, I just did not give any thought to the question. If a young, vivacious girl developed a neurosis in the course of her unsatisfying marriage, with cardiac anxiety, etc., nobody asked to know the reason for the inhibition which kept her from achieving sexual gratification *in spite of all*. As time went on, she would develop a full-fledged hysteria or compulsion neurosis. The first cause of the neurosis was the moral *inhibition*, its driving force the *unsatisfied sexual energy*.

The solution of many problems ramify from this point. There were, however, serious obstacles to the immediate and vigorous undertaking of such solutions. For seven years, I believed that I was working altogether as a Freudian. Nobody had any idea that these questions were the beginning of a dangerous mingling of basically incompatible scientific views.

ORGASTIC POTENCY

The case of the waiter who was not cured threw into doubt the correctness of Freud's formula of therapy. The other case revealed unmistakably the actual mechanism of cure. For a long time, I tried to harmonize these antitheses. Freud, in his "History of the Psychoanalytic Movement," relates how he overheard Charcot tell a colleague the story of a young woman suffering from severe symptoms, whose husband was impotent or very clumsy in the sexual act. The colleague apparently not understanding the connection, Charcot suddenly exclaimed with great vivacity: "*Mais, dans des cas pareils, c'est toujours la chose génitale, toujours! toujours! toujours!*" "I know," says Freud, "that for a moment I was almost paralyzed with amazement, and I asked myself, 'But, if he knows that, why does he never say so?'" A year after this experience with Charcot, the Viennese physician Chrobak referred a patient to Freud. She was suffering from severe anxiety attacks and, having been married for eighteen years to an impotent man, was still a virgin. Chrobak commented, "We know only too well what the only prescription for such cases is, but we cannot prescribe it. It is 'Rx. Penis normalis, dosim. Repetatur.'" Which means, the hysterical patient's trouble is that she has no genital satisfaction. Thus, Freud's attention was called to the sexual etiology of hysteria, but he avoided the full implication of these statements. They seem banal and sound like folklore. My contention is that every individual who has managed to preserve a bit of naturalness knows that there is only one thing wrong with neurotic patients: the *lack of full and repeated sexual satisfaction.*

Instead of simply investigating and confirming this fact and to take up the fight for its recognition, I was for years entangled in the psychoanalytic theories which *distract* one from this. Most of the theories evolved by the psychoanalysts since the publication of Freud's *The Ego and the Id* have had only *one* function: that of making the world forget the implication of Charcot's statement, "In these cases, it is always a matter of genitality, always, always, always." Such facts as that the genital organs of the human do not function normally, and therefore real satisfaction is impossible for both sexes; that this is the basis of most of the existing psychic misery; that it even leads to relevant conclusions with regard to cancer; all this was too simple to be recognized. Let us see whether I am indulging in monomanic exaggeration.

The following facts were confirmed again and again in my private practice as well as at the psychoanalytic clinic and the psychiatric-neurological hospital:

The severity of any kind of psychic disturbance is in direct relation to the severity of the disturbance of genitality.

The prognosis depends directly on the possibility of establishing the capacity for full genital satisfaction.

Among the hundreds of patients I observed and treated within a few years, there was *not one woman* who did not suffer from a complete absence of vaginal orgasm. Among the men, roughly 60 to 70 per cent showed gross genital disturbances, either in the form of erective impotence or premature ejaculation. This inability to obtain genital gratification—which should be the most natural thing in the world—thus proved a symptom which was never absent in female patients, and rarely absent among the males. To the rest of the men, who were seemingly genitally healthy, but otherwise neurotic, I gave no further thought at first. Such loose clinical thinking was entirely in line with the psychoanalytic concept of that time, that impotence or frigidity was *"only one symptom among many others."*

In November, 1922, I had given a paper before the Psychoanalytic Society on the "Limitations of memory during analysis." It aroused much interest, because all therapists tortured themselves about the fundamental rule (of free association) which patients did not follow, and about the recollections which patients ought to have brought and did not. All too frequently the "primal scene" was an arbitrary reconstruction which carried little conviction. I wish to emphasize here that Freud's formulation regarding the existence of traumatic experiences between the ages of one and four cannot be doubted. All the more important was a study of the shortcomings in the method of reaching them.

In January 1923, I reported the case of an elderly woman with a tic of the diaphragm, whose condition improved after genital masturbation had become possible to her. My report met with approval and general concurrence.

In October 1923, I gave a paper on "Introspection in a case of schizophrenia." This patient had particularly good insight into the mechanism of her delusions of persecution, and confirmed the finding of Tausk concerning the role of the genital influencing apparatus.

After three years' study of the subject, I gave my first comprehensive paper on "Genitality from the point of view of psychoanalytic prognosis and therapy" in November 1923. While I was talking, I became increasingly aware of a chilling of the atmosphere of the meeting. I used to speak well, and thus far had always found my audience attentive. When I finished, there was an icy stillness in the room. After a pause, the discussion began. My assertion that the genital disturbance was an important, and perhaps the most important symptom of the neurosis, was erroneous, they said. Even worse, they said, was my contention that an evaluation of genitality provided prognostic and therapeutic criteria. Two analysts bluntly asserted that they knew any number of female patients with a completely healthy sex life! They seemed to me more excited than their usual scientific reserve would have led one to expect.

In this controversy, I started out by being at a disadvantage. I had had to admit myself that among the male patients there were many with an apparently undisturbed genitality, though the same was not true of the female patients. I was searching for the *source of energy* of the neurosis, for its somatic core. This core could be nothing but dammed-up sexual energy. But I could not imagine what should cause the stasis if potency was present.

Two misleading concepts dominated psychoanalysis at that time. First, a man was called "potent" when he was able to carry out the sexual act. He was considered "very potent" when he was capable of carrying out the sexual act several times during one night. The question as to how many times a night a man "can do it" is a favorite topic of conversation among men in all walks of life. Roheim, a psychoanalyst, even went so far as to state that "with a slight exaggeration, one could say that the woman obtains real gratification only if after the sexual act she suffers from an inflammation (of the genital)."

The second misleading concept was the belief that a partial impulse—such as the impulse to suck the maternal breast— could be dammed up by itself, isolated from other impulses. This concept was used to explain the existence of neurotic symptoms in the presence of "complete potency"; it corresponded to the concept of mutually independent erogenous zones.

In addition, the psychoanalysts denied my assertion that genitally healthy female patients were not to be found. A woman was considered genitally healthy when she was capable of a clitoris orgasm. The sex-economic differentiation of clitoris excitation and vaginal excitation was unknown. In brief, nobody had any idea of the *natural function of the orgasm.* There remained a doubtful group of genitally healthy men who seemed to invalidate all my assumptions regarding the prognostic and therapeutic role of genitality. For, there was no doubt: *If my assumption was correct* that the disturbance of genitality formed the source of energy of the neurotic symptoms, *then not a single case of neurosis with undisturbed genitality would be found.*

In this case, I had the same experience that I later often had in making scientific discoveries. A series of clinical observations had led to a general assumption. This assumption had gaps here and there, and was vulnerable to what seemed to be valid objections. And one's opponents rarely miss an opportunity to detect such gaps and to take them as a basis for rejecting the whole. As du Teil once said, "Scientific objectivity is not of this world, and perhaps of none." Objective collaboration on a problem is scarcely to be hoped for. But, unintentionally, my critics often helped me along, just by their objections "on fundamental grounds." So it was at this time. The objection that genitally healthy neurotics existed in great numbers, made me scrutinize "genital health." It is unbelievable yet true that an exact analysis of genital behavior beyond such vague statements as "I have slept with a man, or a woman" was strictly taboo in psychoanalysis of that time.

The more exactly I had my patients describe their behavior and sensations in the sexual act, the firmer became my clinical conviction that all of them, *without exception,* suffered from a *severe* disturbance of genitality. This was especially true of those men who bragged the loudest about their sexual conquests and about how many times a night they "could do it." There was no doubt: they were erectively very potent, but ejaculation was accompanied by little or no pleasure, or even the opposite, by disgust and unpleasant sensations. An exact analysis of the phantasies accompanying the act revealed mostly sadistic or self-satisfied attitudes in the men, anxiety, reserve or masculinity in women. To the so-called potent man, the act had the significance of conquering, piercing or raping the woman. They wanted to give proof of their potency, or to be admired for their erective endurance. This "potency" could easily be destroyed by laying bare its motives. It seemed to cover up serious disturbances of erection or ejaculation. In *none* of these cases was there as much as a trace of *involuntary behavior* or *loss of alertness* during the act.

Slowly groping ahead, I thus learned, bit by bit, to recognize the signs of *orgastic impotence*. It took another ten years before I understood the disturbance well enough to be able to describe it and to develop a technique for its elimination.

The study of this disturbance remained the central clinical problem of sex-economy and is far from being concluded. It plays a similar role in sex-economy to that played by the Oedipus complex in psychoanalysis. One who does not thoroughly understand it cannot be regarded as a sex-economist. He will not comprehend its implications and consequences. He will not understand the distinction between healthy and sick, nor will he understand the nature of pleasure anxiety; he will understand neither the pathological nature of the child-parent conflict, nor the basis of marital unhappiness. He may become a sex-reformer, but he will never really alter sex misery. He may admire the bion experiments, may even imitate them, but he will never do sex-economic research upon life-processes. He will never comprehend religious ecstasy and certainly not Fascist irrationalism. He will continue to believe in the antithesis of nature and culture, instinct and morals, sexuality and achievement. He will not be able to solve in any real sense one single question of pedagogy. He will never comprehend the identity of the sexual process and the life process, and, therefore, also the sex-economic theory of cancer. He will consider healthy what is sick, and sick what is healthy. He will, finally, misinterpret the human longing for happiness and overlook the human *fear* of happiness. In brief, he may be anything but a sex-economist, one who knows that man is the only biological species which has destroyed its own natural sex function, and that that is what ails him.

I shall present the orgasm theory in the way in which it developed, i.e., not systematically. Thus, its inner logic will more readily become evident. It will be seen that no human brain could possibly invent these interconnections.

Up until 1923, the year when the orgasm theory was born, sexology and psychoanalysis knew only of an *ejaculative* and an *erective* potency. But, without the inclusion of the economic, experiential and energy aspects, the concept of sexual potency has no meaning at all. Erective and ejaculative potency are nothing but indispensable prerequisites for *orgastic potency*. Orgastic potency is the *capacity for surrender to the flow of biological energy without any inhibition*, the capacity for *complete discharge of all dammed-up sexual excitation* through *involuntary pleasurable contractions of the body*. Not a single neurotic individual possesses orgastic potency; the corollary of this fact is the fact that the vast majority of humans suffer from a character-neurosis.

The intensity of pleasure in the orgasm (in the sexual act which is free of anxiety and unpleasure, and unaccompanied by phantasies) *depends on the amount of sexual tension concentrated in the genital;* the pleasure is all the more intense the greater in amount and the steeper the "drop" in the excitation.

The following description of the orgastically satisfying sexual act covers only some typical, biologically determined phases and modes of behavior. It does not take into account the preliminaries which present no general regularity. Furthermore, the fact should be borne in mind that the bioelectric processes of orgasm are as yet unexplored; for this reason, this description is of necessity incomplete.

A. *Phase of voluntary control of the excitation*

1.* Erection is pleasurable, and not painful as it is in the case of priapism ("cold erection"), spasm of the pelvic floor or of the spermatic duct. The genital is not over-excited, as it is after prolonged periods of abstinence or in the case of premature ejaculation. The genital of the woman becomes hyperemic and, through ample secretion of the genital glands, moist in a specific way; that is, in the case of undisturbed genital functioning, the secretion has specific chemical and physical properties which are lacking when the genital function is disturbed. An important criterion of orgastic potency in the male is the

---

* The arabic figures (1-10) in the text correspond to the arabic figures in the legend to the diagram.

urge to penetrate. For, there may be erections without this urge, as is the case, e.g., in many erectively potent narcissistic characters, and in satyriasis.

2. The man is spontaneously gentle, that is, without having to cover up opposite tendencies, such as sadistic impulses, by a forced kind of gentleness. Pathological deviations are: aggressiveness based on sadistic impulses, as in many compulsion neurotics with erective potency; inactivity of the passive-feminine character. In the "onanistic coitus" with an unloved object the gentleness is absent. The activity of the woman normally differs in no way from that of the man. The widely prevalent passivity of the woman is pathological and mostly due to masochistic phantasies of being raped.

3. The pleasurable excitation, which during the preliminaries has maintained about the same level, suddenly increases

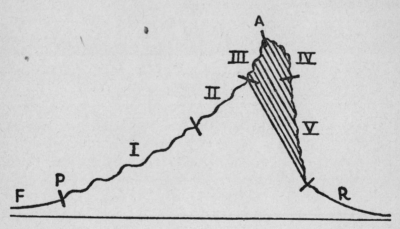

Diagram of the typical phases of the sexual act with orgastic potency, in both sexes.

F = forepleasure (1, 2). P = penetration (3). I (4, 5) = phase of voluntary control of increase in excitation in which voluntary prolongation is as yet harmless. II (6 a-d) = phase of involuntary muscle contractions and automatic increase in excitation. III (7) = sudden and steep ascent to the acme (A). IV (8) = orgasm. The *shaded* part represents the phase of *involuntary body contractions*. V (9, 10) = steep "drop" of the excitation. R = relaxation. Duration, about five to twenty minutes.

—both in the man and in the woman—with the penetration of the penis. The man's sensation of "being sucked in" corresponds to the woman's sensation that she is "sucking the penis in."

4. In the man, the urge to penetrate very deeply increases; without, however, taking the sadistic form of wanting to "pierce through" the woman, as in the case in compulsive characters. As a result of *mutual, slow, spontaneous and effortless* frictions the excitation is concentrated on the surface and the glans of the penis, and the posterior parts of the vaginal mucous membrane. The characteristic sensation which precedes ejaculation is still completely absent, in contradistinction to cases of premature ejaculation. The body is as yet less excited than the genital. Consciousness is completely concentrated on the perception of the pleasure sensations; the ego participates in this activity in so far as it attempts to exhaust all possibilities of pleasure and to attain a maximum of tension before orgasm occurs. Needless to say, this is not done by way of conscious intention, but quite spontaneously and differently for each individual, on the basis of previous experience, by a change in position, the manner of friction and rhythm, etc. According to the consensus of potent men and women, the pleasure sensations are all the more intense the slower and more gentle the frictions are, and the better they harmonize with each other. This presupposes a considerable ability to identify oneself with one's partner. Pathological counterparts are, e.g., the urge to produce violent frictions, as occurring in sadistic compulsive characters with penis anesthesia and inability to have an ejaculation; or the nervous haste of those suffering from premature ejaculation. Orgastically potent individuals never talk or laugh during the sexual act—with the exception of words of tenderness. Both talking and laughing indicate a serious lack of the capacity for surrender, which requires an undivided absorption in the sensations of pleasure. Men to whom surrender means being "feminine" are always orgastically disturbed.

5. In this phase, interruption of friction is in itself pleasur-

able, due to the particular sensations of pleasure which appear
when one is at rest; the interruption can be accomplished without mental effort; it prolongs the sexual act. When one is at
rest, the excitation decreases a little, without, however, completely subsiding, as it does in pathological cases. The interruption of the sexual act through retraction of the penis is not
unpleasurable, provided it occurs after a period of rest. With
continued friction, the excitation keeps increasing above the
level previous to the interruption, and begins to spread more
and more to *the whole body,* while the excitation of the genital
remains more or less at the same level. Finally, as a result of
another, usually sudden, increase of genital excitation, there
sets in the second phase:

B. *Phase of involuntary muscle contractions*

6. In this phase, a *voluntary* control of the course of excitation is *no longer possible.* It shows the following characteristics:

a. The increase in excitation can no longer be controlled
voluntarily; rather, it takes hold of the whole personality and
produces tachycardia and deep expirations.

b. Bodily excitation becomes more and more concentrated
upon the genital, a "melting" kind of sensation sets in, which
may best be described as a radiation of excitation from the
genital to other parts of the body.

c. This excitation results first in involuntary contractions of
the total musculature of the genital and of the pelvic floor.
These contractions occur in waves: the crests of the waves
occur with the complete penetration of the penis, the troughs
with the retraction of the penis. However, as soon as the retraction goes beyond a certain limit, there occur immediately spas-
modic contractions which expedite ejaculation. In the woman,
there occurs in this case a contraction of the smooth musculature of the vagina.

d. In this stage, interruption of the sexual act is absolutely
unpleasurable, for both man and woman; instead of occurring
rhythmically, the muscular contractions which lead to the

orgasm as well as to the ejaculation, occur, in the case of interruption, in the form of spasms. This results in intensely unpleasant sensations and occasionally in pain in the pelvic floor and the lower back; in addition, as a result of the spasm, ejaculation occurs earlier than in the case of an undisturbed rhythm.

The voluntary prolongation of the first phase of the sexual act (1 to 5 in the diagram) to a moderate degree is harmless, and rather serves to intensify pleasure. On the other hand, interruption or voluntary modification of the course of excitation in the second phase is harmful, because here the process takes place in reflex form.

7. Through further intensification and an increase in the frequency of the involuntary muscular contractions, the excitation increases rapidly and steeply up to the acme (III to A in the diagram); normally, the acme coincides with the first ejaculatory muscular contraction in the man.

8. Now occurs a more or less intense clouding of consciousness; the frictions become *spontaneously more intensive*, after having subsided momentarily at the point of the acme; the urge to "penetrate completely" becomes more intense with each ejaculatory muscle contraction. In the woman, the muscle contractions take the same course as in the man; experientially, the difference is only that during and immediately after the acme the healthy woman wants to "receive completely."

9. The orgastic excitation takes hold of the whole body and results in *lively contractions of the whole body musculature*. Self-observations of healthy individuals of both sexes, as well as the analysis of certain disturbances of orgasm, show that what we call the release of tension and experience as a motor discharge (descending portion of the orgasm curve) is predominantly the result of a *flowing back of the excitation from the genital to the body*. This flowing back is experienced as a *sudden decrease* of the tension.

The acme thus represents the point at which the excitation changes its direction: up to the point of the acme, the direction is toward the genital, and at the point of the acme it turns into the opposite direction, i.e., toward the whole body. *The complete flowing back of the excitation toward the whole body is what constitutes gratification.* Gratification means two things: shift of the direction of flow of excitation in the body, and unburdening of the genital apparatus.

10. Before the zero point is reached, the excitation tapers off in a gentle curve and is immediately replaced by a *pleasant bodily and psychic relaxation;* usually, there is a strong desire for sleep. The sensual relations have subsided; what continues is a grateful tender attitude toward the partner.

In contradistinction, the orgastically impotent individual experiences a leaden exhaustion, disgust, repulsion, or indifference, and occasionally, hatred toward the partner. In the case of satyriasis and nymphomania, sexual excitation does not subside. Insomnia is one of the most important indications of lack of gratification; on the other hand, it would be erroneous to assume necessarily the existence of satisfaction if the patient reports that he or she goes to sleep immediately after the sexual act.

Looking back over the two main phases of the sexual act, we see that the first phase (F and I in the diagram) is characterized mainly by the *sensory,* the second phase (II to V) by the *motor* experience of pleasure.

The involuntary contractions of the organism and the complete discharge of the excitation are the most important criteria of orgastic potency. The part of the curve drawn in shaded lines (diagram, p. 44) represents the *involuntary* vegetative release of tension. There are partial releases of tension which are *similar* to an orgasm; they used to be taken for the actual release of tension. Clinical experience shows that man—as a result of the general sexual repression—has lost the capacity for *ultimate vegetatively involuntary surrender.* What I mean by "orgastic potency" is exactly this ultimate, hitherto unrecognized portion of the capacity for excitation and release of tension. Orgastic potency is the biological primal and basic function which man has in common with all living organisms. All feelings about nature derive from this function or from the longing for it.

Normally, that is, in the absence of inhibitions, the course of the sexual process in the woman is in no way different from that in the man. In both sexes, the orgasm is more intense if the peaks of genital excitation coincide. This occurs frequently in individuals who are able to concentrate their tender as well as their sensual feelings on a partner; it is the rule when the relationship is undisturbed by either internal or external factors. In such cases, at least *conscious* phantasies are completely absent; the ego is undividedly absorbed in the perception of pleasure. The *ability to concentrate oneself with one's whole personality on the orgastic experience, in spite of possible conflicts, is a further criterion of orgastic potency*.

Whether *un*conscious phantasies are also absent, is difficult to say. Certain indications make this probable. Phantasies which cannot be permitted to become conscious, can only be disturbing. Among the phantasies which may accompany the sexual act one has to distinguish phantasies which are in harmony with the actual experience from those that contradict it. If the partner is able to draw upon himself all sexual interests at least for the time being, unconscious phantasy activity becomes unnecessary; the latter, by its very nature, stands in opposition to the actual experience because one phantasies only that which one cannot obtain in reality. There is such a thing as a *genuine transference* from an original object to the partner. If the partner corresponds in his essential traits to the object of the phantasy, he can replace the object of the phantasy. The situation is different, however, when the transference of sexual interests takes place *in spite of the fact* that the partner does *not* correspond in his fundamental traits to the object of the phantasy; when it takes place only on the basis of a neurotic searching for the original object, without the inner ability to establish a *genuine* transference; in that case, no illusion can eradicate a vague feeling of insincerity in the relationship. Whereas in the case of genuine transference there is

no reaction of disillusionment after the sexual act, it is inevitable here; here, we can assume, unconscious phantasy activity
during the act was not absent, but served the purpose of maintaining the illusion. In the former case, the original object—its
place having been taken by the partner—lost its interest and,
with it, its power of creating phantasies. In the case of genuine
transference there is none of the overestimation of the partner;
those characteristics which are at variance with the original
object are correctly evaluated and well tolerated. Conversely,
in the case of false neurotic transference, there is excessive
idealization, and illusions predominate; the negative qualities
are not perceived and phantasy activity is not allowed to rest,
lest the illusion be lost.

The harder the imagination has to work in order to bring
about an equivalence of the partner with the ideal, the more
does the sexual experience lose in intensity and sex-economic
value. Whether and to what extent incompatibilities—which
occur in any relationship of some duration—diminish the intensity of the sexual experience, depends entirely on the nature of
these incompatibilities. They will be the more likely to lead to
a pathological disturbance, the stronger the fixation upon the
original object, the greater the incapacity for genuine transference, and the greater the effort that has to be made to overcome
the aversion toward the partner.

Sexual Stasis: The Source of Energy of the Neurosis

In the psychoanalytic clinic, I had—ever since clinical experience had called my attention to it in 1920—carefully observed
and taken notes on the disturbances of genitality. In the course
of some two years, I had collected sufficient material to warrant the conclusion: *The disturbance of genitality is not*, as was
previously assumed, *one* symptom among others, *but it is* the
symptom of the neurosis. Gradually, everything began to point
in one direction: the neurosis is not merely the result of a *sexual*

disturbance in the broader sense of Freud; it is rather, the
result of a *genital* disturbance, in the strict sense of *orgastic
impotence.*

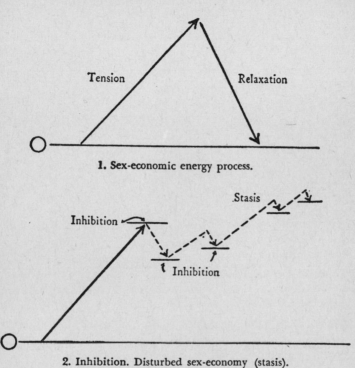

1. Sex-economic energy process.

2. Inhibition. Disturbed sex-economy (stasis).

If I had again restricted sexuality to mean exclusively genital
sexuality, I would have reverted to the old, erroneous concept
of sexuality before Freud: sexual is only what is genital. Instead
of this, in amplifying the concept of genital function by that of
orgastic potency, and by defining it in terms of energy, I extended the psychoanalytic theories of sex and of libido further
along their proper lines of development. I argued as follows:

1. If every psychic disturbance has a core of dammed-up
sexual energy, then it can be caused only by a disturbance of
orgastic satisfaction. *Impotence and frigidity thus are the key
to an understanding of the economy of the neuroses.*

2. *The energy source of the neurosis lies in the differential between accumulation and discharge of sexual energy.* The neurotic psychic apparatus is distinguished from the healthy one by the constant presence of undischarged sexual energy. This is true not only of the stasis neuroses (actual neuroses of Freud) but for all psychic disturbances, with or without symptom formation.

3. Freud's therapeutic formula is correct but incomplete. The first prerequisite of cure is, indeed, to make the repressed sexuality conscious. However, though this alone *may* effect the cure, it *need not* of necessity do so. It does so only if at the same time the *source of energy, the sexual stasis,* is eliminated; in other words, *only if the awareness of instinctual demands goes hand in hand with the capacity for full orgastic gratification.* In that case, the pathological psychic growths are deprived of their energy at the source (*principle of energy-withdrawal*).

4. The supreme goal of a causal analytic therapy, therefore, is the establishment of orgastic potency, of the ability to discharge an amount of sexual energy equal to that accumulated.

5. Sexual excitation is definitely a *somatic* process; neurotic conflicts are of a *psychic* nature. A slight conflict, in itself normal, will produce a *slight* disturbance of the sexual energy equilibrium. This slight stasis will re-enforce the conflict, and this in turn the stasis. In this way, psychic conflict and somatic stasis mutually increase each other. The central psychic conflict is the sexual child-parent relationship. It is present in every neurosis. It is the *historical* experiential *material* that furnishes the *content* of the *neurosis.* All neurotic phantasies stem from the infantile sexual attachment to the parents. But the child-parent conflict could not produce an enduring disturbance of the psychic equilibrium if it were not continually nourished by the actual stasis which this conflict itself originally produced. Sexual stasis is, therefore, the etiological factor which—constantly present in the immediate situation—affords to the neurosis, not its content, but its *energy.* The historical pathological incestuous attachment to parents and siblings loses its strength

when the energy stasis in the immediate situation is eliminated; in other words, when full orgastic gratification takes place in the immediate present. *The pathogenicity of the Oedipus complex*, therefore, depends on *whether or not there is a physiologically adequate discharge of sexual energy*. Thus, actual neurosis (stasis neurosis) and psychoneurosis are interwoven, and cannot be thought of as independent of each other.

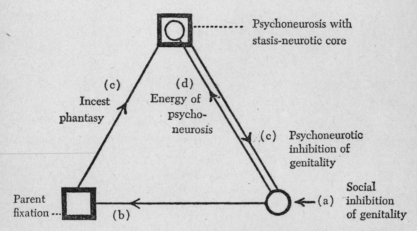

Diagram: Interrelation of infantile psychic content of the neurotic conflict on the one hand and sexual stasis on the other.

   a. Social inhibiion of genitality, resulting in stasis (○).
   b. Stasis results in fixation to parents (historical content, □).
   c. Incest phantasy.
   d. Energy source of the neurosis.
   e. Psychoneurosis maintains stasis (*present-day stasis of energy*).

6. *Pregenital* (oral, anal, muscular, etc.) sexuality differs in its dynamics basically from *genital* sexuality. If non-genital sexual behavior is continued, the genital function becomes disturbed. The resulting sexual stasis, in turn, activates pregenital phantasies and behavior. These, as found in the neuroses and perversions, are not only the cause of the genital disturbance, but at least as much its result. (This is the beginning of the distinction between *natural* [primary] and *secondary* drives

which I formulated in 1936.) This finding, *general sexual disturbance is* a result *of genital* disturbance, i.e., simply, of orgastic impotence, was the most important finding with regard to the theory of instinct and the theory of culture: Genital sexuality, as I understood it, was a function which was unknown and not in keeping with the usual concepts of human sexual activity; no more than "sexual" and "genital" are the same, or "genital" in sex-economy and "genital" in common parlance.

7. Furthermore, a question which had been on Freud's mind a good deal found a simple solution. Psychic disturbances present only "qualities." And yet, one senses everywhere the so-called "quantitative" factor, i.e., the *strength* and *force*, the *energy cathexis* of psychic experiences and activities. In a meeting of the inner circle, Freud counselled foresight. We had to be prepared, he said, that one of these days the psychotherapy of the neuroses would meet a dangerous competitor, a future *organotherapy*. Nobody could as yet have an idea as to what it would be like, but one could already hear the footsteps of its exponents behind one, he said. Psychoanalysis would have to be placed upon an organic foundation. A true Freudian intuition! When Freud said this, I knew immediately that the solution of the problem of quantity in the neurosis also included the solution of the problem of organotherapy. The avenue of approach to the problem could only be the treatment of the physiological sexual stasis. I had already started on this road. Not until five years ago did the efforts to solve the problem bear fruit in the form of the basic principles of the *character-analytic technique of vegetotherapy*. In between lay fifteen years of hard work and difficult struggles.

Between 1922 and 1926 the orgasm theory was formulated and consolidated, bit by bit, followed by the technique of character-analysis. Every bit of future experience, therapeutic successes as well as failures, confirmed the theory which had taken form by itself from those first decisive observations. The ways in which the work was to branch out soon became clear: The clinical work with patients led in *one* direction to *experimental* work in sex-economy, in *another* direction to the question: *Whence does social suppression of sexuality originate, and what is its function?*

Much later, i.e., only after 1933, the first line of problems resulted in a biological side-branch of sex-economy, namely, bion research, sex-economic cancer research, and the investigation of the orgone radiation. The second line, about seven years later, split up into sexual sociology and sex policy on the one hand, and political psychology and mass psychology on the other.*

The orgasm theory determined the psychological, psycho-therapeutic, physiological-biological and the sociological sectors of sex-economy. I am far from claiming that this structure of sex-economy could replace such specialized disciplines as the above. The claim which sex-economy can make today, however, is that of being an inwardly consistent, scientific theory of sex, from which a variety of aspects of human life may expect stimulating revivification. This claim makes imperative a detailed presentation of this structure in all its ramifications. Since the life process is identical with the sexual process—an experimentally proven fact—the wide ramification of sex-economy is a logical necessity. *In everything living, sexual vegetative energy is at work.* This statement is dangerous, just because it is simple and absolutely correct. If it is to be applied correctly, it must be kept from becoming a platitude or a catch phrase. One's followers are in the habit of making things easy for themselves. They take over all that has been acquired through hard toil, and work with it with as little disturbance to themselves as possible. They do not take the pains of applying again and again all methodological subtleties. They become stultified, and the problem with them. I hope I shall succeed in saving sex-economy from this fate.

---

* *Cf.* my books, *Die Sexualität im Kulturkampf* (The Sexual Revolution), *Der Einbruch der Sexualmoral*, and *Die Massenpsychologie des Faschismus* (*The Mass Psychology of Fascism*).

III. THERAPY

1. ON THE TECHNIQUE OF CHARACTER-ANALYSIS

INTRODUCTORY REVIEW

Our therapeutic method is determined by the following basic theoretical concepts. The *topical* standpoint determines the technical principle that the unconscious has to be made conscious. The *dynamic* standpoint determines the rule that this has to take place not directly but by way of resistance analysis. The *economic* standpoint and the psychological structure determine the rule that the resistance analysis has to be carried out in a certain order according to the individual patient.

As long as the topical process, the making conscious of the unconscious, was considered the only task of analytic technique, the formula that the unconscious manifestations should be interpreted *in the sequence in which they appeared* was correct. The dynamics of the analysis, that is, whether or not the making conscious also released the corresponding affect, whether the analysis influenced the patient beyond a merely intellectual understanding, that was more or less left to chance. The inclusion of the dynamic element, that is, the demand that the patient should not only remember things but also experience them, already complicated the simple formula that one had to "make the unconscious conscious." However, the dynamics of the analytic affect do not depend on the contents but

From *Character Analysis*, third enlarged edition, 1949. First presented at the 10th International Psychoanalytic Congress, Innsbruck, 1927.

on the resistances which the patient puts up against them and on the emotional experience in overcoming them. This makes the analytic task a vastly different one. From the topical standpoint, it is sufficient to bring into the patient's consciousness, one after the other, the manifest elements of the unconscious; in other words, the guiding line is the *content* of the material. If one also considers the dynamic factor one has to relinquish this guiding line in favor of another which comprehends the content of the material as well as the affects: that of the *successive resistances.* In doing so we meet, in most patients, with a difficulty which we have not yet mentioned.

CHARACTER ARMOR AND CHARACTER RESISTANCE

a) The inability to follow the fundamental rule.

Rarely are our patients immediately accessible to analysis, capable of following the fundamental rule and of really opening up to the analyst. They cannot immediately have full confidence in a strange person; more importantly, years of illness, constant influencing by a neurotic milieu, bad experiences with physicians, in brief, the whole secondary warping of the personality have created a situation unfavorable to analysis. The elimination of this difficulty would not be so hard were it not supported by the character of the patient which is part and parcel of his neurosis. It is a difficulty which has been termed "narcissistic barrier." There are, in principle, two ways of meeting this difficulty, in especial, the rebellion against the fundamental rule.

One, which seems the usual one, is a direct education to analysis by information, reassurance, admonition, talking-to, etc. That is, one attempts to educate the patient to analytic candor by the establishment of some sort of positive transference. This corresponds to the technique proposed by Nunberg. Experience shows, however, that this pedagogical method is very uncertain; it lacks the basis of analytic clarity and is exposed to the constant variations in the transference situation.

The other way is more complicated and as yet not applicable in all patients, but far more certain. It is that of *replacing the pedagogical measures by analytic interpretations*. Instead of inducing the patient into analysis by advice, admonitions and transference manoeuvres, one focuses one's attention on the actual behavior of the patient and its meaning: *why* he doubts, or is late, or talks in a haughty or confused fashion, or communicates only every other or third thought, why he criticizes the analysis or produces exceptionally much material or material from exceptional depths. If, for example, a patient talks in a haughty manner, in technical terms, one may try to convince him that this is not good for the progress of the analysis, that he better give it up and behave less haughtily, for the sake of the analysis. Or, one may relinquish all attempts at persuasion and wait until one understands why the patient behaves in this and no other way. One may then find that his behavior is an attempt to compensate his feeling of inferiority toward the analyst and may influence him by consistent interpretation of the meaning of his behavior. This procedure, in contrast to the first-mentioned, is in full accord with the principle of analysis.

This attempt to replace pedagogical and similar active measures seemingly necessitated by the characteristic behavior of the patient, by purely analytic interpretations led unexpectedly to the analysis of the *character*.

Certain clinical experiences make it necessary to distinguish, among the various resistances we meet, a certain group as *character resistances*. They get their specific stamp not from their content but from the patient's specific way of acting and reacting. The compulsive character develops specifically different resistances than does the hysterical character; the latter different resistances from the impulsive or neurasthenic character. The *form* of the typical reactions which differ from character to character—though the contents may be the same—*is determined by infantile experiences just like the content of the symptoms or phantasies.*

b) Whence the character resistances?

Quite some time ago, Glover worked on the problem of differentiating character neuroses from symptom neuroses. Alexander also operated on the basis of this distinction. In my earlier writings, I also followed it. More exact comparison of the cases showed, however, that this distinction makes sense only insofar as there are neuroses with circumscribed symptoms and others without them; the former were called "symptom neuroses," the latter, "character neuroses." In the former, understandably, the symptoms are more obvious, in the latter the neurotic character traits. But, we must ask, are there symptoms without a neurotic reaction basis, in other words, without a neurotic character? The difference between the character neuroses and the symptom neuroses is only that in the latter the neurotic character also produced symptoms, that it became concentrated in them, as it were. If one recognizes the fact that the basis of a symptom neurosis is always a neurotic character, then it is clear that we shall have to deal with character-neurotic resistances in *every* analysis, that every analysis must be a character-analysis.

Another distinction which becomes immaterial from the standpoint of character-analysis is that between chronic neuroses, that is, neuroses which developed in childhood, and acute neuroses, which developed late. For the important thing is not whether the symptoms have made their appearance early or late. The important thing is that the neurotic character, the reaction basis for the symptom neurosis, was, in its essential traits, already formed at the period of the Oedipus phase. It is an old clinical experience that the boundary line which the patient draws between health and the outbreak of the disease becomes always obliterated during the analysis.

Since symptom formation does not serve as a distinguishing criterion we shall have to look for others. There is, first of all, insight into illness, and rationalization.

The lack of insight into illness is not an absolutely reliable but an essential sign of the character neurosis. The neurotic symptom is experienced as a foreign body and creates a feeling of being ill. The neurotic character trait, on the other hand, such as the exaggerated orderliness of the compulsive character or the anxious shyness of the hysterical character, are organically built into the personality. One may complain about being shy but does not feel ill for this reason. It is not until the characterological shyness turns into pathological blushing or the compulsion-neurotic orderliness into a compulsive ceremonial, that is, not until the neurotic character exacerbates symptomatically, that the person feels ill.

True enough, there are also symptoms for which there is no or only slight insight, things that are taken by the patient as bad habits or just peculiarities (chronic constipation, mild ejaculatio praecox, etc.). On the other hand, many character traits are often felt as illness, such as violent outbreaks of rage, tendency to lie, drink, waste money, etc. In spite of this, generally speaking, insight characterizes the neurotic symptom and its lack the neurotic character trait.

The second difference is that the symptom is never as thoroughly rationalized as the character. Neither a hysterical vomiting nor compulsive counting can be rationalized. The symptom appears meaningless, while the neurotic character is sufficiently rationalized not to appear meaningless or pathological. A reason is often given for neurotic character traits which would immediately be rejected as absurd if it were given for symptoms: "he just is that way." That implies that the individual was born that way, that this "happens to be" his character. Analysis shows this interpretation to be wrong; it shows that the character, for definite reasons, had to become that way and no different; that, in principle, it can be analyzed like the symptom and is alterable.

Occasionally, symptoms become part of the personality to such an extent that they resemble character traits. For example, a counting compulsion may appear only as part of general orderliness or a compulsive system only in terms of a compulsive work arrangement. Such modes of behavior are then considered as peculiarities rather than as signs of illness. So we can readily see that the concept of disease is an entirely fluid one, that there are all kinds of transitions from the symptom as an isolated foreign body over the neurotic character and the "bad habit" to rational action.

In comparison to the character trait, the symptom has a very simple construction with regard to its meaning and origin. True, the symptom also has a multiple determination; but the more deeply we penetrate into its determinations, the more we leave the realm of symptoms and the clearer becomes the characterological reaction basis. Thus one can arrive—theoretically—at the characterological reaction basis from any symptom. The symptom has its immediate determination in only a limited number of unconscious attitudes; hysterical vomiting, say, is based on a repressed fellatio phantasy or an oral wish for a child. Either expresses itself also characterologically, in a certain infantilism and maternal attitude. But the hysterical character which forms the basis of the symptom is determined by many—partly antagonistic—strivings and is expressed in a specific attitude or *way of being*. This is not as easy to dissect as the symptom; nevertheless, in principle it is, like the symptom, to be reduced to and understood from infantile strivings and experiences. While the symptom corresponds essentially to a single experience or striving, the character represents the specific way of being of an individual, an expression of his total past. For this reason, a symptom may develop suddenly while each individual character trait takes years to develop. In saying this we should not forget the fact that the symptom also could not have developed suddenly unless its characterological neurotic reaction basis had already been present.

The totality of the neurotic character traits makes itself felt in the analysis as a compact *defense mechanism* against our therapeutic endeavors. Analytic exploration of the development of this character "armor" shows that it also serves as a definite economic purpose: on the one hand, it serves as a protection against the stimuli from the outer world, on the other hand against the inner libidinous strivings. The character armor can perform this task because libidinous and sadistic energies are consumed in the neurotic reaction formations, compensations and other neurotic attitudes. In the processes which form and maintain this armor, anxiety is constantly being bound up, in the same way as it is, according to Freud's description, in, say, compulsive symptoms. We shall have to say more later about the economy of character formation.

Since the neurotic character, in its economic function of a protecting armor, has established a certain *equilibrium*, albeit a neurotic one, the analysis presents a danger to this equilibrium. This is why the resistances which give the analysis of the individual case its specific imprint originate from this narcissistic protection mechanism. As we have seen, the mode of behavior is the result of the total development and as such can be analyzed and altered; thus it can also be the starting point for evolving the technique of character-analysis.

c) *The technique of analyzing the character resistance.*

Apart from the dreams, associations, slips and other communications of the patients, their attitude, that is, *the manner* in which they relate their dreams, commit slips, produce their associations and make their communications, deserves special attention.* A patient who follows the fundamental rule from the beginning is a rare exception; it takes months of character-analytic work to make the patient halfway sufficiently honest in his communications. The manner in which the patient talks, in which he greets the analyst or looks at him, the way he lies on the couch, the inflection of the voice, the degree of conventional politeness, all these things are valuable criteria for judging the latent resistances against the fundamental rule, and understanding them makes it possible to alter or eliminate them

---

* *Footnote, 1945:* The *form* of expression is far more important than the *ideational content.* Today, in penetrating to the decisively important infantile experiences, we can make use of the form of expression *exclusively.* Not the the ideational contents but the form of expression is what leads us to the biological reactions which form the basis of the psychic manifestations.

by interpretation. The *how* of saying things is as important "material" for interpretation as is *what* the patient says. One often hears analysts complain that the analysis does not go well, that the patient does not produce any "material." By that is usually meant the content of associations and communications. But the manner in which the patient, say, keeps quiet, or his sterile repetitions, are also "material" which can and must be put to use. There is hardly any situation in which the patient brings "no material"; it is our fault if we are unable to utilize the patient's behavior as "material."

That the behavior and the form of the communications have analytic significance is nothing new. What I am going to talk about is the fact that these things present an avenue of approach to the analysis of the character in a very definite and almost perfect manner. Past failures with many cases of neurotic characters have taught us that in these cases the form of the communications is, at least in the beginning, always more important than their content. One only has to remember the latent resistances of the affect-lame, the "good," over-polite and ever-correct patients; those who always present a deceptive positive transference or who violently and stereotypically ask for love; those who make a game of the analysis; those who are always "armored," who smile inwardly about everything and everyone. One could continue this enumeration indefinitely; it is easy to see that a great deal of painstaking work will have to be done to master the innumerable individual technical problems.

For the purpose of orientation and of sketching the essential differences between character-analysis and symptom-analysis, let us assume two pairs of patients for comparison. Let us assume we have under treatment at the same time two men suffering from premature ejaculation; one is a passive-feminine, the other a phallic-aggressive character. Also, two women with an eating disturbance; one is a compulsive character, the other a hysteric.

Let us assume further that the premature ejaculation of both men has the same unconscious meaning: the fear of the paternal penis in the woman's vagina. In the analysis, both patients, on the basis of their castration anxiety which is the basis of the symptom, produce a negative father transference. Both hate the analyst (the father) because they see in him the enemy who frustrates their pleasure; both have the unconscious wish to do away with him. In this situation, the phallic-sadistic character will ward off the danger of castration by insults, depreciation and threats, while the passive-feminine character, in the same case, will become steadily more passive, submissive and friendly. In both patients, the character has become a resistance: one fends off the danger aggressively, the other tries to avoid it by a deceptive submission. It goes without saying that the character resistance of the passive-feminine patient is more dangerous because he works with hidden means: he produces a wealth of material, he remembers all kinds of infantile experiences, in short, he seems to co-operate splendidly. Actually, however, he camouflages a secret spitefulness and hatred; as long as he maintains this attitude he does not have the courage to show his real self. If, now, one enters only upon *what* he produces, without paying attention to his way of behavior, then no analytic endeavor will change his condition. He may even remember the hatred of his father, but he will not *experience* it unless one interprets consistently the meaning of his deceptive attitude *before* beginning to interpret the deep meaning of his hatred of the father.

In the case of the second pair, let us assume that an acute positive transference has developed. The central content of this positive transference is, in either patient, the same as that of the symptom, namely, an oral fellatio phantasy. But although the positive transference has the same content in either case, the form of the transference resistance will be quite different: the hysterical patient will, say, show an *anxious* silence and a shy behavior; the compulsive character a *spiteful* silence or a cold, haughty behavior. In one case the positive transference is warded off by aggression, in the other by anxiety. And the form of this defense will always be the same in the same patient: the hysterical patient will always defend herself anxiously, the compulsive patient aggressively, no matter what unconscious content is on the point of breaking through. That is, *in one and the same patient, the character resistance remains always the same and only disappears with the very roots of the neurosis.*

In the character armor, the *narcissistic defense* finds its concrete chronic expression. In addition to the known resistances which are mobilized against every new piece of unconscious material, we have to recognize a constant factor of a *formal* nature which originates from the patient's character. Because of this origin, we call the constant formal resistance factor "character resistance."

In summary, the most important aspects of the character resistance are the following:

The character resistance expresses itself not in the content of the material, but in the formal aspects of the general behavior, the manner of talking, of the gait, facial expression and typical attitudes such as smiling, deriding, haughtiness, over-correctness, the *manner* of the politeness or of the aggression, etc.

What is specific of the character resistance is not *what* the patient says or does, but *how* he talks and acts, not *what* he gives away in a dream but *how* he censors, distorts, etc.

The character resistance remains the same in one and the same patient no matter what the material is against which it is directed. Different characters present the same material in a different manner. For example, a hysteric patient will ward off the positive father transference in an anxious manner, the compulsive woman in an aggressive manner.

The character resistance, which expresses itself formally, can be understood as to its content and can be reduced to infantile

THERAPY 67

experiences and instinctual drives just like the neurotic symptom.*

During analysis, the character of a patient soon becomes a resistance. That is, in ordinary life, the character plays the same role as in analysis: that of a psychic protection mechanism. The individual is "characterologically armored" against the outer world and against his unconscious drives.

Study of character formation reveals the fact that the character armor was formed in infancy for the same reasons and purposes which the character resistance serves in the analytic situation. The appearance in the analysis of the character as resistance reflects its infantile genesis. The situations which make the character resistance appear in the analysis are exact duplicates of those situations in infancy which set character formation into motion. For this reason, we find in the character resistance both a defensive function and a transference of infantile relationships with the outer world.

Economically speaking, the character in ordinary life and the character resistance in the analysis serve the same function, that of avoiding unpleasure, of establishing and maintaining a psychic equilibrium—neurotic though it may be—and finally, that of absorbing repressed energies. One of its cardinal functions is that of binding "free-floating" anxiety, or, in other words, that of absorbing dammed-up energy. Just as the historical, infantile element is present and active in the neurotic symptoms, so it is in the character. This is why a consistent dissolving of character resistances provides an infallible and immediate avenue of approach to the central infantile conflict.

What, then, follows from these facts for the technique of character-analysis? Are there essential differences between character-analysis and ordinary resistance analysis? There are. They are related to

a) the selection of the sequence in which the material is interpreted;

_____

* By the realization of this fact, the formal element becomes included in the sphere of psychoanalysis which, hitherto, was centered primarily on the content.

b) the technique of resistance interpretation itself.

As to a): If we speak of "selection of material," we have to expect an important objection: some will say that any selection is at variance with basic psychoanalytic principles, that one should let oneself be guided by the patient, that with any kind of selection one runs the danger of following one's personal inclinations. To this we have to say that in this kind of selection it is not a matter of neglecting analytic material; it is merely a matter of *safeguarding a logical sequence* of interpretation which corresponds to the structure of the individual neurosis. All the material is finally interpreted; only, in any given situation this or that detail is more important than another. Incidentally, the analyst always makes selections anyhow, for he has already made a selection when he does not interpret a dream in the sequence in which it is presented but selects this or that detail for interpretation. One also has made a selection if one pays attention only to the content of the communications but not to their form. In other words, the very fact that the patient presents material of the most diverse kinds forces one to make a selection; what matters is only that one select *correctly* with regard to the given analytic situation.

In patients who, for character reasons, consistently fail to follow the fundamental rule, and generally where one deals with a character resistance, one will be forced *constantly to lift the character resistance out of the total material* and to dissolve it by the interpretation of its meaning. That does not mean, of course, that one neglects the rest of the material; on the contrary, every bit of material is valuable which gives us information about the meaning and origin of the disturbing character trait; one merely postpones the interpretation of what material does not have an immediate connection with the transference resistance until such time as the character resistance is understood and overcome at least in its essential features. I have already tried to show what are the dangers of giving deep-reaching interpretations in the presence of undissolved character resistances.

As to b): We shall now turn to some special problems of character-analytic technique. First of all, we must point out a possible misunderstanding. We said that character-analysis begins with the emphasis on and the consistent analysis of the character resistance. It should be well understood that this does not mean that one asks the patient, say, not to be aggressive, not to deceive, not to talk in a confused manner, etc. Such procedure would be not only un-analytic but altogether sterile. The fact has to be emphasized again and again that what is described here as character-analysis has nothing to do with education, admonition, trying to make the patient behave differently, etc. In character-analysis, we ask ourself *why* the patient deceives, talks in a confused manner, why he is affect-blocked, etc.; we try to arouse the patient's interest in his character traits in order to be able, with his help, to explore analytically their origin and meaning. All we do is to lift the character trait which presents the cardinal resistance out of the level of the personality and to show the patient, if possible, the superficial connections between character and symptoms; it is left to him whether or not he will utilize his knowledge for an alteration of his character. In principle, the procedure is not different from the analysis of a symptom. What is added in character-analysis is merely that we isolate the character trait and confront the patient with it repeatedly until he begins to look at it objectively and to experience it like a painful symptom; thus, the character trait begins to be experienced as a foreign body which the patient wants to get rid of.

Surprisingly, this process brings about a change—although only a temporary one—in the personality. With progressing character-analysis, that impulse or trait automatically comes to the fore which had given rise to the character resistance in the transference. To go back to the illustration of the passive-feminine character: the more the patient achieves an objective attitude toward his tendency to passive submission, the more aggressive does he become. This is so because his passive-feminine attitude was essentially a reaction to repressed aggressive impulses. But with the aggression we also have a return of the infantile castration anxiety which in infancy had caused the change from aggressive to passive-feminine behavior. In this way the analysis of the character resistance leads directly to the center of the neurosis, the Oedipus complex.

One should not have any illusions, however. The isolation of such a character resistance and its analytic working-through usually takes many months of sustained effort and patient persistence. Once the breakthrough has succeeded, though, the analysis usually proceeds rapidly, with *emotionally* charged analytical experiences. If, on the other hand, one neglects such character resistances and instead simply follows the line of the material, interpreting everything in it, such resistances form a ballast which it is difficult if not impossible to remove. In that case, one gains more and more the impression that every interpretation of meaning was wasted, that the patient continues to doubt everything or only pretends to accept things, or that he meets everything with an inward smile. If the elimination of these resistances was not begun right in the beginning, they confront one with an insuperable obstacle in the later stages of the analysis, at a time when the most important interpretations of the Oedipus complex have already been given.

I have already tried to refute the objection that it is impossible to tackle resistances before one knows their *infantile* determination. The essential thing is first to see through the *present-day* meaning of the character resistance; this is usually possible without the infantile material. The latter is needed for the *dissolution* of the resistance. If at first one does no more than to show the patient the resistance and to interpret its present-day meaning, then the corresponding infantile material with the aid of which we can eliminate the resistance soon makes its appearance.

If we put so much emphasis on the analysis of the *mode* of behavior, this does not imply a neglect of the contents. We only add something that hitherto has been neglected. Experience shows that the analysis of character resistances has to assume first rank. This does not mean, of course, that one would only analyze character resistances up to a certain date and then begin with the interpretation of contents. The two phases—resistance analysis and analysis of early infantile experiences—overlap essentially; only in the beginning, we have a preponderance of character-analysis, that is, "education to analysis *by* analysis," while in the later stages the emphasis is on the contents and the infantile. This is, of course, no rigid rule but depends on the attitudes of the individual patient. In one patient, the interpretation of the infantile material will be begun earlier, in another later. It is a basic rule, however, not to give any deep-reaching interpretations—no matter how clear-cut the material—as long as the patient is not ready to assimilate them. Again, this is nothing new, but it seems that differences in analytic technique are largely determined by what one or the other analyst means by "ready for analytic interpretation." We also have to distinguish those contents which are part and parcel of the character resistance and others which belong to other spheres of experiencing. As a rule, the patient is in the beginning ready to take cognizance of the former, but not the latter. Generally speaking, our character-analytic endeavors are nothing but an attempt to achieve the greatest possible security in the introduction of the analysis and in the interpretation of the infantile material. This leads us to the important task of studying and systematically describing the various forms of characterological transference resistances. If we understand them, the technique derives automatically from their structure.

d) Derivation of the situational technique from the structure of the character resistance (interpretation technique of the defense).

We now turn to the problem of how the situational technique of character-analysis can be derived from the structure of the character resistance in a patient who develops his resistances right in the beginning, the structure of which is, however, completely unintelligible at first. In the following case the character resistance had a very complicated structure; there were a great many coexistent and overlapping determinations. We shall try to describe the reasons which prompted me to begin the interpretation work with one aspect of the resistance and not with any other. Here also we will see that a consistent and logical interpretation of the defenses and of the mechanisms of the "armor" leads directly into the central infantile conflicts.

A Case of Manifest Inferiority Feelings

A man 30 years of age came to analysis because he "didn't get any fun out of life." He did not really think he was sick but, he said, he had heard about psychoanalysis and perhaps it would make things clearer to him. When asked about symptoms, he stated he did not have any. Later it was found that his potency was quite defective. He did not quite dare approach women, had sexual intercourse very infrequently, and then he suffered from premature ejaculation and intercourse left him unsatisfied. He had very little insight into his impotence. He had become reconciled to it; after all, he said, there were a lot of men who "didn't need that sort of thing."

His behavior immediately betrayed a severely inhibited individual. He spoke without looking at one, in a low voice, haltingly, and embarrassedly clearing his throat. At the same time, there was an obvious attempt to suppress his embarrassment and to appear courageous. Nevertheless, his whole appearance gave the impression of severe feelings of inferiority.

Having been informed of the fundamental rule, the patient began to talk hesitatingly and in a low voice. Among the first communications was the recollection of two "terrible" experiences. Once he had run over a woman with an automobile and she had died of her injuries. Another time, as a medical orderly during the war, he had had to do a tracheotomy. The bare recollection of these two experiences filled him with horror. In the course of the first few sessions he then talked, in the same monotonous, low and suppressed manner about his youth. Being next to the youngest of a number of children, he was relegated to an inferior place. His oldest brother, some twenty years his senior, was the parents' favorite; this brother had traveled a good deal, "knew the world," prided himself on his experiences and when he came home from one of his travels "the whole house pivoted around him." Although the content of his story made the envy of this brother and the hatred of him obvious enough, the patient, in response to a cautious query, denied ever having felt anything like that toward his brother. Then he talked about his mother, how good she had been to him and how she had died when he was 7 years of age. At this, he began to cry softly; he became ashamed of this and did not say anything for some time. It seemed clear that his mother had been the only person who had given him some love and attention and that her loss had been a severe shock to him. After her death, he had spent 5 years in the house of this brother. It was not the content but the tone of his story which revealed his enormous bitterness about the unfriendly, cold and domineering behavior of his brother. Then he related in a few brief sentences that now he had a friend who loved and admired him very much. After this, a continuous silence set in. A few days later he related a dream: *He saw himself in a foreign city with his friend; only, the face of his friend was different.* The fact that the patient had left his own city for the purpose of the analysis suggested that the man in the dream represented the analyst. This identification of the analyst with the friend might have been interpreted as a beginning positive transference. In view of the total situation, however, this would have been unwise. He himself recognized the analyst in the friend, but had nothing to add to this. Since he either kept silent or else expressed his doubts that *he* would be able to carry out the analysis, I told him that he had something against

me but did not have the courage to come out with it. He denied
this categorically, whereupon I told him that he also never had
had the courage to express his inimical impulses toward his
brother, not even to think them consciously; and that apparently he had established some kind of connection between
his older brother and myself. This was true in itself, but I
made the mistake of interpreting his resistance at too deep a
level. Nor did the interpretation have any success; on the
contrary, the inhibition became intensified. So I waited a few
days until I should be able to understand, from his behavior,
the more important present-day meaning of his resistance.
What was clear at this time was that there was a transference
not only of the hatred of the brother but also a strong defense
against a feminine attitude (*cf.* the dream about the friend).
But an interpretation in this direction would have been in-
advisable at this time. So I continued to point out that for some
reason he defended himself against me and the analysis, that
his whole being pointed to his being blocked against the analysis. To this he agreed by saying that, yes, that was the way
he was generally in life, rigid, inaccessible and on the defensive. While I demonstrated to him his defense in every
session, on every possible occasion, I was struck by the monotonous expression with which he uttered his complaints. Every
session began with the same sentences: "I don't feel anything,
the analysis doesn't have any influence on me, I don't see how
I'll ever achieve it, nothing comes to my mind, the analysis
doesn't have any influence on me," etc. I did not understand
what he wanted to express with these complaints, and yet it
was clear that here was the key to an understanding of his
resistance.*

Here we have a good opportunity for studying the difference

---

* *Footnote, 1945:* The explanation given here is insufficient, although it is
psychologically correct. Today we know that such complaints are the immediate expression of muscular armoring. The patient complains about affect-
lameness because of a block in his plasmatic currents and sensations. The
disturbance, then, is primarily of a *biophysical* nature. Orgone therapy eliminates the block in motility not with psychological but with biophysical means.

between the character-analytic and the active-suggestive education to analysis. I might have admonished him in a kindly way to tell me more about this and that; I might have been able thus to establish an artificial positive transference; but experience with other cases had shown me that one does not get far with such procedures. Since his whole behavior did not leave any room for doubt that he refuted the analysis in general and me in particular, I could simply stick to this interpretation and wait for further reactions. When, on one occasion, the talk reverted to the dream, he said the best proof for his not refuting me was that he identified me with his friend. I suggested to him that possibly he had expected me to love and admire him as much as his friend did; that he then was disappointed and very much resented my reserve. He had to admit that he had had such thoughts but that he had not dared to tell them to me. He then related how he always only *demanded* love and especially recognition, and that he had a very *defensive* attitude toward men with a particularly masculine appearance. He said he did not feel equal to such men, and in the relationship with his friend he had played the feminine part. Again there was material for interpreting his feminine transference but his total behavior warned against it. The situation was difficult, for the elements of his resistance which I already understood, the transference of hatred from his brother, and the narcissistic-feminine attitude toward his superiors, were strongly warded off; consequently, I had to be very careful or I might have provoked him into breaking off the analysis. In addition, he continued to complain in every session, in the same way, that the analysis did not touch him, etc.; this was something which I still did not understand after about four weeks of analysis, and yet, I felt that it was an essential and acutely active character resistance.

I fell ill and had to interrupt the analysis for two weeks. The patient sent me a bottle of brandy as a tonic. When I resumed the analysis he seemed to be glad. At the same time, he continued his old complaints and related that he was very much bothered by thoughts about death, that he constantly was afraid that something had happened to some member of his family; and that during my illness he had always been thinking that I might die. It was when this thought bothered him particularly badly one day that he had sent me the brandy. At this point, the temptation was great to interpret his repressed death wishes. The material for doing so was ample, but I felt that such an interpretation would be fruitless because it would bounce back from the wall of his complaints that "nothing touches me, the analysis has no influence on me." In the meantime, the secret double meaning of his complaint, "nothing touches me" ("*nichts dringt in mich ein*") had become clear; it was an expression of his most deeply repressed transference wish for anal intercourse. But would it have been justifiable to point out to him his homosexual love impulse—which, it is true, manifested itself clearly enough—while he, with his whole being, continued to protest against the analysis? First it had to become clear what was the meaning of his complaints about the uselessness of the analysis. True, I could have shown him that he was wrong in his complaints: he dreamed without interruption, the thoughts about death became more intense, and many other things went on in him. But I knew from experience that that would not have helped the situation. Furthermore, I felt distinctly the armor which stood between the unconscious material and the analysis, and had to assume that the existing resistance would not let any interpretation penetrate to the unconscious. For these reasons, I did no more than consistently to show him his attitude, interpreting it as the expression of a violent defense, and telling him that we had to wait until we understood this behavior. He understood already that the death thoughts on the occasion of my illness had not necessarily been the expression of a loving solicitude.

In the course of the next few weeks it became increasingly clear that his inferiority feeling connected with his feminine transference played a considerable role in his behavior and his complaints. Yet, the situation still did not seem ripe for interpretation; the meaning of his behavior was not sufficiently clear. To summarize the essential aspects of the solution as it was found later:

a) He desired recognition and love from me as from all men who appeared masculine to him. That he wanted love and had been disappointed by me had already been interpreted repeatedly, without success.

b) He had a definite attitude of envy and hatred toward me, transferred from his brother. This could, at this time, not be interpreted because the interpretation would have been wasted.

c) He defended himself against his feminine transference. This defense could not be interpreted without touching upon the warded-off femininity.

d) He felt inferior before me, because of his femininity. His eternal complaints could only be the expression of this feeling of inferiority.

Now I interpreted his inferiority feeling toward me. At first, this led nowhere, but after I had consistently held up his behavior to him for several days, he did bring some communications concerning his boundless envy, not of me, but other men of whom he also felt inferior. Now it suddenly occurred to me that his constant complaining could have only one meaning: "The analysis has no influence on me," that is, "It is no good," that is, "the analyst is inferior, is impotent, cannot achieve anything with me." *The complaints were in part a triumph over the analyst, in part a reproach to him.* I told him what I thought of his complaints. The result was astounding. Immediately he brought forth a wealth of examples which showed that he always acted this way when anybody tried to influence him. He could not tolerate the superiority of anybody and always tried to tear them down. He had always done the exact opposite of what any superior had asked him to do. There appeared a wealth of recollections of his spiteful and deprecatory behavior toward teachers.

Here, then, was his suppressed aggression, the most extreme manifestation of which thus far had been his death wishes. But soon the resistance reappeared in the same old form, there were the same complaints, the same reserve, the same silence. But now I knew that my discovery had greatly impressed him, which had *increased* his feminine attitude; this, of course, resulted in an intensified defense against the femininity. In analyzing the resistance, I started again from the inferiority feeling toward me; but now I deepened the interpretation by the statement that he did not only feel inferior but that, because of his inferiority, he felt himself in a female role toward me, which hurt his masculine pride.

Although previously the patient had presented ample material with regard to his feminine attitude toward masculine men and had had full insight for this fact, now he denied it all. This was a new problem. Why should he now refuse to admit what he had previously described himself? I told him that he felt so inferior toward me that he did not want to accept any explanation from me even if that implied his going back on himself. He realized this to be true and now talked about the relationship with his friend in some detail. He had actually played the feminine role and there often had been sexual intercourse between the legs. Now I was able to show him that his defensive attitude in the analysis was nothing but the struggle against the surrender to the analysis which, to his unconscious, was apparently linked up with the idea of surrendering to the analyst in a female fashion. This hurt his pride, and this was the reason for his stubborn resistance against the influence of the analysis. To this he reacted with a confirmatory dream: he lies on a sofa with the analyst, who kisses him. This clear dream provoked a new phase of resistance in the old form of complaints that the analysis did not touch him, that he was cold, etc. Again I interpreted the complaints as a depreciation of the analysis and a defense against surrendering to it. But at the same time I began to explain to him the economic meaning of this defense. I told him that from what he had told thus far about his infancy and adolescence it was obvious that he had closed himself up against all disappointments by the outer world and against the rough and cold treatment by his father, brother and teachers; that this seemed to have been his only salvation even if it demanded great sacrifices in happiness.

This interpretation seemed highly plausible to him and he soon produced memories of his attitude toward his teachers. He always felt they were cold and distant—a clear projection of his own attitude—and although he was aroused when they beat or scolded him he remained indifferent. In this connection he said that he often had wished I had been more severe. This wish did not seem to fit the situation at that time; only much later it became clear that he wished to put me and my prototypes, the teachers, in a bad light with his spite. For a few days the analysis proceeded smoothly, without any resistances; he now remembered that there had been a period in his childhood when he had been very wild and aggressive. At the same time he produced dreams with a strong feminine attitude toward me. I could only assume that the recollection of his aggression had mobilized the guilt feeling which now was expressed in the passive-feminine dreams. I avoided an analysis of these dreams not only because they had no immediate connection with the actual transference situation, but also because it seemed to me that he was not ready to understand the connection between his aggression and the dreams which expressed a guilt feeling. Many analysts will consider this an arbitrary selection of material. Experience shows, however, that the best therapeutic effect is to be expected when an immediate connection is already established between the transference situation and the infantile material. I only ventured the assumption that, to judge from his recollections of his aggressive infantile behavior, he had at one time been quite different, the exact opposite of what he was today, and that the analysis would have to find out at what time and under what circumstances this change in his character had taken place. I told him that his present femininity probably was an avoidance of his aggressive masculinity. To this the patient did not react except by falling back into his old resistance of complaining that he could not achieve it, that the analysis did not touch him, etc.

I interpreted again his inferiority feeling and his recurrent attempt to prove the analysis, or the analyst, to be impotent; but now I also tried to work on the transference from the brother, pointing out that he had said that his brother always played the dominant role. Upon this he entered only with much hesitation, apparently because we were dealing with the central conflict of his infancy; he talked again about how much attention his mother had paid to his brother, without, however, mentioning any subjective attitude toward this. As was shown by a cautious approach to the question, the envy of his brother was completely repressed. Apparently, this envy was so closely associated with intense hatred that not even the envy was allowed to become conscious. The approach to this problem provoked a particularly violent resistance which continued for days in the form of his stereotyped complaints about his inability. Since the resistance did not budge it had to be assumed that here was a particularly acute rejection of the person of the analyst. I asked him again to talk quite freely and without fear about the analysis and, in particular, about the analyst, and to tell me what impression I had made on him on the occasion of the first meeting.* After much hesitation he said the analyst had appeared to him so masculine and brutal, like a man who is absolutely ruthless with women. So I asked him about his attitude toward men who gave an impression of being potent.

This was at the end of the fourth month of the analysis. Now for the first time that repressed attitude toward the brother broke through which had the closest connection with his most disturbing transference attitude, the envy of potency. With much affect he now remembered that he had always condemned his brother for always being after women, seducing them and bragging about it afterwards. He said I had immedi-

---

* Since then I am in the habit of soon asking the patient to describe my person. This measure always proves useful for the elimination of blocked transference situations.

ately reminded him of his brother. I explained to him that obviously he saw in me his potent brother and that he could not open up to me because he condemned me and resented my assumed superiority just as he used to resent that of his brother; furthermore, it was plain now that the basis of his inferiority feeling was a feeling of impotence.

Then occurred what one always sees in a correctly and consistently carried-out analysis: *the central element of the character resistance rose to the surface.* All of a sudden he remembered that he had repeatedly compared his small penis with the big one of his brother and how he had envied his brother.

As might have been expected, a new wave of resistance occurred; again the complaint, "I can't do anything." Now I could go somewhat further in the interpretation and show him that he was acting out his impotence. His reaction to this was wholly unexpected. In connection with my interpretation of his distrust he said for the first time that he had never believed anyone, that he did not believe anything, and probably also not in the analysis. This was, of course, an important step ahead, but the connection of this statement with the analytic situation was not altogether clear. For two hours he talked about all the many disappointments which he had experienced and believed that they were a rational explanation of his distrust. Again the old resistance reappeared; as it was not clear what had precipitated it this time, I kept waiting. The old behavior continued for several days. I only interpreted again those elements of the resistance with which I was already well acquainted. Then, suddenly, a new element of the resistance appeared: he said he was *afraid of the analysis because it might rob him of his ideals*. Now the situation was clear again. He had transferred his castration anxiety from his brother to me. He was afraid of me. Of course, I did not touch upon his castration anxiety but proceeded again from his inferiority feeling and his impotence and asked him whether his high ideals did not make him feel superior and better than everybody else. He admitted this openly; more than that, he said that he was really better than all those who kept running after women and lived sexually like animals. He added, however, that this feeling was all too often disturbed by his feeling of impotence, and that apparently he had not become quite reconciled to his sexual weakness after all. Now I could show him the neurotic manner in which he tried to overcome his feeling of impotence: he was trying to recover a feeling of potency in the realm of ideals. I showed him the mechanism of compensation and pointed out again the resistances against the analysis which originated from his secret feeling of superiority. I told him that not only did he think himself secretly better and cleverer than others; it was for this very reason that he resisted the analysis. For if it succeeded, he would have taken recourse to the aid of somebody else and it would have vanquished his neurosis, the secret pleasure gain of which had just been unearthed. From the standpoint of the neurosis this would be a defeat which, furthermore, to his unconscious, would mean becoming a woman. In this way, by progressing from the ego and its defense mechanisms, I prepared the soil for an interpretation of the castration complex and of the feminine fixation.

The character-analysis had succeeded, then, in penetrating from his mode of behavior directly to the center of his neurosis, his castration anxiety, the envy of his brother because of his mother's favoritism, and the disappointment in his mother. What is important here is not that these unconscious elements rose to the surface; that often occurs spontaneously. What is important is the logical sequence and the close contact with the ego-defense and the transference in which they came up; further, that this took place without any urging, purely as the result of analytic interpretation of the behavior; further, that it took place with the corresponding affects. This is what constitutes a consistent character-analysis; it is a thorough working through of the conflicts assimilated by the ego.

In contrast, let us consider what probably would have happened without a consistent emphasis on the defenses. Right at the beginning, there was the possibility of interpreting the passive-homosexual attitude toward the brother, and the death wishes. Undoubtedly, dreams and associations would have provided further relevant material for interpretation. But without a previous systematic and detailed working through of his ego-defense, no interpretation would have affectively penetrated; the result would have been an intellectual knowledge of his passive desires alongside with a violent affective defense against them. The affects belonging to the passivity and the murderous impulses would have continued to remain in the defense function. The final result would have been a chaotic situation, the typical hopeless picture of an analysis rich in interpretations and poor in results.

A few months' patient and persistent work on his ego-defense, particularly its form (complaints, manner of speech, etc.) raised the ego to that level which was necessary for the assimilation of the repressed, it loosened the affects and brought about their displacement in the direction of the repressed ideas. One cannot say, therefore, that in this case two different techniques would have been feasible; there was only one possibility if one was to alter the patient *dynamically*. I trust that this case makes clear the different concept of the application of theory to technique. The most important criterion of an orderly analysis is the giving of *few* interpretations which are to the point and consistent, instead of a great many which are unsystematic and do not take into consideration the dynamic and economic element. If one does not let oneself be led astray by the material, if, instead, one evaluates correctly its dynamic position and economic role, then one gets the material later, it is true, but more thoroughly and more charged with affect. The second criterion is a continuous connection between present-day situation and infantile situation. While in the beginning the various elements of the content coexist side by side without any order, this changes into a logical sequence of resistances and contents, a sequence determined by the dynamics and structure of the individual neurosis. With unsystematic interpretation, one has to make one new start after another, guessing rather than knowing one's way; in the case of character-analytic work on the resistances, on the other hand, the analytic process develops as if by itself. In the former case, the analysis will run smoothly in the beginning only to get progressively into more and more difficulties; in the latter case, the greatest difficulties are met in the first few weeks and months of the treatment, to give way progressively to smooth work even on the most deeply repressed material. The fate of every analysis depends on its introduction, that is, the correct or incorrect handling of the resistances. The third criterion, then, is that of tackling the case not in this or that spot which happens to be tangible but at the spot which hides the most essential ego-defense; and the systematic enlarging of the breach which has been made into the unconscious; and the working out of that infantile fixation which is affectively most important at any given time. A certain unconscious position which manifests itself in a dream or an association may have a central significance for the neurosis and yet may at any given time be quite unimportant with regard to its technical significance. In our patient, the feminine attitude toward the brother was of central pathogenic significance; yet in the first few months the technical problem was the fear of the loss of the compensation for the impotence by high ideals. The mistake which is usually made is that of attacking the central pathogenic point of the neurosis which commonly manifests itself somehow right at the beginning. What has to be attacked instead are the respective important present-day positions which, if worked on systematically, one after the other, lead *of necessity* to the central pathogenic situation. It is important, therefore, and in many cases decisive, *how, when* and from which side one proceeds toward the central point of the neurosis.

What we have described here as character-analysis fits without difficulty into Freud's theory of resistances, their formation and dissolution. We know that every resistance consists of an id-impulse which is warded off and an ego-impulse which wards it off. Both impulses are unconscious. In principle, then, one would seem to be free to interpret first either the id-impulse or the ego-impulse. For example: If a homosexual resistance in the form of keeping silent appears right at the beginning of the analysis, one can approach the id-impulse by telling the patient that he is occupied with thoughts about loving the analyst or being loved by him; one has interpreted his positive transference, and if he does not take flight it will, at best, take a long time before he can come to terms with such a forbidden idea. The better way, then, is to approach first the *defense of the ego* which is more closely related to the conscious ego. One will tell the patient at first only that he is keeping silent because—*"for one reason or another,"* that is, without touching upon the id-impulse—he is defending himself against the analysis, presumably because it has become somehow dangerous to him. In the first case one has tackled the id aspect, in the latter case the ego aspect of the resistance, the defense.

Proceeding in this manner, we comprehend the negative transference in which every defense finally results, as well as the character, the armor of the ego. The superficial, more nearly conscious layer of *every* resistance must of necessity be a negative attitude toward the analyst, no matter whether the warded-off id-impulse is hatred or love. The ego projects its defense against the id-impulse to the analyst who has become a dangerous enemy because, by his insistence on the fundamental rule, he has provoked id-impulses and has disturbed the neurotic equilibrium. In its defense, the ego makes use of very old forms of negative attitudes; it utilizes hate impulses from the id even if it is warding off love impulses.

If we adhere to the rule of tackling resistances from the ego side, we always dissolve, at the same time, a certain amount of negative transference, of hatred. This obviates the danger of overlooking the destructive tendencies which often are extremely well hidden; it also strengthens the positive transference. The patient also comprehends the ego interpretation more easily because it is more in accordance with conscious experience than the id interpretation; this makes him better prepared for the latter which follows at a later time.

The ego defense has always the same form, corresponding to the character of the patient, whatever the repressed id-impulse may be. Conversely, the same id-impulse is warded off in different ways in different individuals. If we interpret only the id-impulse, we leave the character untouched. If, on the other hand, we always approach the resistances from the defense, from the ego side, we include the neurotic character in the analysis. In the first case, we say immediately *what* the patient wards off. In the latter case, we first make clear to him *that* he wards off "something," then, *how* he does it, what are the means of defense (character-analysis); only at last, when the analysis of the resistance has progressed far enough, is he told —or finds out for himself—what it is he is warding off. On this long detour to the interpretation of the id-impulses, all corresponding attitudes of the ego have been analyzed. This obviates the danger that the patient learns something too early or that he remains affectless and without participation.

Analyses in which so much analytic attention is centered upon the attitudes take a more orderly and logical course while the theoretical research does not suffer in the least. One obtains the important infantile experiences later, it is true; but this is more than compensated for by the emotional aliveness with which the infantile material comes up *after* the analytic work on the character resistances.

On the other hand, we should not fail to mention certain unpleasant aspects of a consistent character-analysis. It is a far heavier burden for the patient; he suffers much more than when one leaves the character out of consideration. True, this has the advantage of a selective process; those who cannot stand it would not have achieved success anyhow, and it is better to find that out after a few months than after a few years. Experience shows that if the character resistance does not give way a satisfactory result cannot be expected. The overcoming of the character resistance does *not* mean that the character is altered;

that, of course, is possible only after the analysis of its infantile sources. It only means that the patient has gained an objective view of his character and an analytic interest in it; once this has been achieved a favorable progress of the analysis is probable.

e) The loosening of the character armor.

As we said before, the essential difference between the analysis of a symptom and that of a neurotic character trait consists in the fact that the symptom is, from the beginning, isolated and objectively looked at while the character trait has to be continually pointed out so that the patient will attain the same attitude toward it as toward a symptom. Only rarely is this achieved easily. Most patients have a very slight tendency to look at their character objectively. This is understandable because it is a matter of loosening the narcissistic protection mechanism, the freeing of the anxiety which is bound up in it.

A man of 25 came to analysis because of some minor symptoms and because he suffered from a disturbance in his work. He showed a free, self-confident behavior but often one had the impression that his demeanor was artificial and that he did not establish any genuine relationship with the person to whom he talked. There was something cold in his manner of talking, something vaguely ironical; often he would smile and one would not know whether it was a smile of embarrassment, of superiority or irony.

The analysis began with violent emotions and ample acting out. He cried when he talked about the death of his mother and cursed when he described the usual upbringing of children. The marriage of his parents had been very unhappy. His mother had been very strict with him, and with his siblings he had established some sort of relationship only in recent years. The way in which he kept talking intensified the original impression that neither his crying nor his cursing or any other emotion came out really fully and naturally. He himself said that all this was not really so bad after all, that he was smiling all the time about everything he was saying. After a few hours, he began to try to provoke the analyst. For example, he would, when the analyst had terminated the session, remain lying on the couch ostentatiously for a while, or would start a conversation afterwards. Once he asked me what I thought I would do if he should grab me by the throat. Two days later, he tried to frighten me by a sudden hand movement toward my head. I drew back instinctively and I told him that the analysis asked of him only that he say everything, not that he do things. Another time he stroked my arm in parting. The deeper meaning of this behavior which could not be interpreted at this time was a budding homosexual transference manifesting itself sadistically. When, on a superficial level, I interpreted these actions as provocations, he smiled and closed up even more. The actions ceased as well as his communications; all that remained was the stereotyped smile. He began to keep silent. When I pointed out the defensive character of his behavior, he merely smiled again and, after some period of silence, repeated, obviously with the intention of making fun of me, the word "resistance." Thus the smiling and the making fun of me became the center of the analytic work.

The situation was difficult. Apart from the few general data about his childhood, I knew nothing about him. All one had to deal with, therefore, were his modes of behavior in the analysis. For some time, I simply waited to see what would be forthcoming, but his behavior remained the same for about two weeks. Then it occurred to me that the intensification of his smile had occurred at the time when I had warded off his aggressions. I tried to make him understand the meaning of his smile in this connection. I told him that no doubt his smile meant a great many things, but at the present it was a reaction to the cowardice I had shown by my instinctive drawing back He said that may well be but that he would continue to smile He talked about unimportant things, and made fun of the analysis, saying that he could not believe anything I was telling him

It became increasingly clear that his smile served as a protection against the analysis. This I told him repeatedly over several sessions but it was several weeks before a dream occurred which had reference to a machine which cut a long piece of brick material into individual bricks. The connection of this dream with the analytic situation was all the more unclear in that he did not produce any associations. Finally he said that, after all, the dream was very simple, it was obviously a matter of the castration complex, and—smiled. I told him that his irony was an attempt to disown the indication which the unconscious had given through the dream. Thereupon he produced a screen memory which proved of great importance for the further development of the analysis. He remembered that at the age of about five he once had "played horse" in the backyard at home. He had crawled around on all fours, letting his penis hang out of his pants. His mother caught him doing this and asked what on earth he was doing. To this he had reacted merely by smiling. Nothing more could be learned for the moment. Nevertheless, one thing had been learned: his smile was a bit of mother transference. When I told him that obviously he behaved in the analysis as he had behaved toward his mother, that his smile must have a definite meaning, he only smiled again and said that was all well and good but it did not seem plausible to him. For some days, there was the same smile and the same silence on his part, while I consistently interpreted his behavior as a defense against the analysis, pointing out that his smile was an attempt to overcome a secret fear of me. These interpretations also were warded off with his stereotyped smile. This also was consistently interpreted as a defense against my influence. I pointed out to him that apparently he was always smiling, not only in the analysis, whereupon he had to admit that this was his only possible way of getting through life. With that, he had unwillingly concurred with me. A few days later he came in smiling again and said: "Today you'll be pleased, Doctor. 'Bricks,' in my mother-tongue, means horse testicles. Swell, isn't it? So you see, it is the castration complex."

I said that might or might not be true; that, in any case, as long as he maintained this defensive attitude, an analysis of the dreams was out of the question; that, no doubt, he would nullify every association and every interpretation with his smile. It should be said here that his smile was hardly visible; it was more a matter of feeling and an attitude of making fun of things. I told him he need not be afraid of laughing about the analysis openly and loudly. From then on, he was much more frank in his irony. His association, in spite of its fun-making implication, was nevertheless very valuable for an understanding of the situation. It seemed highly probable that, as happens so often, he had conceived of the analysis in the sense of a danger of castration; at first he had warded off this danger with aggression and later with his smile. I returned to the aggressions in the beginning of the analysis and added the new interpretation that he had tried to test me with his provo-cations, that he wanted to see how far he could go, how far he could trust me. That, in other words, he had had a mistrust which was based on an infantile fear. This interpretation im-pressed him visibly. He was struck for a moment but quickly recovered and again began to disavow the analysis and my interpretations with his smiling. I remained consistent in my interpretations; I knew from different indications that I was on the right track and that I was about to undermine his ego defense. Nevertheless, he remained equally consistent in his smiling attitude for a number of sessions. I intensified my interpretations by linking them up more closely with the assumed infantile fear. I told him that he was afraid of the analysis because it would revive his infantile conflicts which he thought he had solved with his attitude of smiling but that he was wrong in this belief because his excitation at the time when he talked about his mother's death had been genuine after all. I ventured the assumption that his relationship with his mother had not been so simple; that he had not only feared and ridiculed but also loved her. Somewhat more serious than usually, he related details concerning the unkindness of his mother toward him; one time when he had misbehaved she even hurt his hand with a knife. True, he added, "Well, according to the book, this is again the castration complex, isn't it?" Nevertheless, something serious seemed to go on in him. While I continued to interpret the manifest and latent meaning of the smiling as it appeared in the analytic situation, further dreams occurred. Their manifest content was that of symbolical castration ideas. Finally he produced a dream in which there were horses, and another where a high tower arose from a fire truck. A huge column of water poured from the tower into a burning house. At this time, the patient suffered from occasional bedwetting. The connection between the "horse dreams" and his horse game he realized himself, although accompanied by smiling. More than that, he remembered that he had always been very much interested in the long penes of horses; he thought that in his infantile game he had imitated such a horse. He also used to find a great deal of pleasure in urinating. He did not remember whether as a child he used to wet his bed.

On another occasion of discussing the infantile meaning of his smile he thought that possibly his smile on the occasion of the horse game had not been derisive at all but an attempt to reconcile his mother, for fear that she might scold him for his game. In this way he came closer and closer to what I had now been interpreting for months from his behavior in the analysis. The smiling, then, had changed its function and meaning in the course of time: originally an *attempt at conciliation*, it had later become a *compensation of an inner fear*, and finally, it also served as a means of *feeling superior*. This explanation the patient found himself when in the course of several sessions he reconstructed the way which he had found out of his childhood misery. The meaning was: "Nothing can happen to me. I am proof against everything." It was in this last sense that the smile had become a defense in the analysis, as a protection against the reactivation of the old conflicts. The basic motive of this defense was an infantile fear. A dream which occurred at the end of the fifth month revealed the deepest layer of his fear,

the fear of being left by his mother. The dream was the following: "I am riding in a car, with an unknown person, through a
little town which is completely deserted and looks desolate.
The houses are run down, the windowpanes smashed. Nobody
is to be seen. It is as if death had ravaged the place. We come
to a gate where I want to turn back. I say to my companion
we should have another look. There is a man and a woman
kneeling on the sidewalk, in mourning clothes. I approach them
to ask them something. As I touched them on the shoulder they
jump and I wake up, frightened." The most important association was that the town was similar to that in which he had lived
until he was four years of age. The death of his mother and the
infantile feeling of being left alone were clearly expressed. The
companion was the analyst. For the first time, the patient took
a dream completely seriously, without any smiling. The character resistance had been broken through and the connection
with the infantile had been established. From then on, the
analysis proceeded without any special difficulty, interrupted,
of course, by the relapses into the old character resistance as
they occur in every analysis.

It goes without saying that the difficulties were far greater
than may appear from this brief synopsis. The whole resistance
phase lasted almost six months, characterized by derision of
the analysis for days and weeks on end. Without the necessary
patience and the confidence in the efficacy of consistent interpretation of the character resistance, one often would have
been inclined to give up.

Let us see whether the analytic insight into the mechanism
of this case would justify some other technical procedure. Instead of putting the emphasis consistently on the mode of
behavior, one might have thoroughly analyzed the patient's
scarce dreams. Possibly he might have had associations which
one could have interpreted. It may not be important that previous to the analysis the patient did not dream or forgot all his
dreams and did not produce any dreams with a content relevant to the analytic situation until after the consistent interpre-

tation of his behavior. One might object that the patient would have produced these dreams spontaneously anyhow; this cannot be argued because it cannot be proved one way or the other. At any rate, we have ample experience which teaches us that such a situation as presented by our patient can hardly be solved by passive waiting alone; if so, it happens by accident, without the analyst having the reins of the analysis in his hand. Let us assume, then, that we had interpreted his associations in connection with the castration complex, that is, tried to make him conscious of his fear of cutting or of being cut. *Perhaps* this would have finally also led to a success. But the very fact that we cannot be sure that it would have happened, that we must admit the accidental nature of the occurrence, forces us to refute such a technique which tries to circumvent an existing resistance as basically un-analytic. Such a technique would mean reverting to that stage of analysis where one did not bother about the resistances, because one did not know them, and where, consequently, one interpreted the meaning of the unconscious material directly. It is obvious from the case history that this would mean, at the same time, a neglect of the ego defenses.

One might object again that while the technical handling of the case was entirely correct one did not understand my argument; that all this was self-evident and nothing new, that this was the way all analysts worked. True, the general principle is not new; it is nothing but the consistent application of resistance analysis. Many years of experience in the Technical Seminar showed, however, that analysts generally know and recognize the principles of resistance technique, while in practice they use essentially the old technique of the direct interpretation of the unconscious. This discrepancy between theoretical knowledge and practical action was the source of all the mistaken objections to the systematic attempts of the Vienna Seminar to develop the consistent application of theory to therapy. If they said that all this was trite and nothing new, they had their theoretical knowledge in mind; if they objected that it was all wrong and not "Freudian" analysis, they thought of their own practice, which, as we have said, was quite different.

A colleague once asked me what I would have done in the following case: For the past four weeks he had been treating a young man who kept consistently silent but was otherwise very nice and showed a very friendly behavior before and after the analytic session. The analyst had tried all kinds of things, had threatened to break off the analysis and finally, when even dream interpretation failed, had set a date for the termination of the analysis. The scarce dreams had been filled with sadistic murder. The analyst had told the patient that, after all, he should realize from his dreams that in his phantasy he was a murderer. But it did not help. The colleague was not satisfied with my statement that it was incorrect to interpret such deep material in the presence of an acute resistance, no matter how clearly the material might appear in a dream. He thought there was no other way. When I told him that, first of all, the silence should have been interpreted as a resistance, he said that could not be done, for there was no "material" available to do it with. Is not the behavior itself, the silence during the hour in contrast to the friendly attitude outside, "material" enough? Does not this situation show clearly the one thing at least, that the patient expresses, with his silence, a negative attitude or a defense? And that, to judge from his dreams, it is a matter of sadistic impulses which, by his over-friendly behavior, he tried to compensate and camouflage? Why does one dare to deduce certain unconscious processes from a slip such as a patient's forgetting some object in the consultation room, and why does one not dare to deduce the meaning of the situation from his behavior? Is the total behavior less conclusive material than a slip? All this did not seem plausible to my colleague; he continued to insist that the resistance could not be tackled because there was "no material." There could be no doubt that the interpretation of the murderous impulses was a technical error; it could only have the effect of frightening the patient and of putting him all the more on his guard.

The difficulties in the cases presented in the Seminar were of a very similar nature: It was always the same underestimation of the complete neglect of the behavior as interpretable material; again and again the attempt to remove the resistance from the id side instead of by analysis of the ego defense; and finally, almost always, the idea—which was used as an alibi— that the patient simply did not want to get well or that he was "all too narcissistic."

In principle, the loosening of the narcissistic defense is not different in other types than in the one described. If, say, a patient is always affectless and indifferent, no matter what material he may be presenting, then one is dealing with the dangerous affect-block. Unless one works on this before anything else one runs the danger of seeing all the material and all the interpretations go to waste and of seeing the patient become a good analytical theorist while otherwise he remains the same. Unless one prefers in such a case to give up the analysis because of "too strong narcissism" one can make an agreement with the patient to the effect that one will continue to confront him with his affect-lameness but that, of course, he can stop whenever he wants to. In the course of time—usually many months, in one case it took a year and a half—the patient begins to experience the continued pointing out of his affect-lameness and its reasons as painful, for in the meantime one has acquired sufficient means of undermining the protection against anxiety which the affect-lameness presents. Finally the patient rebels against the danger which threatens from the analysis, the danger of losing the protective psychic armor and of being confronted with his impulses, particularly with his aggression. This rebellion activates his aggressivity and before long the first emotional outburst in the sense of a negative transference occurs, in the form of an attack of hatred. That achieved, the road becomes clear. When the aggressive impulses make their appearance, the affect-block is breached and the patient becomes capable of being analyzed. The difficulty consists in bringing out the aggressivity.

The same is true when narcissistic patients express their character resistance in their way of talking; they will talk, for example, always in a haughty manner, in technical terms, always highly correctly or else confusedly. Such modes of talking form an impenetrable barrier and there is no real experiencing until one analyzes the mode of expression itself. Here also, the consistent interpretation of the behavior results in narcissistic indignation, for the patient does not like to be told that he talks so haughtily, or in technical terms, in order to camouflage his feeling of inferiority before himself and the analyst, or that he talks so confusedly because he wants to appear particularly clever and is unable to put his thoughts into simple words. In this manner, one makes an important breach in the neurotic character and creates an avenue of approach to the infantile origin of the character and the neurosis. Of course, it is insufficient to point out the nature of the resistance at one time or another; the more stubborn the resistance, the more consistently does it have to be interpreted. If the negative attitudes against the analyst which are thus provoked are analyzed at the same time the risk of the patient's breaking off the analysis is negligible.

The immediate effect of the analytic loosening of the character armor and the narcissistic protection mechanism is twofold: First, the loosening of the affects from their reactive anchoring and hiding places; second, the creation of an avenue of approach to the central infantile conflicts, the Oedipus complex and the castration anxiety. An enormous advantage of this procedure is that one not only reaches the infantile experiences as such, but that one analyzes them in the specific manner in which they have been assimilated by the ego. One sees again and again that one and the same piece of repressed material is of different dynamic importance according to the stage which has been reached in the loosening of the resistances. In many cases, the affect of the infantile experiences is absorbed in character defenses; with simple interpretation of the contents, therefore, one may be able to elicit the memories but not the corresponding affects. In such cases, interpretation of the infantile material without *previous* loosening of the affect energies which are absorbed in the character is a serious mistake. It is responsible, for example, for the hopelessly long and relatively useless analyses of compulsive characters.* If, on the other hand, one first frees the affects from the defense formations of the character, a new cathexis of the infantile impulses takes place automatically. If the line of character-analytic resistance interpretation is followed, remembering without affect is practically out of the question; the disturbance of the neurotic equilibrium which goes with the analysis of the character from the very beginning makes it practically impossible.

In other cases, the character has been built up as a solid protective wall against the experiencing of infantile anxiety and has served well in this function, although at the expense of much happiness. If such an individual comes to analysis because of some symptom, this protective wall serves equally well as character resistance and one realizes soon that nothing can be done unless this character armor which covers up and absorbs the infantile anxiety is destroyed. This is the case, for example, in "moral insanity" and in many manic, narcissistic-sadistic characters. In such cases one is often confronted with the difficult question whether the symptom justifies a deep-

---

* The following case illustrates the decisive importance of the neglect of a mode of behavior. A compulsive character who had been in analysis for twelve years without any appreciable result and knew all about his infantile conflicts, such as his central father conflict, talked in the analysis in a peculiarly monotonous, sing-song intonation and kept wringing his hands. I asked him whether this behavior had ever been analyzed, which was not the case. One day it struck me that he talked as if he were praying, and I told him so. He then told me that as a child he had been forced by his father to go to the synagogue and to pray. He had prayed, but only under protest. In the same manner he had also prayed—for twelve long years—before the analyst: "Please, I'll do it if you ask me to, but only under protest." The uncovering of this seemingly incidental detail of his behavior opened the way to the analysis and led to the most strongly hidden affects.

reaching character-analysis. For one must realize that the character-analytic destruction of the characterological compensation temporarily creates a condition which equals a breakdown of the personality. More than that, in many extreme cases such a breakdown is inevitable before a new, rational personality structure can develop. One may say, of course, that sooner or later the breakdown would have occurred anyhow, the development of the symptom being the first sign. Nevertheless, one will hesitate about undertaking an operation which involves so great a responsibility unless there is an urgent indication.

In this connection another fact must be mentioned: character-analysis creates in every case violent emotional outbursts and often dangerous situations, so that it is important always to be master of the situation, technically. For this reason, many analysts will refuse to use the method of character-analysis; in that case, they will have to relinquish the hope for success in a great many cases. A great many neuroses cannot be overcome by mild means. The means of character-analysis, the consistent emphasis on the character resistance and the persistent interpretation of its forms, ways and motives, are as potent as they are unpleasant for the patient. This has nothing to do with education; rather, it is a strict analytic principle. It is a good thing, however, to point out to the patient in the beginning the foreseeable difficulties and unpleasantness.

f) On the optimal conditions for the analytic reduction of the present-day material to the infantile.

Since the consistent interpretation of the behavior spontaneously opens the way to the infantile sources of the neurosis, a new question arises: Are there criteria to indicate *when* the reduction of the present-day modes of behavior to their infantile prototypes should take place? This reduction, we know, is one of the cardinal tasks of analysis, but this formulation is too general to be applied in everyday practice. Should it be done as soon as the first signs of the corresponding infantile material appear, or are there reasons for postponing it until a certain

later time? First of all it must be pointed out that in many cases
the purpose of the reduction—dissolution of the resistance and
elimination of the amnesia—is not fulfilled: either there is no
more than an intellectual understanding, or the reduction is
refuted by doubts. This is explained by the fact that—as is the
case with the making conscious of unconscious ideas—the topical process is complete only if combined with the *dynamic-
affective* process of the becoming conscious. This requires the
fulfillment of two conditions: first, the main resistances must be
at least loosened up; second, the idea which is to become conscious—or, in the case of the reduction, is to enter a new association—must become charged with a certain minimum of affect.
Now, we know that the affects are usually split off from the
repressed ideas, and bound up in the acute transference conflicts and resistances. If, now, one reduces the resistance to the
infantile situation before it has fully developed, as soon as there
is only a trace of its infantile origin, then one has not fully
utilized its affective energies; one has interpreted the content
of the resistance without also having mobilized the corresponding affect. That is, dynamic considerations make it necessary
not to nip the resistance in the bud, but, on the contrary, to
bring it to full development in the transference situation. In the
case of chronic, torpid character incrustations there is no other
way at all. Freud's rule that the patient has to be brought from
acting out to remembering, from the present day to the infantile, has to be complemented by the further rule that *first*
that which has become chronically rigid must be brought to
new life in the actual transference situation, just as chronic
inflammations are treated by first changing them into acute
ones. With character resistances this is always necessary. In
later stages of the analysis, when one is certain of the patient's
cooperation, it becomes less necessary. One gains the impression that with many analysts the immediate reduction of as yet
completely immature transference situations is due to the fear
of strong and stormy transference resistances; this fits in with
the fact that—in spite of better theoretical knowledge—resist-

ances are very often considered something highly unwelcome and only disturbing. Hence the tendency to circumvent the resistance instead of bringing it to full development and then treating it. One should not forget the fact that the neurosis itself is contained in the resistance, that with the dissolution of every resistance we dissolve a piece of the neurosis.

There is another reason why it is necessary to bring the resistance to full development. Because of the complicated structure of each resistance, one comprehends all its determinations and meanings only gradually; the more completely one has comprehended a resistance situation, the more successful is its later interpretation. Also, the double nature of the resistance—present-day and historical—makes it necessary first to make fully conscious the forms of ego defense it contains; only after its present-day meaning has become clear should its infantile origin be interpreted. This is true of the cases who have already produced the infantile material necessary for an understanding of the resistance *which follows.* In the other, more numerous cases, the resistance must be brought to full development for no other reason than that otherwise one does not obtain enough infantile material.

The resistance technique, then, has two aspects: *First, the comprehension of the resistance from the present-day situation through interpretation of its present-day meaning; second, the dissolution of the resistance through association of the ensuing infantile material with the present-day material.* In this way, one can easily avoid the flight into the present-day as well as into the infantile, because equal attention is paid to both in the interpretation work. Thus the resistance turns from an impediment of the analysis into its most potent expedient.

g) Character-analysis in the case of amply flowing material.

In cases where the character impedes the process of recollection from the beginning, there can be no doubt about the indication of character-analysis as the only legitimate way of introducing the analysis. But what about the cases whose character admits of the production of ample memory material in the beginning? Do they, also, require character-analysis as here described? This question could be answered in the negative if there were cases without a character armor. But since there are no such cases, since the narcissistic protection mechanism always turns into a character resistance—sooner or later, in varying intensity and depth—there is no fundamental difference between the cases. The practical difference, though, is this: In cases such as described above, the narcissistic protection mechanism is at the surface and appears as resistance immediately, while in other cases it is in deeper layers of the personality so that it does not strike one at first. But it is precisely these cases that are dangerous. In the former case one knows what one is up against. In the latter case, one often believes for a long period of time that the analysis proceeds satisfactorily, because the patient seems to accept everything very readily, shows prompt reactions to one's interpretations, and even improvements. But it is just in these patients that one experiences the worst disappointments. The analysis has been carried out, but the final success fails to materialize. One has shot all one's interpretations, one seems to have made completely conscious the primal scene and all infantile conflicts; finally the analysis bogs down in an empty, monotonous repetition of the old material, and the patient does not get well. Worse still, a transference success may deceive one as to the real state of affairs, and the patient may return with a full relapse soon after his discharge.

A wealth of bad experiences with such cases suggested as a rather self-evident conclusion that one had overlooked something. This oversight could not refer to the contents, for in that respect these analyses left little to be desired; it could only be an unrecognized latent resistance which nullified all therapeutic endeavor. It was soon found that these latent resistances consisted precisely in the great willingness of the patients, in the lack of manifest resistances. In comparing them with successful cases, one was struck by the fact that these analyses had shown a constantly even flow, never interrupted by violent emotional outbursts; more importantly, they had taken place in almost constant "positive" transference; rarely, if ever, had there been violent negative impulses toward the analyst. This does not mean that the hate impulses had not been analyzed; only, they did not appear in the transference, or they had been remembered without affect. The prototypes of these cases are the narcissistic affect-lame and the passive-feminine characters. The former show a lukewarm and even, the latter an exaggerated "positive" transference.

These cases had been considered "going well" because they procured infantile material, that is, again because of a one-sided overestimation of the contents of the material. Nevertheless, all through the analysis, the character had acted as a severe resistance in a form which remained hidden. Very often, such cases are considered incurable or at least extremely difficult to handle. Before I was familiar with the latent resistances of these cases, I used to agree with this judgment; since then, I can count them among my most gratifying cases.

The character-analytic introduction of such cases differs from others in that one does not interrupt the flow of communications and does not begin the analysis of the character resistance until such time as the flood of communications and the behavior itself has unequivocally become a resistance.

2. THE BREAKTHROUGH INTO THE VEGETATIVE REALM

The orgasm theory had confronted me with the question: What was to become of the sexual energy that was *liberated* in the therapeutic process? The world strictly opposes all requirements of sexual hygiene. The natural instincts are *biological* facts which can neither be effaced from the earth nor be basically altered. Like everything living, man needs first of all satisfaction of his hunger and gratification of his sexual instinct. Society as it is today, impedes the first and denies the second. That is, there is a *sharp conflict between natural demands* and certain *social institutions*. Caught as he is in this conflict, man gives in more or less to one side or the other; he makes compromises which are bound to fail; he escapes into illness or death; or he rebels—senselessly and fruitlessly—against the existing order. In this struggle, human structure is molded.

Human structure contains the biological as well as the sociological demands. Everything that is signified by position, fame and authority, defends the sociological demands against the natural demands. I was amazed to see how one could so thoroughly overlook the enormous importance of the natural demands. Even Freud, though he himself had discovered quite a considerable part of it, became inconsistent. To him, instincts soon became nothing but "mythical entities"; they were "undeterminable," though "rooted in chemical processes."

The contradictions were enormous. In clinical therapeutic work, everything was determined by the instinctual demands, and practically nothing by society. On the other hand, there were "society and culture" with their "reality demands." True, man was fundamentally determined by his instincts, but at the same time the instincts had to adapt themselves to a sex-negating reality. True, the instincts sprang from physiological sources, but at the same time the individual had an "eros" and a "death instinct," fighting each other. There was, with Freud, an absolute dualism of instincts. There was no connection between sexuality and its alleged biological counterpart, the death instinct; there was only antithesis. Freud psychologized biology when he assumed biological "tendencies," i.e., forces with this or that "intention." Such views were metaphysical. Their criticism was justified by later experimental proof of the simple functional nature of instinctual life. It was impossible

From *The Function of the Orgasm*, vol. I of *The Discovery of the Orgone*, 1948.

to understand neurotic anxiety in terms of the theory of eros and death instinct. Finally, Freud gave up the libido-anxiety theory.

The biological "repetition-compulsion" beyond the pleasure principle was supposed to explain masochistic behavior. A will to suffer was assumed. This was in keeping with the theory of the death instinct. In brief, Freud transferred laws which he had discovered in the functioning of the psyche to its biological foundation. As society was considered to be constructed like an individual, there arose a methodological overburdening of psychology which could not hold water, and which, in addition, paved the way for speculations on "society and Thanatos." Psychoanalysis began to claim increasingly that it could explain all existence; at the same time it was shying away more and more from a correct sociological and physiological, as well as a purely psychological, comprehension of the single object, Man. Yet, there could be no doubt that what made man different from the other animals was *a specific interlacing of biophysiological, sociological and psychological processes*. The correctness of this *structural principle* of my theory was proven by the solution of the problem of masochism. From there on, psychic structure revealed itself, bit by bit, as a dynamic unification of biophysiological and sociological factors.

THE PROBLEM OF MASOCHISM AND ITS SOLUTION

According to psychoanalysis, the pleasure in suffering pain was simply the result of a biological need; "masochism" was considered an instinct like any other, except that it had a peculiar goal. In therapy, nothing could be done with such a concept. For, if one told a patient that "for biological reasons" he *wanted* to suffer, everything remained as it was. Orgasmotherapy confronted me with the question as to why the masochist turned the otherwise easily understandable demand for pleasure into a demand for pain.

A drastic occurrence in my practice cured me from an erroneous formulation by which psychology and sexology had been misled. In 1928 I treated a man who suffered from a masochistic perversion. His lamentations and his demands to be beaten blocked any progress. After some months of conventional psychoanalytic work my patience wore thin. One day, when he asked me again to beat him, I asked him what he would say if I actually did. He beamed with happy anticipation. I took a ruler and gave him two hard slaps on the buttocks. He yelled loud; there was no sign of pleasure whatsoever, and from that time on such demands were never repeated. However, his lamentations and passive reproaches persisted. My colleagues would have been horrified had they learned of this happening; but I had no regrets. All of a sudden I realized that—contrary to general belief—pain is far from being the instinctual goal of the masochist. When beaten, the masochist, like any other mortal—experiences *pain*. A whole industry (procuring instruments of torture, pictures and descriptions of masochistic perversions, and prostitutes to satisfy them) flourishes on the basis of that mistaken concept of masochism which it helps to create.

But the question remained: *If the masochist does not strive for pain, if he does not experience it as pleasure, why, then, does he ask to be tortured?* After much effort, I discovered what is at the basis of this perverse behavior—at first glance a truly fantastic idea: The masochist *wishes to burst and imagines that the torture will bring this about. In this manner alone does he hope to obtain relief.*

The masochistic lamentations revealed themselves as the expression of a painful *inner tension* which could not be discharged. They were open or disguised entreaties for *liberation* from the instinctual tension. As the masochist—due to his pleasure-anxiety—is unable actively to bring about gratification, he expects the orgastic release, the very thing he is most deeply afraid of, in the form of a *liberation from the outside*, provided by somebody else. The desire to burst is opposed by an equally deep fear of the very same thing. The masochistic tendency to *self-depreciation* began to appear in an entirely new light. *Self-aggrandizement* is, as it were, a biopsychic erection, a fantastic expansion of the psychic apparatus. A few years later I learned that it is based upon the perception of bio-electrical charges. The opposite is self-depreciation. The masochist shrivels up because of his fear that he may expand to the point of *bursting*. Behind the masochistic self-depreciation works impotent ambition and an inhibited wish to be great. The masochist's provoking to punishment became clear an an expression of the deep *wish to be brought to gratification against his own will.* Women with a masochistic character never have sexual intercourse without the phantasy of being seduced or raped. The man is to force them—*against their own will*—to the very thing they anxiously long for. They cannot do it themselves because they feel that it is prohibited or charged with intense guilt feelings. The well-known vindictiveness of the masochist, whose self-confidence is seriously impaired, finds an outlet in placing the other person in a bad light or in provoking him into cruel behavior.

Masochists frequently have the peculiar idea that their skin, particularly that of the buttocks, gets "warm" or "burning." The desire to be scratched with hard brushes or to be beaten until the skin breaks, is nothing but the desire to end a tension by bursting. That is, the attendant pain is by no means the goal; it is only an unpleasant accompaniment of the liberation from a doubtless actual tension. Masochism is the prototype of a *secondary* drive, and an emphatic demonstration of what results from the repression of natural drives.

In the masochist, orgasm anxiety is present in a *specific form*. Other patients either do not permit any sexual excitation to occur in the genital itself, as in the case of compulsion neurotics; or they escape into anxiety, as in the case of hysterics. The masochist, however, persists in pregenital stimulation; he does not elaborate it into neurotic symptoms. This increases the tension, and consequently, along with simultaneously increasing incapacity for discharge, the orgasm anxiety, also. Thus, the masochist finds himself in a vicious circle of the worst kind.

The more he tries to work himself out of the tension, the more he gets entangled in it. At the moment when orgasm should occur, the masochistic phantasies undergo an acute intensification; often they do not become conscious until this very moment. The man may imagine that he is being pulled through a fire, the woman, that her abdomen is being slashed or her vagina burst. To many, this is the only way of reaching a modicum of gratification. To be *forced* to burst means to resort to external help in attaining relief from tension.

Since the fear of orgastic excitation is part of every neurosis, masochistic phantasies and attitudes are to be found in every case of neurosis. The attempt to explain masochism as a perception of an internal death instinct, as a result of a fear of death, was in strict contradiction with clinical experience. As a matter of fact, masochists develop very little anxiety—as long as they can engage in masochistic phantasies. They do develop anxiety if and when hysterical or compulsion-neurotic mechanisms take the place of the masochistic phantasies. On the contrary, full-fledged masochism is an excellent means of avoiding anxiety, since it is always *the other person* who does the bad things or causes them to be done. In addition, the double significance of the idea of *bursting* (desire for and fear of orgastic release) satisfactorily explains every detail of the masochistic attitude.

The desire to burst (or the fear of it) which I soon found in all patients, was puzzling. It did not fit into customary psychological concepts. An idea must have a certain origin and a certain function. We are used to derive ideas from concrete impressions; the idea originates in the outer world and is relayed to the organism by the sense organs in the form of a perception; its energy derives from inner, instinctual sources. Such an external origin could not be found for the idea of bursting, which made it difficult to coordinate. At any rate, I was able to record some important findings:

Masochism is not a biological instinct. It is the result of a disturbance in gratification, and an ever unsuccessful attempt to overcome this disturbance. *It is a result, and not the cause, of the neurosis.*

Masochism is the expression of a sexual tension which cannot be discharged. Its immediate cause is pleasure-anxiety, that is, fear of orgastic discharge.

It consists in an attempt to bring about the very thing that is most deeply dreaded: the pleasurable relief from tension, which relief is being experienced and feared as a process of bursting.

The understanding of the mechanism of masochism opened an avenue of approach into biology. Human pleasure-anxiety became understandable as the result of a fundamental alteration of the *physiological* pleasure function. Suffering and wanting to suffer are the results of having lost the organic capacity for pleasure.

With this, I had hit upon the dynamics of all religions and philosophies of suffering. When, as sex counselor, I had to deal with a great many Christian people, I began to see the connection. Religious ecstasy follows exactly the model of the masochistic mechanism: the religious individual expects from God, an omnipotent figure, the relief from an inner sin, that is, an inner sexual tension; a relief which the individual is unable to bring about himself. The relief is desired with *biological* energy. But at the same time, it is experienced as "sin," and so the individual does not dare to bring it about himself. Somebody else has to do it—in the form of a punishment, an absolution, a deliverance, etc. About this, more will be said in another place. The masochistic orgies of the Middle-Ages, the inquisition, the religious castigations, tortures and acts of expiation betrayed their function: they were *unsuccessful, masochistic attempts at sexual gratification.*

The masochist differs in his disturbance of the orgasm in that he inhibits pleasure at the moment of highest excitation and keeps on inhibiting it. In so doing, he creates a contradiction between the tremendous expansion which is about to occur and the reverse direction. In all other forms of orgastic impotence, the inhibition sets in *before* the acme of excitation. This

fine detail, though seemingly only of academic interest, decided the fate of my later scientific work. My notes of the years
between 1928 and about 1934 show that my biological experimental work up to the bion research had this finding as a
starting point. I cannot possibly present the whole story. I will
have to simplify, or, rather, impart those first phantasies of
mine which I never would have dared to publish, had they not
been confirmed by the experimental and clinical work of the
ensuing ten years.

The Functioning of a Living Bladder

The fear of bursting and the desire to be made to burst had
been discovered in one specific case of masochism. Later on I
found it in all masochists, and—without exception—in all patients
to the extent to which they had masochistic tendencies. The refutation of the concept of masochism as a biological instinct went
far beyond a criticism of Freud's theory of the death instinct.
I kept asking myself: what is the origin of this idea of bursting,
which, in all patients, makes its appearance shortly before the
establishment of orgastic potency?

I soon found that in most cases this idea appears in the form
of a kinesthetic perception of the state of the body. In outspoken cases there is regularly the idea of the body as a *taut
bladder*. The patients complain about being taut, filled up, as
if they were going to burst, to explode. They feel "blown up,"
"like a balloon." They dread any loosening of their armor because it makes them feel as if they were being "pricked open."
Some patients express a fear of "melting away," of "dissolving,"
of losing their "hold on themselves," their "contour." They cling
to the rigid armoring of their movements and attitudes as a
drowning person clings to a board. Others have the strongest
desire to "burst." Many a case of suicide occurs on this basis.
The more acute the sexual tension becomes, the more distinct
become these sensations. They promptly disappear when the
orgasm anxiety is overcome and sexual relaxation can take

place. Then the hard features of the character disappear, the
person becomes "soft" and yielding and at the same time develops an elastic sort of strength.

The crisis in a successful character analysis occurs just at
this point; when intense preorgastic sensations are prevented
from taking their normal course by spasms of the musculature
which are caused by anxiety. At a time when the excitation has
reached its peak and calls for unhampered discharge, pelvic
spasm has an effect similar to that of pulling the emergency
brake when going at 100 miles an hour; everything goes helter-
skelter. Something like that happens to the patient in the genuine process of getting well. He has to make his choice: either
to let go entirely of his bodily inhibitory mechanisms, or, to
fall back into his neurosis. *The neurosis is but one thing: the
sum total of all the inhibitions of the natural sexual pleasure
which in the course of time have become mechanical.* All other
manifestations of the neurosis are the result of this *original*
disturbance. Around 1929 I began to grasp the fact that the
original pathogenic conflict of mental disease (the conflict between striving for pleasure and moral frustration) is structurally
anchored in a physiological way in the muscular disturbance.
*The psychic conflict between sexuality and morality works in
the biological depths of the organism as a conflict between
pleasurable excitation and muscular spasm.*

Masochistic attitudes attained great significance for the sex-
economic theory of the neuroses: they represent this conflict in
pure culture. Compulsion neurotics and hysterics—who avoid
the orgastic sensation by way of developing anxiety or neurotic
symptoms—regularly go through a phase of masochistic suffering in the process of getting well. This occurs at a time when
the fear of sexual excitation has been eliminated to a sufficient
extent so that they allow preorgastic genital excitation to occur,
without, however, as yet allowing the *acme of* excitation *without inhibition, i.e., without anxiety.*

Masochism, furthermore, became a central problem in *mass
psychology.* The question as to how this problem may be prac-

tically solved in the future seemed of decisive significance. The
working millions suffer the most severe deprivations of all
kinds. They are being dominated and exploited by a few people in power. Masochism flourishes like a weed in the form of
the diverse patriarchal religions, as ideology and practice,
smothering every natural claim of life. It keeps people in a
profound state of humble resignation. It frustrates their attempts to cooperative rational action and makes them forever
afraid of taking the responsibility for their existence. This is the
stumbling block of even the best intentions for a democratization of society.

Freud explained the chaotic and catastrophic social conditions as the result of the death instinct at work in the society.
The psychoanalysts contended that the masses were *biologically* masochistic. The need for a police force, so some said, was
a natural expression of the biological masochism of the masses;
people are indeed submissive to authoritarian governments as
is the individual to the powerful father.

Since, however, rebellion against the dictatorial authority,
the father, was considered as neurotic, the adjustment to his
demands and institutions, on the other hand, as normal, the
refutation of this theory required the demonstration of two
facts: *First,* the fact that there exists no *biological* masochism;
and *second,* that the adjustment to contemporaneous reality
(in the form, e.g., of irrational education or irrational politics)
is in itself neurotic.

I had no preconceived idea in this direction. The demonstration of these facts resulted from the interplay of many
observations—far from the furious mêlée of ideologies. They
resulted from the simple answer to an almost stupid question:
*How would a bladder behave if it were blown up with air from
the inside, and could not burst?* Let us assume that its membrane would be tensile, but could not be torn. This picture of
the human character as an armor around the living nucleus was
highly relevant. The bladder, if it could express itself in its
state of insoluble tension, would complain. In its helplessness,

it would look for the causes of its suffering on *the outside*, and would be reproachful. It would ask to be pricked open. It would provoke its surroundings until it had achieved its aim as it conceives this. *What it could not bring about spontaneously from the inside, it would passively, helplessly, expect from the outside.*

Let us think of the biopsychic organism, whose energy discharge is disturbed, in terms of an *armored* bladder. The membrane would be the character armor. The stretching takes place as the result of continuous production of inner energy (sexual energy, biological excitation). The biological energy presses towards the outside, be it to pleasurable discharge, be it towards contact with people and objects. The urge for expansion is synonymous with a *direction from within outward.* It is opposed by the force of the surrounding armor. This armor not only prevents the bursting, but, in addition, exerts a pressure *from without towards the inside.* It results in a rigidity of the organism.

This picture was in accord with the physical processes of *internal pressure* and *surface tension.* With these concepts I had come into contact when, in 1926, I reviewed for the psychoanalytic journal a most significant book by Fr. Kraus,* the famous Berlin internist.

The neurotic organism lent itself exceedingly well to the comparison with a taut, peripherally armored bladder. This peculiar analogy between a physical phenomenon and the characterological situation stood the test of clinical observation. The neurotic patient has become rigid at the body periphery, at the same time having retained his "central"

---

* Kraus, Fr., *Allgemeine und spezielle Pathologie der Person.* I. Teil: *Tiefenperson.* Leipzig, Thieme, 1926. Pp. 252. *Translator's note:* The findings and concepts of Kraus, at the time of their publication, were revolutionary, i.e., at variance with the usual mechanistic thinking in medicine. Consequently, they met with little understanding. G. R. Heyer, in one of his books on psychosomatic medicine, states frankly that the book was too difficult for him to understand. Most critics, however, simply declare that Kraus is "all wrong," without, however, going to the trouble of really studying his works or of proving or disproving his findings.

vitality with its demands. He is not at ease "within his own skin," he is "inhibited," "unable to realize himself," "hemmed in" as if by a wall; he "lacks contact," he feels "tight enough to burst." He strives with all his might "towards the world," but he is "tied down." More than that: he is so little able to stand the difficulties and disappointments in life, and the efforts to establish contact with life are so painful, that he prefer to "withdraw into himself." That is, the functional direction of "towards the world, out of the self," is opposed by another direction, that of "away from the world, back into the self."

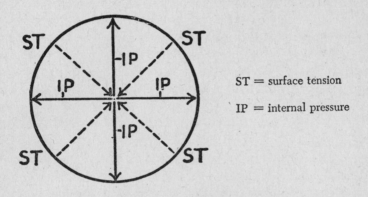

ST = surface tension

IP = internal pressure

The equation of something highly complicated with something simple seemed fascinating. The neurotically armored organism cannot burst like an ordinary bladder in order to get rid of its tension. It has only two ways out: either to become "masochistic," or else "healthy," that is, *able to admit the orgastic discharge of the dammed-up energy.* This orgastic discharge consists in a decrease of tension by way of a "discharge to the outside" in the form of contractions of the total body. The question still remained as to *what it was* that was discharged to the outside. I was far from the present knowledge of the functioning of biological energy. I thought of orgasm with its discharge of substances from the body also in terms of proliferations from a highly tensed bladder; after the detachment of the proliferating body, the surface tension and the internal pressure decrease. Plainly, the ejaculation of the semen alone could not account for this; for, ejaculation, if not accompanied by pleasure, does *not* reduce the tension.

I had no reason to regret this bit of speculation. It was to lead to very concrete facts. In this connection, a little occurrence at the Berlin Psychoanalytic Congress in 1922 may be worth mentioning. As a result of studying Semon and Bergson, I had engaged in a scientific phantasy. One should, I said to some of my friends, take Freud's picture of the "sending out of libido" literally and seriously. Freud had likened the sending out and retracting of psychic interest to the putting out and retracting of pseudopodia in the ameba. The putting forth of sexual energy is plainly visible in the erection of the penis. I thought that erection was functionally identical with the putting out of pseudopodia in the ameba, whereas, conversely, erective impotence, due to anxiety and accompanied by shrinking of the penis, was functionally identical with the retraction of the pseudopodia. My friends were horrified at such muddled thinking. They laughed at me, and I was offended. But thirteen years later, I was able to establish experimental proof for this assumption. I will have to show how the facts led to this proof.

The Functional Antithesis of Sexuality and Anxiety

The comparison of erection with protrusion of pseudopodia on the one hand, and the shrinking of the penis with their retraction on the other, led to the assumption of a functional antithesis between sexuality and anxiety. This antithesis was expressed in the *direction* of biological functioning. I could not rid myself of that idea. Since, through my experiences, everything I had learned from Freud about the psychology of instincts had come into a state of flux, the picture just mentioned linked itself with the very important question as to the biological basis of psychic functioning. Freud had postulated a physiological foundation for psychoanalysis. His "unconscious" was

deeply rooted in the biophysiological realm. In the depths of
the psyche the clear-cut psychic tendencies gave way to mysterious workings which could not be fathomed by psychological
thinking alone. Freud had attempted to apply to the sources
of life the psychological concepts derived from psychoanalytic
investigation. This led inevitably to a personification of the
biological processes and to the re-instatement of such metaphysical concepts as had previously been eliminated from psychology. In studying the function of the orgasm, I had learned
that, in the somatic realm, it is not admissible to think in terms
derived from the psychic realm. Every psychic occurrence has,
in addition to its causal determination, a *meaning* in terms of a
relation to the environment. To this corresponded the psychoanalytic *interpretation*. However, in the physiological realm,
there is no such "meaning," and its existence cannot be assumed
without re-introducing a supernatural power. *The living simply
functions*, it has no "meaning."

Natural science attempts to exclude metaphysical assumptions. Yet, if unable to explain the why and how of biological
functioning, one is apt to look for a "purpose" or a "meaning"
to put into the function. I found myself right back in the problems of the early period of my work, in the problems of mechanism and vitalism. I avoided a speculative answer, but I had
as yet no method for the correct solution of the problem. I was
acquainted with dialectic materialism, but did not know how
to apply it to investigation in the natural sciences. True, I had
given Freud's discoveries a functional interpretation, but the
inclusion of the physiological foundation of psychic life raised
the new question as to the *correct method*. To say that the soma
influences the psyche, is correct, but one-sided. That, conversely, the psyche influences the soma, is an everyday observation. But it is inadmissible to enlarge the concept of the psyche
to the extent of applying its laws to the soma. The concept that
psychic and somatic processes are mutually independent, and
only in "interaction," is contradicted by daily experience. I had
no solution to the problem. Only one thing was clear: *the*

*experience of pleasure, that is, of expansion, is inseparably
linked up with living functioning.*

It was at this point that my recently developed concept of
the masochistic function came to the rescue. I reasoned: The
psyche is determined by *quality*, the soma by *quantity*. In the
psyche, the determining factor is the *kind* of an idea or wish;
in the soma, however, it is the *amount* of energy at work. Insofar, psyche and soma were different. But the study of the
orgasm showed that the *quality of a psychic attitude depended
on the amount of the underlying somatic excitation.* The idea
of sexual intercourse and its pleasure is intense, colorful and
vivid in a state of intense somatic excitation. After gratification, however, the idea can be reproduced only with difficulty.
I had in mind the picture of an ocean wave which, rising and
falling, influences the movements of a piece of wood floating on
its surface. It was no more than a vague idea that psychic life
emerges and submerges from the underlying biophysiological
process, depending on what stage of this process happens to be
current. This wave-like process seemed to be represented in the
appearance and disappearance of consciousness at the time of
waking up or falling asleep. It was all rather obscure and
intangible. What was clear was only that the biological energy
dominates the psychic as well as the somatic. *There is functional unity.* True, biological laws can apply in the psychic
realm, but the converse is not true. This necessitated a critical
evaluation of Freud's concepts of the instincts.

Visual imagination is doubtless a psychic process. There are
unconscious ideas which can be deduced from their outward
manifestations. The unconscious itself, according to Freud, cannot be grasped. But if it "dips into" the biophysiological realm,
it must be possible to grasp it by way of a method which grasps
the *common factor* which dominates the *whole* biopsychic
apparatus. This common factor cannot be the "meaning"; nor
can it be the "purpose"; these are *secondary* functions. From a
consistent functional point of view, there is, in the biological
realm, no purpose, no aim; only *function* and *development*,

following certain laws. There remained the *dynamic structure*, the *balance of forces*. This is valid in all realms; this was something one could hold on to. What psychology calls "tension" and "relaxation" is an antithesis of forces. My idea of the bladder, as simple as it was, was entirely in accord with the concept of *unity of the psychic and the somatic*. Along with unity, there is, at the same time, antithesis. This concept was the germ of my theory of sex.

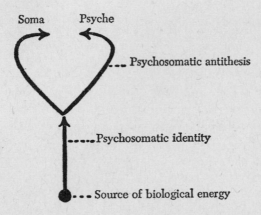

Diagram: Psychosomatic identity and antithesis.

Back in 1924, I had assumed that in the orgasm an excitation concentrates at the *periphery* of the organism, especially at the genital organs, and then flows back to the *vegetative center* where it ebbs away. Unexpectedly, a cycle of ideas was completed. What formerly had appeared as psychic excitation, could now be described as biophysiological current. After all, internal pressure and surface tension of a bladder are nothing but the functions of the *center* and the *periphery* of an organism. They are functionally opposed to each other. Their reciprocal strength determines the "fate" of the bladder, just as balance of sexual energy determines psychic health. *"Sexuality"* could be nothing else than *the biological function of expansion* ("out of the self") *from center to periphery*. Conversely, *anxiety* could be nothing but the reverse direction *from periphery to center* ("back into the self"). Sexuality and anxiety are one and the same process of excitation, only in opposite directions.

Soon, the connection of this theory with a multitude of clinical facts became clear. In sexual excitation, the peripheral vessels are dilated; in anxiety, one feels a tension within one—(in the center)—as if one were going to burst; the peripheral vessels are contracted. In sexual excitation, the penis expands, in anxiety it shrinks. The "biological energy center" is the source of the functioning energy; at the periphery is the functioning itself, in the contact with the world, in the sexual act, in the orgastic discharge, in work, etc.

These findings are already beyond the confines of psychoanalysis. They upset a good many concepts. The psychoanalysts could not follow, and my position was so prominent that my divergent views could not exist within the same organization without complication. Freud had refused to accept my attempt to view the processes of libido as part of the autonomic system. Being in the front line of psychoanalysis, I was not on the best terms with the official psychiatrists and other clinicians. Due to their mechanistic and unanalytic thinking, they would have understood little of what I said. Thus, the new-born theory of sex found itself alone, in a wide and empty space. I was encouraged by the multitude of confirmatory findings which experimental physiology provided for my theory. It seemed to reduce to a common denominator the unrelated findings amassed by generations of physiologists. A central point in these findings was the antithesis of sympathetic and parasympathetic.

What is "Biopsychic Energy"?

After sixty years of sexology, forty years of psychoanalysis, and almost twenty years of my own work against the background of the orgasm theory, this unanswered question still confronted the clinician who was called upon to treat human sexual disturbances. Let us recall the starting point of the orgasm theory. Neuroses and functional psychoses are maintained by excessive, not properly discharged sexual energy. "Psychic energy," it used to be called. What it really was, nobody knew. Doubtless, psychic disturbances had their root in the "somatic realm." What nourished the pathological psychic growths could only be the damming-up of energy. Only the elimination of *this energy source of the neurosis* by way of establishing full orgastic potency seemed to protect the patient against future relapse. Prevention of psychic disturbances on a mass basis without a knowledge of their somatic basis was inconceivable. The correctness of the statement, "with a satisfactory sex life, there are no neurotic disturbances," could not be doubted. This contention, naturally, has individual as well as social consequences; the significance of its implications is obvious. But, in spite of Freud, official science refused to concern itself with sexuality. Psychoanalysis itself eschewed the question more and more. Preoccupation with this question also bordered too much upon all the ordinary effusions of a pathological, distorted kind of sexuality, with that somewhat pornographic coloring which is typical of today. Only the sharp distinction between natural and pathological sexual manifestations, between "primary" and "secondary" drives, made it possible to persevere and to stick to the problem. Cogitation alone would not have led to a solution, nor the integration of all the excellent and pertinent data which appeared in increasing numbers in the modern physiological literature after about 1925 and were collected in Müller's *Die Lebensnerven*.

As always, clinical observation led on in the right direction. In Copenhagen, 1933, I treated a man who put up especially strong resistances against the uncovering of his passive-homosexual phantasies. This resistance was manifested in an extreme attitude of stiffness of the neck ("stiffnecked"). After an energetic attack upon his resistance he suddenly gave in, but in a rather alarming manner. For three days, he presented severe manifestations of vegetative shock. The color of his face kept changing rapidly from white to yellow or blue; the skin was mottled and of various tints; he had severe pains in the neck and the occiput; the heartbeat was rapid; he had diarrhea, felt worn out, and seemed to have lost hold. I was disturbed. True, I had often seen similar symptoms, but never that violent. Something had happened here that was somehow inherent in the therapeutic process but was at first unintelligible. *Affects had broken through somatically after the patient had yielded in a psychic defense attitude.* The stiff neck, expressing an attitude of tense masculinity, apparently had bound vegetative energies which now broke loose in an uncontrolled and disordered fashion. A person with a balanced sex-economy would be incapable of producing such a reaction. Such a reaction presupposes a continuous inhibition and damming-up of biological energy. It was the musculature that served this inhibitory function. When the muscles of the neck relaxed, powerful impulses broke through, as if propelled by a spring. The alternating pallor and redness of the face could be nothing but a movement to and fro of the body fluids, an alternating contraction and relaxation of the blood vessels. That fitted in very well with my concept of the functioning of the biological energy. The direction of "out of the self—toward the world" kept alternating rapidly with the opposite direction of "away from the world—back into the self." The musculature can, by contracting, inhibit the blood flow; it can, in other words, reduce the movement of the body fluids to a minimum.

This finding checked with earlier observations and those in recent cases. Soon, I had a multitude of facts which could be summed up in the formulation: *Sexual energy can be bound by chronic muscular tensions. The same is true of anger and anxiety.* I found that, whenever I dissolved a muscular inhibition or tension, one of the three basic biological excitations made its appearance: *anxiety, anger or sexual excitation.* True, I had been able to bring this about before, by way of dissolving purely characterological inhibitions and attitudes. The difference lay in the fact that now the break-through of biological energy was more complete, more forceful, more thoroughly experienced, and it occurred more *rapidly*. Also, it was accompanied in many patients by a spontaneous dissolution of the characterological inhibitions. These findings, though first made in 1933, were not published until 1935 in a preliminary form, and in 1937 in a more definite form.* Soon, some decisive questions of the mind-body problem clarified themselves:

The character armor now showed itself to be *functionally identical* with muscular hypertension, the muscular armor. The concept of "functional identity" which I had to introduce means nothing but the fact that muscular and character attitudes serve the same function in the psychic apparatus; they can influence and replace each other. Basically, they cannot be separated; in their function they are identical.

Concepts which are arrived at by the unification of facts immediately lead on to other things. If the character armor expressed itself through the muscular armor and vice versa, then the unity of psychic and somatic functions was comprehended and became capable of being *influenced* in a practical way. From now on, I was able to make *practical* use of this unity. When a character inhibition would fail to respond to psychic influencing, I would work at the corresponding somatic attitude. Conversely, when a disturbing muscular attitude proved difficult of access, I would work on its characterological expression and thus loosen it up. A typical friendly smile, e.g., which impeded the work, could be eliminated by describing the expression as well as by disturbing the muscular attitude. That was an enormous step forward. The further development of this technique into the vegetotherapy of today took another six years.

---

* Wilhelm Reich, *Psychischer Kontakt und Vegetative Strömung. Beitrag zur Affektlehre und charakteranalytischen Technik.* Sex-Pol-Verlag, 1935.

Wilhelm Reich, *Orgasmusreflex, Muskelhaltung und Körperausdruck. Zur Technik der charakteranalytischen Vegetotherapie.* Sex-Pol-Verlag, 1937.

The loosening of the rigid muscular attitudes resulted in peculiar somatic sensations: involuntary trembling, jerking of muscles, sensations of hot and cold, itching, crawling, prickling sensations, goose flesh, and the somatic perception of anxiety, anger and pleasure. To comprehend these manifestations, I had to break with all the old concepts of psychosomatic interrelationship. These manifestations were not the "result," the "causes," or the "accompaniment" of "psychic" processes; they were simply *these processes themselves in the somatic sphere*.

I brought together into one concept as *"vegetative currents"* all those somatic manifestations which—in contrast to the rigid muscular armor—are characterized by movement. Immediately the question arose: *Are these vegetative currents only movements of body fluids, or more than that?* Purely mechanical movements of fluids, it is true, could account for the sensations of hot and cold, for pallor and blushing, but they could not account for such manifestations as formication, prickling sensations, shuddering, or the "sweet," "melting" quality of pre-orgastic sensations of pleasure, etc. The problem of orgastic impotence was still unanswered: *the genital may be filled with blood, and yet, any trace of pleasurable excitation may be absent.* That means, sexual excitation is by no means identical with, or produced by, blood flow. Furthermore, there are anxiety states without any special pallor of the face or the rest of the body. The feeling of constriction in the chest (anxiety, *angustiae*), the feeling of "oppression," could not be ascribed solely to congestion in the central organs. Otherwise, one would experience anxiety after a good meal, when the blood is concentrated in the abdomen. *There must be something in addition to the blood flow, something that, according to its biological function, produces anxiety, anger or pleasure.* The blood flow can only play the role of an essential means. Perhaps this unknown "something" does not occur when the flow of the body fluids is somehow impeded. This marks an unformed stage in my thinking on the problem.

THE ORGASM FORMULA:
TENSION → CHARGE → DISCHARGE → RELAXATION

The unknown "something" I was looking for could be nothing but *bio-electricity*. This occurred to me one day when I tried to understand the physiology of the sexual friction between penis and vaginal mucous membrane. Sexual friction is a fundamental biological process; it occurs wherever in the animal kingdom procreation takes place by means of two separate sexes. In this process, two body surfaces are in mutual friction; this results in biological excitation as well as in congestion, expansion, "erection." The Berlin internist Kraus, on the basis of pioneering experiments, found the body to be governed by electrical processes. The body consists of innumerable "border surfaces" between membranes and electrolytic fluids of various densities and compositions. According to a well-known law of physics, electrical tensions develop at the border between conducting fluids and membranes. As there are differences in density and in the structure of the membranes, there are differences in the tensions at the border surfaces and, consequently, differences of potentials of various intensity. Potential differences may be likened to the difference in energy of two bodies at different heights. In falling, the higher one can perform more work than the lower one. The same weight, say, of 1 kilogram, will drive a pile deeper into the ground when falling from a height of 3 meters than when falling from a height of 1 meter. The "potential energy of position" is greater, and consequently the "kinetic energy" is greater when this potential energy is released. The principle of difference of potential can be applied without difficulty to the differences in electrical tensions. When a highly charged body is connected by a wire with a less highly charged one, a current will flow from the former to the latter; static electrical energy changes into current (i.e., moving) energy. There occurs an equalization between the two charges, just as the level of water in two containers becomes the same when they are connected.

by a pipe. This equalization of energy always presupposes a *difference* in potential energy. Now, our body consists of innumerable inner surfaces with different potential energies. Consequently, the electrical energy in the body is in constant motion from places of higher potential to places of lower potential. The carriers of the electrical charges in this continuous process of equalization are the particles of the body fluids, the ions. They are atoms carrying a certain amount of electrical charge; according to whether they move towards the negative or positive pole, they are called kations or anions. What has all this to do with the problem of sexuality? A great deal!

Sexual tension is felt in the whole body, but particularly strongly at the heart and in the abdomen. Gradually, the excitation concentrates at the genitals. They fill with blood, and electrical charges occur at the surface of the genitals. We know that a delicate touch of one sexually excited part of the body produces excitation in other parts. Tension or excitation increases with friction. It reaches its peak in the *orgasm*, a state in which *involuntary contractions of the musculature of the genitals and the body as a whole* take place. It is a well-known fact that muscular contraction is accompanied by the discharge of electrical energy. This discharge can be measured and represented in the form of a graphic curve. Some physiologists think that the nerves store up energy which is discharged in the muscular contraction; not the nerve, but only the muscle, which is capable of contraction, can discharge energy. With sexual friction, energy is first stored up in both bodies, and then discharged in the orgasm. *Orgasm must then be a phenomenon of electrical discharge.* The structure of the genitals is peculiarly adapted for this; great vascularity, dense nerve ganglia, erectibility, and a musculature particularly capable of spontaneous contractions.

On closer investigation of the process, one discovers a peculiar four-beat:

1. The organs fill with fluid: erection with *mechanical tension*.

2. This leads to an intense excitation, which I assumed to be of an electrical nature: *electrical charge*.

3. In the orgasm, the electrical charge or sexual excitation is discharged in muscular contractions: *electrical discharge*.

4. This is followed by a relaxation of the genitals through a flowing back of the body fluids: *mechanical relaxation*.

This four-beat: MECHANICAL TENSION → ELECTRICAL CHARGE, → ELECTRICAL DISCHARGE → MECHANICAL RELAXATION I termed the *orgasm formula*.

The process described by it we can picture to ourselves in a simple way. I come back here to the functioning of a filled elastic bladder about which I had been thinking some six years previous to the discovery of the orgasm formula. Let us compare two spheres, a rigid one of metal, and an elastic one, say, a pig's bladder, or an ameba.

The metal sphere would be hollow, the pig's bladder, however, would contain a complex system of fluids and membranes of different densities and conductivity. Furthermore, the metal sphere would receive its electrical charge *from without*, say, from a static machine; the pig's bladder, on the other hand, would contain an automatically working charging apparatus in the center, that is, it would spontaneously be charged *from*

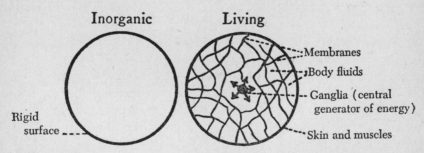

Inorganic	Living

Rigid surface - - - -

Membranes
Body fluids
Ganglia (central generator of energy)
Skin and muscles

Electrical energy	*Electrical energy*
on surface only, evenly distributed, supplied from outside; whole system rigid.	in the whole body, unevenly distributed, supplied from inside source; whole system capable of expanding and contracting.

Diagram of inorganic and organic, living, sphere.

within. According to fundamental laws of physics, the charge of the metal sphere would be equally distributed over the surface, and only the surface. The pig's bladder, however, would be charged through and through; due to the differences in density and the variety of fluids and membranes, the charge would vary from one place to another; furthermore, the charges would be in continuous motion from places of higher potential to places of lower potential. But, generally speaking, one direction would predominate: that *from the center*, the source of the electrical energy, *to the periphery*. For this reason, the bladder would more or less continually expand and contract. From time to time it would—like the vorticella—return to the spherical shape in which—the content remaining the same—the surface tension is lowest. In case of too great an inner energy production, the bladder would discharge the energy by way of a few contractions, that is, it would be able to *regulate* the energy. This discharge of energy would be extremely pleasurable, because it eliminates dammed-up tension. In the state of longitudinal expansion, the bladder could execute various rhythmical movements, such as an alternating expansion and contraction, the motion of a *worm* or of intestinal peristalsis:

Or the whole body might make a *serpentine* motion:

In these motions, the organism of the electrical bladder would form a *unity*. If it could feel, it would experience this *rhythmic alternation* of expansion and contraction as pleasurable; it would feel like an infant that hops up and down rhythmically with joy. In the course of these movements, the bioelectrical energy would constantly be in a state of tension—charge and discharge—relaxation. It could be converted into heat, mechanical, kinetic energy, or into work. Such a bladder, like the infant, would feel one with the environment, the world, objects. Various bladders, if there were such, would have immediate contact with each other, as each would identify the experience of its own rhythm and motion with that of the others. They would not be able to understand the contempt for natural movements, nor would they understand unnatural behavior. The continuous inner energy production would *guarantee development,* as is the case with the budding of plants or with progressive cell division after the addition of energy by fertilization. More than that, there would be no end to development. Work would take place within the framework of general biological activity, *and not against it.*

Longitudinal expansion over long periods of time would tend to make the bladder maintain this shape and might lead to the development of a supportive apparatus (skeleton) in the organism. This would make impossible a return to the spherical shape, but *flexion and extension* would still be entirely feasible; that is, the energy metabolism would still be present. True enough, the presence of such a skeleton would make the organism less protected against harmful inhibitions of motility. But in itself it would by no means constitute an inhibition. Such an inhibition could be compared only with the tying down of a snake at *one* point of its body. A snake, if tied down at any point of its body, would lose the rhythm and the unity of the organic wave-like motion even in those parts of the body that are still free:

The animal and human body in fact resembles this bladder we just described. To complete the picture, we have to introduce an automatically working pump mechanism which makes the fluid circulate in a steady rhythm *from center to periphery and back:* the cardiovascular system. Even in the lowest de-

velopmental stages, the animal body possesses a central apparatus for the production of bio-electricity. In the metazoa, this
apparatus consists of the so-called *vegetative ganglia*, con-
glomerations of nerve cells which are placed at regular intervals and are connected by fine strands with all organs and their
parts. They regulate the involuntary life functions and are the
organs of *vegetative feelings and sensations*. They form a connected unit, a so-called "syncytium," and are at the same time
divided into two groups with an opposite function: *sympathetic
and parasympathetic.*

Our imaginary bladder can expand and contract. It could expand to an extreme degree and then relax by way of a few
contractions. It could be limp or tense, relaxed or excited. It
could concentrate the electric charges together with the fluids
carrying them at one time more in one place, at another time
in another. It could keep certain parts constantly tense, and
others in constant motion. If one were to compress it in one
place, it would immediately show increased tension and charge
in another place.

*If one were to compress it over its entire surface, i.e., to make
expansion impossible* while at the same time its inner production of energy would continue, it would experience constant
anxiety, i.e., a feeling of oppression and constriction. If it could
talk, it would implore us to "deliver" it from this painful state.
It would not care what would happen to it, provided *one* thing;
that *motion* and *change* would replace its rigid, compressed
state. As it could not bring this about itself, somebody else
would have to do this *for it*. This might be done by being
thrown around in space (gymnastics), by being kneaded (mas-
sage), if need be by being pricked open (phantasy of being
made to burst), by being injured (masochistic beating phantasy,
harakiri), and, if everything else fails, by melting, dissolution
(nirvana, sacrificial death).

A society consisting of such bladders would create the most
perfect philosophies about the ideals of the "state of painless-
ness." As every expansion caused by pleasure or tending to-

wards pleasure could be experienced only as painful, the bladder would develop fear of pleasurable excitation (*pleasure-anxiety*) and, in addition, evolve theories about the "evil," "sinful," "destructive" quality of pleasure. In short, it would be the image of the ascetic of the twentieth century. As time went on, it would come to dread any thought of the possibility of the relaxation so much longed for; then it would hate it, and finally punish it with death. It would band together with others of its kind into a society of peculiarly stiff creatures and think up rigid rules of life. The only function of these rules would be to keep the inner production of energy at a minimum; in other words, to maintain the adherence to a quiet, well-trodden path and to accustomed reactions. Any surplus of inner energy which could not find its natural outlet in pleasure or motion, they would try to master in some inadequate way. They would, for example, introduce sadistic behavior and ceremonials with much conventionality and little sense to them (e.g., religious compulsive behavior). *Realistic* goals are reached by their own appropriate pathways and for this reason compel motion and unrest in those who seek them.

The bladder might be overtaken by sudden convulsions in which the dammed-up energy is discharged; i.e., it might develop *hysterical* or *epileptic* seizures. It also might become completely rigid and dried up like a catatonic *schizophrenic*. Whatever else it might show, this bladder would always be suffering from *anxiety*. Everything else is the inevitable result of this anxiety, be it religious mysticism, belief in a Führer or senseless readiness to die. Since everything in nature moves, changes, develops, expands and contracts, this *armored* bladder would behave towards nature in a strange and antagonistic way. It would think of itself as "something very special," as belonging to a "better race," e.g., because of wearing a stiff collar or a uniform. It would represent "a culture" or "a race" which are incompatible with "nature." It would consider nature as "low," "demoniacal," "animal," "unrestrained" or "undignified." But since it could not help feeling some last traces of this nature in itself, it would also gush over it, sentimentalize it, e.g. as "sublime love." To think of nature in terms of bodily contractions would mean blasphemy. At the same time this bladder would create pornography without a sense of contradiction.

The formula of tension and charge gathered together thoughts that had cropped up earlier during the study of classical biology. Its theoretical soundness had to be checked. On the part of physiology, my theory was substantiated by the well-known fact of *spontaneous contractions* occurring in muscles. The muscle contraction can be produced by electrical stimuli. But it occurs also when one—as did Galvani—injures the muscle and connects the severed end of the nerve with the muscle at the point of injury. The contraction is accompanied by a measurable *action current*. There is also a normal current in an injured muscle. It shows itself when the middle of the muscle surface is connected with the injured end by way of a conductor, say, a copper wire.

The study of muscle contractions has been an important field of physiological investigation for decades. I could not understand why muscle physiology failed to make the connection with the facts of *general* animal electricity. If one puts two nerve-muscle preparations together in such a way that the muscle of one touches the nerve of the other, and if one then makes the first muscle contract by applying an electric current, the second muscle also contracts. This first muscle contracts in response to the electrical stimulus and develops itself a biological action current. This in turn acts as an electrical stimulus for the second muscle, which responds with a contraction, thereby developing another biological action current. Since the muscles in the animal body are in contact with each other and are connected through the body fluids with the *total organism*, every muscle action is bound to have a stimulating influence upon the total organism. This influence, of course, will vary according to the site of the muscle, the initial stimulus and its strength; but there is always an influence upon the total organism. A prototype of this influence is the orgastic contraction of the genital musculature; a contraction which is so powerful that it transmits itself to the whole organism. Nothing about this was to be found in the literature; yet, it seemed to be of decisive significance.

Detailed examination of the cardiac action curve confirmed my assumption that the tension-charge process governs the cardiac function also, in the form of an electric wave which runs from the auricle to the apex. Prerequisite for the beginning of the contraction is the *filling* of the auricle with blood. The result of the charge and discharge is the propulsion of the blood through the aorta due to the contraction of the heart.

Drugs that gain bulk in the intestine have a cathartic effect. This gaining in bulk acts upon the muscles like an electrical stimulus. They contract and relax in a rhythmical wave, thus emptying the intestines. The same is true of the urinary bladder; it fills up with fluid; this leads to contraction and emptying of the content.

This description contains an extremely important fundamental fact which may serve as a paradigm for the refutation of teleological thinking in biology. The urinary bladder does not contract "in order to fulfill the function of micturition" due to some divine will or supernatural biological power; it contracts by reason of a very simple *causal principle:* because *its mechanical filling produces contraction.* This principle holds for any other function. One does not have sexual intercourse "in order to produce children," but because fluid congestion produces a bio-electric charge in the genital organs and presses for discharge. This is accompanied by the expulsion of the sexual substances. In other words, not "sexuality is in the service of procreation," but procreation itself is an incidental result of the tension-charge process in the genitals. This fact is disappointing to the adherents of an eugenic moral philosophy, but it is, nevertheless, a fact.

In 1933, I happened upon an experimental paper by the Berlin biologist Hartmann. In special experiments concerning the sexuality of gametes, he showed that the male and the female function in copulation is not fixed. That is, a weak male gamete may act like a female towards a male stronger than itself. Hartmann did not answer the question as to what determines the grouping of gametes of the same sex, their "copulation," if you will. He assumed "certain, as yet unknown, substances." I realized that it was a matter of electrical processes. A few years later, I was able to demonstrate the mechanism of the grouping by way of an electrical experiment with the bions. It is *bioelectrical* forces that are responsible for the fact that the grouping in the copulation of the gametes takes place in a certain way and not otherwise. At the same time somebody sent me a newspaper clipping about experiments done in Moscow. Some scientist (I am unable to locate his name) had succeeded in demonstrating that egg- and sperm cells result in male and female individuals, respectively, depending on their electrical charge.

Procreation, then, is a function of sexuality, and not vice versa, as heretofore assumed. Freud had postulated this with regard to psychosexuality, when he separated the concepts of "sexual" and "genital." But for reasons which I never understood, he again placed "genitality in puberty" in the "service of procreation." Hartmann provided the proof for the fact that procreation is a function of sexuality and not vice versa, in the field of biology. The consequence of these findings for a moralistic evaluation of sexuality is evident. It is no longer possible to consider sexuality as an unwelcome by-product of the preservation of the race. I was able to add a third argument, based on experimental studies by various biologists: the division of the egg, too, like cell division in general, is an orgastic process; it follows the law of tension and charge.

When the egg is fertilized and has taken up the *energy* of the sperm, it at first becomes *tensed*. It takes up fluid, its membrane becomes taut. That means, internal pressure and surface tension increase simultaneously. The greater the pressure within this bladder represented by the egg, the more difficult it becomes for the surface to "keep it together." These are still entirely processes originating from the antithesis between internal pressure and surface tension. A purely physical bladder, if further expanded, would *burst*. In the egg cell, on the other hand, a process begins to take place which is characteristic of the functioning of the living substance: *the stretching results in contraction*. The growth of the egg cell is due to the taking up of fluid and can proceed only up to a certain point. The nucleus begins to "radiate," i.e., to produce energy. Gurwitsch termed this phenomenon *"mitogenetic radiation"* (mitosis means division of the nucleus). Later on, I learned to judge the vitality of bion cultures by observing the degree of certain kinds of radiation in their center. In the cell, extreme filling, that is, mechanical tension, is accompanied by an *electrical charge*. At a certain point, the membrane begins to contract; this takes place at the greatest circumference of the sphere, and at the point of maximal tension; this is the equator, or any meridian, of the sphere. As can easily be observed, the contraction is not a gradual and steady, but a struggling, conflictful process. The tension in the membrane opposes the pressure from within which thus becomes increasingly intense. It can easily be seen how internal pressure and surface tension mutually increase each other. This results in a visible vibrating, undulation and contracting:

The indentation goes farther and farther, the inner tension continues to increase. If the cell could talk, it would express *anxiety*. There is only one way of relieving this inner pressure (aside from bursting): the *division* of the *one big bladder* with its taut surface *into two smaller bladders in which the same volume content is surrounded by a much larger and consequently less taut membrane*. Egg division, thus, *corresponds to a process of relaxation*. The nucleus, in its spindle formation, has previously gone through the same process. Spindle formation is regarded by many biologists as an electrical phenomenon. If we were able to measure the electric condition of the nucleus after cell-division, we would most likely find a discharge. The "reduction division" in which half the chromosomes (which had been doubled in the process of spindle formation) are extruded, would point in that direction. Each of the daughter cells now contains the same number of chromosomes. Reproduction is complete.

Cell division, thus, also follows the four-beat of the orgasm formula: tension → charge → discharge → relaxation. It is the most significant biological process. The orgasm formula, then, can be called the *"life formula."*

In those years, I did not want to publish anything about this. I limited myself to hints in clinical presentations and only published a little paper, *"Die Fortpflanzung als Funktion der Sexualität"* (1935), based on the experiments of Hartmann. The subject seemed of such decisive importance that I did not want to publish it without special experiments which would either confirm or disprove my hypothesis.

PLEASURE (EXPANSION) AND ANXIETY (CONTRACTION): BASIC ANTITHESIS OF VEGETATIVE LIFE

By 1933, my concepts of the unity of psychic and somatic functioning had clarified themselves in the following direction: The fundamental biological function of *pulsation*, i.e., of expansion and contraction can be demonstrated in the psychic as well as the somatic sphere. There were two series of antithetical phenomena, the elements of which corresponded to different depths of biological functioning.

Impulses and sensations are not created by the nerves, but only transmitted by them. They are biological manifestations of the organism as a whole. They are present in the organism long before the development of an organized nervous tissue. Protozoa show the same fundamental actions and impulses as metazoa, although they possess as yet no organized nervous system.* Kraus and Zondek succeeded in demonstrating the important fact that chemical substances can not only stimulate or depress the functions of the autonomic nervous system, but also *can take their place*. Kraus, on the basis of his experiments, arrives at the conclusion that the action of the nerves, of drugs and of the electrolytes can replace each other in the biological system with regard to hydration and dehydration of the tissues (as we have seen, the basic functions of living substance).

The following table shows the action of the sympathetic and parasympathetic from the point of view of the total function:

VEGETATIVE GROUP	GENERAL EFFECT ON TISSUES	CENTRAL EFFECT	PERIPHERAL EFFECT
Sympathetic Calcium (group) Adrenalin Cholesterin Hi-ions	Decreased surface tension Dehydration *Striated muscle: paralyzed or spastic* Decreased electrical irritability Increased O_2-consumption Increased blood pressure	Systolic Heart muscle stimulated	Vasocon- striction
Parasympathetic Potassium (group) Cholin Lecithin OH-ions	Increased surface tension Hydration (tumescence of tissues) *Muscle: increased tonicity* Increased electrical irritability Decreased O_2-consumption Decreased blood pressure	Diastolic Heart muscle relaxed	Vasodilation

The findings tabulated here show the following facts:

1. The antithesis between the potassium (*parasympathetic*) group and the calcium (*sympathetic*) group: expansion and contraction;

2. The antithesis of *center* and *periphery* with regard to excitation;

---

* *Translator's note:* It may be argued here that the finding of a "silver line system" in ciliates is at variance with this statement. Though the silver line system "may well be a mechanism whereby coordination is effected throughout the organism" (Calkins), and while a unitary functioning of the organism is hardly conceivable without some kind of coordinating mechanism, the silver line system, nevertheless, is not a nervous system.

3. The functional identity of sympathetic and parasympathetic functions with those of chemical stimuli;

4. The dependency of the innervation of the individual organs on the functional unity and antithesis of the total organism.

As has been stated, all biological impulses and sensations can be reduced to the fundamental functions of *expansion* (elongation, dilatation) and *contraction* (constriction). *What is the relationship between these two fundamental functions and the autonomic nervous system?* Upon detailed examination of the highly complicated vegetative innervation of the organs, one finds the *parasympathetic* operative wherever there is *expansion, elongation, hyperemia, turgor and pleasure.* Conversely, the *sympathetic* is found functioning wherever the organism *contracts,* withdraws blood from the periphery, where it shows palor, *anxiety or pain.* If we go one step further, we see that the parasympathetic represents the direction of expansion, "out of the self—toward the world," pleasure and joy; the sympathetic, on the other hand, represents the direction of contraction, "away from the world—back into the self," sorrow and pain. The life process takes place in a constant alternation of expansion and contraction.

Further consideration shows the *identity* on the one hand of parasympathetic function and *sexual* function; on the other hand of sympathetic function and the function of *unpleasure* or anxiety. We may see that the blood vessels during pleasure dilate at the periphery, the skin reddens, pleasure is felt from mild pleasurable sensations to sexual ecstasy; while in a state of anxiety, pallor, contraction of the blood vessels and unpleasure go hand in hand. In pleasure, "the heart expands" (parasympathetic dilatation), the pulse is full and quiet. In anxiety, the heart contracts and beats rapidly and forcibly. In the first case, it drives the blood through wide blood vessels, its work is easy; in the second case, it has to drive the blood through constricted blood vessels, and its work is hard. In the first case, the blood is predominantly distributed in the peripheral vessels;

in the second case, the constricted blood vessels dam it up in the direction of the heart. This makes it immediately evident why anxiety is accompanied by the sensation of oppression, and why cardiac oppression leads to anxiety. It is the picture of cardiovascular hypertension, which plays such an important role in organic medicine. This hypertension *corresponds to a general condition of sympatheticotonic contraction in the organism.*

	Anxiety syndrome	*Pleasure syndrome*
Peripheral vessels	Constricted	Dilated
Heart action	Accelerated	Retarded
Blood pressure	Increased	Decreased
Pupil	Dilated	Constricted
Secretion of saliva	Decreased	Increased
Musculature	Paralyzed or spastic	In a state of tonus, relaxed

On the highest, i.e., psychic level, biological expansion is experienced as pleasure, contraction as unpleasure. On the instinctual level, expansion and contraction function as sexual excitation and anxiety, respectively. On a deeper physiological level, expansion and contraction correspond to the function of the parasympathetic and sympathetic, respectively. According to the discoveries of Kraus and Zondek, the parasympathetic function can be replaced by the potassium ion group, the sympathetic function by the calcium ion group. We thus get a convincing picture of a *unitary functioning in the organism, from the highest psychic sensations down to the deepest biological reactions.*

The following table presents the two series of functions according to their depth:

Pleasure	*Unpleasure and anxiety*
Sexuality	Anxiety
Parasympathetic	Sympathetic
Potassium	Calcium
Lecithin	Cholesterin
OH-ions, cholin	H-ions, adrenalin
(hydrating bases)	(dehydrating acids)
Function of expansion	*Function of contraction*

On the basis of this formula of unitary-antithetical psychosomatic functioning, some seeming contradictions of automatic innervation became clear. Previously, the autonomic innervation of the organism had seemed to lack order. Muscles are made to contract one time by the parasympathetic, the other time by the sympathetic. Glandular function is one time stimulated by the parasympathetic (genital glands), another time by the sympathetic (sweat glands). A table showing the opposition of sympathetic and parasympathetic innervation of the autonomically functioning organs will make this apparent lack of order even clearer:

Functioning of the Autonomic Nervous System

Sympathetic Action	Organ	Parasympathetic Action
Inhibition of m.spincter pupillae: *Dilation of pupils*	Musculature of iris	Stimulation of m.sphincter pupillae: *Narrowing of pupils*
Inhibition of lachrymal glands: *"Dry eyes"*	Lachrymal glands	Stimulation of lachrymal glands: *"Bright eyes"*
Inhibition of salivary glands: *"Dry mouth"*	Salivary glands	Stimulation of salivary glands: *"Mouth waters"*
Stimulation of sweat glands: *"Cold sweat"*	Sweat glands	Inhibition of sweat glands: *Dry skin*
Contraction of arteries: *"Cold sweat"; pallor*	Arteries	Dilatation of arteries: *Redness of skin, increased turgor,* without sweating
Stimulation of arrectores pilorum: *Hair is "raised"; "Gooseflesh"*	Arrectores pilorum	Inhibition of arrectores pilorum: *Skin smooth*
Inhibition of contracting musculature: *Relaxation of bronchi*	Bronchial musculature	Stimulation of contracting musculature: *Bronchial spasm*
Stimulates heart action: *Palpitation, tachycardia*	Heart	Depresses heart action: *Heart quiet, pulse slow*
Inhibits peristalsis Reduces secretion of digestive glands	Gastrointestinal tract; liver, pancreas, kidneys; all digestive glands	*Stimulates peristalsis and secretion of digestive glands*

Sympathetic Action	Organ	Parasympathetic Action
Stimulates secretion of adrenalin	Adrenals	*Inhibits secretion of adrenalin*
Inhibits musculature which opens bladder, stimulates sphincter: *Inhibits micturition*	Urinary bladder	Stimulates musculature which opens bladder, inhibits sphincter: *Stimulates micturition*
Stimulates smooth musculature, reduces secretion of all glands, decreases blood supply: *Decreased sexual sensation*	Female sex organs	Relaxes smooth musculature, stimulates secretion of all glands, increases blood supply: *Increased sexual sensation*
Stimulates smooth musculature of the scrotum, reduces glandular secretion, decreases blood supply: *Flaccid penis. Decreased sexual sensation*	Male sex organs	Relaxes smooth musculature of the scrotum, stimulates glandular secretion, increases blood supply: *Erection. Increased sexual sensation*

In the course of the demonstration of the two directions of biological energy, a fact has become apparent to which until now we have paid little attention. Up to now, we have a clear picture of the *vegetative periphery*. However, the place is not defined where the biological energy becomes concentrated as soon as an anxiety state occurs. There must be a *vegetative center*, from which the bio-electric energy originates and to which it returns. This question brings us to certain well-known facts of physiology. The abdominal cavity, the well-known seat of the emotions, contains the generators of biological energy. They are large centers of the autonomic nervous system, particularly the solar plexus, the hypogastric plexus and the lumbrosacral or pelvic plexus. A glance at a diagram of the vegetative nervous system shows that the vegetative ganglia are densest in the abdominal and genital regions. The following diagrams show the functional relationships between *center* and *periphery*:

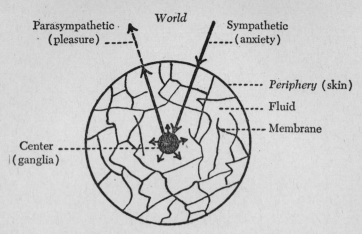

Parasympathetic	Sympathetic
Swelling, expansion	Shrinking
Increased turgor (surface tension)	Decreased turgor (surface tension)
Central tension low	Central tension high
Opening up	Closing up
"Toward the world, out of the self"	"Away from the world, back into the self"
Sexual excitation; skin warm, red	Anxiety, pallor, cold sweat
"Streaming" from center to periphery	"Streaming" from periphery to center

Parasympatheticotonia, relaxation	←	Life process oscillating between	→	Sympatheticotonia, hypertension

Diagram a): The basic functions of the vegetative nervous system.

The attempt to bring order into what seemed a chaos was successful when I began to examine the vegetative innervation of each organ in terms of the biological functions of expansion and contraction *of the total organism.* In other words, I asked myself how this or that organ would normally function in pleasure and anxiety, respectively; and what kind of autonomic innervation would be found in each case. Thus, the seemingly contradictory innervation, when examined *in terms of the function of the total organism,* revealed itself as entirely orderly and understandable.

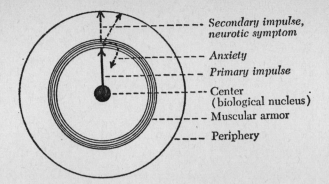

Diagram *b): The same functions in an* armored *organism. Inhibition of primary impulse, resulting in secondary impulse and anxiety.*

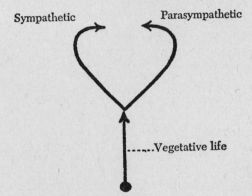

Diagram *c): Unity and antithesis in the vegetative nervous system.*

This can be most convincingly demonstrated by the antagonistic innervation of the "center," the heart, and the "periphery," the blood vessels and muscles. The parasympathetic stimulates the blood flow in the periphery by dilating the blood vessels, but inhibits the heart action; conversely, the sympathetic inhibits the blood flow in the periphery by contracting the vessels, but stimulates the heart action. In terms of the total organism, this antagonistic innervation is understandable, for in anxiety the heart has to overcome the peripheral constriction, whereas in pleasure it can work peacefully and slowly. There is a *functional antithesis between center and periphery.*

The fact that the same nerve (the sympathetic) inhibits the salivary glands and simultaneously stimulates the outpouring of adrenalin, and thus produces anixety, is meaningful in terms of the unitary sympathetic anxiety function. Similarly, we see in the case of the urinary bladder that the sympathetic stimulates the muscle that prevents micturition; the action of the parasympathetic is the reverse. Similarly, in terms of the whole, it is meaningful that, in a state of pleasure, the pupils, as a result of parasympathetic action, are contracted, acting like the diaphragm of a camera, and thus increase acuity of vision; conversely, in a state of anxious paralysis, the acuity of vision is diminished through a dilation of the pupils.

The reduction of autonomic innervation to the basic biological functions of expansion and contraction of the total organism was, of course, an important step forward and at the same time a good test of my biological hypothesis. The parasympathetic, then, always stimulates the organs—regardless of whether it is in the sense of tension or relaxation—when the *total organism* is in a state of pleasurable expansion. Conversely, the sympathetic stimulates the organs in a biologically meaningful way when the total organism is in a state of anxious contraction. The life process, in especial respiration, can thus be understood as a constant state of pulsation in which the organism continues to alternate, pendulum-like, between parasympathetic expansion (expiration) and sympathetic contraction (inspiration). In formulating these theoretical considerations, I had in mind the rhythmic behavior of an ameba, a medusa or a heart. The function of respiration is too complicated to be briefly presented here in terms of these new insights.

If this biological state of pulsation is disturbed in one or the other direction, that is, if either the function of expansion or that of contraction predominates, then a disturbance of the biological equilibrium in general is inevitable. Long continuation in a state of expansion is synonymous with general *para-sympatheticotonia;* conversely, long continuation in a state of anxious contraction is synonymous with *sympatheticotonia.* Thus, all somatic conditions which are clinically known as cardiovascular hypertension, become understandable as conditions

Expansion and movement   Return to spherical shape upon a strong electrical stimulus.

Plasma currents in the ameba with expansion and contraction.

of a chronically fixed sympatheticotonic attitude of anxiety. In the center of this general sympatheticotonia is orgasm anxiety, that is, the fear of expansion and involuntary contraction.

The physiological literature contained a wealth of data regarding the complicated mechanisms of autonomic innervation. The achievement of my sex-economic theory was not that of having discovered new facts in this field, but, to begin with, only that of having reduced generally known innervations to a generally valid basic biological formula. The orgasm theory could claim to have made an essential contribution to an understanding of the physiology of the organism. This unification led to the discovery of new facts.

I published a résumé of these findings under the title *"Der Urgegensatz des vegetativen Lebens"* in the "Zeitschrift für Politische Psychologie und Sexualökonomie" which was founded in Denmark in 1934, after the break with the International Psychoanalytic Association. It was not until several years later that this article was taken cognizance of in biological and psychiatric circles.

The painful incidents at the 13th International Psychoanalytic Congress in Lucerne, 1934, were reported in some detail in the periodical just mentioned, so that I shall give here only the highlights for general orientation. When I arrived in Lucerne, I learned from the secretary of the German Psychoanalytic Society, of which I was a member, that I had already been expelled in 1933, after moving to Vienna. Nobody had found it necessary to inform me of the reasons for this expulsion; more than that, I had not even been notified of the fact. Finally, I found out that my book on Fascist irrationalism [*Massenpsychologie des Faschimus*. Verlag fur Sexualpolitik, 1933, P. 292.] had placed me in such a position, through the publicity involved, that my membership in the International Psychoanalytic Association seemed no longer desirable. Four years later, Freud had to flee from Vienna to London, and the psychoanalytic groups were smashed by the Fascists. In the interest of my independence, I later did not avail myself of the possibility of becoming again a member of the International Association by joining the Norwegian society.

3. THE EXPRESSIVE LANGUAGE OF THE LIVING IN ORGONE THERAPY

THE FUNCTION OF EMOTION

The concept of "orgone therapy" comprises all medical and pedagogical techniques operating with the "biological" energy, the orgone. True, the cosmic orgone energy was not discovered until 1939, but, long before this discovery the established goal of character-analysis was the liberation of "psychic energy," as it was then called, from the character armor and muscular armor, and the establishment of orgastic potency. The reader

From *Character Analysis*, third enlarged edition, 1949.

who is familiar with orgone biophysics knows the development
of character-analysis (from 1926 to 1934) into "vegetotherapy"
(from 1935 on). It was not sensationalism which caused such
diverse terms to be coined within one and the same branch of
science. Rather, a consistent application of a natural-scientific
energy concept in the field of psychic processes led, of necessity, to new terms for new techniques in the successive stages
of development.

The fact that it was sex-economically oriented psychiatry
which provided the access to the cosmic energy must be
regarded as a great triumph for *orgonomic functionalism*.
Although the orgone energy is a strictly physical form of energy,
there are good reasons why it was discovered by a psychiatrist
and not a physicist. The logic of this discovery within the
realm of biopsychiatry is shown in its development, as presented in *The Discovery of the Orgone*, vol. I: *The Function of
the Orgasm*.

When, in 1935, the orgasm reflex was discovered, the accent
in character-analytic work shifted to the *somatic* realm. The
term "vegetotherapy" represented the fact that now my therapeutic technique influenced the character neurosis in the *physiological realm*. We spoke of "character-analytic vegetotherapy,"
indicating the simultaneous work on the psychic and somatic
apparatus. This term had its disadvantages, which, at that time,
could not be helped. For one thing, it was too long. It contained
the term, "vegetative," which sounded correct in German but
reminded one of "vegetables" in English. Finally, it still represented a division of the organism into a psychic and a somatic
part, which was in contradiction with our unitary concept of
the organism.

These conceptual difficulties were ended by the discovery of
the orgone. *The cosmic orgone energy functions in the living
organism as specific biological energy*. As such, it governs the
total organism and expresses itself in the emotions as well as
the purely biophysical organ movements. Thus psychiatry, for
the first time and with its own means, had found roots in objec-

tive natural-scientific processes. This statement calls for some amplification:

Up to the discovery of the orgone, psychiatry always had to turn to inorganic physics in its attempts to give an *objective* and *quantitative* basis to its psychological contentions. Neither mechanical brain lesions nor the chemicophysical processes in the organism, nor the obsolete concepts of the cerebral localisation of sensations and ideas ever succeeded in satisfactorily explaining emotional processes. In contradistinction, orgone biophysics, from the very beginning, was concerned with the central problem of all psychiatry, the *emotions*. Literally, "emotion" means "moving out," "protruding." It is not only permissible but necessary to take the word "emotion" literally in speaking of sensations and movements. Microscopic observation of amebae subjected to slight electric stimuli renders the meaning of the term "emotion" in an unmistakable manner. *Basically, emotion is an expressive plasmatic motion.* Pleasurable stimuli cause an "emotion" of the protoplasm from the center towards the periphery. Conversely, unpleasurable stimuli cause an "emotion"—or rather, "remotion"—from the periphery to the center of the organism. These two basic directions of biophysical plasma current correspond to the two basic affects of the psychic apparatus, pleasure and anxiety. As the experiments at the oscillograph have shown, the physical plasma motion and the corresponding sensation are functionally identical. They are indivisible; one is not conceivable without the other. But, as we know, they are not only functionally identical, but at the same time antithetical, for a biophysical plasma excitation results in a sensation, and a sensation is expressed in a plasmatic motion. These facts, today, provide a sound fundament of orgone biophysics.

No matter whether we release the emotions from the character armor by way of "character-analysis," or from the muscular armor by way of "vegetotherapy," in either case we cause plasmatic excitations and motions. What moves is essentially the orgone energy with which the body fluids are charged. *The mobilization of the plasmatic currents and emotions, then, is identical with the mobilization of orgone energy in the organism.* It is clearly evidenced by vasomotor changes. In every case, whether we produce memories, dissolve defense mechanisms or muscular spasms, we work on the orgone energy of the organism. The difference lies merely in the efficacy of the various methods; a memory will not produce affect outbreaks like the dissolution of, say, a diaphragmatic block.

All this will explain why the term "orgone therapy" includes character-analysis and vegetotherapy.* The common goal is the mobilization of the patient's plasmatic currents. In other words, we cannot split up a living organism into character attitudes, muscles and plasma functions if we take our *unitary* concept of the organism seriously, in a practical way.

In orgone therapy, we work on the biological depth, the plasma system, the "biological core" of the organism. The reader will realize that this is a decisive step. We have left the realm of psychology, including "depth psychology," and have even gone beyond the physiology of the nerves and muscles into the realm of the protoplasmatic functions. These steps are to be taken very seriously; they have far-reaching practical and theoretical consequences, for they change our biopsychiatric techniques basically. We no longer work merely on individual conflicts and special armorings but on the *living function* itself. As we gradually learn to understand and influence this function, the purely psychological and physiological functions are influenced automatically. Schematic specializing is thus excluded.

Plasmatic Expressive Movements and Emotional Expression

It is difficult to give a strict functional definition of "the living." The concepts of traditional psychology and depth psy-

---

* The purely physiological orgone therapy by means of the orgone accumulator is discussed in *The Discovery of the Orgone*, vol. II: *The Cancer Biopathy*.

chology are bound up with *word* formations. The living, however, functions beyond all verbal ideas and concepts. Verbal language is a biological form of expression on a high level of development. It is by no means an indispensable attribute of the living, for the living functions long before there is a verbal language. Depth psychology, therefore, operates with a function of recent origin. Many animals express themselves by sounds. But the living functions beyond and before any sound formation as a form of expression.

The process of word formation itself shows the way in which the living "expresses itself." The term "expression," apparently on the basis of organ sensations, describes precisely the language of the living: *The living expresses itself in movements,* in *"expressive movements."* The expressive movement is an inherent characteristic of the protoplasm. It distinguishes the living strictly from the non-living systems. The term means, literally, that something in the living system "presses itself out" and, consequently, "moves." This can mean nothing but the movement of the protoplasm, that is, expansion and contraction. The literal meaning of "emotion" is "moving out," which is the same as "expressive movement." The physical process of plasmatic emotion or expressive movements always goes with an immediately understandable *meaning* which we call the *emotional expression.* The movement of the plasm, then, has an expression in the sense of an emotion, and the emotion or the expression of an organism is bound to movement. The latter part of this sentence will require some qualification, for we know from orgone therapy that many people present an expression which is caused by immobility and rigidity.

All this is not a play with words. It is clear that language, in the process of word formation, depends on the perception of inner movements and organ sensations, and that the words which describe emotional states render, in an *immediate* way, the corresponding expressive movements of living matter.

Even though language reflects the state of plasmatic emotion in an immediate way, it cannot itself reach this state. The living not only functions before and beyond word language; more than that, it has *its own specific forms of expression which cannot be put into words at all.* Every musical individual knows the state of emotion created by great music; yet, it is impossible to put this emotion into words. Music is wordless. Nevertheless, it is an expression of movement and creates in the listener the expression of being "moved." The wordlessness of music is generally considered either a sign of mystical spirituality or of deepest emotion incapable of being expressed in words. The natural-scientific interpretation is that musical expression comes from the very depths of the living. What is described as the "spirituality" of great music, then, is an appropriate description of the simple fact that seriousness of feeling is identical with contact with the living *beyond the confine of words.*

Thus far, science has had nothing decisive to say about the nature of musical emotional expression. Doubtless, the artist speaks to us in the form of wordless expressive movements from the depth of the living function; but what he expresses in music or painting he could no more put into words than can we. More, he guards against attempts to translate the expressive language of art into word language; he is much concerned about the purity of his expressive language. He thus confirms the orgone-biophysical contention that the living, beyond any word language and independent of it, has its own expressive language. Let us illustrate from everyday experience in orgone therapy.

The patients come to the orgone therapist full of problems. To the experienced eye, these problems are directly visible in their expressive movements and the emotional expression of their bodies. If one lets the patient talk at random, one will find that the talking *leads away* from the problems, that it *obscures* them in one way or another. In order to arrive at a true evaluation, one has to ask the patient *not* to talk for a while. This measure proves highly fruitful. For as soon as the patient ceases to talk, the bodily expression of emotion becomes clearly manifest. After a few minutes of silence, one usually comprehends the outstanding character trait, or, more correctly, the plas-

matic emotional expression. While the patient, during his talking, seemed to smile in a friendly manner, now, in silence, the
smile turns into an empty grin the mask-like character of which
will soon become obvious even to the patient. While the patient, talking, seemed to talk about his life with a restrained
seriousness, now, in silence, an expression of, say, repressed
anger will appear in chin and neck.

These examples may suffice to show that *word language very
often also functions as a defense:* the word language obscures
the expressive language of the biological core. In many cases
this goes so far that the words no longer express anything and
the word language is no longer anything but a meaningless
activity of the respective muscles. Long experience has convinced me that in many psychoanalyses of years' duration, the
treatment became the victim of this pathological kind of word
language. This clinical experience can—and must—be applied to
the social scene: innumerable speeches, publications and political debates do not have as their function the disclosing of vital
questions of life but of drowning them in verbiage.

Orgone therapy is distinguished from all other modes of
influencing the organism by the fact that the patient is asked
to express himself *biologically* while word language is eliminated to a far-reaching degree. This leads the patient to a depth
from which he constantly tries to flee. Thus one learns, in the
course of orgone therapy, to understand the language of the
living and to influence it. The primary expressive language of
the living protoplasm is not present in "pure" form; if the
patient's mode of expression were "purely" biological, he would
have no reason for seeking the help of the orgone therapist.
We must first penetrate through layers of pathological, unnatural modes of expression before arriving at the *genuine* biological mode of expression. After all, human biopathy is nothing
but the sum total of all distortions of the natural modes of
expression of the living organism. By disclosing the pathological
forms of expression we learn to know human biopathy in a
depth which is inaccessible to the therapeutic techniques work-

ing with word language. Unfortunately, *the biopathy, with its distorted expression of life, is outside the realm of language and concepts.*

Orgone-therapeutic work on the biopathy, therefore, takes place essentially outside the realm of word language. Of course, we also use the spoken word; but the words do not refer to the ideational concepts of everyday, but to *organ sensations.* It would be perfectly useless, for example, to try to make the patient understand his condition in terms of, say, physiology. We cannot say to him, "Your masseter muscles are in a state of chronic contraction, that is why your chin does not move in talking, why your voice is monotonous, why you cannot cry; you have to swallow constantly in order to suppress an impulse to cry." True, the patient would understand such statements intellectually, but that would not change his condition.

We work on a biologically deeper level of understanding. It is not very important, anyhow, just what *individual* muscles are contracted. It would be useless, for example, to press on the masseter muscles; the only reaction would be ordinary pain. *We work with the expressive language.* Only when we have *felt* the facial *expression* of the patient are we also in a position to understand it. To "understand" it means here, quite strictly, to know which emotion is "expressed" in it. In that, it makes no difference whether the emotion is actively mobile or whether it is held back, immobile. We have to inquire as to what is the difference between a mobile and a held-back emotion.

In "feeling" the emotional expression of a patient we operate with primary biological functions. If, in a flock of birds, one becomes restless and, "sensing danger," flies off, the whole flock will do so, irrespective of whether or not the other birds have noticed the cause of the restlessness. The panic reaction among animals is based on an involuntary reproduction of the emotional expression of anxiety. It is not difficult to cause people on the street to stop and scan the sky if one acts as if one were observing something very interesting in the sky. These examples may suffice.

The emotional expression of the patient produces in our organism an involuntary *imitation*. Imitating, we feel and understand the expression in ourselves and with that in the patient. Since every motion has an expression and thus discloses the emotional state of the protoplasm, the language of expression becomes an essential means of communication with the patient's emotions. As already stated, the word language *disturbs* the language of expression. By "character attitude" we mean the total *expression* of an organism. This is literally identical with the total *impression* which the organism makes on us.

The emotional expression may greatly vary, in its details, from individual to individual. There are no two individuals with exactly the same speech, the same respiratory block or the same gait. Nevertheless, some general types can be easily distinguished. In depth psychology, we distinguish the "neurotic" and the "genital" character, on the basis of the type of muscular and character armor. We call a character neurotic when the organism is governed by a rigid armor which the individual cannot alter or eliminate. We speak of a genital character when the emotional reactions are not inhibited by rigid automatisms, when, in other words, the individual is capable of reacting biologically, according to the situation in which he finds himself. These two basic character types can be equally sharply distinguished in the realm of biological functioning:

Once one has learned to understand the language of biological expression, the kind of armor and the extent of its rigidity are not difficult to evaluate. The total expression of the armored individual is that of "holding back." This expression has to be taken literally: *the organism expresses the fact that it is holding back*. The shoulders are pulled back, the thorax pulled up, the chin is held rigid, respiration is shallow, the lower back is arched, the pelvis is retracted and "dead," the legs are stretched out stiffly or lack expression; these are some of the main attitudes of total holding back. Schematically, it can be represented as follows:

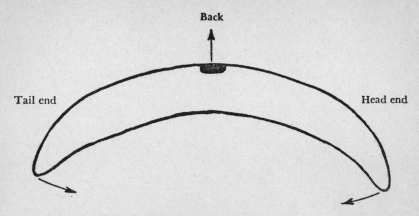

Back

Tail end   Head end

The basic biophysical attitude of the unarmored *organism*

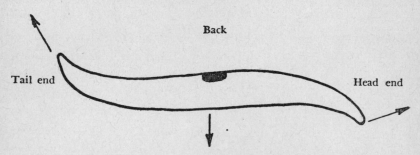

Back

Tail end   Head end

The basic biophysical attitude of the armored *organism:*
"holding back"

This basic bodily attitude is most clearly expressed in the "arc de cercle" of hysteria and the "opisthotonus" of stuporous catatonia. One can readily see that this basic attitude of the armored organism is not a voluntary manifestation but is autonomqus. The armored individual does not himself feel the armor as such. If one tries to describe it to him in words he usually does not know what one is talking about. What he feels is not the armoring itself but only the distortion of his perceptions of life: he feels himself uninterested, rigid, empty, or he complains about nervous unrest, palpitations, constipation, insomnia, nausea, etc. If the armoring is of long standing and has also influenced the tissues of the organs, the patient will come to us with peptic ulcer, rheumatism, arthritis, cancer or angina pectoris. This brief enumeration may suffice here, since the clinical facts have been presented elsewhere. What we are concerned with here is to penetrate to *the functions of the biological depth* and to deduce from them the functioning of the living.

The armored individual is incapable of dissolving his armor. He is also incapable of expressing the primitive biological emotions. He knows the sensation of tickling but not that of orgonotic pleasure. He cannot emit a pleasurable sigh or imitate it. If he tries, he will produce a groan, a repressed roar or an impulse to vomit. He is incapable of letting out an angry yell or convincingly imitating a fist hitting the couch in anger. He is incapable of full expiration: the movements of his diaphragm (as Xrays readily show) are very limited. If asked to move the pelvis forward, he is incapable of doing so, and often even of understanding what one asks of him; he may even execute the opposite motion, that of retracting the pelvis, a motion which expresses holding back. The tension of the peripheral muscle and nervous system is shown in an exaggerated sensitivity to pressure. It is impossible to touch certain parts of an armored organism without producing intense symptoms of anxiety and nervousness. What is commonly called "nervousness" is the result of this hypersensitivity of highly tensed muscles.

The total holding back results in the incapacity for the plasmatic pulsation in the sexual act, that is, orgastic impotence. This in turn results in a stasis of sexual energy, and from this follows all that which is comprised by the term "biopathy."

The central task of orgone therapy is the destruction of the armor, in other words, the reestablishment of plasma mobility. In the armored individual, the function of pulsation is more or less restricted in all organs. The task of orgone therapy is that of reestablishing the full capacity of pulsation. This is done, biophysically, by dissolving the attitude of holding back.

Ideally, the result of orgone therapy is the appearance of the *orgasm reflex*. As we know, this reflex, next to respiration, is the most important motor manifestation in the animal kingdom. At the moment of the orgasm, the organism "gives itself over" completely to its organ sensations and involuntary pulsations. Therefore, the motion of the orgasm reflex inevitably contains the expression of "giving." It would, of course, be useless to preach the patient "to give," because he is incapable of doing so. If he were not, he would not need our help. Nor do we let him practise the attitude of "giving," for no such voluntary technical measure could possibly bring about the *involuntary* attitude of giving. *The living functions autonomously, beyond the realms of language, intellect or volition.* It functions according to certain natural laws which we will have to examine. As we shall soon see, the orgasm reflex, with its expression of giving, is the key to an understanding of *basic* natural processes which go far beyond the individual and even the living itself. The reader who is to follow this presentation with understanding will have to be prepared for a serious excursion in the realm of cosmic energy. He will fail to achieve understanding and will be disappointed if he has not freed himself completely from the concept of sexuality as portrayed by the night club.

We have already sufficiently studied the functions of the orgasm in the realms of psychology and physiology to concentrate our attention here exclusively on the basic natural phenomenon, "orgasm." Peculiarly enough, *in the orgasm the organism constantly tries to bring together the embryologically important mouth and anus.* Its form is the following:

Back

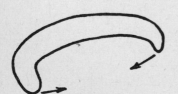 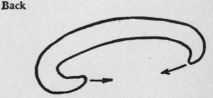

Front

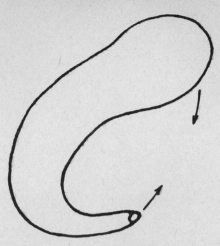

The emotional expression of the orgasm reflex

As we said, the attitude of the orgasm reflex is that of "giving." The organism gives itself over to its plasmatic excitations and sensations of streaming; also, it gives itself over completely to the partner in the sexual embrace, without any kind of reserve, holding back or armoring. All biological activity is reduced to the basic function of plasmatic pulsation. In man, all thinking and phantasy activity cease.

The emotional expression of giving is clear. *What is not clear is the function of the orgastic convulsion.* It consists in alternating contractions and expansions of the total body plasma. *What function has the approximation of the two ends of the torso in the orgastic convulsion?* At first glance, it does not seem to convey any "meaning." The expression of this movement seems incomprehensible. If we are correct in stating that every organismic movement has an *understandable* expression, this does not seem to apply in the case of the orgastic convulsion. We are unable to find in the orgasm a comprehensible expression which could be translated into word language.

Instead of engaging in natural-philosophical speculations about this problem, we must give the natural-scientific answer that, while the orgastic convulsion seems incomprehensible, it

still must have a hidden expression. For, like any other movement of the living, it is a pure *expressive* movement and, consequently, must also show an emotional expression.

In due course, we shall arrive at an astounding but conclusive answer to this basic question of the living function. But
before finding this answer we must collect and correctly interpret a great number of biological manifestations. The answer
lies beyond the individual biological organism and yet is in no
way mystical, metaphysical or spiritualistic. It answers the
riddle as to the *concrete* manner in which the animal and the
plant are connected with the cosmic orgone energy. Thus it
also answers the question as to why orgastic longing is not only
the deepest longing but why it is, characteristically, a *cosmic
longing*. True, that the organism is a bit of cosmos is generally
known but what has remained unknown so far is *how*. Let us
return to orgone-therapeutic experience:

The task of orgone therapy is that of enabling the human
organism to give up the automatism of holding back and, instead, to "give." As long as the two embryonic ends of the torso
bend backwards instead of forwards, towards each other, the
organism is incapable of giving itself to any experience, be it
work or pleasure. Since it is the muscular armoring which prevents any kind of giving, of surrender, and which causes biopathic restriction of living functioning, this muscular armor has
to be dissolved. Only this will achieve our therapeutic goal;
neither psychoanalysis, suggestion, praying or gymnastics will.
Nor do we inform the patient concerning the therapeutic goal;
we know from experience that he will inevitably develop the
total orgasm reflex if we succeed in dissolving the muscular
armor. In the course of every treatment we see that *the basic
function of the muscular armor is that of preventing the orgasm
reflex from taking place*.

The numerous manifestations of the muscular armor and the
corresponding character armor have been described elsewhere.
Here, I would like to introduce a new point of view which
makes the character and muscular armor comprehensible on

the level of the most primitive life functions. It is based on observations over some ten years, so that I can take full responsibility for their significance in biophysics.

THE SEGMENTAL ARRANGEMENT OF THE ARMOR

In psychiatry, it has been known for decades that the somatic disturbances of hysteria do not correspond to the anatomy and physiology of muscles, nerves and blood vessels but to emotionally significant organs. Pathological blushing, for example, is usually restricted to face and neck, although the blood vessels run essentially lengthwise. Similarly, sensory disturbances in hysteria do not correspond to a certain nerve path, but to emotionally significant regions of the body.

In dissolving the muscular armor, we meet the same phenomenon: the individual muscular blocks do not correspond to an individual muscle or nerve. If, now, one looks for some rule which these blocks must inevitably follow, one finds that the muscular armor has a *segmental* arrangement.

Segmental function is a much more primitive mode of living functioning than that found in highly developed animals. It is most clearly seen in worms. In the higher vertebrates, only the segmental structure of the spine which corresponds to the segments of the spinal cord and the spinal nerves, and the segmental arrangement of the autonomic ganglia, indicate the origin of the vertebrates from segmentally functioning primitive organisms.

I am trying to give here a rough sketch—it can be no more than that—of the segmental structure of the muscular armor. This description is based on many years' observation of armor reactions.

Since the body of the patient is held back and since the goal of orgone therapy is that of reestablishing the plasmatic currents in the pelvis, it is necessary to start the dissolution of the armor in the regions farthest away from the pelvis. Thus, the work begins with the facial expression. At the head, at least two segmental armorings can be clearly distinguished: one including forehead, eyes and the cheekbone region, the other including lips, chin and throat. A segmental structure of the armor means that it functions in front, at the sides and in the back, that is, like a *ring*.

Let us call the first armor ring the *ocular*, the second the *oral* ring. In the ocular armor segment we find a contraction and immobilization of all or most muscles of the eyeball, the lids, the forehead, the tear glands, etc. This is expressed in immobility of the forehead and the eyelids, empty expression of the eyes or protruding eyeballs, a masklike expression or immobility on both sides of the nose. The eyes look out as from behind a rigid mask. The patient is unable to open his eyes wide, as if imitating fright. In schizophrenics, as a result of contracted eyeball muscles, the expression of the eyes is empty or as if staring into the distance. Many patients have been unable to cry for many years. In others the eyes represent a narrow slit. The forehead is without expression, as if "flattened out." Very often, there is myopia, astigmatism or other visual disturbances.

The dissolution of the ocular segment of the armor takes place by one's having the patient open his eyes wide, as if in fright; with that, forehead and eyelids are mobilized and express emotions. This usually includes the upper parts of the cheeks, particularly if one has the patient make grimaces. The pulling up of the cheeks usually results in a "grin" which has the character of a spiteful provocation.

The segmental character of this muscle group is shown in the fact that every emotional action in this region also influences other parts, while the oral segment remains uninfluenced. The opening wide of the eyes as in fright will, for example, mobilize the forehead or bring about a grin in the upper parts of the cheeks, but it will not provoke, say, the biting impulses which are held back in the rigid chin.

Armor segments, then, comprise those organs and muscle groups which are in functional contact with each other, which can induce each other to participate in expressive movement.

The next-following segment is that which remains unaffected by the expressive movements of the neighboring region.

The segmental structure of the armoring is always *transverse* to the torso, never along it. The only remarkable exception to this are the arms and legs. They clearly function coupled with the corresponding segments of the torso, that is, the arms with the segment comprising the shoulders and the legs with the segment comprising the pelvis. We shall keep this exception in mind; its explanation will be found in a definite biophysical context.

The second or oral armor segment comprises the musculature of the chin, the throat and the occipital musculature, including the annular muscle of the mouth. They form a functional unit, for dissolution of the chin armoring results in clonisms in the lips and the corresponding emotions of crying or the desire to suck. Similarly, production of the gag reflex may mobilize the total oral segment.

The emotional expressions of crying, angry biting, of yelling, sucking and grimacing of every kind are dependent on the free mobility of the ocular segment. For example, it will be found difficult to mobilize an impulse to cry by mobilizing the gag reflex if one has not previously mobilized the ocular segment. And even after the dissolution of the two uppermost segments it may still be difficult to liberate the crying impulse as long as the third and fourth segment, in neck and thorax, are still in a state of spastic contraction. This difficulty in the liberation of emotions discloses an extremely important biophysiological fact:

1. The armorings are segmental, in rings at right angles to the spine.

2. The plasmatic streamings and emotional excitations which we produce are along the body axis.

The inhibition of the emotional language of expression, then, works at right angles to the direction of the orgonotic streaming.

Since the orgonotic streamings can unite in the orgasm reflex only when they can pass freely *along* the total organism, and since, furthermore, the armorings are in segments at right angles to the movement of the currents, it is clear that the orgasm reflex cannot establish itself until after the dissolution of all the segmental armor rings. This is why the feeling of the unity of all body sensations does not make its appearance until the first orgastic convulsions occur. They herald the breakdown of the muscular armor. The orgonotic streamings which break through with each new dissolution of an armor ring are a great help in the work of dissolving the armor. For the liberated energy, which tries spontaneously to stream longitudinally, meets the still existing transverse contractions; this conveys to the patient the unmistakable feeling of a "block," a feeling which was very weak or entirely absent as long as there were no free plasmatic streamings.

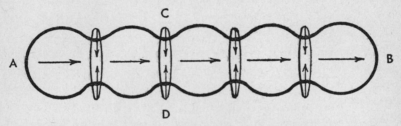

The direction of orgonotic streaming is transverse to the armor rings

The reader will realize that these processes are a matter of primary functions of the plasma system, processes not only beyond any word language, but representing *basic* processes of the life apparatus. It is a matter of phylogenetically primordial functions. *The segmental structure of the muscular armor represents the worm in man.*

The movements of the worm are based on waves of excitation running from the tail end to the front. The waves of excitation progress continually from segment to segment until they reach the front end. At the tail end, one wave motion after the other develops with locomotion. The segments alternate rhythmically and regularly between contraction and expansion. In worms and caterpillars, locomotion is inextricably connected with this plasmatic wave-like motion. Since it can be nothing else, we must conclude that *it is the biological energy itself which moves in this wave-like manner*. This contention is confirmed by the observation of the inner movements of bions. The wave-like movement of the body orgone is slow and corresponds, in its tempo and expression, entirely to the emotional excitations of the pleasure function which we experience subjectively as wave-like.

In the armored human organism, the orgone energy is bound up in the chronic muscular spasms. After the loosening of the armor ring, the body orgone does not immediately begin to stream freely. What appears at first is clonisms, together with prickling and crawling sensations. This indicates that the armoring is loosened and that energy becomes free. Genuine sensations of waves of plasmatic excitation do not appear until a number of armor segments have been dissolved, such as blocks in the musculature of the eyes, mouth, neck and diaphragm. Then we can clearly see *wave-like* contractions in the loosened parts of the body, moving up towards the head and down toward the genital. Very often, the organism reacts to these first streamings and convulsions with renewed armoring. Spasms of the deep throat musculature, reverse peristalsis of the esophagus, diaphragmatic tics and other phenomena clearly show the struggle going on between streaming impulse and armor block. Since more energy was liberated than the patient is able to discharge, and since there are still numerous spasms which prevent plasmatic streaming, acute anxiety develops. These manifestations confirm the orgone-biophysical concept of the antithesis of pleasure and anxiety (*cf. The Discovery of the Orgone*, vol. 1). Here, however, I have to stress a phenomenon which has as yet not been described clearly enough:

As soon as the first armor blocks are dissolved we find that, with the orgonotic streamings and sensations, the expression of "giving" develops more and more. However, still existing armorings prevent its full development. Then, it is as if the organism were trying to overcome the remaining blocks *by force*. In this process, the rudimentary expression of "giving" turns into one of *hatred*. This process is typical and deserves close attention.

When, for example, the armoring of the mouth region is sufficiently dissolved to stimulate an impulse to cry, while at the same time the armoring in the throat and the chest remain in full force, we see the lower part of the face begin to give in to the crying without being able to let it come through. The crying expression may change into a hateful grin. It is an expression of desperation, of utter frustration. This is an illustration of the following general fact: AS SOON AS THE EXPRESSION OF GIVING MEETS ARMOR BLOCKS, SO THAT IT CANNOT FREELY DEVELOP, IT CHANGES INTO DESTRUCTIVE RAGE.

The armoring of the *third* segment is found mainly in the deep neck musculature, the platysma and the sternocleidomastoid muscles. One only has to imitate the attitude of holding back anger or crying to understand the emotional function of the armoring of the neck. The spastic contraction of the neck segment also includes the tongue. This is easy to understand anatomically, since the muscles of the tongue insert mainly on the cervical bone system. Thus we find spasms in the musculature of the tongue in a functional connection with the depression of the Adam's apple and the contraction of the deep and superficial neck musculature. The movements of the Adam's apple show clearly how an anger or crying impulse, without the patient's being aware of it, is literally "swallowed down." This mechanism of suppressing emotions is very difficult to handle therapeutically. One cannot get with one's hands at the larynx muscles as one can with the superficial neck muscles. The best means of interrupting this "swallowing" of emotions is the elicitation of the *gag reflex*. With this reflex, the wave of excitation in the esophagus runs counter to that occurring in the "swallowing" of rage or crying. If the gag reflex develops fully or the patient even reaches the point of actually vomiting, the emotions which are held back by neck armoring are liberated.

Here, we realize again the significance of the longitudinal course of the excitation: The gagging reflex goes with an expansion of the diaphragm, that is, elevation of the diaphragm and expiration. Work on the neck armoring brings with it a loosening of the fourth and fifth armor segments. It follows that we cannot dissolve one armor segment after the other, cleanly separated one from another, in a mechanical manner. Rather, we work on a unitary life system the total plasma function of which is hindered by transverse armor rings. However, loosening of one armor segment leads, as a result of the motion produced, to the mobilization of armor rings above or below. For this reason, it is also impossible to give a mechanical description of the process of dissolving the muscular armor.

I am turning now to the *fourth* or chest segment. Although, again, the armor functions of this segment can be subdivided, it is better to treat the chest as a whole. The chest armoring is expressed in a chronic attitude of inspiration, shallow breathing and immobility of the thorax. As we know, the attitude of inspiration is the most important means of suppressing *any* kind of emotion. The armoring of the chest is particularly important not only because it is a main part of the total armoring of the organism but also because here the biopathic disease symptoms assume a particularly dangerous character.

The muscles that take part in the armoring of the chest are the intercostal muscles, the large chest muscles (pectoral muscles), the shoulder muscles (deltoid muscles) and the muscles on and between the shoulder blades. The expression of the chest armoring is essentially that of "self-control" and "restraint." The shoulders, which are pulled back, literally express "holding back." Together with the neck armoring, the chest armoring expresses suppressed "spite" and "stiff-neckedness" (again to be taken literally). In the absence of an armor, the expressive movement of the fourth segment is that of "free-flowing feeling." In the presence of an armor, the expression is that of "immobility" or "being unmoved."

The chronic expansion of the thorax goes with a tendency to

increased blood pressure, palpitations and anxiety, in severe cases of long standing also to enlargement of the heart. Various kinds of heart disease result either directly from the chronic expansion or indirectly as a result of the anxiety syndrome. Pulmonary emphysema is an immediate result of the chronic expansion of the thorax. Presumably, we have to look here also for the disposition to pneumonia and tuberculosis.

The emotions arising from the chest segment are essentially those of "raving rage" and "heart-breaking crying," of "sobbing" and "intolerable longing." These natural emotions are alien to the armored individual. His rage is "cold"; crying he considers "unmanly," "childish" or "unseemly"; longing he considers "soft," indicating a "lack of character."

It is from the plasmatic emotions of the chest that most emotional expressive movements of the arms and hands originate. These limbs are, biophysically speaking, extensions of the chest segment. In the artist who is capable of freely developing his longings, the emotion of the chest is directly extended into identical emotions and expressive movements of the arms and hands. This is true for the violinist and pianist as well as the painter. In the dancer, the main expressive movements derive from the total organism.

Armoring of the chest results in "awkwardness" of the arms and is largely responsible for the expression of "hardness" and "inaccessibility." The total armoring of the head, neck and chest segments gives the organism in the patriarchal cultural milieu—particularly in Asiatics of the "higher castes"—an atmosphere of "distinction." To this correspond the ideas of "stalwart character," "inaccessibility," "distance," "superiority" and "restraint." Militarism everywhere makes use of the expression embodied in the armoring of head, neck and chest. It goes without saying that these attitudes are based on the armoring, and not vice versa.

In certain patients we meet a syndrome stemming from the armoring of the chest which produces a particularly complicated system of difficulties. These patients complain, typically, of a "knot" in the chest. It seems to be a matter of a spasm in the esophagus similar to the globus hystericus in the pharynx. It is difficult to say whether the trachea is also involved, but it seems likely. This "knot," as becomes evident during its dissolution, contains the emotions of angry yelling or anxiety. To dissolve this "knot," it is often necessary to press down the chest and have the patient yell at the same time. The inhibition of the chest organs usually extends to an inhibition of those arm movements which express "reaching-for-something" or "embracing." It should be noted that these patients are not paralyzed, mechanically; they are capable of moving their arms very well. *But as soon as the movement of the arms becomes associated with the expression of longing or desiring, the inhibition sets in.* In severe cases, the hands, and even more so the fingertips, lose their orgonotic charge, become cold and clammy, and sometimes quite painful. It is likely that Raynaud's gangrene is based on this specific anorgonia. In many cases it is simply an impulse to choke someone which is armored off in the shoulder blades and the hands and which is responsible for the constriction in the fingertips.

The lives of such patients are characterized by a general lack of initiative and by work disturbances based on the inability to use their hands freely. In women, the chest armoring is often expressed in a lack of sensitivity in the nipples. Disturbances in sexual gratification, and disgust of nursing are an immediate result of this armoring.

Between the shoulder blades, in the region of the trapezius muscles, one finds two painful muscle bundles the armoring of which gives the impression of suppressed spite which, together with the pulled-back shoulders, is best expressed in the words, "I won't."

In the armored chest, the intercostal muscles show an exaggerated sensitivity to tickling stimuli. That this is not simply "an aversion to being tickled" but a biopathic overexcitability is shown in the fact that it disappears with the dissolution of the chest armor. In a certain case, the character attitude of inaccessibility had essentially the function of the expression, "Don't touch me, I'm ticklish."

I have, of course, no idea of ridiculing these character attitudes. We do not impute the banality of so many "dignified" attitudes but find them in their biological expression, whether we want to or not. A general may be a "dignified" person; we do not want to magnify or minimize him. But we are entitled to regard him as an animal which is armored in a certain way. I would not object if some scientist were to reduce my scientific curiosity to the biological function of a puppy sniffing at everything. I would be glad to be compared, biologically, to an alive, friendly puppy, for I do not have the ambition to distinguish myself from the animal.

The fact must be emphasized that the establishment of orgastic potency is out of the question without the previous dissolution of the chest armor and without liberating the emotions of raving rage, of longing and genuine crying. The function of giving surrender is most closely linked to the plasmatic motility of the chest and neck segments. Even if it were possible to mobilize the pelvic segment by itself, the head, instead of falling backwards, would inevitably move forward, in a defensive movement, as soon as the slightest sensation of pleasure was felt in the pelvis.

The armoring of the chest, as explained elsewhere, is a central part of the muscular armor as a whole. It was developed at the time of critical conflicts in the life of the child, probably long before the pelvic armor. It is easy to understand, therefore, that the traumatic memories of mistreatments of all kind, of frustrations in love and of disappointments in parents, appear in the course of dissolving the chest armor. The eliciting of memories is not important in orgone therapy; they help little if they appear without the corresponding emotion. The emotion in the expressive movements is ample for an understanding of the misery suffered by the patient, and finally the memories come up by themselves if one works correctly. It remains a riddle that unconscious memory functions can depend on the processes of plasmatic excitation, that memories are preserved, so to speak, in the plasmatic readiness for action.

Let us now turn to the fifth, the *diaphragmatic* segment. This segment, which comprises the diaphragm and the organs under it, is independent of the chest segment in its functioning. This is shown in the fact that the diaphragmatic block may persist even though the chest has become mobile and rage and crying have broken through. Xray fluoroscopy readily demonstrates the immobility of the diaphragm. True, with forced breathing one will find that the diaphragm moves better than before the dissolution of the chest armor. The block, however, consists in the fact that there is *no spontaneous diaphragmatic pulsation.* There are, then, two stages in the process of dissolving the diaphragmatic block:

In dissolving the chest armor, the patient was made to force his breathing voluntarily. In this process, of course, the diaphragm is also mobilized, but its movement is not spontaneous. As soon as the breathing is no longer being forced, the movement of the diaphragm ceases, and with that the respiratory movements of the chest. In order to take the second step, that of bringing about *spontaneous* pulsation of the diaphragm, we must get the emotional expression of the diaphragmatic armoring. This demonstrates again that one cannot reactivate any emotional functions by mechanical means. Only the biological *expressive motion* can dissolve the armor ring.

The fifth armor segment is a contraction ring over the epigastrium, the lower end of the sternum, along the lower ribs to the posterior insertions of the diaphragm, that is, to the tenth, eleventh and twelfth thoracic vertebrae. It comprises essentially the diaphragm, the stomach, the solar plexus, pancreas, liver, and two always plainly evident muscle bundles alongside the lower thoracic vertebrae.

This armor ring is expressed in a lordosis of the spine. As a rule, it is possible to put one's hand between the hollow back of the patient and the couch. The anterior costal margin sticks out in a rigid manner. The patient is more or less incapable of bending his spine forward. The fluoroscopic screen shows the immobility of the diaphragm under ordinary conditions and a very limited mobility with forced breathing. If one asks the patient to breathe, he will always breathe *in;* expiration as a *spontaneous* action is foreign to him. If one asks him to breathe out, he has to make much of an effort. If he succeeds, in a measure, to breathe out, the body automatically assumes some such attitude as opposes the breathing out. For example, the head is shoved forward, or the oral armor ring becomes more sharply contracted; the shoulder blades are pulled back or the arms are brought stiffly to the sides of the body; the pelvic musculature is contracted and the lower back arched more strongly.

The diaphragmatic block is the central armoring mechanism in this region. For this reason, the dissolution of this block is a central therapeutic task.

One asks oneself why precisely the dissolution of the armoring in the diaphragmatic segment is so particularly difficult. The bodily expression says clearly—though the patient is unaware of this—that the organism refuses to let the diaphragm swing freely. If the work on the upper segments was done correctly, the dissolution of the diaphragmatic block will sooner or later succeed. For example, forced breathing in the chest segment or repeating eliciting of the gag reflex will push the organism in the direction of the orgastic contraction; the same is true of irritation of the shoulder muscles by pinching.

Theoretically speaking, the reasons for this strong resistance against the full pulsation of the diaphragm are clear enough: the organism defends itself against the sensations of pleasure or anxiety which inevitably appear with diaphragmatic movement. But we should not forget for a moment that this is a rationalistic, psychologistic and finalistic statement. It implies that the organism "thinks" rationally, in somewhat the following manner: "This bothersome physician asks me to let the diaphragm swing. If I give in, I am going to have the sensations of anxiety and pleasure which I experienced at the time when my parents punished me for my pleasure sensations. I have reconciled myself to the situation as it is, and so I'm not going to give in."

But the living does not think rationalistically, does not do or not do things "in order to . . ." It functions according to the primary plasmatic emotions the function of which is the gratification of biological tensions and needs. One would inevitably go astray were one to translate the language of the living *immediately* into the word language of consciousness. To emphasize this is important because that rationalistic thinking which has given risen to mechanistic civilization has extinguished the understanding of the *basically different* language of the living function.

I shall illustrate these new phenomena as they appeared in a particularly clear clinical case: A patient who had an extraordinary intellectual understanding of orgone therapy and who had already achieved a great deal of dissolution of his upper armoring, was confronted with the task of breaking through the diaphragmatic armor. The therapeutic situation was quite clear. In the spoken word and in the conscious effort to master the armorings, there was an unequivocal YES. But, every time a small breech had been achieved in the armoring of the diaphragm, the patient's body, from the diaphragm down, began to jerk *sidewise*. It was only after considerable attempts to understand this that the expression of this became clear: The lower part of the body, in its sidewise movement, expressed a resolute NO. One only has to move one's right hand from side to side, as in saying, "No, no," in order to grasp this expression.

One might put on this the psychologistic, or rather mystical, interpretation that the plasma, beyond the word language, says NO to a thing which "the cortex" and the word language affirms. Such an interpretation of the process would be erroneous and would not bring us one step closer to an understanding of the living and its expressive language. The abdomen and the pelvis of the patient did not "consider" the task demanded of the organism; they did not "decide" not to give in. The interpretation is a different one, which corresponds better to the expressive language of the living:

The plasmatic movements of a worm, as we said, are *longitudinal*, along the body axis. When the body of the worm, as a result of the orgonotic waves of excitation, moves ahead, we have the "impression" that the worm acts "conscious" of its aim, "volitionally." The emotional expression of the worm can be translated in words of our language which connote "volition" or "affirmation." If, now, we pinch the worm around the middle of its body, thus interrupting the orgonotic excitation as by an armor block, the unitary forward movement ceases, and with it the emotional expression of "volition" or "affirmation." It is replaced by a different kind of motion, say, a bending from *side to side* of the hind part of the body while the front part is pulled in. The immediate impression conveyed by this sidewise movement is one of pain or a violent, "No—don't do that—I don't want it." Let us not forget that we are dealing here with an *impression*, that is, an interpretation which we *experience immediately* while observing the worm. We would act exactly alike if somebody were to grab our torso with huge pincers; we would inevitably pull in head and shoulders and would fight, sidewise, with pelvis and legs.

This interpretation, of course, does not mean that we have joined the subjectivists who claim that we "perceive nothing but our sensations" and that there is no reality corresponding to these sensations. Since everything living is functionally identical, the reactions of the worm to the pinching are identical with our own reactions in the same situation; the pain and the defense are the same reactions. It is this functional identity of man and worm which enables us to be "impressed" by the expression of the writhing worm in the correct, *objectively true* sense. The expression of the worm is what we experience through identification. But we do not experience immediately the pain of the worm and its objection; rather, we perceive an emotional expression which is the same as ours would be in the same painful situation. From this it follows that *we compre-*

hend the expressive motions and the emotional expressions of another living organism on the basis of the identity of our own emotions with those of all that is living.

We comprehend the language of the living *immediately* on the basis of the functional identity of the biological emotions.

After having understood it in this biological language of expression, we also put it in "words," translate it into the word language of consciousness. But the "NO, NO" of word language has no more to do with the language of expression of the living than has the word "cat" with the real cat we see before us. The word "cat" and the specific orgonotic plasma system we see before us have in reality nothing to do with each other. It is merely, as the many terms applicable to the phenomenon "cat" show, one of the loose, exchangeable terms which are applied to real phenomena, motions, emotions, etc.

All this sounds like natural philosophy. The layman is averse to natural philosophy and will be inclined to put this book aside because, he may say, it is "not based on hard reality." This thought is erroneous. I shall have to show how important it is to think *correctly* and to use concepts and words correctly. It will be shown that a whole world of mechanistically thinking biologists, physicists, bacteriologists, etc., in the past 10 years, while the functions of the living were being discovered, actually believed that what was moving there on the street was the word "cat" and not a complicated living organism.

To return to the NO-NO of our patient. The answer to the riddle is this: *When a plasmatic current cannot run along the body because transverse blocks make it impossible, a transverse movement develops which secondarily, in world language, means* NO. This NO of word language corresponds to the NO in the expressive language of the living. It is not by accident that NO is expressed by a sidewise movement of the head and YES by nodding. The NO-NO which our patient expressed by the sidewise movements of his pelvis did not disappear until the diaphragmatic block was dissolved. On the other hand, it made its reappearance every time when this block recurred.

These facts are of eminent significance for an understanding of the body language. Our patient was generally negativistic; his characterological basic attitude was also "NO." He suffered severely from it, he fought against this character attitude, but to no avail. In spite of his conscious and intellectual attempts to say YES, to be positive, his character constantly expressed NO. This characterological NO was not difficult to understand, functionally as well as historically. Like so many children, his severely compulsive mother had given him enemas. Like other children, he suffered this with horror and inner rage. In order to subdue his rage, in order to be able to submit to the torture at all, he "restrained himself," pulling up his pelvic floor, holding his breath, and generally developing the bodily attitude of NO-NO. When the living in him wanted to cry out, NO-NO against this assault, and could not, he acquired an irreparable scar for the rest of his life: the expression of his life system, toward everything and everybody, became a NO-NO. Although this characterological NO-NO was a severe symptom, it was, at the same time, also the expression of a vigorous protest which originally had been rational and justified. But this originally rational protest had assumed the form of a chronic armor and was thus rigid and directed against everything.

As I have shown elsewhere, a traumatic infantile experience can have a present-day effect *only if it is anchored in a rigid* armor. The originally rational NO-NO, in the course of years, turned into a neurotic, irrational NO-NO. This was due to the armoring which, as we saw, expressed a NO-NO. The expression, NO-NO, decreased when, during therapy, the armor was dissolved. With that, the historical assault by the mother also lost its pathogenic significance.

Depth-psychologically, it is correct to say that in this case the affect of defense, of yelling, NO-NO, was "suppressed." In the biological depth, however, it was not a matter of a suppressed NO-NO, *but of the inability of the organism to say* YES. A positive, giving attitude in life is possible only when the organism functions as a total unit, only when the plasmatic excitations with the corresponding emotions can freely pass all organs and tissues. As soon as, however, one single armor block inhibits this function, the expression of giving is disturbed. Then we have infants who cannot give themselves fully to their play, adolescents who fail in school, adults who function like an automobile with the emergency brake on. The observer then has the "impression" of laziness, spite or incapability. The individual with the block experiences himself as "failing in spite of all his efforts." Translated into our expressive language of the living, this means: *The organism always begins, biologically correctly, with achievement, that is, with streaming and giving. During the passage of the orgonotic excitations through the organism, however, the functioning becomes inhibited, and thus the expression of "joyous achievement" turns into an automatic "*NO, *I don't want to."* This means that the organism is not responsible for its non-achievement.

This process has general significance. I chose my clinical examples intentionally from those that have general significance, for the restrictions of human functioning as described will make it possible for us better to understand a number of unfortunate social phenomena which cannot be understood without their *biophysical* background.

Let us, after this long but inevitable digression, return to the fifth armor segment. In the upper segments, we had no great difficulty in discerning the emotional expression. The inhibition of the eye muscles, for example, expresses "empty" or "sad" eyes; a rigid chin may express "suppressed anger"; the "knot in the chest" will dissolve into crying or yelling. Here, in the upper four segments, we understand the emotional expressions *immediately*, and the body language is easily translated into word language. With the diaphragmatic segment, things are more difficult. When this segment is loosened, we are *no longer able to translate the expressive language into word language*. The expression which then comes about leads us into as yet uncomprehended depths of the living function. We meet here the problem as to the concrete manner in which the animal, man, is connected with the primitive animal kingdom and with the cosmic functions of the orgone.

The armor in the diaphragmatic segment can be loosened if the patient repeatedly elicits the gag reflex, without, however, at the same time interrupting his expiration. This measure is successful, however, only if all the armorings in the four upper segments have been previously dissolved so that the orgonotic streamings in the regions of head, neck and chest function freely.

As soon as the diaphragm swings freely, that is, as soon as there is full spontaneous respiration, the torso tends to fold up with each expiration. That is, the upper part of the body tends toward the pelvis, while the upper abdomen recedes. This is the picture of the *orgasm reflex* as it presents itself to us for the first time, although it is still disturbed because the pelvis is not yet loosened. The bending forward of the torso, while the head falls back, immediately expresses "giving, surrender." This is not difficult to understand. What is difficult to understand, however, are the forward convulsions. *The expression of the convulsions in the orgasm reflex is at first incomprehensible. It cannot be translated into word language.* We must assume some basic difference between the expressive movements found thus far and the expression of the total body which appears when the diaphragmatic block is dissolved.

I must ask the reader for a good deal of patience here; the final result will be worth it. I may say that for more than ten years I had to exercise a great deal of patience in order to reach the finding I will have to describe. During these years, I was again and again on the point of giving up the attempt to understand the orgasm reflex, because it seemed so senseless to try to make this basic biological reflex comprehensible. But I stuck to it because I could not admit that, while the living has an immediately understandable expressive language in all other realms, it should express "Nothing" in the orgasm reflex. This seemed too contradictory, too "senseless." I kept telling myself that it was I myself who had stated that the living simply func-

tions, that it has no "meaning"; that perhaps the meaningless-
ness of the orgastic convulsions simply demonstrated this. The
attitude of giving surrender, however, which ushers in the
orgasm reflex, is full of expression and meaning. The orgastic
convulsions themselves are doubtless full of expression. I had
to conclude that natural science had not yet learned to comprehend this general expression of the living. In brief, "an expressive movement without an emotional expression" seemed an
absurdity.

What provided access to the problem was the process of
vomiting which often sets in when the diaphragmatic armoring
is loosened. Just as there is an inability to cry so is there an
inability to vomit. This inability is easy to understand, orgone-
biophysically. The "knot" in the chest, the "swallowing" and
the contraction of the eye muscles prevents crying. In the same
way, the diaphragmatic block, together with the armor rings
above, prevents the peristaltic movement of the body energy
upwards, from stomach to mouth. In many cases of diaphragmatic block there is, together with the inability to vomit, more
or less constant nausea. There can be no doubt that the so-
called "nervous" stomach disorders are the direct result of the
armoring in this region. Vomiting is a biological expressive
movement the function of which achieves exactly what it "expresses": convulsive expulsion of body contents. It is based on
a peristaltic movement of stomach and esophagus in the opposite direction of its normal function, that is, toward the
mouth (antiperistalsis). The gag reflex dissolves the armoring
of the diaphragmatic segment quickly and radically. Vomiting
is accompanied by a convulsion of the body, a rapid folding
in the epigastrium, with a *forward* jerk of head as well as pelvis.
In the colic of infants, vomiting is accompanied by diarrhea.
Energetically speaking, *strong waves of excitation run from
the middle of the body upwards and downwards, toward mouth
and anus.* The corresponding expression is so elementary that
its deep biological nature cannot be doubted; it is only a matter
of also understanding it.

The total movement of the body in vomiting is purely physiologically—though not emotionally—the same as in the orgasm reflex. This is confirmed clinically: the dissolution of the diaphragmatic block inevitably ushers in the first convulsions of the body which subsequently develop into the total orgasm reflex. These convulsions go with deep expiration and a wave of excitation from the diaphragmatic region to the head on the one hand and the genitals on the other.

As we know, the loosening of the upper armor segments is indispensable for the establishment of the total body convulsion. In moving toward the pelvis, the wave of orgonotic excitation typically meets a block in the middle of the abdomen. What happens is either that the abdomen contracts rapidly, or that the pelvis is retracted and held in this position.

The contraction in the middle of the abdomen represents the *sixth* armor ring. The spasm of the large abdominal muscles (Rectus abdominis) goes with a spastic contraction of the lateral muscles (Transversus abdominis) which run from the lower ribs to the upper margin of the pelvis. They can be easily palpated as hard, painful cords. In the back, this segment is represented by the lower sections of the muscles running along the spine (Latissimus dorsi), sacrospinalis, etc. These muscles also can be felt as hard, painful cords. The dissolution of the sixth segment is easier than that of all others. After its dissolution, the way is open to that of the *seventh* or pelvic segment.

The armor of the pelvis comprises in most cases practically all the muscles of the pelvis. The pelvis is retracted and sticks out in the back. The abdominal muscle above the symphysis is painful, as are the adductors of the thigh, the superficial as well as the deep. The anal sphincter is contracted and the anus pulled up. The gluteal muscles are painful. The pelvis is "dead" and expressionless. This expressionlessness is the emotional expression of asexuality. Emotionally, there is no perception of sensations or excitations; the pathological symptoms, on the other hand, are very numerous:

There is constipation, lumbago, various kinds of growth in

the rectum, inflammation of the ovaries, polyps of the uterus, benign and malignant tumors, irritability of the bladder, vaginal anesthesia, anesthesia of the penis surface with irritation of the urethra. There is frequently leukorrhea with the development of protozoa from the vaginal epithelium ("Trichomonas vaginalis"). In the man, anorgonia of the pelvis results in erective impotence or premature ejaculation; in the woman, we find complete vaginal anesthesia or spasm of the vaginal muscles (vaginismus).

There is a specific *pelvic anxiety* and a specific *pelvic rage*. Just like the armoring of the shoulders, the pelvic armor also contains the emotions of anxiety and rage. Orgastic impotence creates *secondary* impulses to achieve sexual gratification by force. Thus, while the impulses of the sexual act begin according to the biological pleasure principle, what happens is this: *the pleasure sensations turn inevitably into rage impulses because the armor does not permit the development of involuntary movements,* of convulsions, in this segment. Thus there develops a painful feeling of "having to get through" which cannot be called anything but sadistic. Like anywhere else in the realm of the living, in the pelvis also *inhibited pleasure turns into rage, and inhibited rage into muscular spasms.* This is easily demonstrated clinically: no matter how far the dissolution of the pelvic armor has progressed, no matter how mobile the pelvis has become, there will be *no pleasure sensations in the pelvis as long as the anger has not been released from the pelvic muscles.*

Just as in other armor segments, there is a "beating" or "piercing" by means of violent forward movements of the pelvis. The corresponding expression is unmistakable. Aside from the expression of anger, there is also one of contempt: contempt of the pelvis and all its organs, contempt of the sexual act and, in particular, of the sexual partner. I say on the basis of ample clinical experience that only in few cases in our civilization is the sexual act based on love. The intervening rage, hatred, sadistic emotions and contempt are part and parcel of the love life of modern man. I am not referring to the clear-cut cases where the sexual act is based on mercenary motives; I am referring to the majority of people in all social strata. On this is based what has become a scientific axiom: *"Omne animal post coitum triste"* ("Every animal is sad after the sexual act"). Man only has committed the error of ascribing his own disappointment to the animal also. The rage and contempt connected with the sexual act is vividly expressed in the common "cusswords" applied to it.

THE EMOTIONAL EXPRESSION OF THE ORGASM REFLEX, AND SEXUAL SUPERIMPOSITION

As we have seen, the pelvic armor has an expression easily translatable into word language, and the emotions released from it speak a clear language. This is true, however, only of the emotions of the armor. It is not true of the expressive movements which regularly appear *after* the dissolution of the anxiety and the rage. These movements consist in gentle forward movements of the pelvis which clearly express desire. It is reminiscent of the rhythmical movements of the tail end of insects, such as bees or wasps, a movement which is particularly clearly seen during the sexual act of such insects as dragonflies or butterflies. The basic form of this movement is the following:

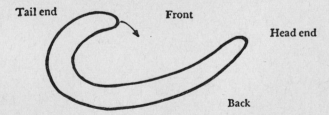

It continues the expression of giving surrender. Subjective perception tells us that his attitude is accompanied by *longing*. The question is: longing for what? and surrender to what?

Word language expresses the goal of the longing and the function of the surrender as follows: As the organism develops the orgasm reflex, the longing for "gratification" makes its unmistakable appearance. The goal is clearly that of the sexual act. In the sexual act one "surrenders" to the pleasure sensation; one "gives oneself" to the partner.

Word language seems to describe this natural phenomenon unequivocally. But it merely *seems* to. Since word language is only a translation of the expressive language of the living, we do not know whether the words "sexual act" and "gratification" really express the function of the orgasm reflex. In addition, the expression of the orgastic *convulsions* cannot be translated into word language. Let us go a step further in doubting the ability of word language to comprehend natural phenomena *immediately*. Our next question will baffle the reader. But after some consideration, he will have to admit that words often obscure processes rather than explain them. The question is the following:

What is the reason for the extraordinary significance of the genital drive? Nobody doubts its elemental power; nobody can avoid it. The whole living world is subject to it. Copulation and the biological functions connected with it form the very basic function of the living which guarantees its continued existence. Copulation is a basic function of the "germ plasm" in the sense of Weissman which is immortal in the strict sense of the word. The species man has simply denied this powerful natural force, but by no means abolished it. We know the terrible tragedies created by this.

The existence of the living is due to the *superimposition* of two orgonotic systems of different sex. We must admit that we have no answer to the simplest of all questions: *What is the origin of this superimposition of two living organisms of different sex? What is its significance and "meaning"? Why is the continued existence of living nature bound up with this form of movement instead of any other?*

The most common form of this movement of sexual super-imposition is the following:

Sexual superimposition goes together with orgonotic lumina-tion of the body cells, with penetration and fusion of two orgonotic energy systems into one functional unity. At the acme of the excitation (= lumination) the two orgone systems, which have become *one*, discharge their energy in clonic convulsions. In this process, highly charged substances (the sperm cells) are discharged which in turn continue the function of superimposi-tion, penetration and fusion.

Word language cannot explain anything here. Its concepts of the process of sexual superimposition derive from the organ sensations which give rise to the superimposition, which accom-pany and follow it. "Longing," "urge," "copulation," "gratifica-tion," etc., are merely pictures of a natural process. In order to understand this natural process we have to find other primary natural processes which have a more general significance than the sexual superimposition of the organisms and which cer-tainly are deeper than the organ sensations to which the con-cepts of word language correspond.

That the orgasm reflex follows natural laws is beyond any doubt. In every successful treatment, it regularly appears when the segmental armorings which prevented it are completely dis-solved. Nor is there any doubt that the sexual superimposition follows natural laws. It occurs inevitably when the orgasm re-flex functions freely and if there are no social obstacles which prevent it.

We shall have to collect a great number of natural phenomena before we understand the expressive language of the living in the orgasm reflex and in the superimposition. The failure of word language here points to a natural function *beyond* the realm of the living. Not, of course, in the sense of the supernatural mystics, but in the sense of a *functional connection between living and non-living nature.*

We must assume that word language can describe only such manifestations of life which can be expressed in terms of organ sensations and the corresponding expressions, such as anger, pleasure, anxiety, annoyance, grief, surrender, etc. The organ sensations and expressive movements, however, are nothing ultimate. At a certain point, the natural law of the non-living substance must of necessity penetrate the living and express itself in it. This cannot be otherwise if the living derives from the non-living and returns to it. While the organ sensations, which correspond specifically to the living, can be translated into word language, those expressive movements of the living which do not specifically belong to the living but which derive from the realm of the non-living, *cannot be put into word language.* Since the living derives from the non-living, and since non-living matter derives from cosmic energy, we must conclude that there are *cosmic energy functions in the living.* The non-translatable expressive movements of the orgasm reflex in the sexual superimposition could, therefore, represent the cosmic orgone function.

I know how far-reaching this working hypothesis is, but it is inevitable. It is a clinical fact that orgastic longing, that is, the longing for superimposition, always goes hand in hand with cosmic longing and cosmic sensations. The mystical ideas of so many religions, the belief in a hereafter and in a transmigration of souls, all derive from cosmic longing; and cosmic longing is functionally anchored in the expressive movements of the orgasm reflex. *In the orgasm, the living is nothing but a bit of pulsating nature.* After all, the ideas of man, of animal in general as "a bit of nature" are widespread and commonly known. But it is easier to use a phrase than to comprehend scientifically wherein this functional identity of the living and of nature consists *concretely*. It is simple to state that the principle of a locomotive is basically identical with that of a primitive wheel-barrow; but it is necessary to state how the principle of the locomotive, in the course of thousands of years, has developed from that of the wheel-barrow.

We find that the problem of the expressive language of the living poses difficult questions. Let us further look for the common features which connect the more highly developed with the lower forms of life.

The technique of orgone therapy has shown us that *in the animal, man, there still functions a worm*. The segmental structure of the armor rings can mean nothing else. The dissolution of this segmental armoring liberates expressive movements and plasmatic currents which are independent of the anatomy of muscles and nerves. They correspond much more closely to the peristaltic movements of an intestine, of a worm or a protozoon.

One still frequently meets the concept that man—in spite of his development from phylogenetically older forms—represents a living being of a *new* kind, without connection with the forms from which he stems. In the segments of the spine and the ganglia, the segmental character, and with that, the worm character of the biological system is clearly expressed. This system, however, is segmental not only morphologically, that is, in its rigid form. The orgone functions and the armor rings also represent *functional* segments. They are not—as one might say of the vertebrae—remnants of a dead past in a new living present. Rather, they represent the most active and important functional apparatus of the present, the core of all biological functions of the animal, man. From the segmental functions derive the biologically important organ sensations and the emotions, pleasure, anxiety and rage. Also, *expansion* and *contraction*, as functions of pleasure and anxiety, are present from the ameba to man. One carries one's head high with pleasure and pulls it in in anxiety, just as does the worm. If the ameba and the worm continue to function in man as a basic part of his emotional functioning, then it is correct to try to connect the basic biological reflex of orgastic superimposition with the simplest plasmatic functions in order to understand it.

As we said, the dissolution of the diaphragmatic block leads inevitably to the first orgastic convulsions. We also said that the limbs represent only continuations of the chest and pelvic segment. *The largest and most important ganglion apparatus is located in the middle of the torso, close to the back.*

Everybody has seen a cat being lifted by being held by the skin of the back. The body of the cat seems doubled up, the head brought close to the pelvis, head and legs hang down limply, somewhat like this:

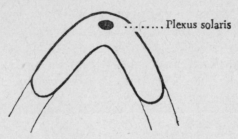

We can conceive of any other animal, including man, in this position. As always when the body assumes a certain attitude, there is an expression. It is not easy to recognize the expression of this attitude immediately. After some observation, we have the picture of a jelly-fish with tentacles.

Biophysics will have to learn to read *forms of movement from bodily forms, and expressions from forms of movements*. More will have to be said about this later. At this point, the similarity with the jelly-fish must suffice. We can go further in this analogy. The central nervous apparatus in the jelly-fish is located in the middle of the back, like the solar plexus in the vertebrates. When the jelly-fish moves, the ends of the body move towards each other and away from each other, in rhythmical alternation. We come to the following assumption:

The expressive movements in the orgasm reflex are functionally identical with those of a living and swimming jelly-fish.

In either case, the ends of the body, that is, of the torso, move towards each other, as if they tended to touch each other. When they are close, we have contraction; when they are as far apart as possible we have expansion or relaxation of the orgonotic system. It is a very primitive form of *biological pulsation*. If this pulsation is accelerated, so that it assumes *clonic* form, we have the expressive movement of the orgastic convulsion before us.

The expulsion of the spawn in fishes and of the semen in higher animals is bound up with this plasmatic convulsion of the total body. The orgastic convulsion is accompanied by high excitation which we experience as the pleasure of the "acme." The expressive movement of the orgasm reflex, then, represents a most important, present-day mobilization of a biological form of movement which goes way back to the jelly-fish. The following drawing shows the bell shape and the jelly-fish-like form of movement:

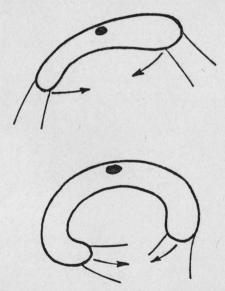

On closer consideration, the functional identity of the jelly-fish movement and orgastic convulsion seems less strange.

When we consider that in the segmental structure of the armor rings and of the emotional functions we met the worm in man, it is not particularly surprising that in the total body convulsion the jelly-fish function is expressed. We have to realize that it is not a matter of dead, archaic remnants from a phylogenetic past, but of *present-day*, bio-energetically highly significant functions in the highly developed organism. The most primitive and the most highly developed plasmatic functions exist alongside each other. The development of complicated functions in the organism, of "higher" functions as we call them, does not change the existence or function of the "jelly-fish in man." It is precisely this jelly-fish in man which represents his unity with the lower animal world. Just as Darwin's theory derived man's origin from the lower vertebrates from his morphology, so does orgone physics reduce the *emotional* functions of man even much further, to the forms of movement of molluscs and protozoa.

What is called "nature in man," then, can be taken out of the realm of mystic and poetic phantasy and can be translated in the concrete language of natural science. It is not a matter of metaphors or analogies, nor of sentimental perceptions, but of concrete, visible and manageable processes of the living.

IV. THE DISCOVERY OF THE ORGONE
—Experimental Investigation of Biological Energy

1. THE DISCOVERY OF THE ORGONE

INTRODUCTION

In the following series of articles on the discovery of the orgone an attempt will be made to present the results of the bion research carried on between 1936 and 1942. A part of these findings was published in my book, *Die Bione* (1938), and in "Bion Experiments on the Cancer Problem" and "Drei Versuche am Statischen Elektroskop" (1939). Since then, nothing has been published on the subject; partly because of the transfer of the laboratory from Oslo to New York, partly because it was necessary first to coordinate the numerous findings. From October 1939 until the summer of 1941, orgone radiation experiments were carried out in cancer mice. In March 1941, orgone therapy experiments were begun in otherwise hopeless cases of human cancer.* Sex-economic cancer research had started long before that, namely in 1933 when the attempt was made to correlate the most important findings of cancer pathology with the sex-economic findings concerning the functions of the vegetative system.

Thus, this series of articles deals with the clinical and experimental findings of almost 10 years. This makes the task an

---

* *Cf.* The next chapter, "The Carcinomatous Shrinking Biopathy."

From the *International Journal of Sex-Economy and Orgone-Research*, vol. I, 1942.

extremely difficult one. On the reader, it makes the demand of his having to become acquainted with the medical concepts of sex-economy; of the author it demands a frank presentation of all uncertainties and shortcomings of this research.

Some readers may ask why this or that experiment was not also carried out, why this or that substance was not also investigated. I am painfully aware of many such gaps. They are, however, not my fault, but largely that of the circumstances under which the work had to be carried on. Several academic organizations which could have lent their financial support considered the whole thing, on the basis of individual, unrelated findings, so fantastic that I had to decide to maintain my independence and to get along without outside help. This is necessary in order to protect the work against misinterpretations before the publication of the total findings. The experimental work consumed practically my whole income; during the years of 1940 and 1941 alone it cost more than $10,000. Adequate research facilities would have required hundreds of thousands of dollars. The limitation in the use of materials, apparatus and experimental set-up simply reflects the limits of my economic capacity. I know that any average physical laboratory aided by government or foundation funds could have applied the findings to an infinite number of materials and set-ups. As well-equipped as my laboratory is in itself, the problems that presented themselves went far beyond its capacities. Nevertheless, the fundamental groundwork has been done which can form the basis for more extensive investigations.

Many of the facts which in orgone biophysics converge into a comprehensible unit can be found in the literature of physics, unrelated and more or less arbitrarily interpreted. The fact of the atmospheric orgone energy, however, is nowhere mentioned. In succeeding articles ample reference will be made to the literature, at a time when we shall discuss the experimental investigation of the connecting links between orgone and electricity. In the course of time, the reader will convince himself that what often appears to be naiveté is actually deliberate exclusion of prejudice and that it leads to decisive new conclusions in the theory of electricity.

THE FUNCTION OF TENSION AND CHARGE

The Function of the Orgasm

Those who are familiar with sex-economy know of the important event which, in 1933, represented the turning point in our research: *the discovery of the biological function of tension and charge.* I should like to give here a brief résumé of these developments.

Clinical investigation had shown us that the function of the orgasm is the key to the problem of the energy in the neuroses. Neuroses are the result of a stasis (damming-up) of sexual energy. This stasis is caused by a disturbance in the *discharge* of sexual energy in the organism. It makes no difference whether this fact is perceived by the ego or not; nor does it matter whether the psychic apparatus misinterprets this process in a neurotic manner, or what kind of ideologies the individual develops around the disharmony in his energy system. Everyday clinical experience leaves no doubt: *The elimination of sexual stasis through orgastic discharge eliminates every neurotic manifestation.* The difficulties involved in this therapeutic task are chiefly of a social nature. It is necessary to point out these simple basic facts again and again.

Sex-economy had known for a long time that the orgasm is a *fundamental biological phenomenon;* fundamental because the orgastic energy discharge takes place at the very roots of biological functioning. This discharge takes place in the form of an involuntary contraction and expansion of the total plasma system. Like the respiratory function, it is a basic function of any animal system. Biophysically speaking, it is impossible to distinguish the total contraction of an ameba from the orgastic contraction of a multicellular organism. The outstanding phenomena are *intensive biological excitation, repeated expansion and contraction, ejaculation of body fluids in the contraction, and rapid reduction of the biological excitation.* In order to comprehend these phenomena as biological functions, we had, of course, to rid ourselves of the lascivious reactions which usually accompany any occupation with sexual functions and autonomic life functions in general; these very reactions, in the form of neurotic attitudes and symptoms, form an important object of our psychiatric work.

In its quickly alternating expansions and contractions, the orgasm shows a function which is composed of tension and relaxation, charge and discharge: *biological pulsation.*

Closer investigation reveals the fact that these four functions appear in a definite four-beat: the mechanical tension, which shows itself as sexual excitation, is followed by a bio-electric charge of the periphery of the organism. This fact was unequivocally demonstrated by measuring the bio-electric potentials occurring with pleasurable excitation of the erogenous zones. When tension and charge have reached a certain degree, there occur contractions of the total biological system. The high peripheral charge of the organism is *discharged.* This is seen objectively in the rapid decrease of the bio-electric skin potential; it is felt subjectively as a rapid decrease in excitation. The sudden shift from a state of high charge into that of discharge is called the "acme." The discharge of bio-electrical energy is followed by a mechanical relaxation of the tissues through a flowing back of body fluids. That we are actually dealing with a discharge of energy is shown, among other things, in the fact that for some time after the discharge the organism is incapable of sexual excitation. This is the condition which, psychologically, we call "gratification." The need for gratification, or, in biophysical terms: *for the discharge of the surplus energy in the organism by way of fusion with another organism*—makes itself felt at more or less regular intervals. These intervals vary from individual to individual as well as from species to species. They usually become shorter in the spring; in animals, one finds the phenomenon of rut or heat, a concentration of this biological need in certain seasons, predominantly the spring. This fact points to a close connection between the function of the orgasm and an energy function of a cosmic nature. The orgastic function, together with the known effects of the sun on the living organism, is one of the phenomena which shows the living organism to be a part of non-living nature.

Thus, the function of the orgasm is expressed in the four-beat: *mechanical tension* → *bio-electrical charge* → *bio-electrical discharge* → *mechanical relaxation*. We shall call it for brief the *function of tension and charge*.

We know from earlier investigations that the function of tension and charge is characteristic not only of the orgasm. It applies to all functions of the autonomic life system. The heart, the intestines, the urinary bladder, the lungs, all function according to this rhythm. *Cell division*, also, follows this four-beat. So does the motion of protozoa as well as metazoa. Worms and snakes show this movement according to the formula of tension and charge particularly clearly, in the movements of their parts as well as their totality.

Thus it is obvious that there is *one* basic law which governs the organism as a whole as well as its autonomic organs. The total organism contracts in the orgasm just as does the heart with every pulse beat; the medusa as a whole contracts just as does the vacuole it contains. This biological basic formula comprehends the essence of living functioning. *The orgasm formula shows itself to be the life formula as such.* This corresponds exactly to our previous formulation that the *sexual process is the productive biological process* per se, in procreation, work, *joie de vivre,* intellectual production, etc. To recognize or to refute this formulation is to understand or to reject sex-economic biophysics.

The mechanical tension of organs through tumescence is easy to understand: it consists in taking up fluid and in a separation of the particles in the biological colloid. Conversely, mechanical relaxation consists in giving off fluid and mutual rapprochement of the particles. The question as to the *nature* of the process of charge and discharge presents a more difficult problem. The possibility of measuring the electrical potentials could easily lead us to discard the whole problem by calling the process one of "electrical charge" and "electrical discharge." After all, electrical energy was measured in the contracting muscle and the "electric eel"; one is even able today to measure the electrical "brain waves." In reporting on my bio-electrical experiments (1934-1936), I gave the changes in potential occurring in pleasure and anxiety in millivolts.

The Postulate of a Specific Biological Energy

Is the specific biological energy identical with electricity? This is not as simple a question as it may appear. Certainly it would be highly satisfying if we could express the function of the orgasm in the familiar terminology of physics. The organism, then, would be nothing but a "particularly complicated electrical machine." It would be very pleasant and convenient to explain the reaction of rheumatic people to weather changes by stating that the "body electricity" was being influenced by the "electric" charges in the air. The attempt has also been made to apply the laws of iron magnetism to the living organism. We say that a beloved person has a "magnetic" attraction, that excitement "electrifies" one. We shall soon see that such analogies are erroneous. In earlier publications, I spoke of "*bio-electricity*," following the usual terminology. No doubt, there is electricity in the organism, in the form of electrically charged colloid particles and ions. Colloid chemistry as well as muscle physiology operate with it. Muscles can be made to contract by the application of an electric current. In combing our hair, we get "electric" sparks.

Nevertheless: *There are a number of phenomena which are completely at variance with the theory of electromagnetic energy.*

First of all, the effects of bodily "magnetism." Many physicians and lay therapists use these magnetic forces in a practical way. But to us, it is not conceivable that these forces which emanate from organic, colloidal, non-metallic material should be magnetic forces. We shall provide experimental proof for the fact that the energy we are dealing with in the living organism is not identical with iron magnetism.

If a faradic current is applied to our body, we experience it as alien to the body, as not "organic." Electrical energy, even in the smallest quantities, produces only disturbances of normal functioning if applied to the muscles, i.e., they show unnatural, uncoordinated, "senseless" contractions. It is altogether impossible to produce, by applying an electrical current, an organic movement which would have the slightest resemblance to the everyday living movements of whole muscle systems or functional muscle groups. The electrical current produces a movement in which the essential characteristic of biological energy is lacking: the movement of a *group* of organs in a *coordinated, functionally meaningful form*. On the other hand, the *disturbances* of biological functioning by the electrical current shows distinctly the character of electrical energy. The resulting movements are rapid, jerky, and angular, exactly like the oscillographic phenomena which one obtains by rubbing an electrode on metal (*cf. The Function of the Orgasm*, p. 348, fig. 7).

If an electric current is applied to a muscle-nerve preparation, the electric current is not expressed as such in the resulting movement. If it did, the smooth muscle would contract just as quickly as the striated muscle. In reality, the smooth muscle does not contract like the striated one, but in the form of a slow, wave-like movement which is characteristic of the smooth muscle. That is, an unknown "something" is interpolated between the electric stimulus and the muscle action. It is only induced by the electric stimulus and manifests itself as a movement which is accompanied by an action current. But this "something" is not electricity.

Our own sensations tell us distinctly that the emotions (which undoubtedly are manifestations of our biological energy) are something basically different from the sensations caused by an electric shock. Our sense organs fail completely to register the electromagnetic waves though the atmosphere is full of them. We feel nothing in the proximity of a radio-transmitter. We do not react to the proximity of a high-tension wire the way a radio apparatus does. If our life energy were electricity, the fact that we react to the wave-lengths of visible light but not to the other wave-lengths would be incomprehensible—since our perceptions are an expression of this life energy. We are insensitive to the electrons of an Xray machine as well as to radium rays. Electrical energy does not convey a biological charge. Thus far it has been impossible to express the potency of vitamins in electrical measurements, although there can be no doubt that they contain biological energy. These examples could be multiplied indefinitely. One might also ask how it is possible that our organism does not get destroyed by all the electromagnetic fields which surround it.

True, we can influence sensitive volt-meters by touching them, but the magnitude of this reaction is so infinitesimal—compared with the energy quantities in the organism—that we cannot see any connection.

We are dealing here with gigantic contradictions, contradictions which are insoluble within the framework of the known forms of energy. They have been occupying the minds of biologists and natural philosophers for a long time. Attempts were made to bridge the gap with concepts which were to make comprehensible the specific *living* functioning. Such attempts were made primarily by the opponents of mechanistic materialism, by the vitalists. Driesch, e.g., tried to solve the problem by introducing the concept of *"entelechy,"* a vital energy pertaining to living matter and governing it. As this energy was not tangible and measurable, his concept was doomed to lead into metaphysics. Bergson's *"élan vital"* also took into account the incompatibility of the known forms of energy and living functioning. His *"force créatrice"* represents an explosive function of matter, manifesting itself most clearly in living functioning. Bergson's hypothesis was directed against mechanistic materialism as well as teleological finalism. It comprehended correctly the basically *functional* character of the living but it lacked empirical substantiation. The force in question was neither measurable nor tangible or otherwise capable of being influenced.

The well-known German physiologist Pflüger, on the basis of the function of cyanide, assumed a connection between life energy and fire. His assumption was correct. Prominent biologists, as for example Kammerer, postulated the existence of a *specific biological energy* which would have no immediate connection with electricity, magnetism and other known forces.

If I should . . . give a scientific credo which as yet is impossible of proof, I must say: the existence of a *specific life force* seems highly probable to me! That is, an energy which is neither heat, electricity, magnetism, kinetic energy (including oscillation and radiation) nor a combination of any or all of them, but an energy which specifically belongs only to those processes that we call "life." That does not mean that this energy is restricted to those natural bodies which we call "living beings"; it is present certainly in the formative process of the crystals. Perhaps, for this reason, it would be better to term it "formative energy" instead of life energy. But this energy is nothing "supra-physical," although it is unlike any of the known physical energies; it is no mysterious "entelechy" (Aristotle, Driesch), but a genuine, natural energy; only, as electrical energy is linked up with electric phenomena, chemical energy with chemical processes, so is this energy linked up with phenomena of life and of the development and change of forms. It certainly follows the law of the conservation of energy; it is convertible into other forms of energy as, for example, heat is converted into kinetic energy and vice versa. (Kammerer, *Allgemeine Biologie*, p. 8).

Kammerer had been led to the problem of a "formative life energy" by his experiments on the heredity of acquired characteristics. The concepts of "inherited substances" and "genes" held dear by the heredity theoreticians only obscured the problem of living functioning, as if devised for the very purpose of blocking any access to the problem. Like a pyramid put on

its tip, their theory consisted of a heap of hypothetical contentions, based on an extremely small basis in fact, and a doubtful
basis at that. One only has to remember the unscientific, un-
warranted and moralizing consequences drawn from the famous "family Kalikak." In reading hereditary hypotheses one has
more the impression of treatises on ethics than of science. The
living function gets smothered in a heap of mechanistic hypotheses. These theories finally degenerated into the disastrous
Hitlerian theory of race.

With the vitalists, the living became a mysterious ghost-like
thing, with the mechanists a lifeless machine. With the bacteriologists, there is, for each living organism, some special germ
"in the air" which as yet nobody has seen. In the second half
of the 19th century, Plouchet undertook the laborious task of
examining the correctness of this theory. Pasteur showed experimentally that liquids which have been exposed to high
temperatures contain no living germs. If he found living organisms, he ascribed their presence to air infection. In his
"Geschichte des Materialismus," Lange criticizes Pasteur's interpretation and points to Plouchet's experiments. Plouchet
passed great quantities of air through water and then examined
it. He invented a special apparatus in which air was blown
against glass plates on which the dust particles were deposited.
He then examined the deposited dust. He carried out these
experiments on glaciers in the Pyrénées, in the catacombs of
Thebes, on land and on the sea in Egypt, and on top of the
cathedral of Rouen. He found all kinds of things, but only
extremely rarely a spore of a fungus or a dead infusorium.
Pasteur's refutation of the primitive theories of spontaneous
generation has been thoroughly misunderstood. There was a
taboo against asking the question as to where the *first* germs of
life came from. In order not to come into conflict with the
assumption of a "Divine Creation," one took recourse to a plasmatic substance which was supposed to reach our planet from
the universe.

None of these schools was ever able to penetrate to the functional problems of the life process or to achieve a connection with experimental physics. The living continued to be an incomprehensible, intangible mysterious something, a special preserve of Divine Providence, like an island in the gigantic field of experimental natural science.

Nevertheless, the sprouting of every plant, the development of every embryo, the spontaneous movement of every muscle and the work done by every biological organism daily demonstrate the existence of gigantic energies governing the working of the living substance. *"Energy" is the capacity to do work.* There is no known energy that could compete with the work of the total life apparatus of our planet. The energies which achieve this work can derive only *from non-living matter* itself. They have remained a closed book to science for thousands of years.

What is the block that kept humans from the comprehension of this energy? Freud's discovery of the function of sexual repression was the first breach in the wall which separated us from a comprehension of the living; the understanding of the manifestations of the unconscious and repressed sexual life was the first step. The second step was a correction of Freud's theory of the unconscious: The repression of the instinctual life is not a natural phenomenon; rather, it is a pathological result of the suppression of natural instincts, in particular, of genital sexuality. An organism which uses most of its energy for keeping living nature hidden in itself must of necessity be incapable of comprehending the living outside of itself. The central manifestation of the living is the genital sexual function. This is what life owes its existence and continuation to. A society of humans which has outlawed the most essential manifestation of this function and has made it unconscious is incapable of guiding the vital functions in a rational manner; they can express themselves only in distorted, pornographic forms. It was only the mystics who—far removed from scientific insight —always kept in contact with the function of the living. Since, thus, the living became the domain of mysticism, serious natural science shrank from occupying itself with it. The biological and physiological literature shows no trace of an attempt to understand the autonomic movement such as it is expressed, e.g., in the movement of a worm. It is too reminiscent of the sexual acts in the animal world. Thus, there is mysticism on the one hand, and mechanistic biology on the other. At the same time, the force of religious feelings in itself points to the existence of a powerful something which the humans, though feeling it, are unable to put into words or to govern. Religion, also, has mystified the living.

The whole problem comes within the realm of natural science only if and when we have an energy function which is measurable and capable of being influenced, which makes the basic functions of the living comprehensible and, at the same time, does not come into conflict with physics.

The functions of the living show that such a specific biological energy would have the following characteristics:

1. It would be basically different from electromagnetic energy and yet have a relation to it.

2. Assuming the origin of the living from the non-living, it would have to exist in non-living nature, independently of the living organism.

3. It would have to explain satisfactorily the relationship between living organisms and non-living nature (respiration, orgasm, nutrition, etc.).

4. Contrary to galvanic electricity—it would function on *organic material* which is a *non-conductor* for electricity, and animal tissues.

5. Its function could not be restricted to isolated nerve cells or cell groups, but would permeate and govern the *total* organism.

6. It would have to explain, in a simple way, the pulsating basic function of the living, *contraction* and *expansion*, as it is expressed in respiration and the orgasm.

7. It would express itself in the production of heat, a characteristic of most living organisms.

8. It would definitely explain the sexual function, i.e., it would make sexual attraction understandable.

9. It would explain why the living organisms have not developed an organ for electromagnetism.

10. It would help to explain the difference between protein that is dead and protein that is alive; that is, it would explain what has to be added to the chemically complicated protein in order to make it *alive*. It would have the capacity of *charging* living matter, i.e., it would act in a *life-positive* sense.

11. It would, finally, have to show us the mechanism of the symmetry of form development, and what is the function of form development in general.

These questions are nothing but the indispensable framework for any discussion of biogenesis and of biophysical problems.

SUMMARY OF THE RESULTS OF THE BION EXPERIMENTS

The biological energy was discovered in a certain culture of bions. Thus, I will have to explain briefly what bions are.*

The bions are forms of transition from inorganic to organic matter; they can develop into organized living forms such as protozoa, cancer cells, etc. They are vesicles filled with fluid and charged with energy; they are clearly visible only with a magnification of over 2000x. "Bion" means the same as "energy vesicle." Their biological characteristics and their energy reactions will be extensively dealt with in a subsequent article.

The bions originate in organic and inorganic matter through a process of swelling. In this process, matter disintegrates into fluid-containing vesicles of about 0.5 to 3 μ. The following substances disintegrate into bions, either by swelling alone or

---

* A detailed presentation of the bion experiments up to 1939 is found in *"Die Bione"* (1938) and "Bion Experiments on the Cancer Problem" (1939). Since 1939, these experiments have been elaborated considerably.

through high temperatures with consecutive swelling: Wood, thus forming humus (wood does not "rot"; if kept in water for weeks on end, it remains sterile, i.e., free of rot bacteria, and the development of protozoa is reduced to a minimum). Further, dried moss and grass; muscle and other animal tissue; wool, coal, soot. Of inorganic substances, according to observations to date, iron and silicates show bionous disintegration. A great many substances consist of bions, i.e., they are made up of energy vesicles: most food stuffs, egg yolk, boiled egg white, milk, cheese, cooked vegetables, meat, vitamins; further, all substances which have been heated to incandescence or owe their existence to such a process: cyanide of potassium, lava, soot, etc. The gonadal cells and the erythrocytes are bions. The chicken embryo develops through organization of the yolk bions, moss from stone bions, protozoa from moss or grass bions. Cancer cells develop from bions which originate from the vesicular disintegration of suffocated or otherwise biologically damaged tissue.

The bions contract and expand, that is, they already show the function of biological pulsation. They move through the microscopic field with slow, jerky or serpentine movements. They react positively to biological stain (Gram, methylene blue, carbol fuchsine, etc.). If viewed with apochromatic lenses at a magnification of at least 2000x, preferably 3-4000x, their content always shows a bluish glimmer, no matter what substance they were derived from. The contents of the vesicles show extremely fine vibrations and refract the light strongly. Under definite strict and difficult conditions, the bions can be cultivated. They show the function of division and fusion.

The motility of bions derived from soot, blood charcoal, blood, muscle tissue, etc., lasts only as long as the fine pulsatory movements, the blue color of the content, and the colloidal suspension lasts. The bions are cataphoretically positive or negative. With the cessation of colloidal suspension and cultivability, the cataphoretic reaction also ceases.

The microphotos (*see* footnote, p. 199) will convey a better impression of the bions and their organization into protozoa than the written word. However, as everywhere else in natural science, only continued microscopic observation will convey a convincing impression of the nature and the living reactions of the bions.

The biological reactions of the bions became comprehensible only by thinking of the bions in terms of a membranous vesicle *containing a certain quantity of energy.* Bions of different origin can permeate each other. Larger vesicles or heaps of vesicles incorporate smaller ones. Bions which emanate a strong blue glimmer kill or paralyze bacteria and small protozoa. They destroy cancer tissue by permeating it. Ameboid cancer cells from mice are paralyzed by certain kinds of bions even at a certain distance. In brief, all these—and other—functions point to enormous energies which are contained in the bions and have a powerful biological effect on their surroundings. This concept found an unexpected confirmation in certain bion cultures which I obtained from sand (see below).

For an understanding of the bions, a knowledge of the following facts is indispensable:

1. All matter—if exposed to high temperatures and made to swell—undergoes a process of vesicular disintegration.

2. High temperatures (autoclavation at 120°C, heating to incandescence, about 1500°C) destroy what life there is. But these same high temperatures produce the energy vesicles which in turn can develop into living bacteria.

3. The energy at work in the bions is not introduced into them artificially from the outside; rather, it originates from the vesicular disintegration of matter itself.

4. An energy vesicle is a minute quantity of matter, containing a quantity of energy derived from this matter.

5. The bions are not complete living beings, but only carriers of biological energy; they are forms of transition from non-living to living.

6. The blue color of the content is the immediate expression

of this energy. As the blue disappears, the essential biological characteristics of the bions disappear also.

7. The bion experiments do not newly "create" artificial life; they only *demonstrate the natural process* by which protozoa and cancer cells develop spontaneously from vesicularly disintegrated matter. They also demonstrate the natural form in which biological energy is contained in humus, in inorganic material, in foodstuffs, blood cells, gonadal cells, etc. The functions of the biological energy in the realm of the living do not become understandable until one first learns to understand them in the realm of the non-living, that is, in the realm of *physics*.

The Cultures of Radiating Sand Bions

In order to completely refute the objection of air infection, I began as early as 1936 to autoclave the bion preparations for ½ hour at 120°C. In doing so, I found that the bionous disintegration was now even more complete than with swelling alone. The blue bions appeared more quickly, the biological stain reaction (Gram, etc.) was more intense. In May 1937, I began to heat coal and earth crystals to incandescence before putting them into the solution which promotes swelling. This procedure accelerated the formation of bions still further. Now, with complete sterility assured, the bionous disintegration of matter could be achieved within a few minutes. No longer did I have to wait for days or weeks until the process of swelling at room temperature finally resulted in bions. To make the substance swell, I used KOH and potassium chloride. For more than 2 years (1937-1939), experiment after experiment confirmed the bionous disintegration of matter and the organization of bacteria and cells from the bions.

In January 1939, one of my assistants demonstrated the heating experiment to a visitor of the laboratory. She took the wrong container from the sterilizer, and instead of earth she heated ocean *sand*. After 2 days there was a growth in the bouillon-potassium-chloride solution, which, inoculated on egg medium and agar, resulted in a yellow growth. This new kind of culture consisted microscopically of large, slightly mobile, intensely blue packets of energy vesicles. The culture was "pure," i.e., it consisted of only *one* kind of forms. At 400x, they looked somewhat like *sarcinae* as they are occasionally found in water. Examination at 2000-4000x showed forms which refracted light strongly, consisted of packets of 6 to 10 vesicles and measured about 10 to 15 μ. In the course of several months, the experiment was repeated 8 times, and 5 times the same forms were obtained.

These bions were termed SAPA (*sa*nd, *pa*cket). They showed some extremely interesting characteristics.

The effect of the SAPA bions on protozoa, bacilli in general and T-bacilli in particular, was much stronger than that of other bions. Brought together with cancer cells, they killed or paralyzed the cells *even at a distance* of about 10 μ. When cancer cells came as close as that to the bions, they would remain, as if paralyzed, in one spot; they would turn around and around in the same spot and finally become immobile. These phenomena were recorded by microfilm.

For weeks, I examined these SAPA bions daily for several hours. After some time, my eyes began to hurt when I looked into the microscope for a long time. As a control experiment, I used a monocular tube; regularly, it was only the eye with which I looked at these cultures that began to hurt. Finally, I developed a violent conjunctivitis and had to see the ophthalmologist. He thought the story "fantastic," gave me some treatment, prescribed dark glasses and prohibited microscopic work for a few weeks. The eyes improved, but now I knew that I was dealing with a radiation. Several months before this occurrence, the Dutch physicist Bon had asked me in a letter whether I had ever observed radiation in my bions. I had to answer in the negative. Dr. Bon had been in a feud with his fellow physicists for years because of his contention that life was a phenomenon of radiation.

Now, I was directly confronted with this fact. I did not know how to approach it. Though I had training in the basic theoretical problems of physics, I had never done any practical work with radiation. This created a considerable difficulty but also had its advantages. For this radiation turned out to be something new with characteristics all of its own. The customary methods of radiation research gave no results. The orgone radiation required the elaboration of special, hitherto unknown methods and apparatus which could be achieved only step by step, by long-continued observation. Routine and schematic methods failed.

In a very primitive manner, I tried at first to test the culture for radiation by holding the test tubes containing them against my palm. Every time I felt a fine prickling, but I was not sure of the sensation. After that, I put a quartz slide on the skin, put some SAPA culture on it, and left it for about 10 minutes. On the spot where the culture had been (separated from the skin by the slide) there developed an anemic spot with hyperemic margin. This experiment I repeated with all my students, whose vegetative reactions I knew well from their training. Those among them who were vegetatively strongly mobile regularly gave a strong positive result; those with less emotional mobility reacted only slightly or not at all. This was a more definite result, but still quite incomprehensible.

So I sought help from the radium physicist of the Cancer Hospital in Oslo, Dr. Moxnes. He tested a culture with the radium electroscope. *There was no reaction.* The physicist declared "there was no radiation." Since his electroscope was designed for radium only, I objected that the negative result meant only that there was no *radium activity*, but not that there was no radiation at all. Because there was no doubt about the existence of the skin reaction. True, why the electroscope failed to react, I did not understand. The rapidity of the skin reaction indicated enormous energies. While the reddening of the skin in response to Xray or radium appears only after days, the SAPA reaction appeared within a few minutes. Incidentally, as will be shown later, the negative reaction at the electroscope found its logical explanation.

The following observations clarified the problems bit by bit:

After two weeks, my left palm was strongly inflamed and very painful. The fact that the cultures exerted a biological influence could no longer be doubted.

Gradually, I began to notice that the air in the room where the cultures were kept became extremely "heavy" and that people who stayed in the room developed headaches if the windows were closed for as short a time as one hour.

One day, in the course of some experiment, I noticed that all metal objects, such as scissors, pincers, needles, etc., were highly magnetic. I could not in the least understand this fact though today it seems a matter of course. I had never observed it before and it was quite unexpected. But after having seen the negative reaction at the physicist's electroscope, I was no longer surprised by unexpected findings.

I tried photographic plates in all kinds of ways: I put culture preparations on top of unwrapped plates in the dark, on plates in plate-holders, on plates partly or completely wrapped in lead, with control plates (without cultures) in the same room. To my great surprise, *all* plates which were in the same room as the cultures were fogged. On some plates there was a darkening corresponding to the joints of the wooden plate-holders, in others at places where the culture had not influenced the plate but where the lead wrapping had not been tight. *But the control plates in the same room were also fogged.* I could not understand it. It was as if the energy were active around the ends of the plate-holder and through the joints. *The radiation seemed to be "present everywhere."* On the other hand, it could have been a matter of an experimental error.

In the course of two decades of clinical and experimental work, I had learned to pay attention to such seemingly incidental ideas as "energy present everywhere." They are inklings of the searching organism, and lead to the goal if combined with rigid objective control. In due time, my inkling was con-

firmed: *The orgone radiation is, in fact, "present everywhere."*
But at that time this had no concrete meaning.

The experiment with the photographic plates seemed to bog
down. If the effect of the radiation was everywhere, its manifestations could not be isolated and controlled; there was no
comparison possible with an object which was not influenced
by it.*

I tried observations in dark basement rooms where I kept the
cultures. In order to increase the intensity, I made dozens of
cultures. The subsequent observations in the dark were somehow "weird." After the eyes had become adapted to the darkness, the room did not appear black, but *gray-blue*. There were
fog-like formations and bluish dots and lines of light. Violet
light phenomena seemed to emanate from the walls as well as
from various objects in the room. When I held a magnifying
glass before my eyes, these light impressions, all of them blue
or gray-blue, *became more intense, the individual lines and
dots became larger*. Dark glasses reduced the impressions.
When I closed my eyes, the blue light impressions continued,
nevertheless. This was confusing. I did not know as yet that
the orgone radiation irritates the optic nerve in a specific manner and produces after-images.

After one or two hours in the basement my eyes hurt and
got red. One evening, I spent five consecutive hours in the
basement. After about two hours, I could distinctly see a radiation from my palm, my shirtsleeves and (in the mirror) my hair.
The blue glimmer was visible as a slowly moving, gray-blue
vapor around my body and around objects in the room. I admit
that I felt frightened. I called Dr. Bon by long distance telephone and told him of my experience. He told me to protect
myself. However, since the radiation seemed to be "everywhere" and seemed to pervade everything, I did not know how
I could protect myself.

I had our friend Dr. F. participate in these observations.

---

* Much later, in the fall of 1940, the photographic demonstration of the
SAPA radiation on Kodachrome film succeeded.

Without knowing anything beforehand, he confirmed most of my observations. For several months, I subjected one person after another to the skin test and the observation in the dark basement. The descriptions I obtained from all these subjects were so uniform that the existence of the radiation could not be doubted. The most difficult task was that of *distinguishing the objective phenomena in the room from the subjective phenomena in the eye.* In the course of the investigations, however, numerous techniques of making this distinction found themselves. Thus, I had people reach for luminous objects in the dark or tell me where an arm was at a given time; I let the subjects turn their eyes away from the light impression until it disappeared, and then to try to find it again. The radiation had a highly irritating effect on the optic nerve. A businessman who had gotten a piece of apparatus for me and once took part in the observations, said: "I feel as if I had been looking into the sun for a long time."

This expression on the part of a layman seemed very significant, especially in connection with the conjunctivitis which many subjects developed. One day I had the sudden idea, *sun energy,* and with that, a simple solution to the problem, though it seemed absurd at first glance: *The SAPA bions had originated from ocean sand. Ocean sand, however, is nothing but solidified sun energy. The process of heating and swelling had liberated this energy from the matter.* I fought down my emotional disinclination to accept such a conclusion. If the radiation in question had an immediate connection with sun energy, many phenomena found a simple explanation; e.g., the irritation of the eyes, the conjunctivitis, the rapid reddening and subsequent tanning of the skin. I had carried on these experiments during the winter and early spring, had not been in the sun, and yet had a strongly tanned body. I felt extremely vigorous and vegetatively alive. Gradually, I lost the fear of the dangerous sequelae of the radiation and worked with it without any attempt at protection.

The existence of an energy with an extraordinarily intense

biological activity could no longer be doubted. The question was, what was the nature of this radiation and what methods of measurement could be employed. One of my co-workers told an assistant of the Bohr Institute in Copenhagen about the SAPA bions. She considered the production of bions from sand so "fantastic" that I preferred not to expose my new discovery to a kind of investigation which was biased by disbelief on principle. In addition, I could offer no other starting points for a qualitative and quantitative determination of the radiation than biological effects and subjective sensations. The negative reaction of the cultures at the Oslo physicist's electroscope also was still unexplained. In addition, this was just after the press campaign of the Oslo pathologists and psychiatrists against the orgasm- and bion research; this campaign had destroyed any possible basis for friendly cooperation. Thus, there seemed to be no avenue of approach to a quantitative determination. There was nothing to do but to leave everything to the spontaneous development of the facts and to chance. This "chance" was not long in coming.

While waiting for it, I spent my time reproducing well-known electroscopic phenomena obtained by rubbing various materials. One day, I was in the process of rigging up a new experimental arrangement which involved high voltage. As an insulation, I put on a pair of rubber gloves which used to be kept in a glass cabinet in my laboratory. When I came near the electroscope with my hands, there was a strong reaction; the electroscope leaf moved up and then *turned to the side, toward the glass wall of the electroscope and adhered to it*. The fact that insulators can be "charged" was known to me. What was amazing was the lateral deflection of the leaf and its tenacious sticking to the glass: non-magnetic aluminum adhered to the glass; glass which is an insulator and which *had not been rubbed*. Whence this effect? It turned out that the gloves had been lying close to a pile of SAPA cultures. As a control I put one glove in the open air in the shade while I experimented with the other, exchanging the two after a while. It was shown that the glove which had been kept in the open air for about 15 minutes did not influence the electroscope; on the other hand, if a previously neutral glove or other rubber object was kept together in a metallic enclosure with the cultures for about ½ hour, it gave a strong electroscopic reaction. The result was the same on a number of consecutive evenings.

Rubber gloves, paper, cotton, cellulose and other organic substances took up an energy from the cultures which gave a reaction at the electroscope. High humidity, ventilation in the shade and touching the substances with the hands for several minutes eliminated the effect.

A first point of departure for the qualitative comprehension of the radiation had been won. The fact that the cultures charged the rubber and other organic substances could not be doubted; I could charge them at any time by bringing them in contact with the cultures and discharge them by ventilating them or putting them in water.

The situation became more complicated when I obtained *new* rubber gloves and found that they, too, gave a reaction at the electroscope, though they had been neither rubbed nor brought into contact with the cultures. That meant that the energy was present not only in the cultures, but "elsewhere" too. This finding disturbed the unequivocal nature of the culture reaction, but seemed important. Again I had the inevitable impression: the radiation is present everywhere.

Here, the statement of one of the experimental subjects, "I feel as if I had been looking into the sun for a long time," came to my aid. *Apparently, the radiation had to do with sun energy. If it was present everywhere, it had to come from the sun.* This suggested the experiment of exposing uncharged rubber gloves to bright sunlight. After 5 to 15 minutes, *it regularly gave a strong reaction at the electroscope.* Now, I had double proof of the solar origin of the energy: first, the consideration that the experiment of heating sand to incandescence had liberated solar energy from the sand; second, the direct charging of insulators by the radiation of the sun. Long-continued irradiation of insulators with ultraviolet light had the same effect.

Further consideration said that if the radiation in question was emitted by bions and by the sun, then it was also present in the living organism. I put uncharged rubber gloves on the abdominal skin of a vegetatively very mobile patient. The result was positive: after 5 to 15 minutes' contact with the abdominal skin, the rubber gave a strong reaction at the electroscope. I repeated the experiment with a number of students and patients. The result was positive every time. In vegetatively sluggish persons and people with poor expiration the reaction was weaker. Increased respiration made it stronger.*

Now, several previously obscure facts became understandable. Obviously, I was dealing with an unknown energy with a specific biological activity. This energy originated from matter which was heated to incandescence and made to swell; it came about probably through disintegration of matter (as in the case of the radiating bions). It was, furthermore, radiated into the atmosphere by the sun; consequently, it was "present everywhere." This solved the seeming contradiction that the rubber was not only charged by the SAPA bions, but that rubber which had not been exposed to the cultures also gave a reaction at the electroscope.

The newly discovered energy is present also in the living organism. *The living organism takes it up from the atmosphere and directly from the sun.*

It was the same energy with which my blue bions—no matter what their origin—killed bacteria and cancer cells; only here the energy was contained within the small blue energy vesicles.

The energy was called *"orgone."* This term indicates the history of its discovery, namely, through the orgasm formula, as well as its biological effect (of charging organic substances).

Now I also understood the blue-gray vapors which I had

---

* Cf. "Drei Versuche am Statischen Elektroskop." Klin. und experim. Berichte, Nr. 7, 1939.

seen in the dark around my head, hands and shirt sleeves: *organic substances absorb the orgone energy and retain it.*

The electroscope of the Oslo physicist had not reacted to the cultures because the electroscope can be activated *only indirectly, via insulators* which have been charged with orgone energy.

The Visualization of the Atmospheric Orgone

In order to study the radiation of the SAPA bions, a closed space had to be constructed which would close in the radiation and prevent it from rapid diffusion into the surroundings. No organic material could be used for this purpose, since, as we have seen, organic material absorbs the radiation. According to my observations, metal, on the other hand, would reflect the radiation and confine it within the enclosed space. However, the metal would reflect the radiation to the *outside.* In order to avoid this, the apparatus had to have *metal walls on the inside, and walls of organic material on the outside.* With this construction, it was to be expected that the radiation from the cultures would be reflected by the inner metal walls, while the outer layer of organic material (cotton or wood) would prevent or at least reduce the reflection to the outside. The front wall of the apparatus was to have an opening with a lens through which the radiation could be observed from the outside.

The apparatus was built and about a dozen culture dishes were put into it. As a magnifying glass I used a film viewer with a cellulose disk; I assumed that the rays would hit this disk and become visible on it. The experiment was successful. It was possible to observe distinctly bluish moving vapors and light, yellowish points and lines. Several experimental subjects confirmed the observations. The result seemed to be unequivocal. But then a completely incomprehensible fact turned up. It was to be expected that the boxlike apparatus after being ventilated and not containing any cultures, would not show any light phenomena. If that were not so, I could not contend that the radiation came *from the cultures.* I did not have the slightest doubt that a control experiment would confirm this expectation.

However, to my greatest surprise, I found exactly the same light phenomena in the empty box, that is, in the absence of cultures. I assumed that the organic part of the enclosure had absorbed radiating energy from the cultures, and that it was this absorbed energy which showed in the control experiment. I took the box apart, dipped the metal plates into water, put in new cotton, ventilated for several days and tried again. My efforts were in vain. *It was impossible to remove the radiation phenomena from the empty box.* Whence came the rays in the box which did not contain any cultures? True, the light phenomena were not as intense as when the box contained cultures, but they were undoubtedly present.

I had another box built, with a glass wall in front, and without organic material. This box I kept carefully away from rooms in which SAPA cultures were kept. Since this box did not have a wall of organic material, the problem of energy absorbed by such material was eliminated.

It did no good. The radiation was still there. After a good deal of understandable puzzlement, I remembered that, after all, something similar had happened with the rubber gloves and the electroscope. Rubber, influenced by the cultures, had deflected the electroscope; water and moving air in the shadow had eliminated the phenomenon; renewed proximity of the rubber with the cultures had always produced it again promptly. But, rubber gloves which had never been near the cultures, and which had not been rubbed, had also produced the phenomenon. From these observations, I had to conclude that the energy which the cultures emitted must be present everywhere. Now, I had to draw the same conclusion from the fact that the box, without containing any cultures, still continued to show the radiation. *Where did it come from?*

Today, at a time when the orgone energy has become measurable and is in practical use with cancer patients, my earlier puzzlement seems unintelligent. After all, I had had the feeling from the beginning that the radiation was present everywhere.

Too, the experiment of charging gloves on the human skin should have prepared me for the existence of radiation in the box even in the absence of cultures.

Being clever afterwards is easy. During the first two years, however, I doubted every one of my observations. Such impressions as "the radiation is present everywhere" or such observations as "spontaneously charged gloves," carried little conviction; on the contrary, they were apt to raise serious doubts. In addition, the continuous doubts, objections and negative findings on the part of physicists and bacteriologists tended to make me take my observations less seriously than they deserved to be taken. My self-confidence at that time—it was just at the end of the infamous Norwegian press campaign that I discovered the radiation—was not particularly strong. Not strong enough to withstand the impact of all the new insights which followed from the discovery of the radiation. So many things began to totter which hitherto had been unshakeable biological and bacteriological convictions: the theory of the air germs; the concept of "body-electricity," the concept that protoplasm was nothing but highly complicated protein, the mechanistic as well as the vitalistic concept of life, etc., etc. Nothing but the logical development of my experiments made me stick.

At a time when the most astounding phenomena have become part of everyday work it is interesting and useful to look back on such uncertainties. It gives one the courage which it takes to go on in spite of disturbing control experiments; not to kill new findings with superficial controls; *to check up oneself on negative control findings;* and, finally, not to give in to the temptation of taking it easy and of saying, "Oh well, it was just an illusion." The existence of the radiation was beyond doubt. I could not expect to be able to explain all the diverse phenomena at once. Even less could I allow myself to avoid the doubts and emotional upheavals which result from such confusing findings.

The explanation that the radiation in the absence of cultures corresponded to the reaction at the electroscope of rubber which had never been near the cultures was, of course, unsatisfactory. There was a void which I was as yet unable to fill.

For several weeks, I kept observing the radiation in the empty box. It remained the same as I had seen it from the first, rain or shine, fog or clear weather, with high relative humidity as well as low, at night as well as during the day. That meant that the radiation could not be the immediate result of the radiation of the sun as was the charge of the rubber exposed to the sun. The radiation came "from everywhere"; it was only impossible to say what this "everywhere" was.

In the summer of 1940 I took a vacation and went to Maine. One night, still under the pressure of this unsolved riddle, I watched the sky above the lake. The moon was low on the Western horizon; on the Eastern sky there were strongly flickering stars. I was struck by the fact that the stars in the West flickered far less than those near the Eastern horizon. If the theory that the flickering of the stars is due to diffused light were correct, then the flickering would have to be the same everywhere or even more intense near the moonlight. But exactly the opposite was the case.

I began to look at individual stars through a wooden tube. Accidentally, I focused the tube on a dark blue spot in the sky between the stars. To my surprise, I saw a vivid flickering and then flashes of fine rays of light. The more I turned the tube in the direction of the moon the less intense were these phenomena. They were most pronounced in the darkest spots of the sky, *between* the stars. It was the same flickering and flashing which I had observed so many times in my box. A magnifying glass used as an eye-piece in the tube magnified the rays. All of a sudden my box lost all its mysteriousness. The phenomenon had found a simple explanation: *The radiation in the box, in the absence of cultures, came from the atmosphere. The atmosphere contains an energy of which I had never heard.* It could not be identical with the "cosmic rays." Nobody had as yet seen the cosmic rays with the naked eye. The physicists contend that the "cosmic rays" reach the earth from far spaces of the universe, that, in other words, they do not originate on our planet itself. True, in recent times, objections to this concept have been voiced. If what the physicists call cosmic rays should prove to be of planetary origin, they would be identical with the orgone radiation. What the physicists call the great power of penetration of the cosmic rays would be simply explained by the fact that the orgone energy *is present everywhere.**

I trained the tube on earth and rock and found the same phenomenon, stronger in one place, less pronounced in another. The clouds showed it also, only more intense. I realized that in the course of my control experiments on the SAPA radiation I had discovered the *atmospheric* orgone energy.

I shall attempt to give a systematic description of the orgone energy in such a manner that everyone can repeat its discovery without having to follow the complicated path over which I was led by my bion experiments. This re-discovery of the orgone will demonstrate many characteristics which are unknown in any other form of energy. Only after a presentation of these findings will we understand the logic which links the "blue bion" and its energy function with the atmospheric energy. Doubtless, the atmospheric orgone could have been discovered without the SAPA bions. But the complicated detour over the bion radiation reveals an insight of far-reaching

---

* Rudolf W. Ladenburg, in "The Nature of Cosmic Rays and the Constitution of Matter," Scientific Monthly, May 1942, states: "... The origin of the primaries of the cosmic rays is still a great puzzle. *We do not know the processes responsible for the production of such immensely energetic particles.* Some of them carry a million times more energy than the most energetic particles we can produce artificially. And as to the question of the constitution of matter our answer is still rather incomplete. We know that all matter consists of atoms, that the atoms consist of tiny nuclei surrounded by electrons and that the nuclei consist of protons and neutrons. *There must be strong forces acting between the protons and neutrons holding the nuclei together. But we do not know what they are. They are not of electrical nature* as we have seen, and many theories have been tried for understanding these forces. The discovery of the meson in the cosmic rays has raised some hope for reaching the goal, but this fundamental problem is still far from being solved." (Italics are mine, W. R.)

importance: *The energy which governs the living is of necessity identical with the atmospheric energy;* otherwise, it would not have led to the discovery of the atmospheric orgone.

The Objective Demonstration of the Orgone Radiation

"Subjective Impressions of Light"?

As children, we used to be fascinated by the light phenomena one can observe with one's eyes closed: small bluish dots would move to and fro in front of our closed eyes. They seemed to come from nowhere and would change their course with every movement of the eyeball; they would move slowly in gentle curves and rhythmically circling movements, somewhat like this:

It would be fun to change the form and course of the dots, e.g., by rubbing the eyes. In this manner, even the color of the dots could be varied: the blue would turn into red, green or yellow. Another part of the game was suddenly to open the eyes, look at a lamp, close the eyes again and watch the after-images. In our imagination, the various forms turned into rainbows, balloons, animal heads or human figures.

As we grew up and studied physics, mathematics and biology, such "games" lost their interest. We had to learn that these subjective visual phenomena were "unreal" and something which had to be distinguished from the objective measurable manifestations of light and its seven colors. These objectively measurable phenomena, in the course of time, drowned out the strong sensations originating in our own organs. These we no longer took seriously. The workaday world required full concentration on concrete tasks; in this, phantasies could be only disturbing. But the subjective light phenomena remained, and many people will ask themselves whether such definite phenomena as the light impressions one can have with one's eyes closed do not reflect a reality after all. The illusionary character of these visual impressions is not as much a matter of course as it may appear.

We learned that the visual impressions with closed eyes were "only subjective," that is, "not real." Scientific research paid no attention to the problem. The subjective impressions were relegated to the realm of "human phantasy." Human phantasy life is at variance with reality and ever changing according to subjective wishes; thus, scientific research had to be based on the objective, realistic basis of experiment. The ideal experiment makes our judgment independent of our subjective phantasies, illusions and wishes. In short, man has no confidence in his perceptive capabilities. In his investigations he rightly prefers to depend on the photographic plate, the microscope or the electroscope.

But in spite of all the progress brought about by our turning from subjective experience to objective observation, it also made us lose an essential quality of research. True, what we observe objectively is existing—but it is unalive, dead. In the interest of scientific objectivity, we have learned to kill the living even before we proceed to make any statements about it. Thus we build, of necessity, a mechanical machine-like picture of the living, a picture in which is lacking the most essential quality, the specific aliveness. The aliveness reminds us too much of the intense subjective sensations of our childhood. These subjective vegetative sensations are at the basis of every kind of mysticism, be it Yoga, or the Fascist "surging of the blood," or the reaction of a spiritist medium, or the ecstasies of a dervish. Mysticism asserts the existence of certain forces and processes which natural science denies or looks at with contempt.

Simple consideration says: *Man cannot feel or phantasy anything which does not actually exist in one form or another. For human perceptions are nothing but a function of objective natural processes within the organism.* Could there not be a reality behind our "subjective" visual impressions after all? Could it be possible that in these subjective impressions we perceive the biological energy within our own organism? Let us see whether this idea is as strange as it seems.

To do away with the subjective visual impression by calling it "phantasy" is erroneous. This "phantasy" takes place in an organism which is governed by certain natural laws; therefore, it must be *real.* We are only just emerging from a period in which medicine called all functional and nervous complaints "unreal" or "imaginary," because they were not understood. But a headache is a headache, and a visual impression is a visual impression, whether we understand it or not.

Of course we will reject the mystical assertions which are based on the *misinterpretation* of vegetative sensations. But that does not justify denying the existence of these sensations. We also have to reject a mechanistic natural science because it divorces the vegetative sensations from the natural processes taking place in the organs. *Self-perception is an essential part of the natural life-process.* It is not nerves here, muscles there and vegetative sensations in a third place; rather, the processes taking place in the tissues form an indivisible *functional unity* with their perception. This is, indeed, one of the essential guiding lines in our therapeutic work. Pleasure and anxiety represent a certain state of functioning of the total organism. We have to distinguish clearly between functional thinking and mechanistic thinking which cuts things apart and will never grasp living functioning. Let us put down four important principles of a *functional* concept of nature:

1. Every living organism is a functional unit; it is not merely a mechanical sum total of organs. The basic biological function governs every individual organ as it governs the total organism.

2. Every living organism is a part of surrounding nature and functionally identical with it.

3. Every perception is based on the consonance of a function within the organism with a function in the outer world; that is, it is based on vegetative harmony.

4. Every form of self-perception is the immediate expression of objective processes in the organism (psychophysical identity).

Nothing is to be expected of the philosophical speculations concerning the reality of our sensations as long as the principle is not recognized that the perceiving *subject* and the observed and perceived *object* form a *functional unity*. Mechanistic science splits up this unity into a *duality*. The mechanistic empiricism of science of today is hopeless, for it excludes sensation completely.

Every important discovery originates from the subjective experiencing of an objective fact, that is, from vegetative harmony. It is only a matter of making the subjective sensation objective, of separating it from the stimulus and of comprehending the source of the stimulus. This is something which we, in our vegetotherapeutic work with the patient, do many times every hour in the process of comprehending the bodily expression of the patient. In this process, we identify ourselves with the patient and his functions. After we have comprehended them vegetatively we let our intellect work and thus make the phenomenon an objective one.

After this discourse on vegetative harmony, let us return to our infantile phantasies and visual impressions. How can we decide *objectively* whether or not our visual impressions with closed eyes correspond to objective processes?

The Flickering in the Sky Made Objective. The Orgonoscope

To begin with, let us try to find out whether similar phenomena can be observed with open eyes and in daylight. If we take plenty of time and observe carefully, we find that this is the case. If we look at a wall or a white door we see a *flickering*. It is as if shadows or fogs were moving more or less rapidly and rhythmically. We resist the temptation of doing away with this observation by calling it "merely a subjective impression" and make up our minds not to give up until we have found out *objectively* whether this flickering is taking place in our eyes or outside of our organism.

To begin with, it is not easy to think of a method of differentiating. We close our eyes. The flickering disappears but is replaced by the movements of forms and color. If we repeat the closing and opening of the eyes, we finally realize that the phenomena are *different* when we have our eyes open from when we have them closed.

We look at the blue sky, looking "as if in the far distance." At first, we see nothing. But if we continue to look carefully, we find to our amazement that the sky shows quite clearly a rhythmical, wave-like flickering. *Is this flickering merely in our eyes, or is it in the sky?* If we follow the phenomenon on different days, under varying weather conditions and at different hours of the day, we find that the kind and intensity of the flickering varies a great deal. In order not to be disturbed by the diffuse light which strikes our eyes from all sides, we repeat our observation at night. The flickering is *more distinct*. It is as if waves ran across the sky. Occasionally, we see a lightning-like dot or line. The flickering can also be seen on dark clouds. If we continue the observation of the sky over a period of weeks, we notice variations in the flickering. On some nights it is only slight, on other nights very intense. The astronomers ascribe the flickering to "diffuse light." We used to accept this explanation as thoughtlessly as many others. But now we must ask ourselves whether the flickering of the stars could not have something to do with the flickering in the sky *between* the stars. Should this be the case, we would have the first indication of the objective existence of a moving unknown something in the atmosphere. Certainly, the flickering of the stars is not a subjective optical phenomenon. The astronomers build their observatories on great heights in order to exclude the flickering of the stars. If it were due to "diffuse light," it would be constant all the time. The variation in intensity cannot be explained on the basis of "diffuse light." The unknown something which makes the star flicker must be moving close to the surface of the earth. It cannot be diffuse light. Such "explanations" only serve to hide the facts. Let us postpone the answer to the problem.

In these observations of the sky, it becomes necessary to delineate a small field of observation. We look at the sky through a metal tube about 2 to 3 feet long and 1 inch in diameter. Through it, we see a circle which appears *lighter* than the surrounding sky. If we keep *both eyes open* and look through the tube with one eye, we see the dark blue night sky and in it a disk of a lighter blue. *Within the disk, we see a flickering and then rapidly appearing and disappearing dots and lines of light.* Close to the moon, these phenomena are less pronounced; it is all the more distinct the darker the general atmospheric background.

Are we again the victim of an illusion? In order to decide this question, we insert an eye-piece with a magnification of about 5x into the tube. Now, the light disk appears larger, the dots and lines are larger and more distinct. *Since we cannot magnify subjective optical impressions, the phenomenon must be objective.* We have now delineated a field of observation and are able to observe the phenomenon under conditions which exclude the objection that it is a matter of diffuse light. In addition, the light disk appears within a black field formed by the dull inside of the tube. The inside walls of the tube show no flickering; it is strictly limited to the light disk; thus, no "subjective" sensation. Without intending to, we have constructed a primitive "*orgonoscope.*" We can improve on it in the following manner:

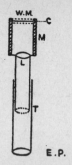

Diagram: Orgonoscope

C: cellulose disk, outside surface dull
W.M.: wire mesh, on both sides of disk
M: metal cylinder, about 4″ long, 2″ wide
L: biconvex lens, about 5x, focused on disk
T: telescopic tube, 1 to 2 feet long, about 2″ wide
E.P.: eye-piece, 5-10x, for additional magnification

We put our tube in front of the mirror of a good microscope with apochromatic lenses, using a 10x object lens and 5x eye-piece. Our eyes have to be adapted to the dark for about half an hour. The microscope shows the light phenomena in the sky very clearly. Every single lightning-like dot is clearly discernible. If we take the eye-piece out of the tube, the flickering is seen on a smaller scale, but stronger; we no longer can distinguish individual dots.

Are the phenomena perhaps to be ascribed to the haze in the atmosphere? If we observe during a foggy or hazy night we find that the phenomena are absent or hardly perceptible. In other words, fog or haze does not produce flickering. *The motion of the light in the field of the microscope or the tube has nothing to do with moving fog.*

On detailed observation, we find that the light phenomena are present all over the sky; they only decrease close to stars or the moon because of the stronger light. They are most intense during clear nights and with a low relative humidity.

If the humidity of the air exceeds 50%, the phenomena decrease in intensity. That is, *humidity absorbs the radiation in the atmosphere,* just as it absorbs the SAPA radiation.

We train our tube at night on various parts of the ground, the sidewalk, loose soil, the lawn, a wall, etc. We see the same movements of light particles. They are more intense on the soil than on the pavement. We look at shrubs at a distance of about a foot, moving the tube sideways toward the shrub and away from it. There can be no doubt that the phenomena are more intense at the leaves than in the surroundings. They seem to emanate from the leaves themselves. We observe flowers. The radiation is more intense at the blossom than at the stalk.

Soil, walls, shrubs, grass, animals, the atmosphere, etc., show the same phenomena, only in different intensities. The conclusion from these findings is inevitable: *The radiation phenomena are present everywhere. The radiating energy varies in density and intensity.* We may have wished to find it in one place and not in the other. Then the whole thing would have been a minor and harmless discovery. But we have to follow the facts, no matter how weird they begin to look to us.

The Construction of a Radiating Enclosure. Objective Visibility

The fact that the orgone radiation is present *everywhere* presents a difficulty in experiment. In order to properly describe a phenomenon, we must isolate it and comprehend it by *comparing* it with something different. We have to construct an enclosed space in which we can separate the energy.

We try to see whether we can find out anything new in a completely darkened room. We adapt our eyes to the darkness for about half an hour. During this time, all subjective light impressions disappear. We see nothing but black, that is, nothing. We look through the tube; we see nothing. In other words, we only confirm the common experience that in an absolute darkroom there is absolute blackness. The radiation disappeared, and we are inclined to give up the "crazy idea." But to follow this inclination would mean not doing research. We cannot simply disregard the fact that on the outside we had established the existence of this peculiar manifestation beyond any doubt. It cannot have simply disappeared. But being convinced of something is one thing; *proving* it is another.

Since we do not know the properties of our atmospheric radiation we have to work with apparatuses such as are used in working with known energies. We might use a "Faraday cage," i.e., a room the walls of which are formed of copper wire mesh. Such a room is free of electromagnetic fields because all electromagnetic waves coming from the outside are caught by the wire net and are grounded. We observe the same principle when we cross a bridge with a metal superstructure in our car: the radio stops working. In this cage, delicate oscillographic experiments can be carried out without interference.

We build such a cage, say, in a corner of the basement. In order to reduce the connection between inner and outer air to a minimum, we build an inside wall of sheet iron, leaving only a few cracks to admit sufficient air for breathing. We sit in the completely dark cage and adapt our eyes.

In the course of about half an hour the complete darkness gives way to a vague shimmer. Our eyes are irritated by peculiar light phenomena. It is as if vapors of a gray-blue color were slowly moving through the room. When we fix our eyes on a certain spot on the wall, we see moving light particles. The longer we stay in the room the more distinct the light phenomena. Within the gray-blue vapors we can distinguish light dots of a deep *blue-violet* color. They are reminiscent of the well-known subjective visual phenomena previous to falling asleep. We begin again to wonder whether the phenomena are inside or outside of our eyes. When we close our eyes, the blue-violet dots do not disappear. Are our optic nerves irritated, or are the light phenomena *not real?* One would expect them to disappear with the closing of the eyes and to reappear with opening them. On the other hand, there are subjective after-images. It is all not so simple. We must ask ourselves: how is it possible for our optic nerves to become irritated in complete darkness, and why can we not get rid of the phenomena in our eyes?

Many experimental subjects develop a conjunctivitis after an hour or more in the Faraday cage. Since, normally, the eyes rest in complete darkness, there must be something in the cage which excites the optic nerve and irritates the conjunctiva.

We repeat our observations in the dark cage, trying to find ways and means of answering some of the questions that arise. For example: Can the bluish-gray and violet light manifestations be magnified with a magnifying glass? We find this to be the case. As they become more distinct, we observe that the light dots appear in two forms: they either fly in our direction or past us. In the first case, there is a succession of the following impressions:

Every light dot seems to become alternatingly larger and smaller, as if it were pulsating. If the light dot flies past us, we have a trajectory something like this:

We may call this trajectory, according to its shape, a spinning wave (*Kreiselwelle*). Its significance will have to be discussed later on. The violet light dots seem to come from the metal walls in *rhythmic* sequence.

After a considerable time—2 to 3 hours—in the cage, we find a bluish-gray shimmer around our white coat and are able to see the contours of another person, even though only vaguely. Let us not be led astray by the "mystical" and "spooky" impression of this phenomenon. There is nothing mystical about it. The radiation seems to adhere to substance, such as cloth and hair. We put some good fluorescent material, such as zinc sulfide, on a swab of cotton and fasten this to the wall. Our observation had been correct. The region of the cotton swab appears lighter than its surroundings. The magnifying glass makes the radiation more distinct; we see flickering and fine rays.

Another observation: A paper disk with a layer of zinc sulfide had been lying in the cage for several days. When we bend it, it emits a strong radiation. For a control, we expose another such disk to fresh air, or we continue the bending for a considerable period of time. In either case, the light phenomena disappear. We leave one of the disks again in the cage for several days. On bending, the light phenomena are again present. That means, that *the paper disk has absorbed orgone*.

We now try to make the orgone in the cage *visible from the outside*. For this purpose, we cut a window about 5 inches square in the front wall of the cage. On the metal inside, we put a fluorescing glass plate across the opening, such as is used, e.g., to make Xrays visible.*

In the opening of the exterior wooden wall we put a tube containing a biconvex lens of a magnification of 5 to 10x. The tube with the lens is removable so that the fluorescing disk can be observed both with and without magnification.

Inside the cage, we mount a green bulb such as is used in developing highly sensitive photographic plates. This bulb gives a steady dim light as a background for the orgone radiation. In this arrangement, we follow a hint given by nature: the orgone radiation is clearly visible against the dimly lighted night sky.

In order to reproduce the flickering of the stars, we drill a few holes of about 1/8" in the wall. Now, we observe the cage from the outside in complete darkness.

---

* Fluorescence, as distinct from luminescence, means light from substances which are influenced by invisible energy particles. In the case of luminescence, the light continues for longer or shorter periods of time even after the substance has been removed from the effective rays. Zinc sulfide is a fluorescent substance, calcium sulfide a luminescent substance.

The light which we perceive through the holes is not steady, but *flickers strongly;* it is not green, but *bluish.*

On the fluorescing disk, strong motion can be observed. There is rapid flickering, and individual lightning-like dots and lines. As time goes on, we can distinguish vapors of a deep violet color which seem to emanate from the openings. The square where the radiation is visible is sharply defined against the black surroundings. The flickering is visible only within the square. The magnifying glass makes it possible to distinguish individual rays. On clear, dry days the phenomena are more intense and distinct than on humid or rainy days. The observation of the radiation within the Faraday cage is greatly improved through the use of the orgonoscope.

How does the energy get inside the cage? After all, the wire mesh is supposed to *ground* all electromagnetic energy. The inside of the cage should be free of any charges; if it were not, one could not carry out delicate electrical experiments in it without interference by electromagnetic forces. We find ourselves confronted by another problem:

Can the energy in the cage possibly be electricity? We have a double task before us:

1. To comprehend the characteristics of the radiating energy "orgone," now made visible.

2. To investigate the connection between orgone and electricity.

The subject of the succeeding article will be the phenomenon of *lumination (Erstrahlung)* of fluorescing gas tubes in the orgone box. Anybody who wishes to follow the succeeding presentations, however, should first convince himself of the visibility of the orgone in its *natural* condition, in the sky, the atmosphere, the soil and the living organism.

Concluded August 1941

2. THE CARCINOMATOUS SHRINKING
BIOPATHY

THE BIOPATHIES

The cancer tumor is no more than a symptom of the cancer
disease. Therefore, local treatment of the tumor—be it operation or irradiation with radium or Xray—affects not the cancer
disease as such, but only one of its visible symptoms. Similarly,
death from cancer is not due to the presence of one or more
tumors. Rather, it is the ultimate expression of the systemic
biological disease "cancer" which is based on a disintegrative
process in the total organism. Medical literature contains no
data concerning the nature of this systemic biological disease.
"Cancer disposition" means nothing but the fact that back of
the cancer tumor there are at work hitherto unknown processes
of a fatal nature. Cancer cachexia, the typical final phase of
cancer, must be considered nothing but the ultimate visible
phase of this general, as yet unknown process called "cancer."
    The term "cancer disposition" is misleading and meaningless.
The term *cancer biopathy*, on the other hand, has a definite
meaning. This series of articles will demonstrate the process
which is the basis of cancer biopathy.
    Under the term *biopathies* we subsume all those disease
processes which take place in the autonomic apparatus. There
is a typical basic disturbance of the autonomic apparatus which
—once it has started—may express itself in a variety of sympto-
matic disease pictures. This basic disturbance, the biopathy,
may result in a cancer (cancer biopathy) but equally well in an
angina pectoris, an asthma, a cardiovascular hypertension, an
epilepsy, a catatonic or paranoid schizophrenia, an anxiety

    From the *International Journal of Sex-Economy and Orgone-Research*, vol. I,
1942.

neurosis, a multiple sclerosis, a chorea, chronic alcoholism, etc. What determines the development of a biopathy into this or that syndrome, we do not as yet know. What interests us here primarily is that which all of these diseases have *in common: a disturbance of the biological function of pulsation in the total organism.*

A fracture, an abscess, a pneumonia, yellow fever, rheumatic pericarditis, acute alcohol intoxication, infectious peritonitis, syphilis, etc., are *not* biopathies. They are not due to a disturbance of the autonomic pulsation of the total vital apparatus; they are circumscribed, and, if they result in a disturbance of the biological pulsation, they do so only secondarily. We shall speak of biopathies only where the disease process *begins* with a disturbance of the biological pulsation, no matter what secondary disease picture it results in. Thus, we can distinguish a "schizophrenic biopathy" from a "cardiovascular biopathy," an "epileptic biopathy" or a "cancer biopathy," etc.

This addition to medical terminology is justified by the fact that we cannot comprehend any of the diverse diseases of the autonomic apparatus unless,

1) we distinguish them from the typical infectious diseases and traumatic surgical diseases;

2) we look for and find their common mechanism, the disturbance of biological pulsation;

3) learn to understand their differentiation into the various disease pictures.

The cancer disease lends itself particularly well to a study of the basic mechanisms of biopathy. In it, we find a great number of disturbances that everyday medical practice has to deal with. It shows pathological cell growth; one of its essential manifestations is bacterial intoxication and putrefaction; it is based on chemical as well as bio-electric disturbances in the organism; it has to do with emotional and sexual disturbances; it results in a number of secondary processes—such as anemia— which otherwise form disease entities by themselves; it is a disease in which civilized living plays a decisive role; it is of concern to the dietitian as well as to the endocrinologist or virus researcher.

The confusing variety of manifestations presented by the cancer disease only hides a common *basic disturbance*. The same is true, as we know, of the neuroses and functional psychoses which—in all their variety of form—have one common denominator: *sexual stasis*.

Sexual stasis represents a fundamental disturbance of biological pulsation. Sexual excitation, as we know, is a primal function of the living plasma system. *The sexual function has been shown to be the productive life function* per se. Thus, a *chronic* disturbance of the sexual function must of necessity be synonymous with a biopathy.

The stasis of biosexual excitation may manifest itself, basically, in two ways. It may appear as an emotional disturbance of the psychic apparatus, that is, as a neurosis or psychosis. But it also may manifest itself *directly* in a malfunctioning of the organs and express itself as organic disease. As far as we know, it cannot produce actual infectious disease.

The central mechanism of biopathy is a disturbance in the discharge of biosexual excitation. This statement calls for the most detailed substantiation. It is not surprising to find that in the biopathy physical and chemical factors are at work as well as emotional factors. The biosexual emotion demonstrates the psychosomatic unity of the total biological system more forcibly than anything else. Thus it is to be expected that disturbances in the discharge of biosexual energy—no matter what their point of manifestation—will result in disturbances of biological functioning, in other words, in a biopathy.

Biopathic Shrinking

Living functioning in man is basically no different from that in the ameba.* Its basic criterion is *biological pulsation*, that is, alternating complete *contraction* and *expansion*. In unicellular

---

* *Cf.* W. Reich, "Der Urgegansatz des vegetativen Lebens," 1934.

organisms, it is readily observed in the form of the rhythmical contraction of the vacuoles or the contractions and serpentine movements of the plasma. In the metazoa it is most readily seen in the cardiovascular system; the pulse beat represents the pulsation unequivocally. In the various organs, it takes a different form, according to their structure. In the intestines, it shows itself as a wave of alternating contraction and expansion, as "peristalsis." In the urinary bladder, the biological pulsation functions in response to the mechanical stimulus exerted by the filling of the bladder with urine. It functions in the striped muscles as contraction, in the smooth muscles as a wave-like peristalsis. In the orgasm, the pulsation takes hold of the total organism in the form of the orgasm reflex.

Neither the pulsatory movements of the organs nor their disturbances such as shock, blocking, shrinking, etc., are compatible with the generally accepted notion that the nerves only transmit impulses while they themselves are rigid and immobile. *The autonomic movements are comprehensible only under the assumption that the autonomic nervous system itself is mobile.* The decisive question as to whether this is a fact can be answered by direct observation. We put small, sufficiently transparent worms under the microscope in such a manner that not only the ganglion but the ganglia *fibers* are in focus. As the worm is in constant motion, one has to learn to keep an autonomic fiber constantly in focus. Thus one can convince oneself that *the autonomic system does indeed expand and contract* and is not rigid. The movements of the nerves are serpentine, slow, wave-like, sometimes jerky. They always precede the corresponding movements of the total organism by a fraction of a second: first, the nerve, and its ramifications, contracts, and then the contraction of the musculature follows. The same is true of the expansion. As the worm dies, the nervous system gradually shrinks; with that, the organism bends. The process of gradual shrinking is occasionally interrupted by a contraction. After a shorter or longer period of complete immobility, the rigid contraction ("rigor mortis") subsides, the organism relaxes together with the nerves, and motion does not reappear.

Biopathic shrinking begins with a chronic preponderance of contraction and inhibition of expansion in the autonomic system. This is most clearly manifested in the respiratory disturbance of neurotics and psychotics: the pulsation (alternating expansion and contraction) of lungs and thorax is restricted; the inspiratory attitude predominates. Understandably enough, the general contraction ("sympatheticotonia") does not remain restricted to individual organs. It extends to whole organ systems, their tissues, the blood system, the endocrine system as well as the character structure. Depending on the region, it expresses itself in different ways: in the cardiovascular system as high blood pressure and tachycardia, in the blood system as shrinking of the erythrocytes (formation of T-bodies, poikilocytosis, anemia), in the emotional realm as rigidity and character armoring, in the intestines as constipation, in the skin as pallor, in the sexual function as orgastic impotence, etc.

At this point, the careful reader will raise an objection. He will ask how one can speak of "shrinking" if it is only a matter of a chronic contraction of the autonomic apparatus. Is there not the possibility that the contraction will subside and that the function of complete pulsation will be restored? Should one not make a distinction between "chronic contraction" of the autonomic system, on the one hand, and its "shrinking" on the other? Could not the shrinking be a *result* of the chronic contraction, a gradual and premature dying off of the vital apparatus?

The objection is correct. *The biopathic shrinking in cancer is, in fact, the result of a chronic contraction of the autonomic apparatus.*

Vegetotherapeutic Considerations

The connecting link between sexual function and cancer disease is formed by the following facts with which sex-economic clinical experience has made us familiar:

1. Poor external respiration which in turn leads to a disturbance of the internal respiration in the tissues.

2. The disturbed function of bio-electrical charge and discharge of the autonomic organs, particularly the sexual organs.

3. The chronic spasms of the musculature.

4. Chronic orgastic impotence.

Up to now, the connection between disturbances in the discharge of sexual energy and cancer has not been investigated. Experienced gynecologists are well aware of the fact that such a connection exists. Respiratory disturbances and muscular spasms are the immediate result of a fear of sexual excitation (orgastic impotence). Organs with poor respiration, organs which are spastic and insufficiently charged, are biologically weakened; thus, they are highly susceptible to cancer-producing stimuli, whatever they may be. On the other hand, organs which function biologically normally are not affected by these same stimuli. This is a necessary and logical assumption.

These clinically well-established facts—deficient biological charge, muscular spasm and deficient external and internal respiration—give the concept of "cancer disposition" a tangible content. I shall now attempt to show how sex-economic clinical experience led to cancer research.

Sex-economic observation of character neuroses showed again and again the significance of *muscular spasms* and the resulting devitalization in the organism. Muscular spasm and deficiency in bioelectrical charge are subjectively experienced as "being dead." Muscular hypertension due to sexual stasis regularly leads to a diminution of vegetative sensations; the extreme degree of this is the sensation of the organ "being dead." This corresponds to a block of biological activity in the respective organ. For example, the blocking of biosexual excitation in the genital always goes with a spastic tension of the pelvic musculature, as is regularly seen in the uterine spasms of frigid women. Such spasms often result in menstrual disturbances, menstrual pains, polyps and fibromata. The spasm of the uterus has no other function than that of preventing the biosexual energy from making itself felt as vaginal sensation. Spasms representing inhibitions of vegetative currents are seen particularly frequently wherever we find *annular* musculature, for example, at the throat, at the entrance to and the exit from the stomach, at the anus, etc. These are also places where cancer is found with particular frequency. The disturbance in biological charge of a gland, a region of the skin or a mucous membrane is produced and maintained by a muscular spasm in the neighborhood of the affected site; the spasm prevents biological energy from charging the respective site.

In a woman whom I treated vegetotherapeutically, Xray showed a beginning cancer of the 4th costal cartilage on the right side. This was due to a chronic spastic contraction of the right pectoralis muscle. This contraction represented a strong holding back in the shoulders because of repressed beating impulses. The woman had never experienced an orgasm and suffered from compulsive flirting.

In vegetotherapy, we see not only character neuroses, but also, of course, schizophrenic, epileptic, Parkinson-like, rheumatic and cancerous disturbances. If an organic disease develops, this may take place during the course of the treatment or afterward; in the latter case, one will remember the signs that foreshadowed the disease. The most frequent finding is *spasms in the pelvic musculature in women*, resulting, in the majority of cases, in benign tumors of the genital organs.

Vegetotherapeutic clinical observations raise the question as to the fate of the somatic sexual excitation when its normal discharge is barred. We know only that the biosexual excitation can be reduced or inhibited by chronic muscular tensions. In female patients, these tensions often show in the form of hard lumps in the uterus. The spasm of the uterus usually spreads to the anal sphincter and the vagina, and beyond that, to the adductors of the thigh. The pelvis is always retracted, the sacral spine often stiff and ankylotic. Lumbago and pathological lordosis are typical manifestations of this condition. In the pelvis, any vegetative sensation is absent. During expiration, the wave of excitation is inhibited by the pulled-up chest and the tense abdomen. The excitation of the large abdominal ganglia does not progress to the genital organs and thus a disturbance of biological functioning necessarily results. The genitals are no longer capable of biological excitation.

Many women who suffer from genital tension and vaginal anesthesia complain of a feeling that "something is not as it should be down there." They relate that during puberty they experienced the well-known signs of biosexual excitation; and that later they learned to fight these sensations by way of holding their breath. Later, so they relate in a typical manner, they began to experience in the genitals a sensation of "deadness" or "numbness," which, in turn, frightened them. As the vegetative sensations in the organs are an immediate expression of the actual biological state of the organs, such statements are of extreme importance for an evaluation of somatic processes. (The fact has to be kept in mind that patients are rarely able to comprehend or describe their organ sensations spontaneously; it takes character-analytic exploration to make them able to do so.)

The generally prevailing sexual inhibition of women explains the prevalence of cancer in the breast and the genital organs. The sexual inhibition may have existed for decades before it manifests itself as cancer.

The following case illustrates in a singularly simple manner the immediate connection between character armoring, muscular spasm and the onset of a cancer tumor.

A man of 45 came to my laboratory because of a complete obstruction of the esophagus by a cancer tumor. He was unable to take solid food at all; liquid food he soon vomited. Xrays showed a shadow the size of a small fist and a complete obstruction in the middle of the esophagus. The patient was rapidly losing weight and strength; there was a severe anemia and T-bacilli intoxication. The anamnesis revealed the following facts: Several months previous to the onset of the complaints, his son had been drafted for the army. This son was the patient's favorite; he became worried and deeply depressed. (He had always had a tendency to depression.) In the course of a few days, he developed a spasm of the esophagus. He had difficulty in swallowing; this disappeared, however, when he took a drink of water. At the same time, he had a sensation of oppression in the chest. These disturbances kept coming and going for some time, until finally they became stationary. The difficulty in swallowing increased rapidly. He went to see a physician who found the constriction and a small tumor. Treatment by Xray did not help, and in the course of a few months the man got to the point of starving to death. I should like to add that he had suffered since childhood from a severe spasm of his jaw musculature; his face had a hard, rigid expression. Correspondingly, his speech was inhibited; as a result of the tension in his jaw muscles, he talked through his teeth.

The extent of the devastating results of the inhibition of the natural biological rhythm—as it is expressed in respiration and the alternation of sexual tension and gratification—can as yet not even be guessed at. Deficient external respiration must of necessity lead to a deficient internal respiration of the organs, that is, a deficient supply of oxygen and elimination of carbon dioxide.

When, some years back, I began to comprehend the significance of the respiratory disturbance for emotional disturbances, I remembered the findings of Otto Warburg* concerning the metabolism in cancer tissue. Warburg found that all the various cancer-producing stimuli have one thing in common: they produce a local oxygen deficiency as a result of which there is a disturbance of respiration in the respective cells. Thus, the cancer cell is a poorly breathing cell. Warburg considers this oxygen lack in the cells one of the causes of cancer, in the following manner. In certain places, only such cells will develop as are capable of overcoming the respiratory disturbance. The cancer cells originate from such cells. It is a matter of a disturbance in the energy metabolism. The respiratory disturbance is characteristic of all known malignant tumors,

---

* Cf., e.g., Biochemische Zeitschr., Bd. 317.

including the Rous' sarcoma. *The metabolism of cancer cells, thus, has to be regarded as an anoxic condition of normally growing cells.* From this correct finding of Warburg we cannot, however, draw the conclusion that the cancer cell is nothing but a normal cell taking on a different mode of growth under the influence of oxygen lack. In reality, the cancer cell is—biologically speaking—basically different from the normal cell. It is nothing but a protozoal formation. (This will be shown in detail elsewhere.)

As stated before, these facts form the connecting link between the autonomic functions and the disease of cancer.

From the Case History of a Cancer Patient. An Attempt at Vegetotherapy

I shall now give the history of a cancer patient which lends itself particularly well to a demonstration of the nature of the shrinking biopathy.

The patient's brother related that her first complaint was a violent pain in the right hip bone. The pain was constant and "pulling." At this time, her weight was about 125 lbs. Her physician diagnosed a sacro-iliac spasm. She was incapable of rising from the examination table. She was given injections of morphine and atropine, to no avail. The pain continued unabated and the patient was unable to leave her bed, where she lay flat and immobile. Three months after the onset, the patient began to vomit. At about the same time, the pain moved to the region of the fifth cervical vertebra. Xrays showed a collapsed vertebra. An orthopedic surgeon put the patient in a plaster cast. He was the first to find a collapse of the 10th dorsal vertebra, a metastasis from a cancer of the left breast. A biopsy confirmed the diagnosis of cancer. The patient was given Xray treatment of the pelvis and the spine and was sterilized by Xray. She was constantly in bed. When she left the hospital after the Xray treatment, the patient weighed 90 lbs.

The hospital case history showed the following data: Four

months before admission, there were pains in the *right hip* which increased with walking and which made it difficult for the patient to sit down. The following is striking: the pains which kept the patient in bed for over two years did *not* set in originally at the place where the tumor was diagnosed. The pains were in the right hip; the primary tumor, however, was in the left breast, and several metastases were in the spine.

The patient also suffered from vomiting. The record states that she would lie flat in bed and was unable to move on account of her pains. She had no enlarged lymph glands. The tumor of the breast measured about 3 x 2 x 6 cm. Her legs showed limited motility, the sacrum was dislocated and stiff. Most of the spine was painful. The hospital diagnosis was: Carcinoma of the left breast with bone metastases. Four months after the onset of the pains, the hospital physician pronounced the case hopeless.

Twenty-six months after the discovery of the breast tumor, the patient was brought to my laboratory, hardly able to walk, being supported by two relatives. The color of her skin, particularly of the face, was ashen gray. The pain in the back, sharply localized at the 12th dorsal vertebra, was violent. The left breast showed a tumor the size of a small apple, hardly movable. Blood examination: Hemoglobin 35%; T-bacilli culture in bouillon strongly positive after 24 hours. There were rot bacteria; the erythrocytes were largely in bionous disintegration and showed T-bodies; there were small nucleated round cells and numerous T-bacilli. The autoclavation test gave predominantly blue bions, but the vesicles were small and showed very little radiation. Inoculation of the bouillon culture on agar resulted in clear-cut T-bacilli growth.* These blood findings pointed to an extreme biological debility of the blood system. Xrays showed the following:

The fifth cervical vertebra is collapsed. No significant findings at the other cervical vertebrae.

---

* *Cf.* "Bion Experiments on the Cancer Problem," 1939.

The dorsal spine shows collapse of the tenth and twelfth vertebra and a narrowing of the joint space between the third and the fourth vertebra. There is also strong suggestion of a metastatic lesion at the medial third of the right ninth rib.

No lesions are present at the lumbar spine, but there are three round areas of lesser density at the right ilium near the sacro-iliac joint which are very suggestive of metastatic lesions, although they might be gas shadows of the cecum.

Conclusions: Multiple metastatic bone lesions.

On the basis of the Xray pictures, the physician to whom I had sent the patient for a general check-up considered the case hopeless. I was less impressed by the Xray pictures than by the biological debility of the blood. Two physicians, friends of the family, declared that the patient would live hardly more than two weeks, while another physician, on the basis of the information from the hospital, thought it was a matter of at most two months.

The Muscular Armor

The vegetative habitus of the patient, when first seen, was as follows: The chin seemed immobile; the patient talked through her teeth, as if hissing. The jaw muscles were rigid, as was the superficial and deep musculature of the neck. The patient held her head somewhat pulled in and thrust forward, as if she were afraid that something would happen to her neck if she were to move her head. This vegetative attitude of head and neck seemed, at first glance, sufficiently explained by the fact that her fifth cervical vertebra was collapsed. She had been wearing a plaster collar for some time, and there was a good reason for fearing a fracture of the cervical spine with rapid or extreme movements. The patient's neurosis made the best of this situation. As was shown later, the fear of moving the neck had been present *long before* the collapse of the vertebra. More than that: this attitude of the neck was part and parcel of *a general vegetative attitude which was not a result but the cause of her cancer disease.*

The reflexes were normal. *Respiration* was severely disturbed. The lips were drawn in and the nostrils somewhat distended, as if she had to draw in air through the nose. The thorax was immobile. It did not perceptibly participate in respiration and remained constantly in an inspiratory position. When asked to breathe out deeply, the patient was unable to do so; more than that, she did not seem to understand what she was asked to do. The attempt to get the thorax into the expiratory position, that is, to push it down, met with a vivid active muscular resistance. It was found that head, neck and shoulders formed a rigid unit, as if any movement in the respective joints were impossible. The patient was able to move her arms only very slowly and with great effort. The handclasp, both left and right, was very weak. The scapular muscles were extremely tense, standing out like taut cords. The muscles between the shoulder blades were sensitive to touch.

The abdominal wall was also tense and reacted to the slightest pressure with a marked resistance. The musculature of the legs seemed thin, as if atrophic, compared with the rest of the musculature. The pelvis was immobilized in a retracted position.

Superficial psychological exploration revealed the following: The patient had been suffering from insomnia for many years previous to the discovery of the cancer. She had been a widow for 12 years. Her marriage, which had lasted two years, had been unhappy. In contradistinction to the many cases of marital misery where the awareness of the unhappiness is absent, the patient had always been fully aware that her marriage was a failure. During the early months of her marriage, she had been much excited sexually and at the same time unsatisfied. Her husband had shown himself to be impotent. When, finally, the sexual act succeeded, he suffered from premature ejaculation, and the patient continued to be unsatisfied. During the first few months, her lack of sexual gratification made her suffer keenly; later, however, she "got used to it." She had always been fully aware of the necessity of sexual gratification, but had found no way of obtaining it. After the death of her husband, she devoted herself to the education of her child, refused any contact with men and withdrew from social activity. Gradually, her sexual excitation subsided. In its place, she developed anxiety states; these she combatted by way of various phobic mechanisms. At the time when I first saw her, she no longer suffered from anxiety states; she appeared emotionally balanced and somehow reconciled to her sexual abstinence and her personal fate in general. She presented the picture of neurotic resignation with which the character-analyst is so familiar; she no longer had any impulse to change her life situation. I avoided going any deeper into the patient's latent conflict and concentrated my attention on the organic changes which soon took place.

The Results of the Orgone Experiment

A detailed presentation of the technique of orgone therapy will be given elsewhere. Here, I shall mention only the essentials.

Our orgone therapy experiments with cancer patients consist in their sitting in an orgone accumulator. The orgone energy which is concentrated in the accumulator penetrates the naked body and is also taken up by way of respiration. The duration of the individual session depends on the atmospheric orgone tension which is measured electroscopically. I began with sessions of 30 minutes.

During the first session the skin between the shoulderblades became red; this was a region which two months later was to play an important role in the patient's functional disease. From the second session on, the reactions in general were more distinct and intense. The pain in the region of the tenth dorsal vertebra regularly decreased *during* the treatment; this improvement usually lasted until the next session. Humid and rainy weather always intensified the pains. During the second session, the redness of the skin spread to the upper part of the back and the chest. When the patient interrupted the irradiation for a few minutes, the redness disappeared, to return as soon as she went back into the box. Beginning with the third session, the patient felt that the air in the box was "closer and heavier." She said, "I feel as if I were filling up," "I have a buzzing around the ears from the inside," "Something clears up in my body." During the third session, she began to perspire, particularly under the arms; she related that during the past few years she had never perspired.

All these reactions of the organism to the orgone radiation are typical in all cancer patients. In one patient one reaction will predominate, in another a different one. Such phenomena as redness of the skin, lowering of the pulse rate, warm perspiration and the subjective sensations of "something in the body getting loose, filling up, swelling," etc., admit of only one interpretation: The cancer habitus is determined by a general sympatheticotonia, that is, vegetative contraction. For this reason, we find in most cancer patients rapid pulse, pallor and dryness of the skin, often with a cyanotic or livid coloration, reduced motility of the organs, constipation, and inhibition of the sweat glands. *The orgone radiation has a vagotonic effect,* that is, it counteracts the general sympatheticotonic shrinking of the organism. In the accumulator, the pulse will come down from 120 to 90 or from 150 to 110 within twenty minutes; this without any medication. Similarly, there is redness of the skin, and perspiration; the peripheral blood vessels dilate and the blood pressure decreases. Expressed in terms of biological pulsation, this means that *the plasma system relinquishes the chronic attitude of contraction and begins to expand vagotonically.* This expansion is accompanied by a reduction of the typical cancer pain.

The cancer pains are usually ascribed to local mechanical tissue lesions caused by the tumor. Doubtless this explanation is correct in one or the other case when the tumor presses on a nerve or a sensitive organ. The typical cancer pain, of which I am speaking here, however, has to be strictly distinguished from these local, mechanically caused pains. Let us call it "vegetative shrinking pain." In order to understand its nature, we have to review a few hitherto generally overlooked facts.

Sex-economy had to give up the view generally held by medicine that the autonomic nerves in metazoa only transmit impulses but are themselves rigid. Such phenomena as the "pulling" pains remain unintelligible unless one realizes that the autonomic nervous system expands and contracts, that, in other words, it is mobile. This is confirmed, as stated before, by direct microscopic observation. We can see the fibers of the autonomic ganglia expand and contract; they move independently of the movements of the total organism; their movements precede those of the total body. The impulses appear first in the movements of the autonomic nervous system and are transmitted secondarily to the mechanical locomotor organs of the organism. This fact sounds revolutionary and strange. Yet it is, really, only a simple conclusion which I had to draw from the functions of pulsation in the organism and which afterward I was able to demonstrate by direct observation. *In the metazoon, the contracting and expanding ameba continues to exist in the form of the contracting and expanding autonomic nervous system.* This autonomic system is nothing but organized contractile plasma. Thus, the emotional, vegetative, autonomic movement is the immediate expression of the plasma current. The prevalent concept of the rigidity of the autonomic nerves is incompatible with every single phenomenon of biophysical functioning, such as pleasure, anxiety, tension, relaxation, and the sensations of pressure, pulling, pain, etc. On the other hand, the contractility of the autonomic nervous system, which forms a functional and histological unity ("syncytium"), explains in a simple manner our subjective vegetative sensations. What we experience as pleasure is an expansion of our organism. The autonomic nerves, in pleasure, actually stretch out toward the world; the whole organism is in a state of vagotonic expansion. In anxiety, on the other hand, we feel a crawling-back into the self, a shrinking and tightness. What we experience here is the actual process of contraction in the autonomic nervous system.

The orgasm we experience as an involuntary expansion and

contraction; this reflects the actual process of expansion and contraction in the total plasma system. The pain in cancer patients reflects the fact that the autonomic nerves retract from the diseased region and "pull" on the tissues. The expression "pulling" pain describes an actual process. It takes a mechanistically rigid, unalive, unbiological and unpsychological attitude to deny the simple and unequivocal fact that our organ sensations are identical with the actual processes in the autonomic system. Such a mechanistic concept relegates our organ sensations to the realm of metaphysics and cannot do justice to a single aspect of the cancer syndrome.

We understand now the seemingly strange phenomenon that in the orgone accumulator cancer pains regularly diminish or disappear. If the pains are not the expression of a local mechanical lesion but of a general contraction of the autonomic nerves, of a "pulling" at the tissues, then we understand that with the vagotonic expansion of the nerves the pulling, and with that the pain, subsides.

This fact reveals an essential effect of the orgone energy: *it charges living tissues and causes an expansion of the autonomic nerves (vagotonia).*

The general vitalization of biological functioning by the orgone radiation is also reflected in the blood picture.

Our patient came with a hemoglobin of 35%. Two days later it was 40%; after four days, 51%; after a week, 55%; after two weeks, 75%, and after three weeks, 85%, that is, normal. The patient got up, took her child back to live with her and, after years of being bedridden, began to work again. She was inclined to overdo things; she went shopping, spending hours at a stretch in department stores. She was free from pain, slept well and felt entirely well. She did her housework all by herself. I had to remind the patient of the fact that she was getting over a very serious illness and had to warn her to take it easy. My warnings were justified. After about 6 weeks, the patient began to feel tired, and the hemoglobin dropped to 63%. The pains in the back did not return, but she began to complain about difficulties in breathing and about a "wandering" pain in the ribs, in the diaphragmatic region. She was prescribed bedrest, and the hemoglobin content soon improved, returning to 83% after another week. The weight remained constant at about 124 lbs. After another four weeks, the hemoglobin was still 85%.

The patient was no longer brought to me by car; she came every day by subway. Her relatives and physicians were amazed. As to the physicians, I met with a peculiar attitude which is incomprehensible from a rational point of view, an attitude which appears when, for a change, the case of a cancer patient is *not* hopeless. They did not ask how the improvement had been brought about. At the beginning, I had sent the patient to a physician who predicted that she would die within a few days. Now, the same patient was up and around and her Xray pictures showed complete ossification in a previously cancerous spine; similarly, the shadows in the pelvic bone had disappeared after two weeks' treatment. Yet, none of the physicians showed any interest in what was going on.

These Xray pictures showed the healing process unequivocally. They confirmed what I had seen so often in my cancer experiments with mice: the orgone energy arrests the growth of the tumor and replaces it by a hematoma which—under favorable conditions—is eliminated by connective tissue or, if the tumor is in a bone, by calcification.

Biological Blood Tests

I shall give here a brief résumé of what will be presented in detail elsewhere: *the orgone energy charges the red blood corpuscles.*

Every individual erythrocyte is an independent orgonotic energy vesicle. It follows the same pulsation and function of tension and charge as the total organism and each of its organs. With a magnification of about 3000x, expansion and contraction of the erythrocytes can easily be observed. Under the influence of adrenalin, the erythrocytes shrink, with potassium chloride they expand; that is, they follow the antithesis of pleasure and anxiety.

Our blood tests in cancer patients are done as follows:

1. Culture test. A blood sample is tested for bacterial growth in bouillon or in a mixture of 50% bouillon plus 50% KCl (0.1 n). The blood of advanced cancer patients *regularly gives a strong growth of T-bacilli* (*cf.* "Bion experiments on the Cancer Problem," 1939).

2. Biological resistance test. A few drops of blood in bouillon and KCl are autoclaved for half an hour at a steam pressure of 15 lbs. Healthy blood withstands the autoclavation better than the biologically devitalized blood of cancer patients. Biologically vigorous erythrocytes disintegrate into large blue bion vesicles. Devitalized erythrocytes in cancer blood disintegrate into T-bodies. *Depending on the degree of devitalization, the content in T-bodies increases and that of blue bions decreases.*

The orgone treatment charges the erythrocytes. This is shown by the fact that the T-reaction changes into a B-reaction; that is, the blood becomes more resistant to destruction by high temperatures.

3. Disintegration in physiological salt solution. A small drop of blood is put on a hanging-drop slide in 0.9% NaCl solution. According to their biological resistance, the erythrocytes disintegrate slowly or rapidly. The more rapidly they disintegrate, and the more rapidly their membrane shrinks and they form bion vesicles on the inside, the lower is their biological resistance. Biologically vigorous erythrocytes can retain their shape for 20 minutes or longer. Disintegration within 1 to 3 minutes indicates extreme biological weakness. In the case of marked anemia, the erythrocytes show the typical T-bodies, i.e., shrinking of the membrane.

4. Blue orgone margin. When observed with apochromatic lenses at a magnification of 2-3000x, biologically vigorous erythrocytes show a wide margin of an intense blue color. Devitalized erythrocytes with a tendency to rapid disintegration show a very narrow margin with a weak blue coloration.

In our patient, the blood tests showed a general biological strengthening of the blood. When the patient first came, the blood cultures were strongly positive, that is, they showed intensive growth of T-bacilli. Three weeks later, the cultures were negative and remained so. The erythrocytes no longer showed shrinking and had a wide margin of deep blue. The autoclavation test resulted in 100% bionous disintegration and no longer in a T-reaction. The disintegration in salt solution now took place very slowly and without the formation of T-bodies.

The patient was free from pain and felt generally well, except that she reacted with malaise to rainy weather. She regularly came for her daily orgone treatment. The blood pressure remained constant about 130/80. The pulse rate was and remained normal. There was only *one* symptom which not only failed to disappear but became more pronounced. This was a respiratory disturbance which at first was ill-defined.

The Appearance of the Cancer Biopathy

I shall proceed now to a description of the cancer biopathy which made its appearance only after the elimination of the tumors and the restoration of the normal blood picture. I did not have the faintest inkling of what I am going to describe here; I experienced it at first with utter amazement and lack of comprehension. It was difficult to understand the connection between the two series of phenomena. What happened was this: After the cure of the local cancer tumors, a general vegetative disease picture appeared which previously had been hidden and which formed the actual background of the cancer disease: the shrinking biopathy.

The patient seemed to have regained her complete physical health. This happy state of affairs lasted about six weeks and was objectively confirmed by the blood tests and the Xray pictures. The tumors had disappeared. The blood remained healthy, the anemia did not recur. The tumor in the left breast was no longer palpable after the eighth orgone irradiation. With purely mechanistic pathological concepts, one would have proclaimed a "cure" of this cancer case. At the same time, however, certain emotional symptoms became more and more pronounced and kept one from jumping to premature conclusions.

At the time when the patient first came she had not felt any sexual desire for a long time. About four weeks after the beginning of orgone therapy I observed in her signs of sexual stasis. Up to that point, she had been gay and full of hope for the future; now, a depression began to set in and she developed signs of stasis anxiety. She began to withdraw from people again. As I learned from her, her attempts to straighten out her sexual situation had failed. She related that for some time now she had been suffering from intense sexual excitation; these excitations were much more intense than those which she had experienced 14 years earlier, at the beginning of her marriage, and which she had fought then. To judge from her description, it was a matter of normal vaginal excitations. During the first two weeks of getting well, she had made a few attempts to establish sexual contact; failing in this, she became depressed and felt physically exhausted. These attempts, which were entirely healthy, were continued for several weeks. One day she asked me whether it would be harmful to have sexual intercourse "once a month." The question had an apprehensive ring to it and was at variance with her sexual knowledge. It pointed to an irrational fear: she began to develop *the fear that a dangerous accident would happen to her in sexual intercourse, since, as she said, "her spine was demolished in two places."* She was afraid of what might result from the violent motions connected with sexual excitation. It is to be noted that this idea did not appear until *after the failure* of her attempts to find a sexual partner. She had met a man who proved impotent. She became furious but fought back her hatred and disillusionment. When another attack of anger would come, she would "swallow her anger." Now, the patient presented the complete picture of a stasis neurosis. The depression became more severe and she suffered from uncontrollable crying spells; she felt "a dreadful pressure in her chest—it goes through and through."

One might have been tempted to explain this "pressure in the chest" on the basis of the collapsed 12th dorsal vertebra.

But simple consideration contradicted this assumption. For six weeks the patient had had no pain in spite of working hard; it was inconceivable that a *mechanical* pressure of the collapsed vertebra on a nerve should now suddenly become effective after not having made itself felt for weeks. What followed showed that the patient was developing an anxiety hysteria. This neurosis made use of the spine lesion as a rationalization. It was to be expected that from now on every psychiatrically untrained physician would ascribe all symptoms to the collapsed vertebra, overlooking the fact that this same vertebra had been no less collapsed at the time when the patient was going around without pain for a number of weeks.

After about ten orgone irradiations, the patient had begun to experience sexual excitation. The orgone energy had charged her biosexually, but she was unable to handle the sexual excitation. The anxiety neurosis which she now developed was only a reactivation of old conflicts; in puberty, she had suffered from similar states. The patient now found herself in the tragic situation of waking up to new life, only to be confronted by a nothingness. As long as she was ill, the tumor and the resulting suffering had absorbed all interest. Indeed, her organism had used up great amounts of biological energy in the fight against the cancer. These energies were now free, and in addition were amplified by the orgonotic charge. In a phase of particularly intense depression the patient confessed that she felt herself ruined as a woman, that she felt herself to be ugly and that she did not see how she could suffer this life. She asked me whether the orgone energy could cure her anxiety neurosis also. This, of course, I had to deny, and the patient understood the reason.

Summarizing the sequence of events, we have the following:

1. In the beginning of the marriage, a severe stasis neurosis due to the husband's impotence.

2. Repression of sexual excitation, resignation, depression and a decade of abstinence.

3. The sexual excitations disappear while the cancer disease develops. As we shall see later, the cancer metastases developed

exactly in those organs which played a dominant part in the muscular armor which repressed the sexual excitation.

4. Elimination of the tumors by the orgone energy, physical recovery of the patient and reappearance of sexual excitability.

5. The high-pitched sexual excitation ends in disappointment; the old stasis neurosis reappears.

This constellation then resulted in a general shrinking of the vital apparatus.

One day there occurred a mishap. The patient left the orgone box and began to dress. She bent over to pick up a stocking and suddenly let out a shriek. We found her pale, with a thready pulse, on the point of fainting. We became frightened because we did not know what had happened. We, too, felt the collapsed vertebra to be a Damocles' sword. Nobody knew when the patient might suffer a fracture of the spine. Just because this fear seemed justified, it lent itself so well to a rationalization of the patient's neurosis. When the patient calmed down it was shown that she had only experienced a fright. For a moment she had believed that by her swift movement she had really broken her spine. Actually she had only suffered a slight strain at the shoulderblade; she had made too swift a movement with a hypertonic muscle. During the next few days, the patient felt well, but four days later she complained of heavy *"pressure in the chest"* and *"weakness in the legs."* During these days, the reflexes were normal. Three days later she again felt more strength in her legs, but the pressure in the chest persisted. On one of the following days, during a conversation in the treatment room, the patient suddenly cried out and doubled up, so that everybody present immediately thought of a fractured vertebra. Yet, all reflexes were absolutely normal. But now there was a new symptom which kept the patient in bed for many months and which deceived a number of physicians.

When the patient doubled up, she stopped breathing; she no longer could breathe out properly and kept gasping for air. I had the impression of a *spastic contraction of the diaphragm,* a diaphragmatic block.

The pain in the lower ribs about which the patient now complained could be ascribed either to this spasm or to the mechanical pressure of the collapsed vertebra on a sensory nerve. *The collapsed 12th vertebra corresponded to the costal insertion of the diaphragm.* What happened during the ensuing months was essentially a clash of opinions as to which of the two interpretations was correct. I advised the relatives to take the patient to the orthopedic surgeon whom she had consulted previously. The surgeon declared that the spine and the pelvis were free of shadows and metastases and that the patient's condition was due to a mechanical lesion at the 12th dorsal vertebra. What had made the metastases disappear he did not inquire about. He prescribed bedrest in a plaster cast. The patient's brother refused to take this advice because he had followed the course of his sister's disease with great understanding and was convinced of the correctness of my interpretation.

It was during this period that I first began to understand the connection between the lesion of the 12th vertebra and the biopathic contracture of the diaphragm. It could be no accident that the diaphragmatic spasm—a symptom so well known to the vegetotherapist—should appear just at this time. There also seemed to be significance in the fact that one of the main metastases had appeared just at the insertion of the diaphragm. This *concurrence of diaphragmatic spasm and lesion of the vertebra* complicated the clinical diagnosis considerably; on the other hand, it opened an avenue of approach to the understanding of the extremely important *connection between emotional muscle spasm and the localization of metastases.* One of the tasks of this series of articles will be to demonstrate the fact that *the localization of a cancer tumor is determined by the biological inactivity of the tissues in its immediate neighborhood.*

The orgone treatment had to be interrupted because the patient was again bedridden. Renewed examination at a cancer hospital and by private physicians revealed calcification of the defects in the spinal column and the absence of cancer growths. The original breast tumor did not reappear. But nobody could foresee whether or not new cancer growths might appear. I saw the patient repeatedly at her home. She complained of violent pains in her lowermost ribs. The pain was neither constant nor definitely localized; it appeared at various places along the costal margin and could always be eliminated by correcting the breathing. The whole thing looked like a neuralgia with a marked hysterical component. The patient lay flat in bed and gave the impression of being completely unable to move. If one tried to move her arms or legs, she would cry out, become pale and would break out in a cold sweat. A few times I succeeded in getting her out of bed into an easy chair by making her breathe deeply for about 10 minutes. The relatives were amazed that I should be able to eliminate the pain so easily. They had seen the tumors disappear and had had this confirmed by outside physicians. As I worked without drugs or injections, my orgone therapy seemed mysterious. In order to counteract this impression, I tried to explain to the relatives the mechanism of the disturbance. They realized very soon that the pain could not be due to the lesion of the vertebra, otherwise it would have been sharply localized and it could not have been eliminated by improved respiration. At that time, I had as yet no idea of the fact that in reality the patient did not have any pain *but a panicky fear of the onset of pain.*

An intercostal injection of an anesthetic was tried at the point where the pains were most violent. The anesthetic had no effect; shortly after the injection the pains appeared at *another* rib. The physicians who had been convinced that the pains were the result of the vertebral lesion finally had to admit that they were essentially "functional." But nobody could tell what was the "meaning" of the "functional" symptom. In addition, to most physicians "functional" means "not organic," that is, "not real but imaginary."

One day I found the patient again in violent "pain." She was gasping for air and produced peculiar groaning sounds. The condition seemed serious, but gave way promptly when the patient succeeded in breathing down and when the spasm of the jaw muscles was released. I turned over the work on the respiration to a colleague because I was going away for two months. He reported later that again and again it had been possible to eliminate the pains by the establishment of full expiration.

The patient was taken to a cancer hospital once more. The hospital physician confirmed again the complete absence of metastases in the bones. He doubted that Xray therapy would eliminate the pains or that a surgical procedure at the nerve of the 12th segment would help. This was 5 months after the initiation of the orgone therapy, and 3½ months after its interruption. When the patient's brother told the hospital physician about the result of the orgone therapy, he became very reserved. He said he could not go into that until it was "recognized by official medicine." He overlooked the fact that he himself was a representative of "official medicine" to which he shifted the responsibility for the recognition of the results of the orgone therapy in this cancer case.

The patient soon returned home and continued to lie flat in bed. The atrophy (of disuse) of her muscles progressed, and the danger of a recurrence of the tumors was considerable. A month later, I saw the patient again. I succeeded again in eliminating the pains by improving respiration. The patient was able to get out of bed but felt very weak. One day, during one of these attempts to stay out of bed, I saw the patient develop severe anxiety; she implored me to be allowed to go back to bed. At that moment, *she had no pains.* I insisted on her staying up. All of a sudden, she began to tremble violently, was scared, broke out in a cold sweat and turned pale. In other words, she experienced a violent, shock-like reaction of the autonomic system to the standing up. I did not let the patient go back to bed because I noticed that *some fear made her want to go back to bed.* A few moments later, there were visible convulsions in the upper abdomen, and she gasped for air; the chronic spasm of the diaphragm dissolved itself into clonic convulsions of the abdominal musculature. After this, she felt greatly relieved and was able to move about freely.

Now, I understood a basic feature of biopathy. The biological charging of her organism by the orgone had resulted in sexual excitations; to these, she had reacted with a contracture of the diaphragm. (The repression of sexual excitation by way of a chronic attitude of inspiration is a phenomenon well known to the vegetotherapist.) This contracture of the diaphragm apparently caused the "pressure in the chest" and the pain-like sensations which were ascribed to the collapsed vertebra. The pressure in the chest disappeared every time I succeeded in overcoming the inspiratory spasm and thus in restoring the pulsatory movement of the diaphragm. But it was just these contractions and expansions of the diaphragm which caused violent anxiety which the patient tried to escape by falling back into the inspiratory attitude. As was shown now, the "danger" of a clonic dissolution of the contracture was too great when the patient was standing up or walking around. *The danger consisted in the violent convulsions which threatened to dissolve the diaphragmatic spasm. She did not dare leave her bed because she was very much afraid of these convulsions.* It was this fear, then, which kept her in bed, although it was not the exclusive motive for staying in bed.

Doubtless, the diaphragmatic spasm created neuralgic pains in the ribs and at the insertion of the diaphragm. But this spasm accounted only in part for her enormous fear of motion; the more important part was her fear that if she moved she would "collapse" or "break her back."

The involuntary convulsions of the diaphragm which threatened to set in when she got up only seemed to justify this fear. Thus, she really did not suffer from acute pains, but from a *tremendous fear of sudden violent pains*. This fear was further increased by the experience of a few months before, when "something seemed to crack when she moved too suddenly."

In other words, she suffered from a misinterpretation of normal vegetative sensations such as accompany the movement of the diaphragm. Her staying in bed was a strong defense mechanism against the fear of "breaking apart." This fear would arise as soon as the diaphragmatic spasm was about to dissolve itself into clonic movements. This she would counter with an intensification of the diaphragmatic contracture. Of course, this fear and her reaction to it had far-reaching physical results, for it led to a general muscular tension which was to prevent any motion; the long duration of the consequent immobility led to an atrophy of the musculature. For example, she was hardly able to lift her arms; when she lifted her left arm, she lifted it with the aid of her right. She was unable to lift her legs and hardly able to bend her knees. The head was kept rigid. Passive movement of the head was strongly resisted. The patient was afraid of "breaking her neck." All physicians had warned her against rapid movements because the fifth cervical vertebra was collapsed.

On one of the following days I found the patient in a very bad condition. In spite of a strong urge to defecate, she had not gone to the bathroom for several days, in order not to have to leave her bed. As on previous occasions, the "pains" disappeared when the patient was made to breathe, and she was able to get up. She had an enormous bowel movement without any difficulty.

I told her brother that I would undertake an attempt at vegetotherapy for two weeks (without remuneration), but that I would have to stop if it showed no results. She moved to my neighborhood and for the next few weeks I worked with her for about 2 hours every day. This work disclosed the phobic background of her biopathic condition.

The Characterological Expression of the Shrinking Biopathy

Six months after the collapse in my laboratory the patient developed a paralysis of the rectum and the bladder. The question was whether this was due to a local mechanical lesion or, as I suspected, to a functional shrinking of the autonomic system. In the first case, emotional motives would be absent and the symptoms would point to a sharply localized lesion. In the second case, one would expect prominent emotional and character disturbances and an inconstancy of the paralytic symptoms.

When I explained to the patient again and again her *fear* of the pains, she became capable of moving in her bed without any pain. In order to be able to move, however, she always first had to mobilize her respiration and to loosen up the spasms of her jaw musculature. As she put it, she always had first "to get rid of the fear of moving." In the case of mechanical lesion of the nerve, this would not have been possible.

When she succeeded in turning on her side or her stomach, she always seemed extremely exhausted. We looked for the reason for this peculiar exhaustion and finally found it in an extreme tension of the musculature of the neck and throat. The patient looked as if her head were being pulled into the thorax. It was the same attitude one involuntarily assumes to protect oneself against a sudden blow on the head. This muscular attitude was completely autonomic; the patient could neither control nor consciously loosen it. When this contraction of the musculature of the neck and throat occurred, respiration ceased and the patient's throat rattled as if she were choking. In order to loosen up the spasm, I had her stick her finger down the throat. To this she promptly reacted with a gag reflex which was so violent that she turned blue in the face. After a while she felt "greatly relieved in the throat."

In connection with these throat reflexes, she began to tell me spontaneously about her anxiety dreams. She dreamed every night, with intense anxiety, that she was falling into an abyss; that she was choking or that something was falling on her and she was being destroyed. With such dreams of falling the vegetotherapist is very familiar. They occur typically toward the conclusion of a character-analysis, at a time when pre-orgastic sensations in the abdomen and the genital begin to appear and are suppressed before becoming conscious. These sensations, if anxiety-laden, are experienced as *falling*. This is based on the following mechanism:

Pre-orgastic excitation is the onset of an involuntary convulsion of the plasma system. If the organism is afraid of this convulsion, it will develop—in the midst of an expansion which should end in a convulsion—a *counteracting contraction,* in other words, an *inhibition of the expansion.* This results in a sensation like that which one experiences when an elevator suddenly starts down or an airplane drops rapidly. *The sensation of falling is the perception of a contraction of the autonomic system in the process of inhibiting an expansion.* The typical falling dreams are often accompanied by a sudden contraction of the total body.

In the case of our patient this means the following: She reacted to vagic sensations of expansion regularly with spastic contractures; her organism became fixated, as it were, in the muscular spasms in the throat and the diaphragm, as if "not to lose hold." The fear of the convulsions diminished considerably when I succeeded in eliminating the spasms by eliciting the gag reflex. Then the movements which she executed in bed no longer resulted in spasms but in pleasurable sensations.

Every plasma current begins with a central contraction (tension) which dissolves itself into a vagic expansion;* the vagic expansion goes with the sensation of pleasure; in the case of orgasm anxiety, it is inhibited and results in muscular spasms. We understand now: *The patient suffered from a spastic reaction to vagic expansion as the result of orgasm anxiety. Biopathic shrinking begins with a spastic restriction of biological pulsation.* It differs from the simple sympatheticotonic stasis neurosis insofar as, here, the impulses to expansion gradually subside, while in the stasis neurosis they maintain their intensity. A sharp distinction, however, cannot be drawn.

---

* This can be directly observed in the ameba limax at a magnification of 2000x.

This mechanism of spastic reaction to vagotonic impulses of expansion functioned in a different manner in the different muscle systems. For example, when I tried to move the patient's arms passively, she always reacted with a contraction of the shoulder musculature and the flexors of the arms; the reaction was similar to the muscular negativism and rigidity in catatonics. The patient presented the picture of a flaccid paralysis of the arms. When I asked her to hit my arm, she was at first unable to do so. But when I made her imagine that she was now letting out her suppressed anger, she was able, within five minutes, to get rid of the paralysis and to hit quite freely. At the end, she experienced pleasure in the motion and the action. The paralysis seemed to have been eliminated to a considerable extent. Thus, the patient was able to overcome her fear of expansion and of the plasmatic pulsation temporarily. This regularly improved her general condition considerably.

The same thing could be observed when I sat her up passively in bed. She always became frightened, began to gasp for breath, turned pale and repeated several times, with an expression of severe anxiety, "You shouldn't have done that." But when I repeated the procedure several times she even became able to sit up by herself. She was absolutely amazed and said, "It's a miracle how this is possible."

From then on, I had the patient continue to elicit the gag reflex, bite the pillow, hit my arm, etc.; all this in order to produce clonic contractions in the musculature of the throat and the shoulders. I knew from vegetotherapeutic experience that biological energy which is bound in spastically contracted musculature can be released only by clonisms. So it was in this patient. After about half an hour of *active* production of various reflexes, *involuntary clonic spasms began to set in in the musculature of the arms and the shoulders.* The legs also began to tremble. This trembling could always be intensified by gentle flexion and extension.

When these spasms appeared for the first time, the patient became very much frightened. She did not know what was going to happen to her. It was the very same fear of involuntary contractions which she avoided by her spastic contractures. After a few minutes, however, she began to enjoy the spasms. Gradually, the musculature of the throat began to participate in the spasms; the patient was afraid she was going to vomit. At one point she looked as if she were going to faint. I asked her to give free rein to the spasms. After a while they became less intense: the biological energy had been discharged. She sank back in the bed exhausted; her face was red, her respiration deep and full. The gag reflex could no longer be elicited, and the patient said, "My throat is peculiarly free—as if a pressure had been taken away." Similarly, the pressure on the chest had disappeared.

On the following day, the patient breathed normally, and I proceeded to relieve the paralysis of the legs by producing clonisms of the leg musculature. This was possible to a certain degree by slowly moving the legs, which were bent at the knees, apart and again together. I had not prepared the patient for the pre-orgastic sensations which are likely to appear with the dissolution of contractures in the leg musculature. All of a sudden, she inhibited her respiration, set her jaw, turned pale and developed a facial expression which I can only describe with the word "dying." The reaction was so violent that I became frightened. There could, however, be no mechanical lesion, for I had moved the legs only very slowly and gently. The patient emitted sounds such as one makes with the most severe pains in the chest. The sounds were a mixture of groaning and rattling. From vegetotherapeutic experience I knew that this was the patient's reaction to vegetative currents in the genital. We know from vegetotherapy that orgastic sensations, when inhibited by orgasm anxiety, are experienced as a *fear of dying;* "dying" in the sense of falling apart, melting, losing consciousness, dissolving, "nothingness."

The patient groaned heavily, was pale and blue, turned her eyes up and seemed exhausted. Never before had I seen the neurotic reaction of dying so realistically. With all the work on disturbances of the orgasm I had done during twenty years, I had still underestimated the depth at which the disturbances of the function of biological pulsation are at work. True, my contention had always been that the orgasm is "basic biological functioning *per se*." But never before had I seen an organism "die" so realistically as a result of orgasm anxiety. I told the relatives that quite possibly the patient would not survive more than a few days. It was clear to me that the shrinking of her vital system might well continue into actual death. This being the case, I would have relinquished any further efforts had it not been for the fact that seven months earlier, when the patient first came to me, she had also been on the point of dying. There was nothing to be lost by going on and a great many insights into the nature of the shrinking biopathy to be gained.

The following day I was called on the telephone by the relatives who said the patient was actually dying, that she was hardly breathing at all and was unable to have a bowel movement. When I saw the patient, she really seemed to be dying. Her face was blue and sunken, she emitted rattling sounds and whispered, "This is the beginning of the end." I found her pulse to be rapid but forceful.

In the course of about fifteen minutes, I was able to establish a good rapport with the patient. I asked her whether she had had—at any time previous to her developing tumors—the feeling that she was going to die. Without any resistance, she related that *as a child she had often rolled her eyes up and played at "dying."* The rattling and groaning sounds which she made now were also familiar to her from her childhood. She used to make them when she felt a constriction in her throat; as she put it, "when something pulled together in her throat." Now it became clear that the localization of *one of the cancer metastases at the fifth cervical vertebra was due to a spasm of the musculature* of the throat which had been present for decades. The sensation of constriction in the throat, the patient continued, went hand in hand with a pulling in of the shoulders and a tension between the shoulderblades, that is, at exactly the region where later the cancer pains developed.

Now that the patient talked with me wide awake and lively, I made her "play at dying." Within a few seconds, she succeeded in producing consciously the same picture by which she previously had been overcome involuntarily. She turned her eyes upward so that the lids were closed except for a narrow slit through which the whites of her eyes were just visible, fixed her chest in the inspiratory position and emitted groaning and rattling sounds. It was not easy to bring her back out of this dying attitude; but the more frequently she assumed this attitude consciously, the easier it became for her to give it up again. This was entirely in accord with vegetotherapeutic experience: *by practice, an autonomic function can be made objective and finally subject to conscious control.*

I asked the patient whether she thought that she was unconsciously committing suicide. She started to cry and said there was no point in going on living. Her illness had ruined her sexual attractiveness; she could never again be happy; and without happiness she did not want to live. I had the patient again elicit the gag reflex. Promptly, the clonic trembling in the arms and the throat reappeared, though not as strongly as the day before. She even succeeded in sitting up by herself, but her legs failed her. I had the impression that the upper part of her body was functioning while the lower part, from the hips down, failed to function.

For several days after this, the patient felt well and gay. One day, however, she suddenly relapsed into the dying attitude. I saw immediately that it was not playacting, but that she was overwhelmed by her biopathic reaction. Her respiration was shallow and labored, her nose pointed, her cheeks were sunken and her throat rattled heavily. I did not understand why this happened just at this point. She complained of violent pains and was completely unable to move. I succeeded again in restoring normal respiration. Again, intense clonic spasms occurred in the throat and the torso, but the lower extremities remained "dead." I had her again elicit the gag reflex. After this, the spasms became more intense.

I noticed that the pelvis tended to participate in the spasms but that she held back. The spasms lasted for about ten minutes and then subsided. While previously one had had the impression of suffocation, now the patient showed definite vagotonic reactions: the face was flushed, the skin over the body was no longer pale. The pains due to the diaphragmatic spasms subsided. After a while, the patient began to talk. She was, as she said, afraid that "something was going to happen down there." She related that up to the time when she came to me for treatment she had occasionally obtained sexual gratification by masturbation. This was a very belated correction of her earlier statement that she had been living in complete abstinence for over 10 years. As early as the first week of the orgone treatment, she had suppressed every impulse to masturbate because of phantasies of sexual intercourse with me. Since then she had not dared to touch her genital. The inhibition of masturbation, together with the phantasy, led to a stasis of sexual excitation, which, furthermore, was intensified by the biological charge by the orgone. The intensification of her sexual needs increased her anxiety. Thus she developed the phantasy that she might break her spine. The straining of the shoulder muscle when she tried to pick up her stocking seemed to confirm this fear, as if she had said to herself, "See, I knew it was going to happen."

The day after she had told me about her masturbation phantasies, I found her in the best of moods, full of hope and without complaints. The talk of the day before had made it possible for her, for the first time in months, to masturbate again. She had experienced a good deal of satisfaction. She was now able to control her diaphragmatic spasm very well. She was constipated, but felt the urge for defecation; only her fear of motion kept her from going to the bathroom. She moved much more easily in bed. She was even able to sit up all by herself, which amazed and pleased her a good deal. For the first time, she understood the chain of causes and events: fear of spinal

fracture → fear of pain → inhibition of respiration by diaphragmatic block → pain in the chest → fear of spinal fracture.
Now, however, the inhibition of motion by the fear of pain did
not set in so readily. The fear did not appear until the motion
required a good deal of effort. We now understood the connection between her fear of spinal fracture and her fear of
"motion."

On the next day, I found the patient again with poor respiration, full of complaints, and assuming the dying attitude. She
could not say what had brought this about. The relatives told
me that the day before she had felt very well until the evening.
Then things had taken a turn for the worse after the following
episode. Her boy was in the bathroom adjoining her room. She
heard a noise and got terribly frightened. All of a sudden she
had the idea *that the boy was closed in in a very small space
and was going to be smothered.* During the night she slept
poorly and had a number of severe anxiety dreams, some of
them falling dreams. All I could do on this day was to improve
her breathing which reduced her complaints about the "pains."

During the next few days, the patient felt much better, being
able to move without pain and to lift her legs. During a treatment hour, she happened to get near to the edge of the bed,
whereupon she became pale, stopped breathing, and cried out.
She was afraid of falling out of bed. Her reaction was clearly
exaggerated and did not correspond to any real danger. She
related spontaneously that the summer before, at the hospital,
she had asked to have an additional bed put at each side of her
bed, because she was afraid of falling out of bed. I lifted her
toward the edge of the bed, and although I held her firmly, she
yelled with fear. The *fear of falling* which was at the basis of
her fear of motion was now quite evident.

On the next day she sat up in bed. She had no pain, but
developed violent anxiety, broke out into a sweat and hysterical crying. She said she was going to die; that she had been
fighting death for so long, but this was the end. She cried for
her boy. She asked me for an injection which would make her

die so that she did not have to suffer any longer. "I don't want to get out of bed, I want to stay right here." After a while, she quieted down and found to her great surprise that she was able to sit up without any effort. But gradually she developed violent clonic spasms all over her body, particularly intense at the shoulders. She was extremely afraid of these spasms; that was the reason for her staying in bed. Whenever she was forced to sit up she felt the spasms coming. She no longer had her fear of falling, but the connection was clear. The violent clonic spasms of her musculature formed the physiological basis of her neurotic fear of falling. During the night, she had nightmares of falling into great depths, of heavy things falling on her, of men attacking and threatening to *choke* her. Now she remembered that she had suffered from exactly the same anxiety states for a long time in adolescence. She also remembered a phobia she used to have at that age. When she would walk on the street and hear footsteps behind her, she would begin to run, for fear that "somebody was after her." This fear usually was so intense that her *legs "failed her"* and she always had the feeling that she was going to fall down. She recognized in this the very same bodily sensation which she experienced when she had to sit up in bed now. Then also, her legs would fail her and she became afraid of falling. With that, she would have the sensation of a spasm of the diaphragm and would be "scared to death."

All this shows unequivocally that the motor paresis of the legs was caused by a phobia, *a phobia which had dominated her as far back as puberty, long before she had developed cancer.* The paresis which she now had developed was nothing but an intensification of this old motor weakness in the legs. This old fear of falling now became associated with the idea of the spinal fracture and was thus thoroughly rationalized. The old phobia of falling was the real forerunner of her later paresis.

The day before she had had to go to the bathroom all the time. The movements of her intestines and bladder were "extraordinarily lively." The previous night she had been restless.

In the late forenoon, she felt unable to urinate. She felt her legs were without sensation. On examination, I found a reduced sensitivity to pin pricks up to the 10th segment. The knee jerk, the Achilles reflex and the abdominal reflexes were normal. I had been told on the telephone that she was unable to move her legs. In reality, the motility of the legs was only reduced, but not absent. The deep sensitivity of the joints of the toes was reduced. It was the picture of a functional paresis. There were no definite symptoms either of a flaccid or of a spastic paralysis. The only point in support of the assumption that the lesion of the 12th vertebra had something to do with it was the fact that the sensory disturbance in the upper abdomen had a fairly sharp upper limit.

The next day, the patient was again able to urinate, but three days later she became unable to control her anal sphincter. The reflexes were normal, but the patient's fear of sitting up returned.

She was again taken to a hospital for a general check-up. Xrays showed the spine, pelvis and legs free from metastases, but there were new metastases in the cranium and in the humerus. That is, *the new tumors made their appearance far away from those regions which showed the paresis. Functional biopathy and carcinomatous growth had nothing to do with each other.*

The patient remained at the hospital for two weeks. No neurological examination was done. The paresis of the legs was considered a result of the vertebral lesions; none of the physicians discovered its functional nature. They told the relatives that the patient would live for two weeks at best.

As nothing was done for the patient at the hospital except that she was given morphine injections, the relatives took her back home. I saw her on the day of her return. She was very apprehensive about her motions and stressed the fact that the hospital physicians had warned her to be extremely cautious in her motions because "the spinal column was pressing on the nerve and it might break." This admonition on the part of the physicians naturally confirmed and reinforced the patient's phobia. The relatives wished me to undertake another experiment with orgone in order to eliminate the tumors of the cranium. On that day, I was not able to palpate any tumors at the cranium.

I observed the patient for another four weeks at her home. During this time, *all reflexes at the legs were normal, the bowels and the bladder functioned normally again.* However, the atrophy of the musculature and the bones progressed rapidly. She had developed a putrid bed sore at the buttocks. The legs moved in reaction to painful stimuli, but showed few spontaneous impulses. She continued to have nightmares of men falling into an abyss, of an elephant charging at her and of being "as if paralyzed," unable to move. During the day, also, she felt anxiety in the eyes and in the chest. The pains had completely disappeared, but the fear of motion and of a spinal fracture persisted.

We had a special orgone accumulator built for her bed. The effect of the orgone showed itself in a reduction of the pulse rate from about 130 to between 80 and 90, in a general feeling of well-being and the disappearance of anxiety. The blood picture, which in the past few months had taken a turn for the worse (50% Hb., T-bodies, positive T-cultures, about 50% T on autoclavation) also improved rapidly. The impulses in the legs increased in frequency and intensity.

Then there occurred a sudden and unforeseeable catastrophe which sealed the fate of the patient. One night, as she moved in bed, she fractured her left femur. She had to be taken to a hospital. The physicians were amazed at the thinness of the femur. They could not understand how the breast tumor could have disappeared. The patient was given morphine, declined during the following four weeks and finally died.

The orgone therapy had prolonged her life for about 10 months, had kept her free of cancer tumors and cancer pains for months and had restored the function of her blood system to normal. The interruption of the orgone treatment by the biopathic paralysis interdicts any conjecture as to a possible favorable outcome. What is certain is that in this case the real cause of death was the biopathic shrinking, and not the local tumors.

This case has given us important insights into the emotional and vegetative background of the cancer disease. Now we are confronted by the important question as to *what takes place in the blood and the tissues as a result of the biopathic shrinking;* in other words, the question as to how the general shrinking of the autonomic system produces local tumors. I may anticipate: *The general result of biopathic shrinking is putrefaction in the blood and the tissues. The cancer tumor is only one of the symptoms of this process of putrefaction.* This finding requires extensive clinical and experimental substantiation; this will be given elsewhere.

CONCLUSION

Let us briefly review our observations. The "dying" of the patient in the biopathic attack did not in the least give the impression of hysteria or simulation. The autonomic system reacted in such fashion that actual death was by no means improbable. The sunken cheeks, the cyanotic color, the faint, rapid pulse, the spasm of the throat, the failure of motility and the general physical debility were dangerous realities.

I venture the statement that each of these attacks was the beginning of an actual cessation of the vital functions. It was possible, by dissolving the spasms and by breaking the diaphragmatic block again and again to interrupt the process of dying. Death was again and again counteracted by vagotonic expansion. This cannot be a matter of *suggestion.* Suggestion in the usual sense could not possibly penetrate into these depths of the biological apparatus. What was possible, however, was to elicit the biological impulses to expansion in various bodily systems and thus, month after month, to arrest the shrinking process again and again. In order to do this, a good rapport with the patient, as a *part* of the vegetotherapeutic technique, was, of course, indispensable. Only in this aspect of the procedure might one be justified in speaking of suggestion.

Let us go back to our familiar diagram of psychosomatic functioning and try to find out at which place in the vital apparatus the biopathy (in contrast to a mechanical lesion), as well as the vegetotherapeutic experiment, takes effect:

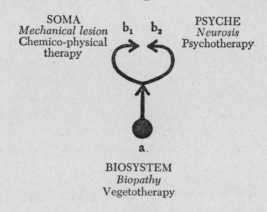

with the captions:

SOMA
Mechanical lesion
Chemico-physical
therapy

b_1 b_2

PSYCHE
Neurosis
Psychotherapy

a.

BIOSYSTEM
Biopathy
Vegetotherapy

Every lasting energy stasis in the *biological system* (a) must of necessity manifest itself in *somatic* as well as *psychic* symptoms (b_1 and b_2). Psychotherapy attacks the psychic symptoms, chemico-physical therapy the somatic symptoms. *Vegetotherapy* has as its starting point the fact that psyche as well as soma have, from a point of view of bio-energy, the same root in the pulsating plasma system (blood and autonomic system). Vegetotherapy thus influences not the psychophysical function itself, but the common basis of psychic as well as somatic functions; it does this by eliminating the *inhibitions of biological functioning*, such as the respiratory block, the inhibition of the orgasm reflex, etc. Thus, vegetotherapy is neither a psychic therapy nor a physiological-chemical one; *it is biological therapy directed at the disturbances of pulsation in the vital apparatus.* Since these disturbances show their effects in all the more superficial layers of the psychosomatic apparatus—for example, as hypertension and cardiac neurosis in the somatic, as phobia in the psychic realm—vegetotherapy, of necessity, reaches these symptoms in the superficial layers also. Vegetotherapy, thus, is the most advanced existing method for the influencing of biopathic disturbances. For the time being, its field is limited to the biopathies. In the cancer biopathy, the vegetotherapeutic treatment of the disturbances of respiration and of the orgasm is supplemented by the *orgone therapy* which is directed at the anemia, the T-bacilli in the blood and the local tumors. As succeeding articles will show, we are fully aware of the enormous complexity of the problem as well as of the largely experimental character of this cancer therapy.

According to the prevalent concepts there are only mechanical or chemical lesions of the somatic apparatus on the one hand and functional disturbances of the psychic apparatus on the other. Sex-economic investigation of the cancer shrinking biopathy reveals a third, more deep-reaching disturbance: *The disturbance of the plasma pulsation at the common biological basis of soma and psyche.* What is fundamentally new here is the finding that *the inhibition of the autonomic sexual function can produce a biopathic shrinking of the autonomic nervous system.* The question remains whether this etiology can be found in all forms of cancer.

There is a general misconception that the organism is divided into two independent parts: one is the physico-chemical system, "soma," which is destroyed by such agents as a cancer; the other is the "psyche" which produces hysterical phenomena, so-called conversion symptoms, in the body, and which "wants" or "fears" this or that and has nothing to do with the cancer. This artificial splitting up of the organism is misleading. It is not true that a psychic apparatus "makes use of somatic phenomena"; nor is it true that the somatic apparatus obeys only chemical and physical laws, but does neither "wish" nor "fear." In reality, *the functions of expansion and contraction in the autonomic plasma system represent the unitary apparatus which makes the "soma" live or die.* Our patient demonstrated *the functional unity of psychic resignation and biopathic shrink-*

ing exceedingly well. In her, life began to function poorly; the function of expansion began to fail. To express it psychologically: there was no impulse behind motion, action, decision and struggle. The vital apparatus was, as it were, fixed in the reaction of anxiety; psychologically, this was represented in her fear that motion might result in a fracture somewhere in the body. Now, motion, action, pleasure and expansion appeared to be "a danger to life." The characterological resignation *preceded* the shrinking of the vital apparatus.

The motility of the biological plasma system itself is damaged by the biopathic shrinking. The fear of motion has its basis exactly in this vegetative shrinking. The plasma system shrinks, the organism loses its autonomic balance and the self-regulation of locomotion. Finally, a shrinking of the body substance sets in.

The inhibition of plasmic motility by the shrinking fully explains all aspects of the disease picture; it explains neurotic anxiety as well as functional paresis, the fear of falling as well as the muscular atrophy, the spasms as well as the biological disturbance which breaks through as "cancer" and finally ends in general cachexia. For it was possible again and again to make the patient develop new living impulses by vegetotherapeutically correcting her breathing. The diaphragmatic spasm is the central defense mechanism in the biopathic disturbance of the organism: The patient really breathes poorly; she really ventilates her tissues insufficiently; the plasmatic locomotor impulses are actually insufficient for the maintenance of co-ordinated movements; the fear of falling and of suffering damage has a real basis and is not "imaginary"; more than that, *the imagined catastrophe of falling has itself a real basis in the restriction of biological motility.* The hysterical, functional character of the paresis thus gains a factual biopathological basis. There is a difference only in degree between hysterical paralysis and paralysis as a result of biopathic shrinking.

In medicine, functional paralyses are usually looked at with some irony; the concept is still prevalent that a functional paralysis is more or less "simulated." I would like to state that functional disturbances of motility are *much more serious and far-reaching* than are paralyses which result from a mechanical lesion. In the case of the mechanical lesion, the biological functioning of the total organism is not affected. *A functional paralysis*, on the other hand, *is the expression of a total biological disturbance*. In this case, the function of plasmatic impulse formation in the biological core of the organism is itself disturbed and may result in a more or less extensive loss of tissue (muscular atrophy, anemia, cachexia, etc.). To say that the mechanical lesion cannot be influenced by suggestion, while the functional disturbance is amenable to suggestion, means nothing. For the "suggestion" which may bring about an improvement in the functional paralysis is in reality nothing but a pleasurable stimulus for the biological system and thus causes it to reach out for new life possibilities and to function again.

The basic disturbance in the functioning of the body plasm, represented by chronic sexual stasis, character rigidity and resignation, and by chronic sympatheticotonia, is to be taken much more seriously than the mechanical lesions. The mechanistic and purely materialistic concepts of medicine of today have to be partly replaced and partly overcome by a functional concept. This functional concept made it possible to make a breach in the wall which hitherto has made the cancer problem inaccessible. Succeeding articles will show to what extent this functional concept is generally applicable. We shall next turn our attention to the local changes in blood and tissues which are caused by the biopathic shrinking.

Concluded February 10, 1942

V. ORGONOMIC FUNCTIONALISM

1. ANIMISM, MYSTICISM, AND MECHANISM

We must ask: Was the ignorance of living functioning only the result of imperfect thought technique and insufficient research data? Or was it the result of a characterological block, unconscious intention, so to speak? The history of science leaves no doubt that the living was not *allowed* to be investigated; that it was the mechanistic-mystical structure of humanity over thousands of years, which with all—but *all*—conceivable means blocked the investigation of the cosmic basis of the living. And there was *method* in this structural intention: First, in the religious taboo on thought which, from the very start, established God and life as unknowable; then in the fact that many religious prohibitions punished knowledge of the living with death. The myth of Adam and Eve has a deep rational meaning: To eat from the tree of knowledge meant to be chased from paradise with fire and sword. It is a *snake*, thus a symbol of the phallus and simultaneously of the biological original movement, which persuades Eve to tempt Adam. They pluck the forbidden apple and eat of it. Shame overcomes them. The sexual symbolism is unequivocal: "Whoever eats of the tree of knowledge knows God and life, and that will be punished," we are warned. *The knowledge of the law of love leads to the knowledge of the law of life, and that of the law of life leads to knowledge of God.* This sequence is true in each feature and is confirmed by the development of the discovery of the cosmic energy in the

From *Ether, God and Devil*, 1949.

273

twentieth century. The punishments which followed this discovery were in complete harmony with the old biblical saying.

It is incorrect that the orgone energy and thus the functional
law which blends living and nonliving nature into *one* were
discovered by me for the first time. In the course of 2,000 years
of human history, men again and again struck upon phenomena
of orgone energy or they developed systems of thought which
were in the direction of orgone energy. That this knowledge
hitherto did not break through lay in the fact that the same
human character traits which created the religious thought
taboo, rendered sterile every advance in the proper scientific
direction. The weapons of destruction were always basically
either mechanistic pseudo-scientific explaining away of the
facts or mystical bowdlerization, where actual bodily violence
was not applied.

I can only bring forth scattered examples from different
epochs, and must leave to the historians a thorough presentation of the systematic war of extermination which the emotional plague waged against the conception of the functional
equation: God = life = cosmic orgone energy = orgonomic
functional law of nature = gravitational law.

Even among the Greeks, there was a rigid and fanatical orthodoxy
which depended as much upon the interest of an arrogant priest-
hood as upon the faith of a salvation-craving multitude. One would
perhaps have completely forgotten this had not Socrates been com-
pelled to drink the hemlock; but also Aristotle fled from Athens so
that the city would not commit another crime against philosophy
["philosophy" in ancient times played the role of contemporary
natural science—W. R.]. Protagoras had to flee, and his manuscript
on the Gods was burned by the state. Anaxagoras was imprisoned
and had to flee. Theodorus the "atheist" and apparently also
Diogenes of Apollonia were persecuted as deniers of God. And all
that happened in humane Athens. From the viewpoint of the masses,
everyone, even the most ideal philosopher, could be persecuted as
an "atheist," for none thought of the Gods as the priestly tradition
prescribed them to think.

So writes Friedrich Albert Lange in his history of materialism. What enabled Greek philosophy to pave the way for the
development of scientic materialism as opposed to superstition?
It was the energetic hypothesis of "soul atoms," thus a scientific
presentiment of the existence of a special energy, the orgone,
which is at the basis of psychic functions.

Materialistic philosophy started not with mechanical, but—
strangely enough—with *psychological* basic questions, exactly
as orgone biophysics had its origin in psychiatric problems of
biological drive dynamics: WHAT IS SENSATION? HOW CAN MAT-
TER PERCEIVE ITSELF? WHAT IS SENSATION BOUND TO? UNDER
WHICH CONDITIONS IS THERE SENSATION AND UNDER WHICH IS
SENSATION ABSENT?

Ancient natural science, distinguished then, and to this day
leading in the right direction in its tendencies, proceeded not
from materialistic, but from *functional* problems, which *included* and did not exclude sensation. In these functional processes, and not in materialistic questions, did the scientific spirit
emerge in contrast to the metaphysical and mystical. In these
questions was kindled the raging battle of the emotional plague
against the equation *God = natural law*. In these questions, and
originally not in the mechanical laws of gravitation, the burning struggle began for the correct conception of the world and
the processes in it. For it was clear to every investigating spirit
that it is solely our *sensation* of the natural processes inside and
outside ourselves, which holds the keys to the deep riddles of
nature. The sensation of living protoplasm is a real phenomenon, *this side of*, and not beyond, human life. Sensation is the
sieve through which all inner and outer stimuli are perceived;
sensation is the connecting link between ego and outer world.
This is indeed well known in natural philosophy as in natural
sciences which are aware of their methods of investigation. All
the more unusual is it that scientific research on just this central
part of its own nature had nothing to say about its essential
tool until a short time ago, and that mysticism could have

occupied the realm of living sensations so completely and so destructively.

Such grotesque facts have always a definite function and a secret intention. Naturally, it would be false to assume that sometime, somewhere, a secret council of armored human beings had held a conference, and decided how the knowledge of sensation, the connecting gate between ego and nature, should be blocked, how mercilessly the revealers of this secret of nature should be punished, persecuted, burned, tortured. No, there was no secret deliberation and there were no decrees. The deadly battle of the emotional plague against the knowledge of the nature of sensation was guided and executed by the *characterological laws* of *armored* human animals.

It was, first of all, the *character-analytic theory of structure* which broke the spell and opened the door for insight into the nature of sensation. The subsequent discovery of the biological energy phenomena within the perceiving organism and the further discovery of the atmospheric orgone energy in the purely physical sense were only the logical results of the *first* act: *The discovery that sensation is a function of excitation, that thus, in other words, a functional identity exists between quantity of an excitation and intensity of a sensation.* With this formulation, sensation itself had become the object of natural-scientific investigation. The further consequences of this discovery speak for themselves.

Sensation is a function of the skin membrane, which demarcates the living system from the surrounding orgone ocean. Through this membrane, the orgonotic living body communicates with all other orgone systems. It is no accident that the sensory nerves develop from the ectoderm, the *outer* germinal layer of the gastrula.

Since this view of nature is a result of the biological constitution of the natural observer, the world picture cannot be separated from the creator of the world picture. In short, *against the natural research which created the atomic bomb stands the natural research which discovered the cosmic orgone energy, sharp, clear, and incompatible.*

It is a matter of deciding the question whether nature is an "empty space with a few widely scattered specks," or whether it is *a space full of cosmic primordial energy, a continuum which functions in a lively way and obeys a generally valid natural law.*

The *technician* of physics, whose thinking was formed by the mechanistic world outlook, believes that all—but *all*—physical problems are essentially solved. His world picture is based on the fact that planes can be guided by fine apparatus so that the living pilot is excluded. The onslaught of the most infamous weapon for murder since human thinking began, he considers the "beginning of a new era of atomic energy." His world is falling to pieces under his feet, but his world picture is tight and compact, filled with "empty space and some small specks." We do not wish to concern ourselves with him any longer, although his opinion represents an essential part of the general thinking. In his ideology, the living has no place. Moreover, the *practical* result of his outlook is *destructive:* in theory, through the exclusion of living substance from all observation, in practice through social murder and war.

It is a different story with the *founders* of this dead and sterile world outlook. The founders of the empty and lifeless universe are clever and learned men. They do not believe that all problems are solved. On the contrary, they freely admit that their physical picture is in urgent need of correction. They are in contradiction with their own theory. According to their own words, they have given up reality and have withdrawn into an ivory tower of mathematical symbols. No reproach is meant when we say that they have withdrawn from the real world into a shadow world, and that they operate only with shadow things and abstract symbols. Each can do and refrain from doing as he pleases so long as he harms no one. Still—does this kind of influence harm no one? Is not the damage proven, since this kind of physics excluded the human being, mystified the living, and, in its direction of research—whether it wished to or not—landed again and again in explosive substances?

I will attempt to describe the sensory apparatus of the mechanistic observer who has built the mechanistic world picture. How does it happen, we must ask, that mechanistic physics is declared bankrupt by its most prominent representatives, but so far has not found the capacity to break through the iron ring of its thinking, in which it feels itself imprisoned? If we remain consistent and make the character structure of the physicist responsible for the mechanistic world picture, then the questions must be raised: How is the mechanistic character structured? What special qualities create the helplessness in natural observation? Whence stems this character structure? And, finally, in what social processes did it arise?

It is not my task here to give a history of mechanistic natural science. It is sufficient to speak from experience and to describe the typical mechanistic physicist as he is revealed to psychiatric investigation.

The typical mechanistic physicist thinks according to the principles of machine construction, which he essentially has to serve. A machine has to be *perfect*. Hence the thinking and acts of the physicist must be "perfect." *Perfectionism* is an essential characteristic of mechanistic thinking. It tolerates no mistakes; uncertainties, shifting situations are unwelcome. The mechanist works on artificial models of nature when he experiments. The mechanistic experiment of the 20th century has lost the essential part of genuine research: the handling and imitation of *natural* processes, which stamped the work of all pioneers in natural science. All machines of the *same type* are alike to the finest details. Deviations are observed as errors. That is fully correct in the realm of machine construction. But this principle, when applied to processes in nature, inevitably leads into confusion. *Nature is inexact. Nature operates not mechanically, but functionally.* Hence the mechanist always misses nature when he applies to it his mechanistic principles. There is a *lawful* harmony in natural functions, which penetrates and rules all being. But this harmony and lawfulness is not the strait-jacket of mechanistic technology into which mechanistic man has forced his character and his civilization. Mechanistic civilization is a *deviation from natural law;* more, it is a *perversion of nature,* a life-inimical variant, as a mad dog represents a sick variant of the species, dog. Hence mechanistic man can find no access to nature, outside the construction of machines.

Natural processes are characterized by the lack of any kind of perfectionism, in spite of the lawfulness of their functions. In a naturally thriving forest, to be sure, a unitary principle of growth functions. Yet there are no two trees, and, in the hundreds of thousands of trees, no two leaves which would be photographically identical. The realm of variation is infinitely wider than the realm of uniformity. Although the unitary natural law functions and is to be detected not only in the basis of all nature, but also in each single and smallest detail, there is nothing in nature that could be traced to perfectionism. Natural processes are *uncertain,* in spite of their lawfulness. Perfectionism and uncertainty are mutually exclusive. One cannot advance the functions of our solar system as a refutation of this assertion. To be sure, the orbits of the sun and the planets have not changed for thousands of years. But thousands of years, indeed millions of years, play only a small role in the natural process. The origin of the planetary system is as uncertain as its future. This is widely known. Thus even the planetary system, this "perfect" mechanism of the astrophysicist, is imperfect, in the "unlawful" fluctuations of thermical periods, sun spots, earthquakes, etc. Neither weather formation nor the tides function according to mechanical laws. The failure of scientific mechanism in these realms of nature is plain; their dependency on the functions of a primordial cosmic energy is basically just as clear. There is a natural law, so much is certain. But this natural law is not mechanical.

Perfectionism is, then, a compulsive correctness of machine civilization, correct *within* but *not outside* the realm of mechanistic functions, of the artificial models of nature. As every-

thing within the thought framework of formalistic logic is
logical and outside this framework is illogical; as everything is
consistent within the framework of abstract mathematics and
outside it has no factual frame of reference; as all principles
within the authoritarian educational system are consistent, but
outside it are unusable and inimical to education, so also is
mechanistic perfectionism unscientific outside its mechanistic
realm, and, as a sham exactitude, constitutes a drag-chain on
natural research. Research without mistakes is impossible. All
natural research is, and was from its very beginning, explora-
tive, "unlawful," labile, eternally reshaping, in flux, uncertain
and unsure, yet still in contact with *real* natural processes. For
these objective natural processes are in all their basic lawfulness variable to the highest degree, *free* in the sense of irregular, incalculable, and unrepeatable.

It is just this freedom intrinsic in nature which makes our
mechanists anxious when they encounter it. The mechanist does
not tolerate uncertainty. However, this freedom is neither metaphysical nor mystical, but *functionally* lawful.

Character-analysis has here gained several decisive insights.
It was important to apply the psychiatric insights into human
reactions to the—in itself—incomprehensible, hate-filled rejection of orgonomic phenomena. In my publications, I have
repeatedly asserted how astonishing it was that the cosmic
orgone energy had been so basically and so consistently overlooked by physicists. This oversight, continuing over centuries,
could be no accident. My psychiatric occupation placed me
in the fortunate position of solving a part of the riddle in the
character-analysis of an extraordinarily gifted, but inhibited
physicist of the classical mechanistic school. The help which he
himself provided in the therapy was of great value.

We found that ever since childhood a vigorous and dreamy
cosmic longing had developed. It had brought him to physics.
The core of this fantasy was the idea of floating quite alone in
the universe among stars. A concrete recollection from the age
of two rooted this fantasy in objective historical processes: As

a small child, the physicist had nightly observed the stars through his window. IIe waited for their appearance with an excitation mixed with anxiety. His "flight into world space" also had the function of allowing him to escape from very painful situations in his parents' home. The severe inhibition, which I mentioned earlier, had its origin precisely in these painful experiences which led him into the universe. At the same time, they remained as lasting inhibitions of his capacity for surrender and as a block on his organ sensations. As we now approached the liberation of his orgastic sensations, severe anxiety developed, an anxiety which formed the core of his work inhibition. It was the same fear of his powerful organ sensations which he had developed as a child. In organ sensation, man experiences the orgone function of nature in his own body. This function was now charged with strong anxiety and consequently was blocked. Our physicist wished to dedicate himself to orgone biophysics, the correctness and significance of which he was convinced. He had observed the orgone in the metal darkroom and described it in detail. Still, when he had to approach the work *practically*, a severe inhibition set in, the same inhibition whose core was the fear of complete letting-go, of entire surrender to his own bodily sensations. In the process of orgone therapy, the sequence of pushing forward and terrified withdrawal was repeated so often and in so typical a fashion that there could be no doubt about the *identity of the fear of organ sensations and the fear of scientific orgone research.*

The hate reactions which developed in the process were exactly the same as those one meets in the usual intercourse with physicists or physicians in questions of orgone energy. Our clinical experience can be generalized: *It is the fear of the autonomic organ sensations which blocks the recognition of orgone energy.*

Self-perception is the most difficult and deepest problem of natural science. The understanding of sensation will also pave the way to the comprehension of self-perception. We recognize the capacity for sensation in living organisms in their *response to stimuli.* The response to stimuli is inseparably knitted with an EMOTION, in other words, with *movement of the protoplasm.* We know that an organism has perceived the stimulus when it answers it with movement. The emotional response to stimuli is functionally identical with the sensation, not only quantitatively but also *qualitatively.* Just as all stimuli which an organism meets can, in principle, be traced to two basic types, pleasurable and unpleasurable, so, in principle, are all sensations reducible to two basic emotions, *pleasure* and *unpleasure.* This fact was already known in pre-Freudian psychology; it was emphasized by Freud in his libido theory. The accomplishment of orgonomy lay in the fact that it succeeded in functionally equating *pleasure* with biological *expansion,* and *unpleasure* or anxiety with biological *contraction.*

Expansion and contraction are at bottom *physical* functions, which are encountered in the *nonliving* realms of nature. Thus, they embrace much wider realms than the emotions. It is to be assumed that there is no emotion without expansion and contraction, but that, on the other hand, expansion and contraction function without emotion, as in the atmospheric orgone. In this way, we arrive at the conclusion that in the development of living matter emotions are added to orgonotic expansion and contraction when certain conditions are fulfilled. A preliminary assumption is that *emotion is tied to the existence and movement of protoplasmic substance within a demarcated system and does not exist without this pre-condition.* But in another connection we will meet a *stimulus sensitivity* of the purely physical orgone energy, when the medium of electromagnetic waves will be discussed.

Many problems await concrete answers. Still, however many unclarities may cloud our view, it is certain that, from now on, sensation and emotion are *within* and no longer outside *physical,* natural-scientific observations, as hitherto. Mechanistic research *must* exclude sensation and perception because it cannot grasp them. But, since sensation and emotion are the immediate and less doubtable experiences of the living organism, they had to strike the attention of ancient natural philosophy and urge an explanation. In his book *The Meeting of East and West*, Northrop has related what significance immediate organ sensation had for the whole natural philosophy of the old Asiatic cultures. For Democritus, sensation was not a metaphysical or mystical function. It was not to be ascribed to any God. It was treated in the framework of physical functions and was ascribed to special, particularly smooth and fine atoms. This ancient concept is far superior to that of "modern" natural science and comes far closer to the natural processes.

The primitive concept of emotional life was not mystical as is the present-day concept, neither spiritualistic nor metaphysical, but *animistic*. Nature was conceived as "animated," but *this animation was modeled after one's own objective experiences of sensation*. The spirits had *earthly* form, the sun and the stars behaved like *actual, living* human beings. The souls of the deceased lived on in real animals. The primitive animistic mind did not change the world inside or outside itself. The sole thing which it did in contrast to the natural-scientific world picture, was that it ascribed *objective* functions to *objective* objects where they did not belong; it transferred its own reality into a foreign one, in short, it *projected*. The primitive mind thought very close to reality when it equated the fruitfulness of the earth with the fruitfulness of a female body, or when it thought of the cloud which gave rain as a perceiving creature. It animated nature according to its own sensations and functions; it *animated* it but it did *not mystify it* as its great-great-grandchild did centuries later. In the strict sense of the term, *"mysticism" signifies here the changing of sense impressions and organ sensations into supernatural and unreal entities*. Anthropology teaches us that the devil with tail and pitchfork, or the angel with wings is a late product of human fantasy and no longer imitates reality but is created from an imagination which distorts reality. "Devil" and "angel" correspond to human structural sensations which already *deviate basically* from those of the animals or primitive men. "Hell," "heaven," formless blue-gray spirits, dangerous monsters, and tiny pygmies are likewise representations of *unnatural, distorted* organ sensations.

The process of animating the surrounding world is the same in animistically thinking primitives and in mystics. Both animate nature through projection of their bodily sensations. *The distinction between animism and mysticism lies in the fact that the first projects natural, undistorted sensations, the second, on the other hand, unnatural, perverted organ sensations.* In both cases, we can reconstruct the emotional structure of the organism from the mythology. But we can also see the radical difference which here appears. It reveals the transition from *one* biological form of existence to *another, basically different* mode of living of the human animal.

We can still characterize animism as a *realistic* natural conception, even if the animating idea and the animated object do not concur in reality. For both idea and object are objective, *unchanged* realities. On the other hand, we cannot regard mysticism as a true natural concept, for in it not only is the outer, but also the individual's inner world distorted, *changed* from natural law. To be sure, a cloud or the sun is not animated in reality; but, for animism, the form and function of the cloud and sun are unchanged. On the other hand, a devil or an angel no longer corresponds—in form or function—to any reality. The sole reality which the mystical kind of animation is based upon is the distorted organ sensation of the armored human being.

This analysis is of decisive significance for the clarification of some basic questions in natural-scientific research. Later, we will meet in Kepler an animistic conception of planetary functions which we should not mistake for mysticism. Kepler has often been accused of mysticism. It is also known that Galileo, who founded the mechanistic laws of functioning, was not on good terms with Kepler. We will also see in Newton an animism whose meaning we will have to understand. It is important to separate onself here from the unfounded feeling of superiority on the part of the mechanists, who explain away as "mysticism" the animistic attempts of a Kepler or Newton to understand the harmonic natural law. We will have to show that our mechanists are far more mystical than they themselves suspect, and are much further removed from nature than was primitive animism. It can be shown historically that mechanism in natural science was not a reaction against the animism of a Democritus or Kepler, but a reaction against the rampant mysticism of the church in the Middle Ages. The Christian Church had exchanged the close-to-nature animism of early scientific workers and the life-closeness of its own founders for mysticism, which was far removed from both nature and life. The mystical bishop condemned the animistic "witch" to the stake. Till Ulenspiegel was a nature-loving animist, Phillip II of Spain a sadistic-brutal mystic. Functional natural science must defend primitive animism against perverse mysticism and take from it all experiential elements which correspond to the *perception of nature.*

Narrow-minded mechanists of natural science now accuse functionalism of "mysticism." This reproach rests on the assumption that whoever tries to understand mysticism is mystical. The mechanist does not understand emotional processes; they are alien to him, within as experience and without as object of research. One will search in vain in any handbook of neurology or organ pathology for an investigation of the emotions. On the other hand, the emotions are the experiential material of mysticism. Thus, whoever—so asserts the narrow-minded conclusion of the mechanists—is concerned with emotions, is mystical. The comprehension of the emotions is so foreign to mechanistic thinking that there is no room in it for their natural-scientific observation. *Functionalism cannot overlook emotion, and it is capable of bringing emotion into the realm of scientific thought.* This the mechanist now mistakes for "mysticism." Above all, it is psychiatrists without a natural-scientific orientation and party-political drifters who condemn orgonomy as mystical, because they do not distinguish mysticism from the investigation of mysticism.

If the mechanistic physician cannot determine any change

in the chemical composition of the blood or any alteration of tissue structure, then no illness exists for him, even if the patient actually dies. The functional physician, the orgone therapist, knows the *bodily* function of emotions. He understands how one can "die from grief." For "grief" is functionally identical with a shrinking of the autonomic nervous system, a protracted shock, so to speak. "Functional fever" is no fantasy of the brain for him, but an objective, *biophysically* unmistakable excitation of the biosystem.

The distinction between animism and mysticism has its significance in the fact that now the *orgone-physical* motility of *living* substance can be distinguished from the *animation* of a *lifeless* substance (= animism), and from the grotesque distortion of organ sensations (= mysticism). For the mystic, a soul "lives" in the body. There is no connection between body and soul, save the one that the soul influences the body and the body the soul. Body and soul are for the mystics (and for the mechanists, in so far as they recognize the psychic at all) sharply separated realms which only stand in an interacting relationship. This is valid for psychophysical parallelism as well as for the mechanistic and the psychologistic causal relationship, body → psyche or psyche → body. Functional identity as the *research principle* of orgonomic functionalism is nowhere so splendidly expressed as in the *unity* of psyche and soma, emotion and excitation, sensation and stimulus. *This unity or identity as the basic principle of the concept of the living excludes completely and conclusively the "other-wordliness" or autonomy of the psychic.* Emotion and sensation *are* and *remain* tied to the orgone-physical excitation. Hence this also excludes any kind of mysticism. For the essence of mysticism is the concept of a supernatural *autonomy* of emotions and sensations. *Therefore, any natural concept which assumes an autonomy of the psychic, no matter what it calls itself, is mystical.* This is valid for mechanism which cannot deny sensation, although it would like to very much, and which cannot comprehend sensation, although it should. It is obviously valid for any kind of outspoken mysticism, especially religious spiritualism. But it is also valid for psychophysical parallelism. Hence psychoanalysis also thinks mystically in so far as it does not see that the drives are concretely rooted in physiologically tangible excitations.

Furthermore, from the sharp distinction between animism and mysticism there follows a sharp distinction in the direction of research:

Animism proceeds from its own organ sensations which express that organs are *moving* and *alive*, or, what amounts to the same thing, *animated*. Although the animist concludes directly from experience, he cannot say anything about the *nature* of sensation, movement, and animation. Motility is the direct experiential material by means of which the child forms his ideas. As long as the child has undisturbed, naturally functioning organ sensations, it can, to be sure, arrive at an incorrect explanation of immobile matter, for the child falsely animates it; but where the healthily perceiving child describes moving, living matter, he will judge *correctly*. If this function is continued later in natural research, then he will, as in the case of a Sigmund Freud, develop the concept that there is a "psychic energy," which is anchored in bodily processes. This judgment is correct, for the psychic is conceived as *motile*, and movement is energy-shifting in the strictest physical sense. The discovery of the orgone proceeded in fact from this correct animistic concept: *Research on the nature of sensation led through thought technique and practical experimentation to the discovery of the physical orgone energy, which has specific biological functions.*

In antithesis, the mystical concepts of psychic motility never led to the discovery of physical energy processes. Not in principle, because the psychic has no connection with the physical world for the mystic. And not in practice, because the mystical human being does not experience his organ sensations directly as does the animistically thinking and feeling child, but *always only as in a distorted mirror*. The mystic may describe the orgonotic currents and excitations, he may often even supply details with an astonishing exactness. But he will never determine them quantitatively, just as one cannot weigh the mirror image of a block of wood on the scales.

We have determined by controlled, clinical experiences that there is always a *wall inserted* between organ sensation and objective excitation in mystical human beings. This wall is objective; it is the muscular armor of the mystic. Every attempt to bring a mystic into *direct* contact with his excitations causes anxiety or even fainting. He can feel the emotion as in a mirror, but *not really*. This assertion is based on an experience which I have often had: If the orgone-therapeutic dissolution of the armor in the mystic is successful, then the "mystical experiences" disappear. *Thus, the existence of a separating wall between excitation and sensation is the basis of the mystical experience.*

The mystical experience is rarely found without brutal-sadistic impulses. Furthermore, to my knowledge orgastic potency is not found in mystics nor mysticism in orgastically potent individuals.

Accordingly, mysticism rests on a blocking of direct organ sensations, and on the re-emergence of these sensations in the pathological perception of "supernatural powers." This is valid for spiritualists, schizophrenics, religious physicists, and for every form of paranoia. If, then, a mystical character, with the given conditions of his structure, tries to describe nature, he will only be able to reach *one* result: A picture of reality in which, to be sure, the real processes are mirrored, not, however, in harmony with objective processes, but *distorted:* as an influence by electric currents in paranoid schizophrenics, as a blue-gray vaporous ghost in spiritualists, as a sensation of the "world spirit" in religious epileptics, as the "absolute" in metaphysics. Each one of these judgments contains a bit of truth: The orgonotic prickling sensations are the "electric currents" of the schizophrenic; the blue color of the orgone is the blue-gray spirit of the spiritualists; the cosmic universality of the orgone energy is the "world spirit" and the "absolute" of the mystical character.

Thus both the animist and the mystic touch on reality. The difference is the distortion of reality into the absolute or grotesque in mystics, the animation of the inanimate in animists. The assertions of the mystics are easy to see through and to refute. Those of the animists are more difficult to refute, and easier to comprehend rationally. The concept spread and confirmed so widely of a harmony in nature is at bottom an animistic concept, which in the mystic is degraded into a personified world spirit or into a godlike universal being. The mystic remains stuck in the absolute. The absolute is intangible. The animist keeps moving. His outlooks are shifting. And, compared with the mystic, he has the advantage that his natural outlook contains a *practical* core of truth. *The animist Kepler, who formulated the planetary harmonic law, is, after centuries, correct with his "vis animalis" which moves the planets.* THE SAME ENERGY WHICH GOVERNS THE MOVEMENTS OF ANIMALS AND THE GROWTH OF ALL LIVING SUBSTANCE ALSO ACTUALLY MOVES THE HEAVENLY BODIES.

In the functional identity of organismic and cosmic orgone is to be sought the origin of all animistic and genuinely religious world concepts. In it, we also have the *rational core* of animism and genuine religiosity before us; we must free this rational core from its mystical wrapping in order to reach the rewarding naked kernel that leads us, in strict natural-scientific fashion, to the *physical* function of the cosmic energy. Under "physical function" is here understood the *orgonomic law of movement* which has to be formulated *orgonometrically*. The poetic and philosophic equation of life sensation and cosmic function is correct, but insufficient to bring the species of the human animal again into harmony with nature inside and outside himself. The human animal can only grasp and learn to love the nature inside and outside himself when he thinks and behaves as nature functions, namely, *functionally* and not mechanistically or mystically.

The world of orgonomic ("energetic") functionalism is a vigorous, free, and still lawful and harmonic world. In it, there is no "empty space" which the mechanistic physicist postulates because he cannot fill nature; in it, too, there is no space full of spirits and phantoms which mysticism believes in but is not able to demonstrate. The world of functionalism is, then, no "shadow world" as it is for the abstract mathematician, but it is a *tangible*, full, *pulsating* world, *perceivable* and *measurable* at the same time.

The abstract mathematician overlooks the fact that his formulae are only able to deal with objective processes because his thinking is a part of the same natural function which he grasps in abstract symbols. For the student of organ sensations it is possible to trace the sources from which the "higher" mathematician draws his insights without knowing it. Even if the functional symbols which he substitutes for the world are arbitrary and not intended to mirror a reality, still there can be no doubt that the *creator* of these functional symbols is a living pulsating orgonotic system who could create no mathematics if he did not pulsate. Hence "higher" mathematics could be presented as the highest product of natural-scientific development only because its rooting in pulsating nature was unknown or unadmitted. The brain of the mathematician is not a specially developed instrument; it is different only in that it can express organ sensations in mathematical form. Thus the mathematical formula is only one means of expression among many, and not the magic wand it appears to be to the warped understanding of mystical human beings. It is the living organism which arranges, regroups, and connects its sensations before it formulates them mathematically.

To the orgone biophysicist, it is well-known that one often finds the solutions of problems in one's sleep for which one struggled in vain during the day. I myself have formulated a whole group of functional equations, which I will have to present in another connection, in a state of half-sleep. I can gladly admit this since I am no representative of the superiority of "pure reason" over the "emotions"; since, furthermore, I know that the human mind is only an executive organ of investigating, living plasma feeling out its environment.

Sensation is, functionally seen, a tester of reality. The slowly feeling, undulating movements of animal antennae or tentacles illustrate what is meant here. Sensation forms the greatest riddle of natural science as death is the greatest plight of the living. Hence, functionalism knows correctly the worth of sensations and values them highly. Since it observes sensation as a *tool*, it is as careful for its cleanliness as a carpenter is for his plane. The functionalist will always keep arranging his perceptual and intellectual activity so that it is in harmony with his "experience." Where the amount of irrationality is small—and it can never be large in any work which investigates nature—one listens to the gentle urgings of the sensations which tell one whether one thinks correctly or falsely, colored by personal interests or clearly, whether one follows irrational inclinations or objective processes. All this has nothing to do with mysticism. It has solely to do with the *cleanliness of the sensory apparatus*, our tool of natural research. This clean condition is no "gift," no special "talent," but a continuous exertion, a prolonged practice in self-criticism and self-control. We learn how to control our sensory apparatus when we have to treat biopathic patients. Without a constantly clear sensory apparatus, without the capacity for cleaning it up when it becomes irrationally blurred, we could not take a step into the depths of human character structure, or mirror natural processes as they are.

Such observations and viewpoints in natural research (and the emotional life of mankind is certainly a part of nature!) are foreign to the chemists, the physicists of the old school, the astronomers and the technicians. They do not know the sensory apparatus with which they explore the world. They are able to control their acts only by experimentation, and experiments without organ sensation have, as we know, led mechanistic natural science nowhere in decisive questions of nature.

That is denied by the technicians of science, but admitted by prominent physicists.

The life function, then, has a manifold significance for us as natural researchers:

It forms, *first of all*, the *basis* of all living activity, and so also that of natural research. It is the harbor from which we undertake our research journeys and into which we return to rest, to shelter results, and to take on new provisions.

The life function is, *secondly*, our tool with which we feel out, investigate, arrange, and understand ourselves and nature around us. (The German word for "understand," *begreifen*, means literally to "feel out" or "touch.") The essential tool is *sensation*, be it inner organ sensation or outer sense perception.

The life function is, *thirdly*, an *object of our research*. The first and most important object is again organ sensations as tools as well as concrete natural phenomena. While we investigate the functioning of the living, we simultaneously investigate a part of external nature. Thus we must, if we proceed carefully through the material which represents the life function, concern ourselves with such functions as are generally, *cosmically valid*. This is a necessary and unavoidable conclusion: *The most general functioning principle is contained in the smallest, special functioning principle.*

Thus the life function becomes, as a part of objective, perceivable nature, a model of distinct, generally valid natural functions which originally have nothing to do with the living in itself. A thundercloud in itself has nothing to do with an ameba. Still it is possible through the observation of definite functions in the ameba to draw conclusions which are also valid for the thundercloud, for instance, the attraction which is exercised by highly-charged thunderclouds on smaller clouds just as it is exercised by an ameba on small bions.

Such strictly ordered and controlled natural research, such interlacing is strange and often horrifying to the mechanist. Under no conditions will he admit a connection between ameba and clouds, and he explains away this kind of thinking as humbug, charlatanry, or mysticism. For this reason, he also does not discover, starting from the energy development of bions in swollen matter, the same kind of energy in the atmosphere. For this reason, he speaks of *one and the same* phenomenon as "heat waves" if, as a meteorologist, he observes in *daylight* the flickering in the atmosphere, even at $-20°C$; as "bad seeing" and "diffused light" if, as an astronomer, he observes the stars *at night*, and as "static electricity" if, as an electrophysicist, he has to deal with the atmosphere. One would have nothing against him if he did not believe that he had solved all riddles with the concept of "ionized cosmic dust." His arrogance makes him a chain on thinking in natural-scientific research; and since the further development of the human race will be determined by its relationship to nature inside and outside itself, and for centuries by nothing else, such ignorant arrogance is also a chain on social development. The situation in which the world finds itself today, 1949, speaks an unequivocal language.

Functional thinking tolerates no static states. For it, all natural functioning is *moving* even where our thought technique deals with rigid structures and immobile forms. It is just this motility and uncertainty in thinking, forever flowing, which places the observer in contact with the natural process. The word "flowing" is valid without limitation for the sensory apparatus of the natural observer; the living knows no static states if it is not subject to immobilization due to armoring. Nature is also "flowing" in every single one of its varied functions as well as in the whole. Nature, too, knows no static states. For this reason, I believe that Bergson, in his splendid concept of the "experience of duration," committed the mistake of postulating the biophysical process as "metaphysics," in opposition to nature as the realm of "science and technology." In essence, Bergson wished to say only one thing with his natural philosophy: Mechanistic natural science is valid in the realm of non-living nature and technical civilization. It leaves us in the lurch when we have to deal with the perceiving living creature and the *act* of natural research in the realm of biophysical processes.

Orgone research has established beyond any doubt the fact that mechanistic natural research failed, not only in the biophysical but also in all the other realms of nature where it was valid, to penetrate to the common denominator of the natural processes. For, as we said already, nature is *functional* in *all* realms, and not only in those of the living. True, there are mechanical laws. But the mechanics of nature is itself a special variation of functional natural processes. This statement will be proven.

If we wish to be consistent in our work hypothesis, as a consequence of which the orgone energy represents the cosmic primordial energy; that from this cosmic energy the three great functioning realms of mechanical energy, dead mass and living matter have resulted through complicated variation processes; that, finally, the cosmic primordial energy *actually* functions in all three main realms in a definite, varied way, then the gigantic task results of deriving the transition of specific variations from the common functioning principle of orgone energy. We can do this in manifold fashion:

We can study the orgone energy in its natural functioning in the atmosphere and in the living organism, comprehend the functional basic principles and pursue them into the higher variations. At the same time, we can, indeed we must, understand concretely the specific variations in and between the three great functioning realms, and concretely bind them together in such a way that the common functioning principles of higher order spontaneously lead us to the common functioning basis of all nature.

This has nothing to do with philosophy, not even with natural philosophy. This task is comparable to that of an engineer who has to build a complicated bridge over a broad stream. He has to connect the two banks and must, in order to fulfill his task, set up *practically* the bridge as a whole as well as bind together the individual cement blocks. We differ from this engineer in that we do not promise to have the bridge fixed and ready by a definite date. We do not know when the bridge will be finished and who will carry it through to the end. But we must direct our attention—to continue the comparison—*simultaneously* at the two banks and at those details of construction which are indispensable for the crossing of the stream. We still do not have to think of the form and material of the accessories, of the arrangement of the lighting for the bridge, etc.

We have sufficiently investigated the cosmic orgone energy in different functioning realms to be able to submit some generally valid principles concerning the common functioning basis of all nature.

In this functioning basis of nature, we find PULSATION as a basic quality of the orgone. It can be analyzed into two antithetical part-functions, *expansion* and *contraction*, or synthesized from them. I know that I express myself here mechanistically. Still, unavoidably, we have to free, for the duration of the observation, the function we are investigating from the general flux of natural functioning, indeed even have to immobilize it, in order to observe it more exactly. However, under no conditions are we permitted to interpret a measure which we had to take because we could not operate without it as an objective quality of the function itself. We are not permitted to ascribe qualities to nature which it only assumed at the moment of investigation but which are not its specific characteristics. It is not a pedantic or superfluous warning to say this. Mechanistic natural science is full of such misinterpretations:

Mechanistic bacteriology colors certain cocci and bacteria with biologically effective stains, in order to make them more visible. In the Gram stain, staphylococci appear blue; tubercle bacilli appear red in eosin. The bacteriologist then speaks of special color reactions of bacteria as if they were specific biological qualities of these creatures. This is wrong, for the staining is an artificial measure for the presentation of the object, and not a specific quality of the creature.

The cancer researcher of mechanistic direction constantly overlooks the true qualities of the cancer cells because he is stuck in the secondary, artificial properties which the cancer cells acquired in the process of investigation.

The mechanistic physicist says that light consists of seven basic colors, that it is "composed" of them. The functionalist says: *If* I have a light ray pass through a prism, it assumes the appearance of a seven-colored scale. Without a prism, or without a grid which is formed by the rain, i.e., without a special artificial influence, light is a unitary phenomenon which has its own special qualities, for instance, that of "illuminating" space. We do not want to forget that we do not really understand anything at all when we say "illuminate."

I can kill an animal and dissect it as I please. No one would think of saying that the animal is made up of the parts into which I have dissected it. This is basically valid as a criticism of EVERY kind of mechanistic research: *The experimental interference changes the object of research.* The staining of cancer tissue extinguishes its living quality. The decomposition of light by a prism only tells us how the light behaves under the influence of refraction but not how light behaves *without* such an influence.

Mechanistic natural science has in wide realms committed the error of thinking that the *changed* qualities of a natural function were identical with its real qualities. I say nothing about the nature of a child of two years when I have it combine triangles and squares. I am only expressing something about the particular situation into which I have placed the child, about how it reacts under this *special* condition. It is a different matter if I first *observe* the child in his natural environment. The child creates for itself its own conditions of life; it does not react to a state set up by me. Hence, the direct observation of nature is more important than experimentation. As controls of my observations, I can set up my experiments in such a way that I investigate *nature* and *not my alteration of nature*.

I observe that plants spontaneously grow better under the

influence of vigorous orgone and water than under the influence of darkness or lack of water. I deal with the *natural* conditions of growth in my experiment when I irradiate seeds with concentrated orgone energy, and then compare the growth with the seeds that have been irradiated less or not at all. But if I apply a chemical medium to these seeds with which they never come in contact in nature, then I have introduced an artificial alteration of the qualities of the seeds. My results may be useful, senseless, or harmful. But I have not investigated any natural process when I introduce conditions into my experiment which were not present in nature. A child does not naturally place square blocks in corresponding holes, but he plays with sand or earth. A cancer cell is not naturally Gram-stained, but has its own natural color. And seeds function in nature on the basis of orgonotic processes and not on the basis of potassium excess.

Every kind of natural observation connects excitation as cause with sensation as result, or, vice versa, sensation as cause with excitation as result. That quantitative changes bring about qualitative changes, and vice versa, is as generally recognized as the fact that the living and non-living influence, condition, and change one another. *Dynamic* thinking, then, is no special property of orgonomic functionalism. That the natural processes influence the cultural processes, and that the cultural processes change nature is a banality for *every* kind of thinking. Exactly so are the interacting functions of animals and plants, men and machines, male and female, science and art, electricity and mechanics, positive and negative electricity, acids and alkalis, feudalism and bourgeois life, mathematics and music, intellect and emotion, thought and experience, etc., known, recognized, understood and practically handled.

The *basic* distinction between orgonomic functionalism and all other techniques consists in the fact that the living organism not only directly connects, but, *moreover, searches for a common, third, and deeper functioning principle.*

From this interlacing of two functions in a third and common functioning principle, it follows simply and logically that:

1. All existing functions will be *simplified* in the advance of knowledge, and not complicated. Here orgonomic functionalism finds itself in sharp contradiction with all other thought techniques. For the mechanist and metaphysicist, the world becomes all the more complicated the more our knowledge about facts and functions increases. For the functionalist, the natural processes become simpler, clear, and more transparent.

2. With the interlacing in the common functioning principle, there is automatically a *direction* of research which penetrates to knowledge of *still simpler and more comprehensive functioning principles.* If one has recognized the common functioning principle of animal and plant, namely the bion, one must, whether one wishes to or not, penetrate to the wider and deeper *common factors,* for instance, the common functioning of the bions which result from *living* matter and the bions which result from *non-living* matter. In this way, one wins a position from which one can investigate non-living and living nature under *one* viewpoint.

We can decide whether we wish to investigate the *special* or the *general*, the *distinguishing* or the *common*, the *variation* or the *basic*. The variation has its own functioning laws which distinguish it from other variations. *Simultaneously*, the variation obeys the general functioning principle of its origin.

In research on the cancer biopathy, functional observation gained a valuable confirmation. A cancer cell in animal tissue is very different from an ameba in a grass infusion. Mechanistic cancer research asserts that the ameba arises from "germs in the air," and it is ignorant of the origin of the cancer cell. "Ameba" and "cancer cell" thus remain two sharply differentiated realms, both without beginning and without end or transition to other realms. On the other hand, for orgonomic functionalism, a rich field of research presented itself in the comparison of cancer cell and ameba.

The *common factors* are far richer than the distinguishing ones. Cancer cell and ameba develop through the natural organization of bions or energy vesicles. The cancer cell is the ameba of animal tissue, and the ameba is the cancer cell of plant tissue. Through the connection of ameba and cancer cell in living tissue which decomposes through distintegration into bions, a functional relationship was established which opened wide the hitherto closed door to research on the cancer cell and, with it, on the cancer disease. Schematically this appears as follows:

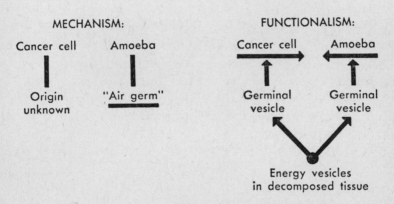

The mechanistic way of thinking prefers the distinguishing, usually overlooks the common, and hence becomes rigid and sharp in its separations. The functional way of thinking is, first of all, interested in the common, since the observation of the common leads deeper and further. For Darwin in his research on the origin of man from the higher animals, it was far more important that the embryos of man, pig, ape, and dog showed so many identities than that they showed this or that fine distinction. In this way, he found the common principle of the development of vertebrates, a principle that is valid for men *and* for apes. For mechanism and mysticism the distinction between man and animal was and forever is the important thing, for instance, man's "non-animal" or "non-sexual" nature. We can study how separating observation *must* degenerate finalistically and mystically: the common is always also that factor which points to the common origin. *Hence research on*

the common functions of different phenomena is also always historical and genetic research. Classifying observation alone, as, say, in purely descriptive biology, cannot lead to any genetic findings. Therefore, the inclination arises to connect the variations by a common *"goal"* or *"purpose"* of their functions. In this way mysticism slips into natural science. And from the mysticism of separating observation emerge the irrational outlooks on life, such as race prejudice or the sexual suppression of children.

It is no accident but well-founded that the life-negating world outlook always emphasized the separating: in nationalism, the distinctions between peoples; in family ideologies, the distinctions between families; in the money principle, the distinctions of wealth; in the authoritarian principle, the distinctions of social hierarchy. On the other hand, the life-affirmative attitude stresses the common: the common biological origin of all human animals, the community of man, animal and nature, the common life interests and needs, etc.

Since functional thinking knows the *mobility* in all processes, it itself is moving and always rich in developmental processes. On the other hand, mechanistic thinking is by its nature rigid, and hence works rigidly on the object of its research, its education, its healing, its social exertion. We don't deny the conservative good will, but we say that he cannot guide living reality. The mechanist cannot be other than conservative or backward. He may think whatever he wishes of his attitudes and intentions: It lies in the *essence* of his thinking to overlook development, to distrust or hate the living, and hence to seek compensation in rigid principles.

It is the essence of the living to function, and thus to be opposed to every kind of rigidity. In nature there is no bureaucracy. Natural laws are functional, and not mechanical laws. Even where the law of mechanics is valid, nature is abundantly rich in variations.

Functionalism is in the position to dissolve contradictions which, to the mechanists, appear as insoluble, through the fact that functionalism grasps the common functioning principle. To give only one example:

Mechanism is not able to bring "society" and the "individual" into harmony; not because it does not wish to, but because it cannot. Hence, it will stress either the interests of society *or* those of the individual. To be sure, it knows that the interests of society are furthered by the fulfillment of the interests of its individuals, and vice versa; yet in its thinking and treatment it is always only the one *or* the other. Thus arises the sharp contradiction between state and individual, in this form insoluble and incompatible.

In the sharp opposition between "religion" and "sexuality" we have another example of mechanistic separation before us. For mechanistic and mystical thinking, religion and sexuality are incompatible. This holds so widely that, as in catholicism, genital pleasure, even in the church-blessed marriage, is a sin. For functionalism, the contradiction is resolved in the following way: The common principle of sexuality and religion is the sensation of nature in one's own organism. When the sexual expressions of nature in the human animal were repressed by the development of patriarchy, a sharp, unbridgeable antithesis arose of *sexuality as "sin"* and *religion as "absolution from sin."* In natural religion, religion and sexuality were ONE: *orgonotic plasma excitation.* In patriarchy, orgonity becomes on the one hand "sin," and on the other, "God." Thus, the functionalist understands the identity of emotions in sexuality and religion, the origin of the splitting-up, the contradiction which arose, the fears of sexuality in religious men and the pornographic degradation of sexuality in men who have repudiated religion. The "mechanist" and the "mystic" are products of this contradiction, remain imprisoned in it, and reproduce this split in their children. Functionalism breaks through the boundaries of the rigid, splitting contradiction through the discovery of the common factors in emotion, origin, and essence of sexuality and religion.

The transgression of the rigid boundaries which mechanism

erects in nature at first leads the functionally thinking observer into uncertainties. Mechanistic, splitting rigidity in observation and in theory-formation serves personal security far more than objective research. I have experienced again and again, in myself and many of my co-workers, that the holding tight to rigid boundaries and laws *has the function of sparing psychic unrest*. While we keep the moving rigid, we feel remarkably less threatened than when we observe a *moving* object.

One of my assistants, who came to me from a biological laboratory, reported that she had there received strict rules for research. She was not permitted to transgress boundaries, and to step outside the "research program." I do not overlook the fact that the inclination of the neurotic character structure for arbitrary action and lack of discipline in thinking and working is at the basis of such rules. But I also do not overlook the result that these rules exclude genuine research work. The bacteriologist is so confined by the limits of sterilization that he forgets that *nature is not sterile*, and *that one must also investigate the decay processes*. We will see in another connection that several decades of cancer research overlooked the simple fact of the putrefaction in cancerous organisms because the boundaries of sterilization could not be transgressed. It is now clear that one becomes uncertain if one works with unsterile preparations. But this uncertainty is an essential discipline in balanced thinking. The "sterile," acquired results must be compared with the "unsterile" facts. That is more difficult, but also more fruitful. It reduces prejudice and permits one to stand closer to reality.

Natural-scientific research by experimentation was a decisive step forward toward *objective* observation. But the *mechanistically* executed experiment has separated the researcher from the direct observation of nature. Man's distrust of his power of judgment and the rationality of his emotions was justifiably so gigantic that he has overburdened the objective experiment. He has refused to investigate tissue in the living state just as he has rejected observation of the atmosphere with the naked eye. "Objective experiments," such as the Michelson-Morley light experiment which did away with the ether, are catastrophic events in scientific research. One can only control the living observer by experimentation, but one cannot replace him. A mechanistically working and thinking character structure in the observer cannot be fructified by experimentation. Hence it was always the rebel against mechanism in science who overstepped sharp boundaries and made his discoveries precisely through his heterodoxy. The rebel simply turned to direct observation and to natural, i.e., functional, connection of the observations. These rebels of natural science were also rebels in thinking; they functioned in a living way, transgressed boundaries, broke down fences, as in the question of the unchangeability of chemical substances, in the relationship between energy and mass, in the relationship between man and animal, etc. One need only think of what psychology has accomplished by the application of direct observation.

Thus functionalism uses the experiment for confirmation of its observations and results of thought. *It does not replace thinking and observation by experimentation.* The mechanist has no confidence in his thinking and observation, and he is correct in having no confidence in them. The functionalist *has* confidence in his senses and in his thinking. He is distinguished from the mystic in that he knows the uncertainties and controls them by experimentation. He is distinguished from the mechanist in that he does not exclude observation, considers *everything* possible, breaks down, through his grasping of relationships, the boundaries between the sciences and always advances in *disciplined* fashion to the *simpler* functioning principle.

Thus the mechanistic scientific worker is so unsure, his operations so complicated and stuck in unessential details without any relationship to the whole, that he does not consider *simple* results correct and turns away from them immediately. The orgone accumulator was rejected by prominent people because "it is *only* a simple metal box."

The mechanistic human structure tolerates uncertainties poorly, avoids long-lasting suspense arising from doubts, and dislikes the flowing and intermeshing functions of nature. Added to this is the fear of the living which will later be discussed in another connection.

Since functionalism always transgresses the boundaries erected by mechanism in nature and distinguishes the common functions from the special variations, it reduces the different facts to functional connections, the functions to energy processes, and the different energy processes to a generally valid functional law of nature. It is unimportant how much it accomplishes at any given time practically or theoretically. Important is the *direction* of research in the observation of nature. *And the research direction*—simplification and unification *or* complication—*is dependent upon the structure of the researcher.*

The mechanistic viewpoint fails if we wish to find the transition from the orgonotic excitations of a human organism to the processes in the tissues of his organs. The visible convulsions and the subjective streaming sensations justify the assumption that there are concrete processes in the tissue substance which correspond to them. But mechanism cannot tell us how we should confirm or control our justified assumption. The processes in the human tissues are not directly observable. The post-mortem dissection and staining of the tissues tell us nothing about the processes in the living state, since dead or dying tissue is *basically* different from the living. The statements of mechanistic pathology are derived from *dead* tissues that, moreover, *have been changed by staining;* for this reason they by-pass the problem of the living and lead into error. Furthermore, mechanism assumes in men and in the higher animals innervations of the tissue functions which supposedly *originate* not in the tissues themselves, but in the "higher centers." If this is true, then nothing can be gained by observations of primitive plasmatic organisms. An ameba has no nerves and possesses no innervations which, from the mechanistic viewpoint, would correspond to those of the higher animals. In this way, mechanistic pathology automatically excludes itself from every kind of comparative observation.

Functionalism has freed itself from these prejudices with their rigid demarcations. Purely in its thought technique, functionalism connects the animal with the protozol tissue, since all living substances must be identical in their common functioning basis. If once the consideration of this identity is accepted, then many experimental possibilities emerge to answer the question:

Have the orgonotic sensations, which are so very familiar to the psychiatrist who is an orgone therapist, an objective, observable basis in animal tissue?

Let us observe flowing amebae. We see currents in the protoplasm which are directed to the periphery when the stimuli are pleasurable and to the center when they are unpleasurable. In other words, the ameba stretches itself toward pleasurable stimuli and creeps back into itself if the stimuli are unpleasurable. Here with one stroke, by the help of a simple observation and correct theory, a solid bridge is constructed from the metazoon to the ameba. The ameba behaves exactly as we could predict on the basis of our clinical observation of emotional behavior in the human animal. What we infer psychiatrically in humans, we observe *directly* in the ameba: *the current of the protoplasm has* "emotional" *significance*. Our theory tells us: *What we perceive subjectively and call "organ sensations," are objective movements of the protoplasm. Organ sensation and plasmatic current are functionally identical*. Hence with regard to the functions of pleasurable expansion and anxious contraction of the protoplasm, man and ameba are functionally identical.

We let amebae die. Their protoplasm increasingly loses motility until it reaches a complete stop. "Death" has occurred. After dying, the protoplasm disintegrates into small bodies which we know so well as "T-bodies" from our investigation of cancerous tissue. Microscopic processes in the protozoa have brought us on the track of the degeneration of tissue in cancerous humans. Moreover, the study of the organization of protozoa from bionously disintegrating grass tissue formed the key to the origin of cancer cells in disintegrating human tissue. Microscopic observations are in harmony with our clinical observations. Tissue disintegrates into bions and further into T-bodies, if it loses biological energy and thus becomes anorgonotic. This can be studied microscopically. Corresponding to this observation are the decline in life activity in the cancerous organism, the typically stale or foul odor, the lessened motility, the resigned character attitude, etc. All this points to a constantly increasing loss of organismic orgone energy. I believe that few judgments of classical medicine rest on such a congruence of different kinds of facts.

A further fact is the existence of orgone energy in the atmosphere. Concentrated in accumulators, this energy can stop the anorgonotic processes in the sick organism and reverse them. Anorgonity of the blood of cancer patients can be cured by orgone therapy. The organism feels itself strengthened, it develops vigorous impulses, gains weight, etc.

We see that the functional connection of facts from different, very separated realms, mastered with different methods of investigation but subordinated to *one* theoretical basic principle, is no wizardry, no magic, but a teachable thought technique. With the help of this thought technique, we bridge broad gaps which hitherto have so severely stymied biology and medicine. It is the primary biological motility, it is the primary emotions which, in a simple way, bring the living of different stages of organization into a UNITY. In principle, we have now become independent of nerve paths and specific glands, since we have placed the problem where it belongs: *in the foundation of living functioning*. Not substance and structure but *movements* and *energy processes* are the guiding lines of our thought technique. Since, now, substances and structure forms are infinitely complicated, while the primitive movements and energy processes of the living, on the other hand, are extremely simple and accessible to observation, we have won a new and very promising position. For the time being, it is just this simplicity of our clinical and experimental position which separates us from our colleagues in mechanistic pathology, who work with chemical substances and structures. The simple appears today incredible, if no longer "unscientific" as it did only a few years ago. I know how alien to complicated thinking the comparison of an ameba with a human organism must seem. But I can assure the reader that to me the rigid boundaries which mechanistic cancer research has erected between the protozoon in grass infusion and the cancer cell in animal tissue appear far more peculiar.

Scientific methods of research demonstrate their correctness not only by the facts which they reveal, but also by the *new* realms of research which they disclose. The mechanistic separation of cancer cell and protozoon has led nowhere. Even more, it has for decades condemned cancer research to sterility. This happened because of a prejudice which has a religious-mystical origin: "The units of the living are cells and cells always have and always will come from cells." Thus arose the error in thought that the cancer cell was only an aberrated body cell. *The cancer cell has nothing in common with the healthy cell* except *one* thing: It is organized from the *disintegrating material of previously* healthy cells.

In opposition to this *cul de sac* of orthodox cancer research, the functional connection of cancer cell with the protozoon in disintegrating grass tissue has opened wide the door for further cancer research.

This basic scientific position spares us very unfruitful discussion about the biochemical results of classical biology. They are of secondary significance for the comprehension of the living and, with it, of the cancer biopathy. An example from the realm of mechanics that is more readily accessible to mechanistic thinking may illuminate what is meant here.

A train consists of a number of coaches which are drawn by a locomotive. The coaches consist of metal, wood, glass, etc.

The locomotive consists of a body and numerous boilers, levers, pistons, etc. We can tell ever so much about the wood, metal, glass, boilers, etc.; we can analyze them ever so exactly and break them down into details: The most exact investigation of this type, carried into infinity, would never tell us anything about the function of the train. This function is solely determined by the fact that the train is able *to move* as a *whole* and can bring me from New York to Boston. Thus if I wish to understand the train, I must understand the *principle of its movement*. The *material* construction of its locomotive and coach is unessential and only of secondary interest, e.g., of interest for traveling comfort and safety, but not for the *principle* of travel.

Classical biology investigates the structures of the living in different variations down to the finest details. It may attain results of ever so neat elegance; but operating in this way it will forever be silent about the *essence* of the living.

This applies to more than biological questions. The discovery of orgone energy reaches far beyond the realm of the living, even if it was made and found its most important application in that domain. The discovery of the orgone is basically to be ascribed to an involved but consistent act of thought. This act of thought was confirmed by the discoveries that it made possible and by the development of experiments which confirmed the thought technique and secured the orgonomic facts. The presentation of this act of thought becomes a basic part of the comprehension of the living. In it, the living grasps itself.

I say: *In the act of thought the living grasps itself*. That is equally valid for the functions of non-living as well as living nature. In the building of a machine the living comprehends the laws and functions of *non-living* nature in their relation to living needs. In the sciences of man, the living tries to understand the functions of the living itself. Thus it always comprehends only a relationship to itself. Were, now, the living in the human animal not armored and hence a victim of mechanistic-mystical degeneration, the result of this mastery of living nature would be in harmony with objective life functions. It would master the material structures of living matter *next* to the laws of living movements. As a consequence of the social tragedy which has befallen the human animal for thousands of years in the form of mechanistic-mystical deterioration, it has only found access to man's mechanical functions, to the construction of the skeleton, the muscles, the blood vessels and nerves, the chemical, materialistic composition of the organism, etc. Since the motile living in man was armored and hence inaccessible, the living principle itself, precisely the MOVING, the very essence of the living, remained a book with seven seals. What rigid mechanistic thinking was not able to accomplish because it observed the living only as an especially complicated machine, mysticism has tried to complete: *The moving in the living was transferred into the beyond*, allegorically in theory, and often literally in the wars of rigid human animals.

As a consequence of his armoring, the armored human being thinks mainly in terms of matter or material particles. He feels the moving as beyond him or supernatural. Language always expresses directly the state of the organ sensations and hence forms an excellent key to how human beings experience themselves. The moving, the plasmatic current, is in fact inaccessible to the rigid human animal; thus it is "beyond," i.e., beyond his ego sensations, or "supernatural," i.e., as an object of eternal longing for the cosmos *beyond* his earthly life. *What the armored individual conceives as "spirit" or "soul" is the motility of the living which is inaccessible to it*. He sees and feels the moving only *as in a mirror*. He describes living motility very correctly, but correctly only in the sense of a correct reflection in a mirror. A large part of the brutality of the mystic can be traced simply to the fact that he feels the living in himself, to be sure, but he never *really* experiences it nor is he able to develop it. Hence he develops the impulse to master the mirror image, to make it palpable and tangible by force. The living in the mirror is a constant provocation, which drives him finally to fury. There it is, the moving, it lives, laughs, weeps, hates, loves . . . but always only in the mirror, actually as unattainable to the ego as the fruit to Tantalus. From this so tragic situation arises every murderous impulse directed against the living.

Mechanism and mysticism supplement one another to form a sharply split-up picture of life, with a body consisting of chemical substances *here* and a spirit or a soul, remarkable and uninvestigable, unattainable as only God himself, *there*.

On the other hand, the unarmored organism experiences itself above all as unitary *motility*. Its organ sensations tell it that the essential in the living is not materialistic. A corpse— from the viewpoint of its material structure—does not look different from a living body. Even the chemical composition shortly after death before putrefaction sets in, is nearly the same as in the living. The difference lies in the *absence of motility*. For this reason, the corpse is strange, indeed hor- rendous to living sensation. *Thus the living is spontaneously mobile*. Now we understand the hopelessness of all mechanistic- mystical thinking. It always bounces against the armor of the individual's own organism, without being able to penetrate it.

On the other hand, the unarmored living will find, feel out, and understand in its own movements the expressive move- ments of the living generally. Therefore the biological science of the unarmored organism must necessarily be basically dif- ferent from the biology of the armored organism. For the former, the moving is the essential; true, the structure is im- portant too, but it is not basic.

Mechanism does not understand the principle of organiza- tion. It does not know the qualities of orgone energy and hence must necessarily introduce a metaphysical principle, if it does not wish to remain mired in pure description. For mechanism, there is a hierarchy of organs in the organism. As the "highest" developmental product, the brain is, together with the nerve apparatus of the spinal cord, the "director" of the whole organ- ism. Mechanism assumes a center from which all impulses are sent out which move the organs. Every muscle has, connected by its respective nerves, its own center in the brain or in the thalamus. *From where the brain itself receives its assignments, remains a riddle.* The organs are the good underlings of the brain. The nerves are the telegraph wires. The *coordination* of the movement of the organism in this description remains veiled and mysterious. Where understanding fails, "purpose," the convenient "IN ORDER TO," enters the picture. The muscles of the shoulder and arm in apes coordinate their movements "IN ORDER TO" grasp. To my knowledge, a center for this coordination has not been assumed or found. And it would not help the situation, for the question *who* assigned the tasks of coordination to *this* center would still remain unsolved.

Since the mechanist does not understand the living, he must take flight into mysticism. Therefore, all mechanistic world pictures are always mystical and *must* be mystical. Mechanistic thinking itself is clearly modeled after the structure of the social patriarchy when it sees the master in the brain, the telegraph wires in the nerves, and the executing subjects in the organs. And behind the brain "works God," or "reason," or "purpose." The situation in natural-scientific comprehension still remains as hopelessly confused as before.

For functionalism, there is no "higher" center and no "lower" executive organ. The nerve cells do not produce impulses but only transmit them. The organism as a whole forms a *natural cooperative of equally important organs of different function.* When natural social work democracy is *biologically* based, we find it modeled after the harmonic cooperation of the organs. Multiplicity and differentiation combine into a unity. *The function itself governs the cooperation.* Every organ lives for itself, functioning in its own realm on the basis of its own functions and impulses. The hand grasps and the gland secretes. *The individual organs are self-active living creatures, equipped with their own sensation and function.* That has been unequivocally confirmed by the experiments on isolated hearts and muscles. Sensation is in no way tied to sensory nerve endings. All plasmatic matter perceives, with or without sensory nerves. The ameba has no sensory or motor nerves, and still it perceives.

Each organ has its own mode of expression, its own specific language, so to speak. Each organ answers to irritation in its own specific way: the heart with change in heart beat, the gland with secretion, the eye with visual impressions and the ear with sound impressions. The specific expressive language of an organ belongs to the organ and is not a function of any "center in the nervous system."

In the contrast between the two basic concepts of the organism, we again clearly recognize the difference between unarmored and armored living. Both take their judgments from the organ sensations of their own organism. The unarmored living grasps directly with the hand. The pianist does not give his hand any assignments. The hand is, *in connection with the whole organism,* the moved and moving, *self-active* organ. One hears with the whole organism, and not only with the ear. The wheel is not the automobile. One travels in the auto, and not on the wheel.

On the other hand, the armored individual feels that his organism consists of individual parts. Every impulse has to penetrate the armor. From this arises the feeling of a "you should" or "thou must." From this also emerges the idea that there is a higher center in the organism which "delegates tasks" to the executive organs. Added to this is the feeling of heaviness, inertia or even paralysis in the limbs as well as in the body as a whole, which forms the basis of the idea that an organ must be activated and moved by assignment. Then it is logical that there is an "ego" which stands behind everything, a mind, a "higher reason" which "guides," "delegates," etc. From there to the state-like concept of human society, or vice versa, from the idea of the absolute state to the mechanistic concept of the organism, is but a step.

In this way arose and constantly arises from the organ sensations of the armored individual his concept of the functions of the living. The splitting up of his organ sensations creates the further fact that he loses the capacity to formulate or to find functional *connections*. This is why brain mythology could rule the scene of natural science for decades, without having the insight that milliards of organisms functioned for countless thousands of years before there was a brain. The terror of the total convulsion, of involuntary movement and spontaneous excitation is joined to the splitting up of organs and organ sensations. This terror is the real stumbling block. For, while the

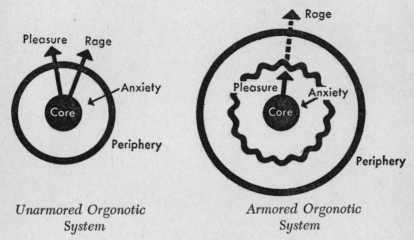

Unarmored Orgonotic   Armored Orgonotic
System   System

splitting up prevents the functional unification of individual functions, the terror is responsible for the fact that the armored being develops fright or rage when another person fills, connects the gaps, comprehends or establishes functional identities.

For the reasons described above, classical biology remained stuck in the cell and did not find the simple path to the demonstration of the cell's organization from bions and its disintegration into bions after death. Armored living is essentially characterized by the fact that it does not feel the moving, the living itself, cannot perceive it, and thus cannot understand it. What one calls the rigidity or the conservatism of traditional science is borne in reality by this incapacity and anxiety of individual leading researchers, who are then followed by the mass of less significant scientists. We know many examples of such dogmata: The indestructibility of the atom, the separation of matter and energy, "all cells from one cell," etc. Much indeed has been written about this. But it is here for the first time that such dogmata have been understood and—through this understanding—shaken. Many such fixed ideas will fall in the further development of functional thinking.

Unquestionably, the most significant distinction between these two types is the development of destructive rage in the armored orgonotic system. Since every plasmatic current and orgonotic excitation, in its striving for contact, hits on a wall, the unmasterable urge arises to break through the wall, under all circumstances and with all means. *In so doing, all life impulses are changed into destructive rage. The organism is driven to break out of the armor with force,* as if it felt itself imprisoned in an iron cell.

I earnestly believe that in the rigid, chronic armoring of the human animal we have found the answer to the question of his so gigantically destructive hatred and his mechanistic as well as mystical thinking. We have found the realm of the DEVIL.

2. THE FUNCTION OF SUPERIMPOSITION

The sexual embrace, if abstracted and reduced to its basic form, represents *superimposition* and the *bio-energetic fusion* of two orgonotic systems. Its basic form is the following:

FIG. 1.

From *Cosmic Superimposition*, 1951.

We have learned to reduce form to movement. Form, to orgonomic functional thinking, is *frozen* movement. We know from ample evidence that the act of superimposition is due to bio-energetic forces acting beyond control. The two orgonotic systems involved are DRIVEN to superimpose by a force which, under natural conditions, i.e., not restricted by outer or inner hindrances, is beyond their control. It is *involuntary* bio-energetic action. Basically, this function cannot be stopped just as the heartbeat or intestinal peristalsis cannot be stopped, except by forceful interference or by death. When two children of different sexes, 3 to 5 years old, superimpose* and their organisms fuse orgonotically, we are not dealing with propagation, since no new individual will result from this fusion. Neither are we dealing here with the "quest for pleasure" in the psychological sense. The pleasure involved in superimposition is the experiential *result*, and not the driving force of the act. Let us forget for a moment all the complicated higher functions which later are added to natural superimposition; let us reduce it all to functioning *beyond* the individual and even the realm of the species; let us penetrate deeply enough to see this function as an energetic event which runs a certain course quite autonomically and with unimpeachable impact; if we do this, then we clearly see in it a *transindividual* happening, something that takes charge of the Living and governs it.

Further careful observation tells us that bio-energetic superimposition is closely linked up with plasmatic excitation and sensations of *energy streamings* in *two* orgonotic systems, be they children, adolescents or grownups. It is absolutely necessary, in order to visualize this function in its proper aspects, to abandon all of the many social, cultural, economic, psychological, and other implications which, in the case of man, have complicated and all but obliterated its original, bio-energetic functioning.

Reduced and abstracted in its purest form, superimposition

---

* Cf. Reich: "Children of the Future, I," *Orgone Energy Bulletin*, October, 1950, pp. 194-206.

in the biological realm appears as the approach through *attraction* and full bio-energetic *contact of two orgonotic* STREAMS. Membranes, organs, fluids, nerves, will-power, unconscious dynamics, etc. must be discounted here, since they do not constitute superimposition. Superimposition of two orgone streams appears as a common functioning principle (CFP) of nature which *fuses* two living organisms in a specific manner—specific to the *basic* natural function, and not to the two organisms. In other words, *superimposition of two orgone energy streams reaches, as a function, far beyond biology.* It governs other realms of nature, too, as it governs living systems. In order to find out which realms of nature *beyond* the living realm are governed by superimposition of two orgone energy streams, we must not deviate from its basic form and movement. Orgonometrically abstracted, it is this:

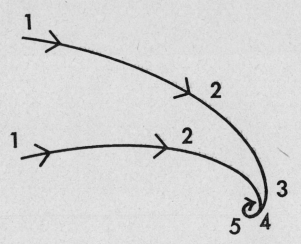

FIG. 2. BASIC FORM OF THE FUNCTION "SUPERIMPOSITION"

Its functional characteristics are:

1. Two directions of energy flow;
2. Convergence ("attraction") and mutual approach of the two energy streams;

3. Superimposition and contact;
4. Merger;
5. Sharp curving of path of flow.

Finding superimposition in realms of *nonliving* nature would be a first decisive step toward finding a *cardinal* root of man in nature; a *common functioning principle* which, already present and working in nature at large, also permeates in a basic fashion the animal kingdom, including man.

The following is a sweeping generalization. It was pointed out at the very beginning that what we are doing here is no more than flying high above a vast territory, the exploration of which will require painstaking, detailed efforts. We are free later on to abandon parts of it or the whole aspect, should it not resist strictest observational and experimental as well as orgonometric scrutiny. We are also free to construct this framework of a future detailed operation, to retain its general features, its layout and its basic characteristics while changing most of its inner detailed constitution. We are free to leave the confirmation or refutation of this construction to others; however, we would have to remind anyone who would approach a task of such magnitude to be well aware of the broad factual background from which the framework of this workshop construction emerged. To those who never dare to look into microscopes or at the sky, who never sit in an orgone energy accumulator and yet are full of fake "authoritative" opinions about orgonomy, we say in advance: Step aside and do not disturb most serious work. Keep quiet, at least!

Years of painstaking observations and functional theory formation have hewn two major pathways into the realm of nonliving nature which revealed the function of superimposition to be at work at the very roots of the universe. The one pathway leads into the *microcosmos*, the other into the *macrocosmos*. Superimposition is the CFP which integrates both into one single natural function.

Let us begin with the microcosmic realm. We shall not dwell too long in it since, though the theoretical outlines seem clearly marked, there are many gaps in details essential to a firm foot-hold. The essence of the microcosmic framework is the following:

In completely darkened, metal-lined orgone energy observation rooms we can observe luminating orgone energy units pursuing certain pathways as they move spinning forward through space. These pathways distinctly show the form of a *spining wave:*

FIG. 3.

This was reported on several occasions many years ago without further elaboration. There is now ample, well-reasoned evidence to the effect that TWO *such spiraling and excited orgone energy units attract and approach each other until they* SUPERIMPOSE, thus:

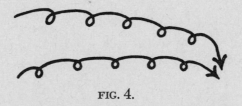

FIG. 4.

It is an essential characteristic of our base of operation to assume that the primordial orgone energy ocean is entirely mass-free; accordingly, mass (*inert* mass at first) emerges from this mass-free energy substratum. It seems logical further to assume:

In the process of superimposition of two mass-free, spiraling and highly excited orgone energy units, kinetic energy is being lost, the rate of spiraling motion decreases greatly, the path of motion is strongly curved and a change takes place from long drawn-out spinning forward toward circular motion on the spot.

Exactly at this point of the process *inert mass emerges from the slowed-down motion of two or more superimposed orgone energy units;* it is immaterial whether we call this first bit of inert mass "atom" or "electron" or something else. The basic point is the *emergence of inert mass from freezing kinetic energy.* This assumption is in full agreement with well-known laws of classical physics. It is also in agreement, as will be shown in a different context, with the quantum theory.

In continuation of our train of thought, we must further assume that the material, chemical *"particles"* which compose the atmosphere, have originally emerged and are still continuously emerging through superimposition of two or more spinning orgone energy units in the orgone envelope of the planet. It matters little at this point in what particular manner the *different* material units are created from primordial orgone energy. We restrict our curiosity to the above-mentioned basic change:

INERT MASS IS BEING CREATED BY SUPERIMPOSITION OF TWO OR MORE SPINNING, SPIRALING ORGONE ENERGY UNITS THROUGH LOSS OF KINETIC ENERGY AND SHARP ENDING OF THE ELONGATED PATH TOWARD CIRCULAR MOTION.

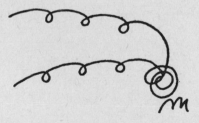

FIG. 5. CREATION OF THE PRIMORDIAL MASS PARTICLE (M) THROUGH ORGONOTIC SUPERIMPOSITION

Hereby a functional relationship is established between the spinning movement of mass-free orgone energy (OR) and inert mass (m) which also characterizes the relationship of heavenly bodies spinning in the surrounding orgone ocean:

Spheres or discs of solid matter spin on a spiraling path within a *faster-moving*, wavy orgone energy ocean, *as balls roll forward on a faster-moving, progressing water wave*. The exact numerical relationship of the two movements, though of great importance, does not matter at this point. What matters is that a functional relationship has been found between the movements of primordial orgone energy and matter which, for the first time in the history of astrophysics, makes comprehensible the fact that heavenly bodies move at all in a spinning manner; furthermore, it makes comprehensible the fact that our sun and our planets more in the same plane and in the same direction, held together in space as a coherent group of spinning bodies. *The spinning wave is the integration of the circular and forward motion* of the planets, of their *simultaneous* rotation on the N-S axis and their movement forward in space. *The moving primal orgone ocean appears as the primordial mover of the heavenly bodies.*

Sharply delineated, new astrophysical problems arise which can not and should not be discussed right away. It is sufficient to have them tentatively formulated:

1. It is *necessary* to assume that the first material particles which were formed (or "created") by superimposition of two or more orgone energy units, from then onward form the material *nucleus of growth of the material body*. It does not matter at present whether these "core" elements of the future heavenly body are of a gaseous or of a solid nature, or whether they possibly go through a process of development from a gaseous to a solid state. What matters is that a *starting point* for the development of a heavenly body from primordial energy has been hypothetically established.

2. A further logical necessity is the assumption of a *GENESIS of the function of gravitational attraction*. The growth of the material core particle of the future heavenly body would be accomplished by way of the *orgonomic potential*: the orgonotically stronger body attracts smaller and weaker systems such as mass-free orgone energy units and

other small bits of primordial matter as they arise in the orgone ocean which surrounds the first growing core. It would be necessary, furthermore, to *distinguish* between the *orgonotic attraction of two energy waves* and the *gravitational attraction* between two material bodies. Thus, primordial orgonotic attraction changes functionally into gravitational mass-attraction.

3. In consequence of points 1 and 2, we would further have to assume that the growing material core would be permanently surrounded by an orgone energy field which from now onward is subject to the gravitational attraction of the material core: this would explain the origin of the *orgone envelope* of the sun (corona) and of the earth. Both are clearly visible and are governed by basic orgonomic functions such as wavy motion from west to east, faster motion of the envelope than the globe, lumination, blueness, and containment within the field of attraction of the material core.

4. The mass-free orgone energy stream which surrounds the material globe must, of necessity, due to the orgonotic attraction exerted upon it by the core, *separate from the general stream of the cosmic orgone energy ocean* since it must follow the rotation on its axis of the material body. Thus, the cosmic ocean, hitherto unitary, *splits up into one major and one minor orgone energy stream.* This assumption will be verified by concrete astrophysical functions. (*Cf.* fig. 6.)

5. The gaseous atmosphere which surrounds the heavenly bodies would necessarily have to emerge through superimposition of mass-free orgone energy units in the revolving orgone energy envelope. This necessary assumption would have to be confirmed in due time by the establishment of the laws which lead from the mass-free orgone energy units toward the atomic weights of the gas particles which constitute the gaseous atmosphere.

6. It follows that concentration and condensation would increase toward the core of the rotating body, the heavier elements being located toward the center and the lighter elements progressively toward the periphery, with the lightest gases,

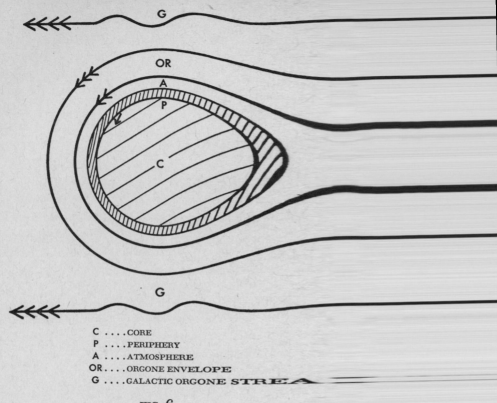

C ....CORE
P ....PERIPHERY
A ....ATMOSPHERE
OR....ORGONE ENVELOPE
G ....GALACTIC ORGONE STREA

FIG. 6.

helium, hydrogen, argon, neon, etc., being I -
treme periphery.

7. In this connection, a most striking fu
must be mentioned which so far has not attr
scientific thinking: *The chemical elements
the gaseous atmosphere* of the planets are i
elements which constitute the living orgono t
are: Hydrogen (H), oxygen (O), nitrogen (N)
and their various molecular groupings suc I
$C_6H_{12}O_6$, etc. This functional identity cannot
out a deep functional significance.

other small bits of primordial matter as they arise in the orgone ocean which surrounds the first growing core. It would be necessary, furthermore, to *distinguish* between the *orgonotic attraction of two energy waves* and the *gravitational attraction* between two material bodies. Thus, primordial orgonotic attraction changes functionally into gravitational mass-attraction.

3. In consequence of points 1 and 2, we would further have to assume that the growing material core would be permanently surrounded by an orgone energy field which from now onward is subject to the gravitational attraction of the material core: this would explain the origin of the *orgone envelope* of the sun (corona) and of the earth. Both are clearly visible and are governed by basic orgonomic functions such as wavy motion from west to east, faster motion of the envelope than the globe, lumination, blueness, and containment within the field of attraction of the material core.

4. The mass-free orgone energy stream which surrounds the material globe must, of necessity, due to the orgonotic attraction exerted upon it by the core, *separate from the general stream of the cosmic orgone energy ocean* since it must follow the rotation on its axis of the material body. Thus, the cosmic ocean, hitherto unitary, *splits up into one major and one minor orgone energy stream.* This assumption will be verified by concrete astrophysical functions. (*Cf.* fig. 6.)

5. The gaseous atmosphere which surrounds the heavenly bodies would necessarily have to emerge through superimposition of mass-free orgone energy units in the revolving orgone energy envelope. This necessary assumption would have to be confirmed in due time by the establishment of the laws which lead from the mass-free orgone energy units toward the atomic weights of the gas particles which constitute the gaseous atmosphere.

6. It follows that concentration and condensation would increase toward the core of the rotating body, the heavier elements being located toward the center and the lighter elements progressively toward the periphery, with the lightest gases,

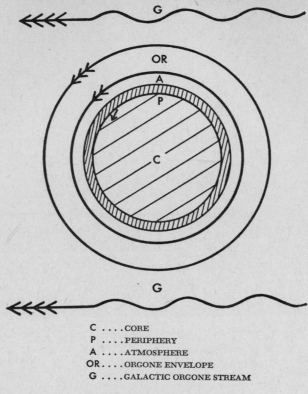

C .... CORE
P .... PERIPHERY
A .... ATMOSPHERE
OR .... ORGONE ENVELOPE
G .... GALACTIC ORGONE STREAM

FIG. 6.

helium, hydrogen, argon, neon, etc., being located at the extreme periphery.

7. In this connection, a most striking functional identity must be mentioned which so far has not attracted attention in scientific thinking: *The chemical elements which constitute the gaseous atmosphere* of the planets are identical with the elements which constitute the living orgonotic systems. They are: Hydrogen (H), oxygen (O), nitrogen (N), and carbon (C), and their various molecular groupings such as CO_2, H_2O, $C_6H_{12}O_6$, etc. This functional identity cannot possibly be without a deep functional significance.

The above-mentioned functional identity concerns only the primordial orgone energy functions and the transformations from primordial mass-free to secondary mass-containing functions. From here onward, but *not* previously, the well-known laws of mechanics and chemistry are fully valid. Also natural laws submit to *evolution*; they have a *genesis*. The problem to be solved in detail is the ORIGIN OF THE MECHANICAL AND CHEMICAL LAWS FROM THE FUNCTIONAL PROCESSES IN THE MASS-FREE PRIMORDIAL ORGONE ENERGY OCEAN.

The advantage of our work-hypothesis, as delineated above, is quite obvious. *Summarily:*

1. It frees us from the clumsy assumption of material bodies rolling in an "empty space," in a merely mathematically approachable action at a distance in a "field." The "field" is *real*, of a *measurable, observable*, and thus *physical* nature. *Space is not empty* but is filled in a continuous manner without gaps.

2. It frees us, furthermore, from the uncomfortable idea that a gravitational attraction which never could be demonstrated, is exerted from the sun over tremendous spaces upon all the planets. **The sun and the planets move in the same plane and revolve in the same direction *due to the movement and direction of the cosmic orgone energy stream in the galaxy*. Thus, the sun does not "attract" anything at all. It is merely the biggest brother of the whole group.**

We have done no more than drawn a sketch of the transition from the microscosmic to the macrocosmic function. We shall later return to superimposition in the macrocosmic realm in greater detail. But first we must acquaint ourselves with some important functions pertaining to the function of superimposition in the *living* realm where it was originally discovered.

We shall concentrate upon *two* basic functions only:

1. *The spinning flow of the orgone energy in the living organism* ("bio-energy");

2. *The superimposition of two orgone energy streams in living bodies: COPULATION*, and the functional meaning of the drive to genital embrace and "ORGASTIC DISCHARGE."

3. THE LIVING ORGONOME (1945)

The formation of living matter in orgone *Experiment XX*
integrates bioenergetic phenomena and points to a single result
of great significance: This experiment reproduced the process
of *primary biogenesis*, thus the *first* arising of plasmatic, living
matter by condensation of mass-free cosmic orgone energy.
This conclusion follows logically: After freezing of a clear solution, bion water of high orgonotic potency, organic forms
develop which have all the properties of the Living: *form,
pulsation, reproduction, growth* and *development*. The theme
is inexhaustible. It is not our task to present it fully at this
point. The reader is again reminded of Columbus's discovery
of America. This discovery did not exhaust all of the future
of America. It only opened the door to a gigantic realm full of
possibilities. The same is true for Experiment XX.

In the following schema, accesses are presented to the manifold functions of nature, views which were opened up by
Experiment XX:

1. Formation of organic forms, plasmatic *"orgonomes"*;
2. Organization of protozoa (*orgonomia*);
3. Formation of bio-chemical matter: coal, sugar, fat;
4. Life- and growth-stimulating effects of the orgone water
solution.

*In the process of the freezing experiment energy is trans-
formed into matter.* This matter becomes alive. On drying, or
burning of the flakes, carbon results; a sweet-tasting, sugary
substance arises in the process. These are gross characteristics
to be elaborated in detail. Frozen orgone energy passes through
all stages of the bionous forms that have been disclosed by
orgone biophysics: T-forms, by taking up free orgone energy,

From *Cosmic Superimposition*, 1951.

develop into PA bions; the PA bions give rise to larger, round forms which look like small "eggs"; many of these "egg forms" elongate and become *bean*-shaped; the bean forms become mobile and form small protozoa: "ORGONOMIA." In their movement and form some among them bear a great similarity to spermatozoa. It is to be assumed that the spermatozoa and eggs in the metazoa are formed in the same manner, by condensation of orgone energy into reproductive cells. The development of bions from *distilled orgone* water leaves no doubt about the *primary* formation of living matter from free orgone energy.

Bion water is yellow in varying intensities up to brown. One thinks in this connection of the production of the *yellow* resin in trees, of *yellow* honey in bees, of the *yellow* of the blood serum of animals, the *yellow* of urine, etc. Of great significance is also the "sugar level" in the living organism. In this way, the gap in biology is slowly being filled which hitherto contained the riddle of how plants can transform "sun energy" into carbohydrates and the solid cellulose forms. "Sun energy" is our orgone energy which is taken up by the plants directly from the earth and from the atmosphere.

Here, the behavior of the leaves of the evergreen ivy is of significance: In winter the leaves lose their *green* color except for the venation which remains green and which corresponds to the branching-out of the vascular system. The rest becomes *yellow-brown* in winter. In spring the green from the leaf's venation spreads slowly over the smooth leaf again. This phenomenon permits the assumption that in winter the biological orgone energy withdraws from the periphery of the leaves, in other words, that it contracts due to cold, exactly as it does in Experiment XX, to expand again in the spring. The withered part of the ivy leaf is "reanimated."

The change from green to yellow in autumn and from yellow to green in spring becomes perfectly comprehensible in terms of orgonotic functioning: *green* is the result, according to classical investigations, of a mixture of *yellow* and *blue*. Blue is the specific color of orgone energy, visible in the atmosphere,

ocean, thunderclouds, "red' blood cells, pr
orthochromatic photographic plates after i
bions.

Now, it seems clear that the turning to
in autumn is due to disappearance of the
and, accordingly, the turning toward gree
ivy is due to new absorption of orgone e
phere. Thus, the green of leaves is the r
resin and the blue orgone energy in the at

Only *one* assumption explains satisfactor
mobile, formed living substance in Expe
process of freezing, the free orgone ener
tracts, exactly as does living plasma. Cont
dependent on the existence of formed mat
all matter formation as a basic function of
energy. *The contraction of the orgone ene*
with a condensation, and the condensation i
formation of material particles of microscop
classical, mechanistic conception a concret
known; accordingly, there can be no conne
getic *movement* and organismic *form.* Org
demonstrate a functional connection betw
ment and form of living matter.

Matter once originated for the first time
the process of matter formation evidently o
One experiences the cosmic origin of one'
emotionally moving equation of "life—earth
mechanistic conception knows only atoms
form salts and organic bodies. It can explai
ment nor the formation of the Living, since
the second have any similarity with mecl
and known geometric forms. *Orgone bioph*
hand, operates with a concrete cosmic ene
the functions of the cosmic energy in the n
in harmony with those in the realm of the

In Experiment XX membranes, and in tl

are formed from free orgone energy; they constitute forms which still cannot be designated as "living beings" in the classical sense, but which already show the typical shape of living organisms. That becomes clear from the illustrations of Experiment XX (*cf.* fig. 3). Most of the flakes have forms similar to those of fishes or tadpoles. If, now, forms are always the expression of (frozen) movement, we are permitted to draw conclusions from these forms to the form of movement of the orgone energy. There is *a basic form of the Living*, which does not agree with any of the known forms of classical geometry. This basic form, seen laterally, appears like this:

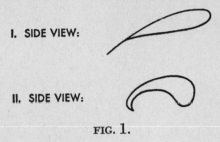

I. SIDE VIEW:

II. SIDE VIEW:

FIG. 1.

And seen from above or below, the living form is typically this:

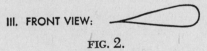

III. FRONT VIEW:

FIG. 2.

Before we proceed to study the energetic function of this form, we want to be convinced that it is in fact *the* basic biophysical form. It is clearly valid for:

Plant seeds: wheat, corn, barley, hay, maize, beans, lentils;

Plant bulbs: potato tubers, almond kernels, apple-, pear-, plum-, peach-pits, etc.;

Animal reproductive cells;

Animal embryos;

All organs of the animal body: heart, urinary bladder, liver, kidney, spleen, lung, brain, testicles, ovary, uterus, stomach;

Single-celled organisms: paramecia, colpidia, vorticellae, cancer cells, human vaginal protozoa (trichomonas vaginalis), etc.;

Animal and plant bodies as total forms: jellyfish, sea stars, reptiles of all kinds; the body form of all kinds of birds, fishes, beetles, mammals including man, etc.;

Trees as a whole and each individual leaf and the blossoms as well as the pollen and pistils of the plants (*cf.* fig. 4).

It is worth noticing that even the organs which grow out of the torso: the arms, legs, fins, wings, the head of the snake, lizard, fox, man, fish, etc., etc., have again the *"orgonome"* *form*. Indeed, even the talons of birds, their beaks, the air-bladders of fish, the horns of oxen, rams, bucks, the binnacles of snails and of shell-fish show the *"orgonome"* *form*.

All this points to the working of a functional natural law: a natural law that manifests itself in a fashion fundamentally different from the geometric laws of classical mechanism.

Access to this cosmic energy law has to be sought in the movement of free orgone energy.

Exactly as the *expressive movements* of the living have an *emotional expression*, which has a significance with regard to the surrounding world, so also the form of the living has in itself an expression. It is a question of reading it *correctly*.

All forms of the living realm can be traced back to the EGG *form, without violating the individual form variations.* This basic form varies according to length, breadth, thickness. It can appear in subdivisions of the same form as in worms; but the basic form remains, whether in entirety or in part, always the same *egg form* as the basic form of the living.

Such a pronounced unanimity of living structure must correspond to a fundamental natural law, and, moreover, to a natural law of cosmic dimension. For the biological basic form is universal, independent of climate or region. It is as if the cosmic orgone energy in its organization into living substance obeyed only *one* law, its *own law of movement*.

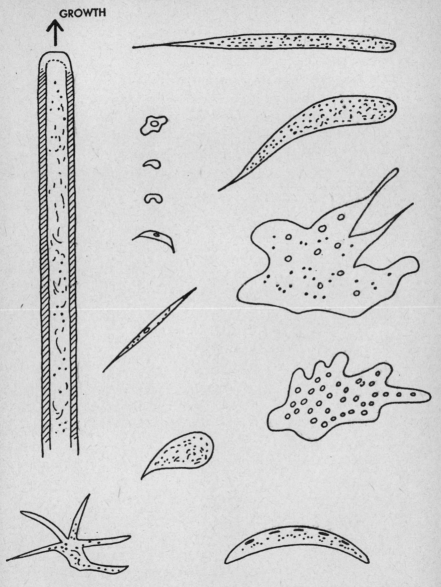

GROWTH

FIG. 3. VARIOUS TYPICAL FORMS OF PLASMATIC FLAKES IN EXP. XX (1945), DRAWN FROM NATURE: BIO-ENERGETIC ORGONOME

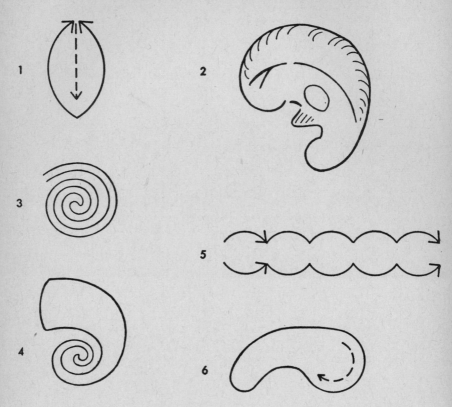

1. Heart; Tree and Plant Leaves; Various Fruits (Plums, etc.); Eggs;
2. Ear; Shells of Oysters, Clams;
3. Ringworm; Snakes;
4. Shell of Snail;
5. Intestines; Worms; Caterpillars;
6. Embryo; Larvae; Stomach; Brain;
   Spleen; Kidney; Liver; Pancreas.

FIG. 4. VARIOUS ORGONOME FORMS, ABSTRACTED

We shall term the specific basic form of the Living

ORGONOME

Its typical basic form is the following generalization of microscopic forms in Experiment XX (fig. 5):

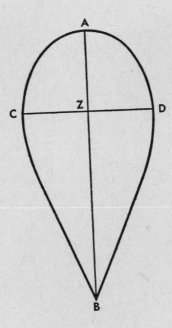

FIG. 5. CLOSED ORGONOME
Basic Form

Trigonometry of the Orgonome

As *orgonome* we wish to designate that geometric form which is represented in the purest form by the hen's egg.

The orgonome is no triangle, no quadrangle, no circle; it is no ellipse, no parabola and no hyperbola. *The orgonome represents a distinct, new kind of geometric figure;* let us try to find out orgonometrically in what way an orgonome arises.

Orgonomy had to concern itself among other things with two fundamental natural phenomena:

1. With the *orgastic convulsion*, and

2. With the *spinning wave (Kreiselwelle)*, named in brief KRW.

We meet the orgastic convulsion in the entire animal kingdom. The KRW confronts us in the observation of the atmospheric orgone energy in the dark room. The blue-violet dots swing along definite trajectories which I have already sketched schematically in "The Discovery of the Orgone" (page 216) as follows:

FIG. 6.

Let us isolate from the KRW-chain an individual wave:

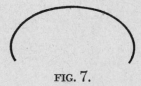

FIG. 7.

If we place two such KRW's with the concave sides facing one another we obtain the known form of the ellipse:

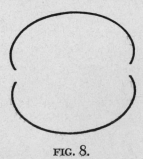

FIG. 8.

On the other hand, if we bend a KRW in the middle at A, and if we bring the two ends of the KRW, B and B', to each other, we have the egg form or the *orgonome form*.

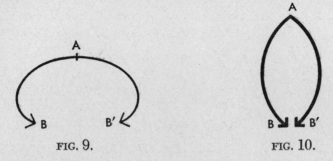

FIG. 9.   FIG. 10.

We could work out the described operation purely trigonometrically without establishing it orgone-physically. However, the orgastic convulsion provides us with a *biophysical* argument which this trigonometric operation fulfills with an important significance. *The most striking phenomenon in the orgasm reflex is the striving of both ends of the body, of the mouth and the genital, to draw near to one another.* This biophysical phenomenon in fact led me on the track of the origin of the orgonome form. In the orgastic convulsion of an animal or in the swimming movement of a jellyfish, the body seems to give way in the middle and to approach its ends to one another.

The relation of a fundamental *biological* movement with a *physical* form of movement may appear arbitrary at first glance. But such a connection is justified if it opens wide for us the door to an obvious lawfulness in biological functioning. To my knowledge, the basic forms of the living body has never been understood. If, now, the orgasm reflex leads to the comprehension of the orgonome form, we are not permitted to recoil from the facts.

The similarity of a KRW to an animal body, observed laterally, is indeed very striking (fig. 9). A detailed elaboration of this similarity cannot be given here, but it has already been worked out.

The membranes of living matter are frozen orgone energy; thus, necessarily, the form of the orgone energy movement must be represented in the form of the living orgonome. If structural form is frozen energy-movement, then, also, the form of movement of the cosmic energy is to be derived from the form of the organ or organism.

Let us return to the orgasm reflex, that richest source of bio-energetic insights.

We found that the orgasm reflex has no expression which can be rendered in words.* Its expressive language, so asserted the conclusion, would be supra-individual, not metaphysical or mystical, but *cosmic. In the orgasm reflex the highly excited organism tries to draw its two body ends close to one another, as if it tended to unite them.* If this explanation is correct, it must also be demonstrable in other realms of orgone physics. It could not be limited to the orgasm reflex.

Let us now observe the form of the living orgonome in its functional connection with the form of the plasmatic currents.

The plasmatic current does not occur continually, but in *rhythmic impulses.* For this reason we speak of PULSATION. The pulsation is readily observed in the blood circulation of all the metazoa. The pulsatory current of the body fluids is the work effect of the organismic orgone energy, an immediate expression of its form of movement. We must derive the mechanical pulsation of body fluids from the functional pulsation of the orgone energy. This conclusion is based on observation of certain protozoa (amebae, cancer cells) in which pulsatory waves of excitation stream over the body and move the protoplasm. In the worms, waves of excitation of pulsatory nature move from tail to head. We see the same phenomenon in certain ameboid cancer cells. The following sketch illustrates the form of movement of the waves of excitation in the protoplasm of these cancer cells.

---

* See Part III, Chapter 3, "The Expressive Language of the Living in Orgone Therapy."

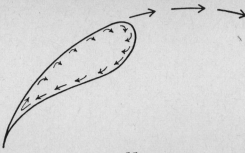

FIG. 11.

We have, accordingly, to distinguish *two kinds* of pulsatory movements in the living:

The pulsatory movement of the orgone energy within the organism and its effect, the pulsatory, mechanical movement of the body fluids. We differentiate them as *functional* and *mechanical* pulsation. *The mechanical pulsation is the result of the functional pulsation of the orgone energy, of its spinning forward in alternating expansion and contraction.*

The movement of fluids is a mechanical one; it can only be the consequence of the pulsatory function of the orgone energy. In the flowing ameba the functional, orgonotic pulsation coincides fully with the pulsing of material fluids. In the colpidia and paramecia, there is a jerky, pulsatory form of movement which is not rectilinear, but *spiraling*, and as a whole curved. We can connect together the individual points of the movement curve and obtain a geometrical figure depicting a "SPIN-NING WAVE" (KRW):

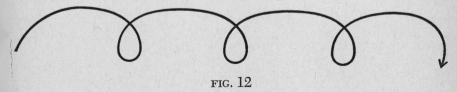

FIG. 12

We see that the curve of the plasmatic current is the same within the body of the cancer cell as it is in the local movement of the whole body of a colpidium. Now let us analyze the curve of the orgonotic plasma current into its individual constituents so that we obtain a form which is similar to the form of all living organs and organisms, seen laterally (*cf.* fig. 9).

This harmony in the form of movement of the bio-energy in the orgonotic wave of excitation and the form of organ, can be no accident. It is obviously governed by a common functioning principle of movement which is lawfully carried over into the individual forms of movements and into the structures. Even in the very elongated ringworm (annelida) where at first nothing can be seen of an orgonome form that turns back on itself, we find the orgonome in the *segments*. The ringworm, moreover, rolls itself into a form which is similar to the orgonome of a snail shell. (*cf.* fig. 4: 3 and 4).

The following diagram illustrates the structuralized, clearly expressed original movement of the organismic orgone energy in the growth of a shell:

FIG. 13. GROWTH OF A SHELL

We can, then, distinguish *three states* of the orgonotic expressive movement:

a. *The spinning movement of the orgonotic waves of excitation of the protoplasm and the locomotion of protozoa.*

b. *The orgonome form of the animal organs and organisms, thus frozen orgone movement,* and

c. *The orgonome form of the animal body in rest as an interphase between energetic motility and material solidity.*

We can now also comprehend the segmentary arrangement

of the orgonotic current in man, and the segmentary sequence of the armoring in the biopathic character more completely from the viewpoint of biophysics:

The plasmatic (mechanical) and the orgonotic (energetic) currents in man, the blood circulation and the waves of excitation, have a rhythmic, wavelike and segmentary character exactly as in the ringworm.

The segmentary arrangement of the armoring is an expression of the immobilization of individual parts of the course of wave excitation, or differently expressed: *One* wave freezes to *one* structured orgonome segment.

Thus the rule of orgone therapy of proceeding in the dissolution of the armoring always from the "head end" and toward the "tail end" or "genital end" acquires its bio-energetic import: As in the ring-worm, the snake and the plasmatic cancer cell, the *orgonotic waves of excitation run always from the tail end over the back to the head, then backward over the chest and abdomen toward the genital*. This course of the orgonotic current is bio-energetically comprehensible for it causes movement of the total body *"forward,"* in the direction of the head. Were we now in orgone therapy to dissolve the armor at the tail end first, the liberated energy would, so to speak, bounce against the segment situated higher up and would not flow on. Dissolution *at the head end first* removes the armor-ring toward *where* the orgonotic excitation has to stream. We move in the direction of the current, thus we first clear the way for the streaming, instead of first un-armoring the original source of this current. The technique of orgone therapy, to be sure, did not proceed from this bio-physical consideration, but followed purely clinical findings, e.g., that it was advantageous to free all bodily energy before the genital is mobilized. But as we now see, the clinical and the bio-energetic aspects of the problem meet harmoniously.

Let us now return to our Experiment XX to learn more about the formation of the living protoplasm into the orgonome. Plasmatic flakes were produced in which first spherical, the *bean-shaped* orgonome forms developed. In the bean-form the orgonome again is clearly expressed. This orgonome is motile.

Its movements also have orgonome-form, as we can readily determine from the spiral lines of the movement.

It is now admissible to conclude that *the orgone energy, at first freely moving in the fluid, is transformed to a very small extent by the process of freezing into matter, in the form of membranes.* Since the movement of the orgone energy is curved, it is understandable that the membranes have a curved shape. Within the membranes further free orgone energy is moving. Its striving is naturally to *stretch* the membrane, *as if it tended to break out of the "sack" in which it is imprisoned.* Naturally, it is not a matter of any "wish" or "tendency," but of a contradiction between the expansive movement of the *free* orgone energy and the enclosing *membrane.* Logical consideration shows us that *from this contradiction between energy-flow and restricting membrane nothing else than a bean-form, our orgonome, can result.*

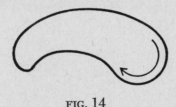

FIG. 14

The formation of the bean-form, of course, does not satisfy in any way the movement of the free orgone within, which strives after *extension of the curve,* thus after *forward movement from the spot.* Thus emerges *local movement* for the first time, the basic line being again long-extended, curved, and rhythmically turned back in on itself.

The development of colpidia from primary germinal vesicles is especially well-suited for the study of plasmatic currents which arise from the liberation of orgone energy in the membranous sack. As soon as a membrane has formed around a heap of bions, the "germinal vesicle" develops. Its inner content reveals vesicular structure and a blue shimmer, and the membrane is taut; but the whole system is still at rest (fig. 15:1). Within the "germinal vesicle" motile impulses are liberated; this is revealed by the fact that sooner or later a *rolling movement* of the vesicles takes place. While the membrane is still at rest, the vesicles first roll at the periphery, in *one* direction along the membrane. The inner connection is slackened. With the rolling movement in one direction goes a mutual attraction and repulsion. After a while the direction of the total movement is reversed: The vesicular content reverses the direction. In this way, the bionous content gains in elasticity (fig. 15:2). The vesicle grows increasingly taut; it becomes larger. *Gradually the form of an egg, our orgonome, takes shape.* The plasmatic current is *divided at one end into two currents.* The two currents converge and are continued in the middle line backwards (fig. 15:3). One can clearly distinguish in the orgonome *two* halves which, each on its own, ever more plainly assume the bean or lateral orgonome form. After several hours of vigorous orgonotic motility of the plasma, the vesicle usually separates into *four* "complete" colpidia. We hitherto could not determine whether the number "four" is lawful or whether division into *two* colpidia also occurs. It is important that *the "head" end of the colpidium is where the originally formed current was directed. The animal swims away locally in the direction of the original orgonotic current* (fig. 15:4).

This current had described an orgonome form. Now, when the local forward movement begins, the current within stops and the animal moves *as a whole* forward in spinning lines which are gently curved. *The curving of the path of movement is synonymous with the curvature of the "back."* The sketches (fig. 15) drawn according to life, illustrate what has been said.

Let us now recapitulate the process in the living orgonome:

1. *The inner motility is supplied by wavelike, undulating, pulsating orgone energy which is confined in a membranous "sack."*

2. *The movement of the orgone energy induces the motility of the structured, bionous substance within the organism.*

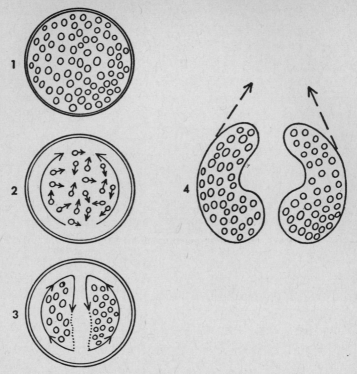

FIG. 15 FOUR DISTINCT PHASES IN THE DEVELOPMENT OF THE
COLPIDIUM

3. *As a consequence of the confinement of the inner orgone
energy movement by the membrane, there arises a curved path
of plasmatic current in which we recognize an orgonome.*

4. *The "energetic" orgonome leads to the formation of the
"material" orgonome. The form of the orgonome preserves the
form of the original energy movement.*

5. *There arises an opposition between the movement of the
orgone energy and the rigid membrane. The membrane at the
head bends the current sharply backward.* Since this happens
at all protusions of the vesicle, the currents converge at the
middle and create in this way a division of the vesicle into four
structural orgonomes.

6. If the division is complete, then separation and *local movement of individual orgonomes occur.* The local movement describes a curved line, a wave movement with alternating long and short half waves. The movement "from position" is obviously dictated by the direction of the orgonotic impulses. It is curved in the sense of the "back." The "front end" lies in the direction of the original orgonotic current.

Orgonotic Superimposition in Copulation of Metazoa

To recapitulate: The specific orgonome form of the living and its organs is the result of an opposition between *free* orgone energy and *frozen* orgone energy that has developed into membranous matter. *The free orgone energy tends continually to go beyond the membrane that confines it and that is closed in on itself. The energetic orgonome is extended and open, the material orgonome is closed.* Since the waves of excitation of the energetic orgonome move within the limits of the closed material orgonome, they necessarily are impeded by the membranous enclosure, as is represented in fig. 16.

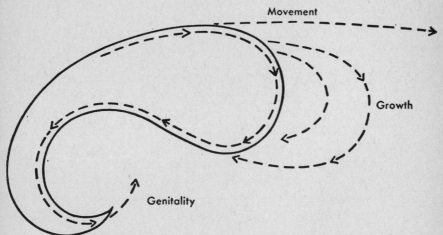

FIG. 16. MOVEMENT, GROWTH AND GENITALITY ARE FUNCTIONAL VARIANTS OF ORGONOTIC WAVES OF EXCITATION

In this way, a *stretching* of the orgonome occurs, in which we recognize the basis of all kinds of GROWTH, especially vivid in the *stretching of the gastrula* to the elongated embryo of a multicellular organism *(metazoa)*. *The function of growth corresponds to the extension of the membranes of the closed orgonome.* That it is in fact a question of the *expansive functions* of the free orgone energy can be seen in the bulging protrusions which initiate the formation of every new organ in the embryo of all kinds of animals. The embryonic protrusions have again typically the orgonome form.

To what extent the *original* wave movement of the energetic orgonome clearly emerges depends upon the subtleness of the structured body membranes and upon the presence or absence of a skeleton. But even where an extensive skeleton and full musculature has obliterated the *outer* phenomenon of the waves of excitation, still there always exists the rhythmic pulse of excitation, the current of blood circulation, and the plasmatic currents which are felt subjectively. *In the orgasm reflex the original form of movement of the energetic orgonome* returns unveiled, embracing *the whole organism.*

The superimposition of two closed orgonomes is the energetic basis of the superimposition of two living organisms during copulation (cf. fig. 18). In so doing, the highly excited tail ends penetrate each other bodily; the two orgonomes flow together into a single highly-charged orgone energy system. It is characteristic of the unity of all processes in the Living that the energy functions of excitation, superimposition, penetration and fusion are carried over into the like functions of the reproductive cells. For spermatozoa and egg cell continue in copulation the function of superimposition and fusion of male and female orgonomes. The division of the living orgonomes into *male* and *female* individuals still remains a riddle from the viewpoint of orgone physics.

Let us try now, on the basis of the orgonome as the biophysical basic form of the living, to comprehend the expressive movement of the orgasm reflex.

The function of the orgasm reflex cannot be, as one could assume from the viewpoint of a "purposiveness," to accelerate the passage of the male semen into the female genital organs. The orgasm reflex is independent of semen discharge for we also find it in the embryo in the typical forward position and convulsion of the tail end; in the whipping, energetic forward-movement of the tail end of many insects, e.g., in wasps, bees, bumblebees; and also in the customary position of the tail end and hindlegs in the species of dogs, cats, and hoofed animals. These examples may suffice to show that in the orgasm reflex it is a question of a far more general life function than fertilization. Mechanistic and finalistic explanations fail here; they are too narrow and do not touch on the core of the phenomenon.

Let us try to understand the function of the orgasm reflex from its expressive movement.

The living orgonome, be it an embryo, an insect or an animal of higher organization, is characterized essentially by this: that *first, the local movement always and lawfully occurs in the direction of the larger and broader front end; that second, the genital organs always and lawfully lie on the ventral side close to the tail end; that third, in the state of orgonotic excitation of the orgonome the genital organ is extended by erection in the direction of the local movement; and that fourth, the movements which effect the penetration and fusion of the male with the female genital organ drive the whole tail end forward in a highly energetic fashion* (cf. fig. 17).

These biological phenomena apply quite generally for the animal kingdom with the exception of animal species which have reached only a little beyond the stage of the primitive orgonome form of the jellyfish.

The form and position of the body (trunk) in the vertebrates shows in what direction the orgonotic waves of excitation occurred during growth: *They ran from the tail end over the long curved back forward to the head end.* They also run during the whole lifetime of the organism in the same direction. That can be subjectively experienced when the sensations of pleasure or anxiety stream over the back; it can be objectively seen in the stroking of an animal's fur. The "hair bristles" through contraction of the mm. erectores pilorum in the direction of the orgonotic wave movement, as they are erected *frontward.*

As we can observe clearly in the sketch (fig. 17), the whole back is gently curved, and in this way *in harmony with the curving of the path of orgonotic waves.* It is to be assumed that the curvature of the wave stream determines the curvature of the back, and not vice versa. But once the material, closed orgonome has formed, then it contains, as earlier presented, the energetic waves of excitation and *forces on them a deviation from the original path of the extended wave.* It is likely that the generally *frontward* formation of secondary protrusions in embryonic growth is due to this deviation of the wave of excitation. The essential fact is above all the *opposition between the material* and the *energetic* orgonome.

So long as the directions of the material and the energetic orgonome are in harmony, there is no contradiction. The body orgone energy does not force its way out beyond the orgonome sack. For this reason there is on the whole length of the back of animals no organ formation.

Growth on the longitudinal axis and local movement appear accordingly as energetic functions of the body orgone energy, as results of its striving to get beyond the confining membranous sack. In so doing, the membrane is stretched and thus forms the *protruding sacks* of the growing organs in their primitive state.

In antithesis to the back where solid and energetic orgonome are in harmony, we find at the front end on the ventral side a plethora of organ formations of different kinds: the forehead, nose, mouth, chin and jawbone, breasts, limbs and genitals. If, now, our functional conception of organ formation is universally valid, then organs must always arise through protrusions of the membranes on the ventral side where the direction of current of the biological energy is turned from its regular

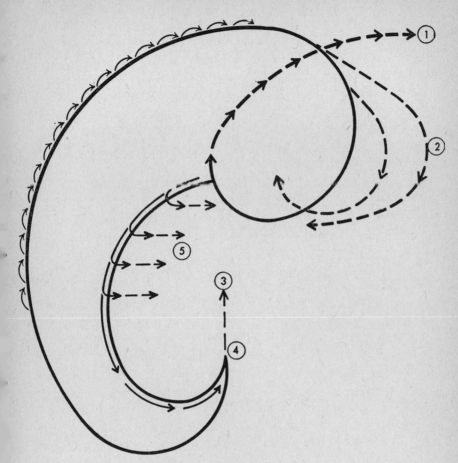

1) Direction of *forward movement*.
   Antenna, optic peduncles, primary brain vesicles
2) Direction of *growth*.
3) *Org-movement* = continuation of direction.
4) *Highest orgonity*, sharpest concentration.
5) Intermediary "break-outs."

FIG. 17. THE ORGASM REFLEX BRINGS THE TAIL END IN THE
FORWARD DIRECTION OF THE ORGONOTIC WAVES

direction, thus where the body orgone has the tendency to "*break out of the sack*" (*cf.* fig. 17).

We see by our sketch that the membranes on the ventral side actually everywhere oppose the original forward direction of the orgone energy waves. Consequently, we find again and again, and moreover at almost regular intervals, as in the arrangement of limbs and breast nipples, a rhythmically recurring "impulse to break through." This contradiction between membrane and energy wave is increased to the highest degree at the tail end. The material tail end is pointed and sharp; the material orgonome bends sharply forward in the direction of forward movement.

The sharp forward motion of the tail end in animals, on the basis of concentrated orgonotic waves of excitation pressing forward, explains "*genital excitation*" and the orgasm reflex in a satisfactory and probably complete way. *The orgastic convulsions of the tail end forward express the sharp pressing-forward of the orgonotic waves of excitation.* The sharpness of the orgonotic excitation at the tail end is explained by the *compression of the orgone waves in a narrow space*, in the pointed and less extensive tail end and particularly in the narrow genital organs. The *orgone* energy at the tail end *turns at the genital in the original direction forward; it brings the genital into high excitation in the forward direction and into erection.*

Let us now analyze *copulation of animals* from the viewpoint of orgonomic functionalism. The orgone, concentrated at the genital end and urging forward, cannot get out of the membrane; it is forced backward again most acutely. *There is only* ONE *possibility of flowing out in the intended forward direction:* BY FUSION WITH A SECOND ORGANISM. *The direction of excitation of the second organism agrees with the direction of the orgone waves in the first.* This is now in fact *fulfilled in orgonotic superimposition*, as the sketch (fig. 18) will show. We see that in the superimposition of the two orgonomes and penetration of the genitals, the hard-pressed and hence "unsatisfied" tail end can allow its orgonotic waves of excitation to flow in the natural direction; it does not have to turn them back sharply; furthermore, the *space is widened* in which the waves can stream.

Our assertion that the orgasm reflex has no direct verbal expression is correct. Its function lies beyond the boundary of speech. Still it has a concrete expression: *Superimposition* follows orgonotic *penetration. The pre-orgastic bodily movements and in particular the orgastic convulsions represent extreme attempts of the free orgone of both organisms to fuse with one another,* TO REACH INTO ONE ANOTHER.

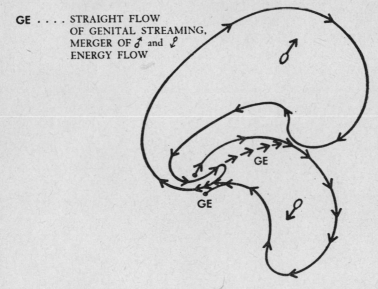

GE . . . . STRAIGHT FLOW
OF GENITAL STREAMING,
MERGER OF ♂ and ♀
ENERGY FLOW

FIG. 18. FUNCTION OF "GRATIFICATION" IN GENITAL
SUPERIMPOSITION

I said earlier that the energetic orgonome always strives to go beyond the material orgonome. *Since now the energy of one organism is pouring into the energy system of the second organism, the free orgone energy in fact succeeds in flowing beyond the limits of the organism, and, fusing with a second orgonotic system, is swinging further.* In this way the tendency to stretching, to widening of the effectual area of the free orgone energy is taken into account. In the acme of excitation, energy in large quantities actually flows out, together with the sexual substances. The subjective sensation of "release" or "satisfaction" (gratification) is connected with this discharge. Since every expression of language mirrors directly the function of the energetic process, these words express exactly what takes place objectively.

Orgastic longing, which plays such a gigantic role in the life of animals, appears now as an expression of this "striving beyond oneself," as "longing" to reach out *beyond* the narrow sack of one's own organism. "We *yonder"*—to use an apt phrase —for the beyond of ourselves. Perhaps here lies the solution of the riddle why the idea of death so often represents the orgasm. In dying, too, the biological energy reaches beyond the boundaries of the material sack which holds it prisoner. The religious idea of "liberating death," of "deliverance beyond" acquires, then, its factual basis. The function which in the naturally functioning organism is fulfilled by the orgasm in sexual superimposition, reappears in the armored organism in the form of the nirvana principle or the mystical idea of salvation. The religious, armored organism expresses it directly: he would like to "free his soul from the flesh." The "soul" represents the orgonotic excitation, the "flesh" the confining tissue. The idea of "sinful flesh" has nothing to do with these facts. It is an idea grown in the pornographic structure of humanity.

Recapitulating, we may call attention to the *simplicity of the functional laws of living nature* as one of their main characteristics. Such far apart functions as *growth, movement* and *genital excitation* can be reduced to the common denominator of the relationship between free orgone energy and the confining membranous sack. The variations of this CFP are determined by the place in the organism where the contradiction acts: *growth* is the result of orgone waves pressing the confining membranes outward at the head end; *genital excitation* is orgone energy pressing forward at the tail end.

We will meet again the function of *Orgonotic Superimposition* in the astrophysical realms of nature. For it is orgonotic superimposition which knits the living organism together with surrounding nature.

VI. ORGONE PHYSICS

THE ORANUR EXPERIMENT

Orgone Energy (OR) Versus Nuclear Energy
(NR)—ORANUR (December, 1950–May, 1951)

Introductory Remarks

It is a common experience in natural-scientific work that one starts some research project with a certain problem in mind to be solved, and that the actual operation forces its way in an entirely different, unexpected direction. Careful vigilance combined with complete lack of preconceived ideas will then achieve important, though unexpected results. The discovery of the radioactivity of pitchblende was made this way, and many other discoveries made in a similar manner are known. This magnificent rationality in true natural inquiry was at work also in the series of Oranur experiments which began toward the end of 1950.

As proposed in the first ORANUR REPORT (*Orgone Energy Emergency Bulletin*, No. 1, December, 1950), the Oranur experiment proper had as its primary objective the investigation of possible anti-nuclear radiation effects in the atmospheric orgone (OR) energy; in other words, the experiments were planned with the prospect of finding a powerful antidote against nuclear (NR) radiation sickness. On the basis of years of previous experimentation and observation, it was assumed that the powerful forces contained in the cosmic OR energy would neutralize NR radiation and mitigate its effects. It was roughly

---

From *The Oranur Experiment.* First Report (1947-1951), 1951.

taken for granted that "radiation sickness" is the effect of *nuclear* radiation acting upon living tissues and blood; this assumption was in accordance with the prevalent view in today's radiological pathology.

Now, the first series of the specific Oranur experiments did not fully reach this goal, although several important and hopeful observations had been made in the intended direction. *However, the main result of the Oranur experiment proper was the nearly complete disclosure of the true nature of a type of radiation sickness which has much in common with what is known about biological effects of atomic energy.* IT WAS FOUND, BEYOND ANY REASONABLE DOUBT, THAT SO-CALLED RADIATION SICKNESS IS NOT, AS HERETOFORE ASSUMED, A DIRECT RESULT OF NR RADIATION UPON LIVING TISSUE BUT AN IMMEDIATE EXPRESSION OF A *severe reaction of the organismic* OR *energy against the action of* NR *radiation.*

To explain these astounding results in familiar terms of medicine:

To a superficial view, an abscess or an inflammation may appear as the direct result of the invasion of virulent bacteria into the organism. However, it is well known in organic pathology that abscess, inflammation, high temperature, etc., are due to strong *defensive* reactions of the organism *against* invading infectious bacteria. Concentration of leucocytes in the invaded area, concentration of blood, and, in severe cases, high-pitched activity of the heat regulation system (high temperature) are the immediate symptoms in infectious disease.

This clinical example may suffice to give the reader an initial idea of the first results we achieved. To continue with the analogy: Steeped in the wrong belief that it is the bacteria which are acting as the specific factors in abscess formation, inflammation and high temperature, we had started with the expectation of finding an effective agent against infectious bacteria. To our great astonishment we discovered that the bacteria are no more than the eliciting cause, mere triggers which stir leucocytes, blood concentration in the area of infection, and the general rise in temperature into action. This reaction *on the part of the organism* to the infection is in itself an attempt at *self-cure*. However, under certain specific conditions, *the process of defensive health reaction can or does turn into the true killer*. We are most probably dealing with an organismic reaction similar to that of *immunization* to an infectious disease.

To anticipate briefly:

RADIATION SICKNESS IS A SPECIFIC PROBLEM OF ORGANISMIC OR ENERGY FUNCTION AND NOT OF NR RADIATION. THE LATTER IS NOT A *specific* CAUSE OF RADIATION SICKNESS. Symptoms which appear in the course of radiation sickness can also come about without the action of NR radiation.

Nausea, hemorrhages, petechiae, general malaise, loss of hair, sclerosis of the skin, decline of the blood function, fatigue, anemia, leukemia and final death are not specific symptoms of radiation sickness. They are to be found singly or in complex syndromes in diseases which were not elicited by overirradiation. In addition to these symptoms, during the Oranur experiment other symptoms were observed which, as far as we know, have not been reported by observers of NR radiation effects. The Oranur experiment has produced some of the well-known NR radiation symptoms, and in addition, symptoms which were specifically related to overirradiation by OR energy.

Thus we did not yet, in this first run, secure a safe antidote to radiation sickness, but we found the true dynamics of this disease and were able to link it up comprehensibly with other disease pictures. These introductory remarks will now be substantiated by concrete facts and observations.

The Oranur experiment proper has left too many questions unanswered to yield a clear-cut picture of all the underlying processes. This is reflected in the presentation which is less compact and systematic than the three preceding reports on the preparatory Oranur experiments. It is hoped that in due time the main body of the Oranur experiment will reach the same degree of clarity and consistency. The urgency of the subject matter made not premature but less elaborate publication necessary.

Before entering the main subject, I would like to express my deep appreciation and my thanks to my assistants, who helped carry the dangerous job through during the five months of experimentation in Oranur. They were fully devoted to their tasks; they took severe criticism at times, with the attitude of the man or woman who knows fully what doing a responsible job means; they have exposed themselves to dangerous hazards and even to possible death without hesitation or complaint; at times they have worked uninterruptedly day and night; and last but not least, they have stood by all through the task as good friends in a team. I am very grateful to all of them, and I would like to express my regret that, without intention, they have become, in these experiments, objects of a dangerous threat to their health and even to their lives.

Basic Premises of the Oranur Project

The Oranur project was inaugurated on several well-known and commonly understood premises.

1. *Atomic energy* (nuclear energy, NR) represents cosmic energy which is free from matter through disintegration of the atom, which is the constituent of the universe in terms of classical and quantum physics. It is energy AFTER MATTER. OR ENERGY, on the other hand, represents cosmic energy BEFORE MATTER, i.e., energy which has *not* been caught in or has not been transformed into solid matter. It is universally present, penetrates everything, surrounds, as the so-called OR energy envelope, our planet and most likely all other heavenly bodies (sun's corona, Saturn's ring, etc.). Cosmic OR energy, moving freely within the living organism, is called BIO-ENERGY or ORGANISMIC OR ENERGY.

2. From many observations over a period of some 15 years, it had been deduced that OR energy and NR energy are antagonistic to each other. NR energy, according to current views,

damages living functions in the form of *"radiation sickness,"* in severe cases with consequent death; in orgonomic terms, NR energy somehow affects bio-energy, rendering it incapable of functioning to various degrees. On the other hand, it was assumed that OR energy, in sufficient concentration and strength, would counteract NR radiation. It seemed most likely that the spontaneous recovery from radiation sickness was to be attributed to the OR energy in the organism getting the upper hand over NR energy.

3. In order to make this interrelationship of atomic and OR energy more readily comprehensible to ourselves and to the world at large, a parallel had been drawn in *psychological* terms many years ago to the age-old notions of the human mind such as the antagonistic functions of "GOOD" and "EVIL," or, meaning the same, of "GOD" and "DEVIL." (*Cf. Ether, God and Devil*, 1949.)

The physical *Life Energy* had been discovered in consequential pursuit of the functions of what is called "LOVE" in the whole animal kingdom. The human mind has always conceived of LOVE as being capable of coping with HATE and DESTRUCTION. It was also always clear that hate can kill love and that love, in its struggle against evil, can turn into hate by mere frustration.

To the experimenter in the Oranur project, the antithesis of OR energy and NR energy easily merged with our psychiatric knowledge about emotional functions, which are, in a deep biophysical sense, truly *physical* functions. OR energy had never shown any ill effects on living organisms; it was shown to be capable of coping with such afflictions as tissue and blood degeneration by charging of the organism to a high bio-energetic level. On the basis of these medical experiences, it was assumed that *"OR Energy"* or *"Life Energy"* represented in strictly physical terms what the layman is used to calling "Good" or "God". Furthermore, it has been found and was secured as a piece of well-founded knowledge that the BIONS or OR ENERGY VESICLES which constitute the living substance also appeared in two antagonistic forms, as PA bions and

T-bions; the PA bions are capable of killing the T- or death bacilli. But it is also true that T-bacilli, highly concentrated or active in bio-energetically weakened tissues, destroy healthy tissue. This was learned from the cancerous shrinking biopathy. (*Cf.* Reich, *The Cancer Biopathy*, pp. 11-63.)

Thus our background of operation contained two series of functions which were antagonistic to each other and were amply represented in human ideology, in microscopic observations and in physical functions. Synoptically:

GOOD	EVIL	Ethics
GOD	DEVIL	Religion
LIFE	DEATH	Biology
PA-BIONS	T-BIONS	Bio-energetics
ORGONE ENERGY (OR)	NUCLEAR ENERGY (NR)	Physics
COSMIC ENERGY	COSMIC ENERGY	Astrophysics, Cosmology
before MATTER	*after* MATTER	

Though no more than a useful framework of thought, this coordination provided a perfect base of operation and a safe guiding line into the dark realms of a dangerous unknown. Its general human and scientific basis seemed broad and firm enough to serve as a reliable outlook onto things to come.

Moreover, extensive work on the cancer problem for the past fifteen years had yielded a rich harvest of various facts about life functions and their counterparts, the forces of evil and destruction. A firm hold had been established with regard to diagnosis of initial decay and degeneration in living systems through such measures as the Reich Blood Tests and the cultivation and microscopic observation of the indicators of death, the T-bacilli (*cf. The Cancer Biopathy*).

Our first report contains the general outline. Now, let us turn to the events proper as they began to develop around the middle of December 1950 to about the end of May 1951. These events, to say it bluntly, represented a severe knockout blow in many directions: With respect to physical functions, with respect to the crucial breakthrough into the concrete experimentation, and with respect to Oranur particularly.

The workers who partook in these first steps of Oranur all became afflicted to various degrees with "Oranur sickness"; experimental mice died; the experimental building was knocked out of function for several months and possibly permanently; all plans which were carefully designed to carry out the project, were thrown over and had to be redesigned; crucial physical concepts tottered. Only the open, free, truly scientific mind will be able to follow this report without prejudice or fear.

SEQUENCE OF EVENTS

On August 30, 1950, I had reported at the annual meeting of the Board of Trustees of The Wilhelm Reich Foundation about the *anti-nuclear* possibilities of OR energy. (*Cf. Orgone Energy Bulletin*, 3/1, January, 1951, pp. 59-60.)

During the first week of December 1950, we began to proceed toward effective action.

The medical orgonomists in New York were alerted through our educational secretary, Dr. Elsworth F. Baker, to stand by after information was given on our plans.

We made it clear, to begin with, that there is at present no remedy known to medicine in cases of decline of organismic functioning, except OR energy as applied in the cancer biopathy. This, naturally, constituted a heavy responsibility which fell on *our* shoulders. We alone were able to find out whether or not OR energy contained any hope in the treatment of NR radiation sickness. The USA faced a dangerous situation in the first days of December 1950, when the disaster in Korea had struck with the evil attack of the Chinese communists; with the hands of the USA bound by the pledge not to bomb their hinterland in Manchuria; with the English allies still doing business with the red dictators; with the helplessness in the face of the tactics of the red fascists who were far superior in the use of all of the most refined methods of the emotional plague, and with the terrible experience of the Chinese aggressors making propaganda through the UN right in the middle of the USA, while their forces marched in Korea. The USA was left holding the bag.

I mention these social events in order to make comprehensible why I felt impelled to step out of my usual reserve and to do something crucial: This was the moment to rush in to help with whatever we had. It was, however, the first time that I started an experiment having in mind a particular purpose to be achieved.

The following steps were taken:

1. On December 15th, an application for the procurement of 20 millicuries Phosphorus P-32 (a radioactive isotope of phosphorus) was dispatched. In an accompanying letter to the AEC in Oak Ridge, Isotope Division, it was pointed out that we would not do any routine experiments with radioactive material such as tracer work or radioactive therapy; that we would solely test the effects of orgone energy on mice injected with P-32. An accompanying chart surveyed the plan of treatment of 80 mice in particular. The main question to be answered was:

CAN ARTIFICIALLY PRODUCED RADIATION SICKNESS BE TREATED OR PREVENTED BY OR ENERGY?

2. Preparations were made at Orgonon for the deposit and disposal of radioactive material P-32, approximately four millicuries per two weeks, was to be kept in a small wooden cabin some fifty feet away from the main students' laboratory building. Since Orgonon is miles away from any habitation area (four miles from Rangeley), there seemed to be no problem with contamination of inhabited areas, water supplies, etc. We planned on burying the carcasses of the animals used in the experiment several feet deep in the ground about 500 yards away from the laboratory and other buildings at Orgonon. Injection and dissection of mice was to be done in a small building, separated from the others, where no one would be present at any other time. The protective devices which we had ordered, the lead aprons we possessed, the lead gloves and the use of strong OR energy accumulators seemed sufficient measures to secure the safety of the personnel at that time.

This was in accordance with what was known at that time about radiation protection. We had no inkling of what was in store for us. In December 1950, before the experiment started, we could not possibly have guessed that all these measures would not work. But as we found out later, *no protection at all was possible in such experimentation as using OR energy versus NR energy.*

3. One of our physicians in New York offered his services in contacting various agencies to find out whatever he could about the different materials and the rules for handling them. We had heard that the AEC was particularly strict in its requirements for the handling of isotopes, and that this strictness was not shared by many commercial or even scientific laboratories. We learned, for instance, in one place, that no lead brick shielding was necessary in handling one or two millicuries of radioactivity. In many years of contacts between orgone physics and classical physics, we have learned that many things are not as exact and commonly agreed upon as it would appear from the claims of exactness; that one cannot find answers to some of the most primitive questions in the routine handbooks of physics, such questions as, for instance, what is the absolute rate of counts per minute (CPM) for a mg. of pure radium. It is essential to state these facts; it is not meant to criticize or to devaluate the labors of our colleagues in other branches of knowledge.

4. While these contacts were made and application forms sent out, I devoted myself to a recapitulation of very old observations which I had made some seven to twelve years ago, of NR radiation and its relationship to OR energy. I also began to prepare my base of operation. First of all, the natural "radioactivity" in all places where the future experimentation was to be performed, had to be monitored, and the instruments had to be prepared and calibrated for action in the main experiment. Here are a few results of these preliminary investigations, December 15-27, 1950:

No.	Background CPM (No NR present)	Orgone-Treated radioactive zinc sulfide CPM	Orgone-Treated 1 mcgr. radium CPM	Distance
Day	A	B	C	
1	40	500	30,000	1 cm.
2	50-70	2-300	20-30,000	" "
3	40-60	3-400	30,000	" "
4	40-50	4-500	30,000	" "
5	40-50	2-300	2-3,000	C dist. 10 cm.
6	60-70	60-70	3-4,000	" " " "
	(within ORACC)*	in ¼" lead 2-300 free		
7	60-70	200 in lead 300 free	3-4,000 3-4,000	" " " " " " " "

* Orgone energy accumulator.

These preliminary results on the BASE may suffice. Lead shielding did not appreciably reduce the activity. The background counts went up when radioactive material was put into an OR energy charger. No attention was paid to this fact, since we knew that OR effects on the GM counter vary greatly.

The background activity in the students' laboratory, where the main experiment was later to be performed, varied between 40-60 CPM. The measurements were made with a SU-5 Survey Meter and a tube Serial No. G-632, Type 6C5, Tracerlab, Inc. (30 mg./cm.^{2} wall thickness).

These examples are only to give an idea of the base functions, and are not a thorough account of the investigation. The high background count of 40-70 CPM was always observed in concentrated OR atmosphere.

We ordered a sample of radio cobalt (CO-60) from Tracerlab for the purpose of calibration of instruments. The counts from this source vary greatly and would have to be established in our laboratory. We had hoped, however, to obtain the counting rate from Tracerlab since we knew that the radioactivity would change and begin to vary a great deal once its source reached the highly charged orgone energy atmosphere at

Background monitoring with SU-5 Beta Gamma Survey Meter, Dec. 15, 1950
to Jan. 10, 1951

Date	Student Lab. CPM	Mouse House CPM	Garage CPM	Observ- atory CPM	Shop CPM	Free Space CPM	Remarks
12-15-50	30-50	30-50	30-50	30-50	30-50	30-50	Normal for Orgonon
12-16-50	30-50	30-50	30-50	30-50	30-50	30-50	,,
12-17-50	30-50	30-40	30-50	50-70	30-40	30-50	,,
12-18-50	30-50	30-50	30-40	50-60	30-50	30-50	,,
12-19-50	40-50	30-50	40-50	40-50	30-50	40-50	,,
12-20-50	30-40	30-40	30-40	30-60*	30-40	30-40	*Preliminary Oranur experiment
12-27-50	30-40	30-40	30-40	50-70*	30-40	30-40	*same
1-3-51	40-50	40-50	50-60	60*	40-50	30-40	*same
1-10-51	30-40	80-90*	30-50	90*	40-50	30-40	Oranur at work since 1-5-51

Orgonon. 2.26 x 10^{-5} millicuries CO-60, with a half life of 5.3 years, arrived on December 28, 1950. The source was not permitted to touch the highly charged students' laboratory and was rushed to a place in the OR energy observatory where no sizable OR effect could reasonably be expected during the short period of a few minutes. At 20h (8 p.m.) in the evening, the background count was still only 40-50, i.e., normal for Orgonon buildings. The source was left within the brass container and yielded 70 CPM and 0.016 MR/H (milli-röntgens per hour) with the SU-5 Survey Meter. The ionization effect on a calibrated aluminum leaf electroscope was rapid within seconds over 10 divisions (90° deflection). Spontaneous discharge rate in ORG time during that period was approximately 180 seconds per one division. Thus the ionization effect appeared quite clearly.

In order to protect the source, it was wrapped in lead foils of altogether some ½" thickness. Now the first surprise came. Three and one-half hours later, at 23:30h, I tested the source again. This time, though far away from any concentrated OR and outside the concrete rock walls of the observatory, the CPM amounted to 150, with the MR/H still at 0.016. *However, the ionization effect was gone. The NR source had no effect whatsoever on the charged electroscope beyond its spontaneous OR discharge rate.* Since the NR source had not been exposed to OR and had carefully been kept away from any OR accumulator, this astounding result could only be explained by the OR activity of the *lead shielding: the lead had been situated in the OR energy laboratory for many years, and although it itself did not give any counts, it most likely had eliminated the ionization effect.* The ionization effect did not return during the following three weeks, even when the source was taken out of its brass container and put naked on the plate of the electroscope. This, then, was a major first result in the direction of the expected OR-versus-NR effect. On December 29, the following day, the NR electroscopic discharge rate was even much slower than the OR rate: 300 (NR) as against 180 (OR) seconds per one division. Until January 2, 1951, the CPM with the source shielded in its capsule of brass, had *risen* to 200, measured with the survey meter *and* the autoscaler (Tracerlab). It varied greatly from one measurement to the next: between 150 and 250 CPM as against 70 upon arrival. Also, the MR/H went up from the initial 0.016 to 0.02 and 0.04 on the second day. It remained at that level for several days, having more than doubled its energy output. Also the background counts had slowly climbed up from 60 CPM on the second day, to 100 on the third day. All this remains to be investigated in greater detail.

The rise in background counts did not disquiet us since for four years I had worked in an atmosphere yielding 40-70 CPM background counts, and surrounding OR activities as high as 20,000 counts PER SECOND in high vacuum; furthermore, it was perfectly clear that it was not the well-shielded tiny amount of NR activity, but the reaction of the OR which was responsible for the increase of the atmospheric energy level. Though the NR source was handled with tongs, and with the use of lead gloves as well as lead apron, precautions far beyond the established health safety requirements, there was already at that early phase no way of protecting oneself against the clear-cut high OR activity, due to its *ability to penetrate everything— lead, cement, brick, metal of any thickness, etc.*

I just had to proceed, hoping that ill effects of high OR charges would continue to be absent.

The CO-60 was put into the "discharge funnel" and inserted in a small 5x OR "shooter" for further OR irradiation of the NR source. On January 4, 1951, I took the NR source out of its container and shielding, and measured it naked with two GM counters. At the autoscaler it yielded 5-6000 CPM at one cm distance from the mica window. The rate *within* its container was around 200-250 CPM, and around 0.04 MR/H measured with the SU-5 Survey Meter. This rate began to change considerably as the days passed. The activity was 7000 CPM on January 8, down to 3000 CPM on the 12th, and somewhat below 5000 CPM, naked, on the 15th.

The counts per time unit were *not* constant; they varied so greatly that the question presented itself as to how constant other radioactivities were. The problem of quantitative *nuclear* radioactivity had never occupied much place in the framework of orgonomic research, with the exception of the most primitive observations, such as scintillation, measurement of small amounts of radioactivity in the calibration of instruments, ionization, etc. But now, when the question of influencing NR by OR had come into sharp focus, it was of crucial importance to determine the constancy of NR radioactivity. Unfortunately, in no book on nuclear radiation which was available, could any definite answer be found.

A vial of radioactive luminescent matter (zinc sulfide) had been kept in a small OR charger for many years. It had lost its ionization effect through OR influence long ago. It still luminated very strongly. I measured the activity with the autoscaler (scale 4096). The result over several consecutive days was nearly constant at 245,760 CPM, increasing occasionally to 307,200 CPM. This seemed a high count for less than a microgram of radium as compared with 500 CPM for 2.26 micrograms of CO-60.

My wristwatch radium dial which had soaked up OR energy for many years, gave between 40,000 and 45,000 CPM in a fairly constant manner. I had worn this watch for years, and no ill effects had ever been observed on my wrist. The count seemed tremendous for the minimal amounts of radium on a dial. It was soon found that the OR influence was quite substantial. Radium dials on wristwatches which had newly been bought and had not been in contact with the OR atmosphere for any appreciable length of time, gave only 3-5000 CPM. We had to assume, but could not safely ascertain, that the distribution of radium on watch dials would be approximately equal. Yet, my wristwatch dial had yielded ten times the count of a newly-arrived wristwatch. This was striking.

The dial on the wristwatch of another worker in the laboratory who had been in much less contact with highly concentrated OR, gave between 5500 and 8000 CPM.

All measurements were done with the same autoscaler 4096, the same GM tube, and at the same distance, i.e., one cm.

These results, confusing as they were, also disclosed a very strong influence of OR upon NR. As in so many other cases, we had to realize that we had to learn anew, from scratch.

ORGONE ENERGY RUNS AMOK (DOR): THE "ORANUR SICKNESS"

In order to save time, we decided to order two milligrams of *pure radium*, and, instead of injecting fluid radioisotopes, to irradiate some of our mice with radium. The radium, in two one milligram units (each 8.3 R/H) and each in a separate ½ inch lead container, arrived on January 5, 1951. The NR sources were measured immediately and gave 245,760 CPM naked at one centimeter (cm.) distance.* One mg. radium was

---

* In the early summer of 1951 we had a third sample of radium, one mg., measured in New York before it was brought up to Orgonon. The count in New York was only 16,000 CPM naked and 7,000 in ½" lead shielding. This we did not know, of course, in January 1951.

designated as a control, to be left untreated; the other was to treated with OR energy. The first, No. I, remained untreated and was put into the garage near the observatory on the hill; the other, No. II, was put into a one-fold, small OR charger on January 5, 1951, at 11:30h. This charger was placed in the 20-fold OR energy accumulator which was located in an 18 x 18 foot OR energy room, lined with sheet iron of gauge 26. The experimental hall of the laboratory measuring 60 x 70 feet surrounds the OR energy room as depicted in the diagram.

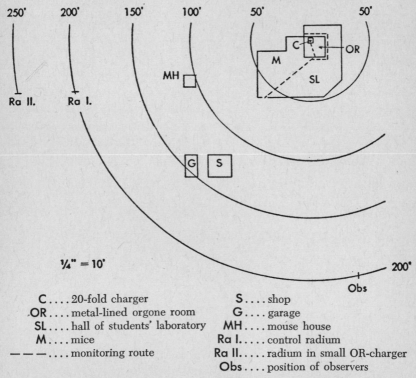

¼" = 10'

C .... 20-fold charger
.OR .... metal-lined orgone room
SL .... hall of students' laboratory
M .... mice
— — — .... monitoring route

S .... shop
G .... garage
MH .... mouse house
Ra I. .... control radium
Ra II. .... radium in small OR-charger
Obs .... position of observers

Sketch showing distances of places in students' laboratory and surroundings from OR energy room and 20-fold charger.

The background count, immediately before the Ra needle was put into the charger, was between 40 and 50 CPM everywhere, i.e., normal for this building.

366 WILHELM REICH

Now we made our first major mistake, which, however, was responsible for the tremendous results we obtained that same day: *I did not measure personally the background count right away after the radium needle was put into the charger.* Had I done so, I would have found a very high count in the hall; I would have immediately taken the Ra needle out of the charger and the hall, and would have missed the whole Oranur effect. I did not personally measure the background count right *after* the beginning of the experiment because I had measured the activity of the radium before with the autoscaler and counter tube (mica window, 2.3 mg./cm.^{2} thickness), and had found a count of only 2457 CPM with the needle *naked* at *one-meter* distance. The 20x accumulator into which the charger containing the needle had been put, measures 5 feet square horizontally, i.e., about 1½ meters. The distance between the outer walls of the 20x accumulator and the metal-lined walls of the OR energy room adds another 6 to 7 feet on each side. This means that the needle of Ra was at a distance of about 10 feet on two sides, and some 16 feet on a third side from the walls of the OR room. We had the notion that the metal lining of the OR energy room itself would add some shielding. There were workers doing their jobs outside in the experimental hall at a distance of an average of some 30 feet (i.e., ca. 10 meters) and more from the shielded radium needle.

Feeling safe about the distance of the radium from the outer hall of the laboratory, we committed a second mistake. We left the needle of Ra in the charger until about 16:30h (in the afternoon of January 5, i.e., 5 hours). We had intended to keep the Ra *continuously* in the shielded place. We had no inkling of the happenings that are now to be recounted.

The background count had been measured at 13h by a technical assistant. It was high, 70 to 80 CPM in the hall. *The assistant failed to report this high background count.* At 16:30h when I came down to the lower laboratory, the air was sticky and heavy. The background count ran up to 80 CPM 50 feet away from the Ra-needle, and amounted to *several hundred* CPM

TABLE OF DISTANCES

No.	Symbol	Place-object	Distance in feet from OR room	Distance in feet from students' laboratory
1	M	mice	40	
2	W	worker's desk	23	
3	MH	mouse house	105	50
4	S	shop	130	75
5	G	garage	145	85
6	NR	control radium	200	150
7	NR+OR	radium in charger	250	200
8	Ob	observer's position	200	160

on the *outside* of the walls of the OR room. The workers were immediately ordered out of the hall. The inside of the OR room was unbearably charged. The walls felt "glowing" 10 to 16 feet away from where the Ra needle was located. The portable survey GM meter "jammed" when I approached the 20x accumulator. There seemed no sense in counting CPM's at that moment. The first thing to do was to take the Ra needle out of the charger in order to calm down the OR reaction. It was not a failure in the battery of the survey meter which had caused the jamming. I remembered similar phenomena when I had worked with highly charged counter tubes in the first GM experiments back in 1947. If the GM meter operated again after having been in the fresh air for a while, the jamming would certainly have been due to blockage of the operation through extreme OR energy action. The GM survey meter actually recovered without repair after a few minutes in the fresh air, counting the normal 30-50 CPM background count in the open air. The radium was deposited within the small charger in a garage some 150 feet away from the metal room. We aired the building right away and hoped that this would remove the high OR charge quickly, to no avail. It still is "active" at this date (May 1951).

The radium itself did not produce any of the effects described above when it was taken outside into the garage. Whereas every one of us could feel the heaviness of the air, the oppression, the pulling pains here and there in the body, headaches and nausea right away within the OR energy building, no such sensations were felt outside in the vicinity of the radium as close as one foot. Furthermore, to our great astonishment, ventilation did not seem to remove the oppressive air from the laboratory building. After one hour ventilation, it was still impossible to enter the OR energy room, the radium having been removed long ago. *This was new.* Usually fresh air would remove any orgonotic overcharge. However, the high background count in the hall came back to nearly normal soon after the removal of the Ra needle. It sank to 60 CPM after half-an-hour's ventilation.

It is essential to acquaint the reader more fully with the subjective sensations which all of us experienced long after the removal of the radium; sensations which came back intensely and typically, and even more intensely as the days passed, whenever we came near the orgone energy laboratory, especially the OR energy room *with no NR material in it.* The OR researcher is professionally required to be free of blocking of his perceptions. He relies on his impressions and sensory reactions to a great extent as guiding posts into new territory, and what he thus finds he controls with objectively operating devices. Both the *subjective* and the *objective* experience are essential and must go together. An emotionally blocked or "dead" researcher would be completely useless in OR research. He would only endanger himself and others.

A penetrating salty taste, turning slightly bitter or sour on the outstretched tongue, was felt by all present everywhere within the building and even outside the building as far as 50 feet. With further experimentation, this unpleasant sensation became more intense and was felt increasingly outside the building in the fresh air.

All workers who partook in the observations developed more

or less severe conjunctivitis within a few minutes after entry into the hall.

All observers reported independently a severe pressure in the depths of the cheek bone in the region of the exit of the II branch of the trigeminus nerve.

Most workers became nauseated, lost appetite later on, felt weak; some to the extent of losing control of balance.

A ringlike pressure around the forehead and back into the occipital region was felt by many observers almost immediately.

The diaphragmatic segment seemed especially sensitive. Pressure, pain, or a strong pulling sensation were felt in the epigastrium.

Some participants became very pale within a few minutes upon entering the hall. Feelings of cold shivers alternated with hot flashes, as manifestations of severe impairment of the vago-sympathetic equilibrium.

In some cases, the skin became mottled, especially on the palms. This may suffice until more is reported about the following events.

THE OR ENERGY ITSELF SEEMED TO HAVE CHANGED INTO A DANGEROUS, DEADLY POWER. We came to call this effect "DOR" (Deadly ORgone).

All work in the building had to be stopped immediately. Nobody was permitted to enter it. Those who had certain chores to fulfill such as cleaning, filling the oil heaters or caring for the mice which were left in the experimental hall, were ordered to work inside only 2 to 3 minutes at a time, then to leave the building and to "air out" for at least 10 minutes. Workers who had shown great sensitivity to the stormy orgone reaction were told to stay away entirely. Orgonomic Reich blood tests were done with all workers each week, except the two maintenance men who, on special personal grounds, refused to have their blood examined. One of them was then prohibited from working in the hall at all, and the other was directed to stay in no longer than 2-3 minutes at a time. The results of the blood tests will be reported separately. They were of great theoretical and practical value and opened up new vistas upon the nature of the common functions of *"Oranur sickness"* and its relation to leukemia.

We repeated the same experiment from January 5-12, daily, for one hour. On Friday, the 12th of January, we undertook the last experiment in this series of daily Oranur experimentation. The *Experimental ONE mg.* of radium was put into the 20x OR charger. It remained there for only half-an-hour. The results of this last experiment were so severe that they deserve to be reported in great detail.

Three experimental observers remained outside the laboratory within about 100 yards. One assistant rushed the experimental piece of radium into the OR energy room and into the 20x charger. We desisted from measuring with the GM survey meter this time, in order to avoid unnecessary additional exposure. A few minutes later, we could clearly see through the large windows that the atmosphere in the laboratory had become "clouded"; it was moving visibly, and shined blue to purple through the glass. As we walked up and down some 100 to 250 feet OUTSIDE the laboratory, all three of us had the same experience, but no one at first dared to mention it. I felt severe nausea, a slight sensation of fainting, loss of equilibrium, clouding of consciousness, and had to make an effort to keep erect on my feet. I saw Dr. S. Tropp, who was with me, getting very pale. He had not said anything, and I had not told him how I felt. Then I asked him how he felt, whether he felt what I felt. He immediately admitted to feeling very ill and faint, with pressure in the forehead, nauseated, cramped in the stomach, and weak. Then I confirmed his experience by mentioning my own reactions. We had both hesitated to tell about it since we were so far outside the experimental hall in the fresh, clear, dry air of a late afternoon in midwinter.

Thereupon, we interrupted the experiment and put the radium away to half a mile distance from the laboratory, within an uninhabited area of 280 acres.

It was perfectly clear, from what we had experienced, that

the *OR energy field of the laboratory had been greatly extended and excited to a dangerous degree far outside the outer walls.* Since there is no sharp borderline anywhere in OR energy functioning, the reaction seemed not only to persist all the time, WITHOUT ANY RADIUM IN THE CHARGER; more, it seemed to extend rapidly. We began to worry about how far this spreading of the Oranur reaction would go and where it would halt. We began to feel responsible for what might happen to the village some four miles away. The closest inhabited building was at least 1½ miles away.

We also wondered what *could* happen if we continued with the Oranur experiment: whether all hope of an *anti*-nuclear effect of OR had gone; whether an explosion was possible if a high concentration of OR would act upon some as-yet-unknown NR material; whether we would recover from the sickness we were suffering from, and whether it would leave any after-effects.

Our eyes burned and the conjunctivae were heavily inflamed. We drove up to the OR observatory some 500 yards away on the hill, took a sharp drink and began separately to write down our physical and emotional experiences. These notes were signed and deposited with the protocols in the archives. Common to all of us were: severe belching, nausea, pressure in the nasal bone structure, in the depth of the eyes, alternating cold and hot flushes, paresthesias, feeling of disequilibrium, wandering pains in the legs, weakness in arms, especially in the ulnar region, dull headache, tension in the pharynx, severe headache.

The morning of that same day we had dissected two OR mice, i.e., formerly *healthy* mice which had been exposed to the Oranur atmosphere. They were very ill and about to die. Both mice showed clearcut bleeding in the subcutaneous tissue, petechiae, an exudate of the fibrinous type at the pleurae, change in the shape and charge of the RBCs in the direction of leukemia (to be described in a separate report), and an increase in white cells. The blood cultures of both mice were T-positive the following day. *We had apparently found the bridge from*

Oranur sickness to leukemia, in the blood picture as well as in the T-picture.

My co-workers left after a rest of about two hours. I went to bed early, tired and worn out and fell asleep immediately, still nauseated.

We had fallen ill with "Oranur sickness."

I slept some five hours soundly and heavily. At 24h I woke up and felt refreshed. I was struck by what appeared to me as *perfect, crystal-clear vision* and a sharp awareness of things around me, as if my OR energy field were particularly wide and active. My eyes were clear and sparkling; the conjunctivae were still slightly injected.

Things now appeared somewhat rosier. I had gone through a similar but lesser experience 12 years ago, in January 1939, when for the first time I had encountered the OR radiation from the SAPA bions in my laboratory in Oslo. Then, too, I first had felt frightened, nauseated, with eyes inflamed; then, too, I had tried in vain to "protect" myself, had called a physicist in Amsterdam for help, and had feared what might happen or develop. Then, too, after a few days things began to look less dangerous. I felt crystal clear in my head, I was tanned on my whole body (with clothes on) in the middle of the northern winter, and then, too, I had lost my fear of the danger involved. I began to learn to rely upon BIO-ENERGY without any protection.

These experiences have been reported at some length in my book, *The Cancer Biopathy.* This time, however, all reactions semed increased a thousandfold. The OR energy seemed to have run amok, possibly even to the extent of a chainlike reaction in the atmosphere, far outside the building. Extreme caution was imperative. In 1939, I had worked quite alone. This time a dozen workers were doing their jobs at Orgonon, and many more were standing by in the New York area.

At one o'clock at night, I turned on the radio in my library. There was no transmission, only a cluttering noise as from a Geiger counter when it reports atmospheric orgone energy action. I thought something had gone wrong with this particular radio. I turned around the plug in the wall outlet. The noise remained. I turned on another radio with the same result. A third radio, result the same. This could not be an innocent coincidence. It occurred to me that I had transferred two micrograms of radio cobalt to the tower above the roof of the observatory building. This tower rests on a 6″ cement floor. Therefore, it seemed unlikely that the radio cobalt acted through the cement floor which was some 60 feet away from the third noisy radio. Then the reaction became understandable: The tower where the radio cobalt (contained within a small 10-fold charger) was located, also housed the antenna structure for the whole building, with wires running from the antenna in the tower through the wall linings to the several outlets in the lower laboratory hall. This effect was now explainable in the following manner. *If it is the atmospheric OR energy which gets excited by nuclear activity and runs wild, then countless discharges take place and make a noise like "static," an approaching thunderstorm, or an operating secondary coil system.* I planned to remove the radio cobalt with the containing charger from the observatory tower the following morning, and to deposit it in the garage some 100 feet away from the north wall. If the noise would stop then, my interpretation could be considered correct. I was right: the noise stopped the following morning and all three radios were operating again. This observation required repetition.

The Oranur effect showed up in the following manner, too. The observatory houses several Geiger counters, one of them designated to record the atmospheric and organismic OR energy action. The latter, the organismic action, is transmitted through a coil of wire, six inches long and five inches wide, which is connected to the grid of the extension amplifier of the GM apparatus. It can be shut off and on at will by means of a switch. The organismic OR reaction appears in the form of a steady sequence of impulses and light flashes at the neon indicator the moment one touches the coil with one's hand.

Strong bio-energy systems produce a reaction on dry, sunny days at about one or at most two inches distance of the palm from the transmitting coil. However, this reaction at a distance *without touching* is very rare, and occurs only on very dry, sunny days. My palms give it only when I feel particularly strong. I went to the GM set-up in order to test the OR field of my hands. I was stunned when the reaction occurred even at a distance of *TWO FEET!* I tested again and again. There was no doubt. The field of my palm had stretched out measurably by some two feet. I was, accordingly, severely *overcharged*, or at least in a state of abnormally high bio-energetic activity.

I am reporting these facts as they happened during those exciting days, without claiming to understand or to explain everything. Many of these facts were in agreement with what I already knew well from former experiences of some fifteen years of operation with OR energy. Others, such as the mass dying of mice, were not explainable as yet. But there could be no doubt whatsoever that the severe reactions were due to OR and *not* NR effects, as already elaborated before. However, if any slight doubt may have bothered us in this respect, it was dispelled in a perfect way when the following happened:

The small amount of radio cobalt, 2.26 microcuries, after having caused the widespread atmospheric disturbance through the antenna, was deposited in the small charger in the garage of the observatory 150 feet away.

Three physicians had arrived from New York for a conference at Orgonon. In order to demonstrate the Oranur effect to them, I asked an assistant to bring in the small charger WITHOUT the radio cobalt sample. The *empty* charger had been on the table no longer than one minute, when all of us began to feel sick, as if affected with seasickness. We felt nauseated, pressure in the head and eyes, twitchings in various parts of the body. The charger was removed right away again, but the effects persisted for about one hour in spite of ample ventilation and our taking stiff drinks. The physicians were quickly convinced of the truth about the first Oranur experiment. I would suggest that anyone who, on whatever grounds, refuses to accept the well worked-out and well reasoned orgonomic functions, subject himself to the atmosphere which emanates from such an empty shooter, or to the atmosphere in the OR room for only twenty minutes, with a small amount of NR in it. Efficient methods of scientific debate such as the one proposed are fully justified in the face of the irrational objections to orgonomy. In science, not opinions, but only experience decides the issue. The only way to reach a valid opinion about OR energy is to use an OR accumulator regularly for a considerable period of time.

Specific Biological Reactions

It became increasingly evident that the workers who were in contact with the Oranur effects reacted in a highly specific manner. It seemed as if the high-pitched charge in the atmosphere *attacked each person at his or her weakest spot.*

One worker had suffered from inflammation of the liver several years ago, and at times developed bloating of the abdomen. This worker complained during the experiment about feelings of being bloated in the abdomen and pains in the liver.

A second worker had been suffering for many years from a hypersensitivity of the skin. It would react to any kind of irritation with erythrodermia. He developed skin inflammation during the experimentation, although he had been free from trouble for many years before that time.

A third worker was prone to develop obesity and an appearance of "being blown-up" when in emotional distress. During the experiment, she looked swollen all over, obese, and sick, as if suffering from some inner secretory dysfunction.

A fourth worker used to suffer from sinusitis and Basedow with protruding eyeballs at times. During the period of the Oranur experiment, she suffered severely from exactly these symptoms, to the point of needing bed rest.

A fifth worker had once suffered from gall bladder trouble.

During the Oranur period, she felt sick in the region of the gall bladder.

A sixth worker had suffered from slight pains in the upper epigastrium years ago. He suffered gravely from exactly this same symptom during Oranur.

A seventh worker, whom I knew well from orgone therapy, had suffered from biopathic fatigue. He reacted during Oranur with severe malaise, weakness, and even a corresponding blood picture. He had to be disconnected from Oranur work completely.

The other workers had reacted only in a general manner, such as malaise, headaches, and brief spells of weakness.

These symptoms had no relation whatsoever to the small (one mg.) NR source. They appeared, in the absence of any NR source, to be due to the presence of an OR system which had been in touch with even small amounts of NR. We know from many years of work with OR, that, in cancer cases, for instance, OR energy would effect exactly the region or organ which had become diseased. This is in itself a major bio-energetic puzzle, not easy to solve.

The importance of these observations is obvious. They opened up the prospect of possible future therapeutic use of OR: *OR could be driven to high activity by NR in desirable amounts, according to the kind and severity of the symptoms to be treated.* This appeared as a major route to be followed in further investigations of Oranur. Elaboration of proper dosage seemed the most crucial task. But little doubt could be maintained about the therapeutic promises of Oranur, in spite of the severe reactions we all had suffered. Not only did all workers return to good health after a few weeks; more, they felt particularly well, strong and active, after Oranur was disrupted. We all had the distinct impression that those who had participated at close range in the experiment, had developed a certain *immunity*, as it were, to the Oranur effects. They no longer reacted as severely when one milligram of radium was brought into the highly charged atmosphere for measurement at the GM counter. They were now able to stop the malaise by "airing" in the open fresh air. The reactions were less severe and did not persist as they had done in the beginning.

During the first two weeks after January 5, 1951, shocklike reactions, swinging back and forth from paleness to "hot shivers" were common to most of us, while later on we all developed splendid color in our faces; people who usually were inclined to paleness, became pink or tanned; eyes inclined to dullness became lustrous and shining. I, personally, who had gone through a similar bio-energetic storm in 1939 when the SAPA bion radiation was discovered, and was more familiar with details of behavior and appearance, felt very vigorous; I needed little sleep, worked much and without effort, better than usual, and I felt a peculiar pleasantness in moving my limbs. Also, I began to develop the ability to work with NR in a highly charged OR atmosphere without any appreciably uncomfortable reactions at all, whereas only two weeks before, the same small amount of NR in a highly charged OR atmosphere was capable of rendering me helpless and disturbed me deeply.

Therefore, the idea of IMMUNIZATION to NR effects, as it were, was no longer strange and no longer contradicted so sharply what we had actually gone through. It appeared that our biosystems had not only adjusted themselves to the high-pitched OR reactions, but even that we could tolerate much more and far better than we could have otherwise.

The great difference between our bio-energetic state in the beginning of the experiment and three weeks later was clearly shown by way of contrast, when some physicians newly arrived from New York, reacted to the presence of a tiny amount (microgram) of NR in a highly charged OR atmosphere, with severe malaise, and even, in one case, with loss of balance. We, on the other hand, who had become adjusted to Oranur, worked easily and efficiently while the two newcomers nearly fainted. These physicians understood instantly what we were talking about. They suggested subjecting everyone who, in a habitual manner, doubted the facts of orgonomy to exactly the same experience. We all agreed that this should be done, if possible.

Overirradiation experiments with mice are being conducted and will be continued until clarity has been obtained as to the possible immunization effects and the dangers involved.

On the basis of what has just been stated, I propose that the following possibility be carefully considered:

Should further experimentation corroborate my observation of what I called *"immunization" by Oranur against NR radiation effect, we would have obtained a most powerful weapon against radiation sickness.* Thought through to its last consequence, it would perhaps be possible to immunize the whole population against NR effects in the following manner. In single, careful steps, the Oranur immunization could be built up by letting people use OR accumulators which had been excited to higher energy levels by small amounts, in micrograms only, of some kind of NR—radium, uranium, radioisotopes, pitchblende, etc.

Through carefully measured progression from low to high Oranur charges, a much higher level of bio-energy functioning could be achieved, and an atomic energy blast would possibly not have the widespread damaging effects upon populations at some distance from the blast as it now threatens to have.

This was at that time, of course, only a proposition based on a few observations, which may well have turned out to be unworkable. We were not aware of the *deadly* quality in Oranur, the now so-called DOR effects, which seems, from what we have learned from our experimental mice, to act in the direction of blood disintegration through dehydration, deformation of RBCs and inner suffocation.

Nearly everything still remains to be investigated and established on a broad and safe basis. This report only points to certain directions; it does not claim final results. Even the slightest hope in a positive direction should not go unmentioned. It may well harbor some answers to the menace of atomic warfare. And as long as we are willing and ready to control our actions and opinions sharply, no harm can come of it.

At this point, the following summary conclusions can be made with surety:

1. NR radiation excites OR energy into high-pitched activity. This is in agreement with the previous experience of many years—that all electromagnetic energy is different from and antagonistic to OR energy.

2. The bio-energetic (orgonotic) systems of the workers who had come into close contact with the area of experimentation were severely affected by the high-pitched orgonotic excitation in the atmosphere.

3. Overirradiation with Oranur can cause severe sickness of the autonomic nervous system and the blood system, to the extent of death.

4. The irritation of OR by NR, even in minimal amounts, seems exorbitant. OR runs wild, as it were. The NR effect on OR has in its subjective aspects the taint of death. *The organismic OR rebels against NR, as if it were NR itself, i.e., deadly.* The otherwise benign OR splits off a deadly branch (DOR), as it were, similar to the development of a lightning from the orgonotic brightness of a sunny day.

5. Since it is the atmospheric Oranur and not NR which causes the sickness, there is *no possibility of protecting oneself, for OR as well as Oranur penetrates everything and cannot be shielded off by any amount of lead bricks, aprons or masks.*

6. The deadly OR effects (DOR) act in a direction observable in leukemia: destruction of the RBC-producing systems, bone, marrow, etc.

7. The Oranur project as a whole appeared doomed if no other than a deadly change of OR is contained in the NR + OR reaction. However, there are other possibilities of great importance entailed in NR + OR:

a. The *health* qualities of Oranur will be obtainable only by careful dosage. If someone had discovered water for the first time in his life while exposed to deathly thirst in a desert, and had immediately poured gallons of water into his stomach, he certainly would have died from the otherwise life-saving element. OR from now on could be stimulated to any *desirable* amount of beneficial Oranur activity simply by a careful regulation of the dose of NR put into the health-giving OR accumulator for a period of time sufficient to stimulate the OR into Oranur reaction.

b. There must be a dividing line separating the beneficial from the *harmful state of excitation* in OR energy for each organism.

8. The theoretical assumption that in the atomic explosion the *atmospheric* OR plays some important role, could not be entirely discarded. The atomic "pile," constructed as it is of metallic (plutonium) and nonmetallic (graphite) material, most likely constitutes a special type of OR accumulation. The chain reaction could thus be due, in some part at least, to OR action, induced by URANIUM influence. These are questions of theory for further practical experimentation, no more than guesses of some probability.

9. Upon thorough clarification of all functions observed so far, it became clear that the death quality in OR which had revealed itself so drastically and had stunned the research staff of The Wilhelm Reich Foundation, fell in line with several bio-energetic phenomena, well-known for a long time:

a. The health-*positive* PA bions become excited and luminate strongly when they are brought into contact with the deadly T-bacilli. PA bions are able to kill T-bacilli, but in this process some of the PA bions themselves lose their healing qualities and degenerate into harmful T-bodies.

b. Highly charged RBCs are capable of attacking cancer tissue, of immobilizing cancer cells and causing their T-disintegration. However, in this process, the healthy RBCs themselves lose their bio-energy charge and disintegrate into T-bodies.

c. It is a well-known and common thing that a healthy, upright, honest man while fighting evil and death, may himself change and develop the qualities of exactly the same evil that he is fighting with all his vigor. It is equally well known that love easily, through frustration, turns into bitter hatred, its exact opposite.

There is a deeply moving quality in these functional identities of such far-apart and various realms of nature. One cannot withstand the impact of this basic unity which pervades all being as one single law: Love, while fighting hate, degenerates into hate, as PA bions fighting T-bacilli, themselves degenerate into T-bodies, and as life-giving atmospheric orgone energy turns into the killer, lightning; thus, also, OR changes into DOR while fighting NR.

The creative possibilities in these antithetical functions are endless. They deserve full devotion on the part of man in learning the appropriate means of using the good against the evil without turning good into evil itself. Thus, also, the moral, social implications of the first Oranur experiment are important enough to have warranted the great risk taken in the performance of the experiment.

ATMOSPHERIC ORANUR CHAIN REACTION

The need to prepare for elaborate routine health measures in handling liquid radioisotopes had become obsolete. There were no means for protection against an atmospheric energy running amok under the irritation exerted by nuclear energy. We had already sent an application to Oak Ridge for admission of one physician to a course on safety measures against NR radiation. It was withdrawn and a second application, ready to be dispatched, was withheld, too.

At the time of these events, I had no knowledge of the atomic explosions in Nevada which were to be carried out some time later. Neither could I possibly have predicted an increase in the background count in the eastern USA and in Canada. Such a thought could not even have occurred to me in connection with our Oranur experimentation. But I was stunned when on February 3, *three weeks later*, the *New York Times* reported an unusually high background count found from Rochester, New York, to Canada *during the last week of January*. Several workers at Orgonon who had participated in the Oranur experiment had the same idea independently: DID OUR ORANUR EXPERIMENT CAUSE THE HIGH COUNT IN THE EASTERN USA?

In order to approach an answer to this question, several points need clarification:

1. The background count at Orgonon had been high: twice to three times the normal of between 20-30 CPM, i.e., 60-90 CPM all through the Oranur experiment. It returned to the normal 20-30 CPM only after the dismantling of all arrangements for OR energy concentration in all research buildings. It returned on a high scale (50-70 CPM) immediately if only a small one-cubic-foot shooter was reassembled, *without the presence of any NR source*. It dropped again when the arrangement was removed. Further, some OR accumulators that had merely been near an OR accumulator which had been in use with Oranur, developed highly radiating Oranur effects.

2. Some physicists at the AEC had suggested that the high counts in the East were due to atomic energy blasts which had taken place in Nevada between January 27 and February 3, 1951. However natural such an explanation seemed to be, we had serious doubts. We had felt responsible for possible chain reactions in the atmospheric energy around Orgonon long before the atomic blasts occurred. We had also, upon realization of the severity and extent of the Oranur reaction far outside the laboratory building, worried about what might happen to the village four miles away.

The area in which the unusually high count had been reported, formed a circle of from 300 to 600 miles around Orgonon as an approximate center. Whether the radioactivity had reached far out into the Atlantic ocean, nobody can tell. But it had reached, according to our assumption, some 600 miles southwest, and farther into eastern Canada. The increase in background count had been reported on February 3, 1951, i.e., three weeks after the strongest Oranur reaction had occurred. If we assume that the Oranur effects had traveled 600 to 700 miles to the west in 21 days, *against* the general west-east direction of the OR energy envelope, the speed had been some 30 to 35 miles per day, or slightly less than 1¼ miles per hour. This seemed entirely within the limits of actual possibilities.

On the other hand, if we assumed that the higher background count in the eastern USA was *not* due to Oranur but was caused by the atomic explosions in Nevada, the following inconsistencies were at hand:

a. The first atomic explosions had occurred *one week before* the high count was reported in the East. However, the latter had already been observed for several days *before* February 3, 1951, i.e., two to three days after the first explosion.

b. The increased radioactivity in the atmosphere at Rochester, New York, was found in snow that had fallen; it was found there only after the snow had been melted. Thus radioactivity had supposedly traveled the 2300 miles (!!) from the Las Vegas area in Nevada to the East in only two or three days, or with a speed of about 1200 miles per day, 50 miles per hour, i.e., with the speed of a whirling hurricane, on clear, windless days, i.e., faster than an average hurricane which progresses forward at a rate of only 10-12 miles per hour. According to our weather charts, the last week in January had been mostly sunny and calm, with no major storms. Obscure as all these things may be, and open to doubt as our guesses surely are, no stone must be left unturned to determine whether the high radioactivity in the atmosphere in the eastern USA during the week of January 26 was due to the atomic blast in Nevada *or* to the Oranur experiment in Maine, that began on December 28, 1950.

c. The increase of atmospheric radioactivity had been noticed *only in the East.* From Rochester, New York, to Las Vegas, Nevada, with the exception of the immediate vicinity of the latter, nothing unusual had been noticed. Is it possible that the radioactive "cloud" traveled with the speed of a major storm over 2300 miles, leaving no trace until it reached the eastern border states, only then manifesting itself in high counts? I believe such an interpretation is far less acceptable than the other one—that Oranur was responsible for the increased atmospheric activity.

d. All reports so far accessible on atomic explosions stress the fact that the high radioactivity lasts only a few seconds, that it reaches only a few miles beyond point zero; and I have heard of no effect as far as 2300 miles, *with an untouched area of some 1700 miles between the blast and the location of increased radioactivity*. On the other hand, some reports from Bikini have it that living organisms remained highly radioactive for years after the explosion in Bikini.

e. Last but not least, a basic consideration which is to be taken into account, and which we should get used to slowly but surely, is, again: *The scope of OR energy in intensity as well as extensity, is to the scope of atomic energy in one or even ten pounds of fissionable material, as is infinity to a grain of sand.* One will most likely miss this critical bird's-eye view if one does not detach oneself from the atomic and electronic hypothesis of the constitution of the universe, at least long enough to compare OR with NR.

EVENTS SINCE FEBRUARY 6, 1951, AT ORGONON

On February 6, 1951, a careful check had been carried through in several widely separated places at and around Orgonon. It was found that the observatory building was highly active, with from 80 to 120 CPM or 2×10^{-2} MR/H in the experimental hall. No NR material was present in the hall. The tiny amount of NR material which had arrived and had been measured on February 3 at 13h, had been removed several hundred yards away from any building and habitation. Several orgonomic blood tests carried through that same day, showed a high degree of overirradiation in myself, in a physician who had taken care of the experimental mice, and in another physician who had ceased working at Orgonon due to Oranur sickness two weeks before. The only NR material that had remained within the confines of the observatory, was a well-shielded scintilloscope for the observation of alpha particles containing an amount of radium of a fraction of a microgram. It was situated in a one-cubic-foot OR charger lined with 26 gauge metal. No other NR material was placed at that time in any OR charger, nor was any such material closer than 200 feet from any OR charger. The two milligrams of radium, within lead shielding, were still placed half-a-mile away from any building; the *experimental* milligram of radium was taken out of the 10-fold small charger. The scintilloscope was removed from the hall to an unused porch on the second floor OUTSIDE THE TWO-FOOT ROCK AND CEMENT WALLS OF THE OBSERVATORY.

The results of the checkup of background count on February 6 were as follows:

The newly built OR charger, inside	30 to 40 CPM
The newly built OR charger, outside	30 to 50 CPM
The 20x OR accumulator within the charger	100 down to 30 to 40 CPM (initial discharge)
The metal-lined box containing the 2 microgr. CO-60 + the scintillation test material	50 to 60 CPM
Dr. S. Tropp's home in Rangeley, 4 mi. away	25 to 35 CPM
The Orgone Institute Press office, Rangeley	35 to 40 CPM
The Country Club road some 2 miles away	30 to 50 CPM
The new road leading to the radium	30 to 50 CPM
The charger containing the shielded radium, close by	20,000 CPM
The charger containing the shielded radium, 100 cm. dist.	1500 to 2000 CPM
The charger containing the shielded radium, 300 cm. dist.	200 to 300 CPM
Student laboratory, outside	40 CPM
Student laboratory, inside (still unusable, May, 1951)	40 CPM
The inside of the OR room	30 to 50 CPM

All Oranur experimentation was intentionally stopped for a period of several weeks in order to carry through all the necessary blood tests. The workers were again ordered to stop working in the students' laboratory where the initial Oranur experimentation had been done, beginning January 5. We were waiting for the clearing of the laboratory. Some work was transferred to the hall of the observatory.

To stop the experiment completely was definitely out of the question. To continue, considering the severe bio-energetic reactions on the part of the workers, was equally impossible. Thus, we found ourselves in a difficult dilemma.

To put the two micrograms of CO-60 into a newly built, remote OR charger, was most tempting. Consideration of the possible effect on the atmosphere held us back. With no atomic blasts in the offing, such an experiment would definitely and irrevocably have decided the question as to whether or not the high counts in the Eastern USA and in Canada had been caused by the blast in Nevada 2300 miles away.

During the afternoon of the sixth of February, 1951, the CPM in the observatory hall came down to 30 to 40 again and continued to be low.

ORANUR RESULTS IN MICE

Shortly before we had started the Oranur experiment, we had begun to investigate leukemia. At the same time, different types of experimental mice were kept for various purposes. When the Oranur experiment began, those mice which were not to be exposed to Oranur were transferred to a small wooden cabin 100 feet away from the main building. The mice which were treated by OR were transferred to the bathroom within the same building. The bathroom is separated from the main hall by a wall of cement sheets on one side and by an empty open hall on the other side. The two remaining sides are toward the free open space.

We had prepared for the Oranur experiment proper a set of forty healthy mice freshly ordered from the breeder. All of them were treated with OR several weeks before the NR experiment started, in accordance with our original plan to test the efficacy of NR- on OR-treated mice. All of these carefully laid plans were completely overthrown by the actual events.

We did not inject any fluid radioactive isotopes. In its place, we exposed a first test group of four mice to a naked radium needle three times for half-an-hour each. Two of these mice had been treated with OR beforehand, and all four of them were treated with OR after NR exposure.

As it turned out, however, all these minute, elaborate details lost their significance with the tremendous impact of the Oranur experiment. It did not matter at all whether we had or had not treated mice prophylactically; neither did it matter whether or not we treated them afterwards with pure OR for half-an-hour or an hour. We soon had to realize that our former habits of careful timing of OR irradiation in terms of minutes had become meaningless, just as the elaborate health protection devices used in the atomic energy project had become meaningless. Our previous arrangements were to the Oranur action effects as would be the fiddling around with a small spark-producing induction coil to a lightning in the sky during a hurricane. The discrepancies between what we had been used to and what we now went through, were quite awesome. Nobody present during the Oranur experiment but had experienced deep fear.

We also had been running some parallel series of cancer experiments with mice and some test groups for various bion and Experiment XX products. To make it brief, all these clinical and experimental differences were wiped cleanly off the table, and it made no difference whatsoever as to what group the special mouse had belonged. The Oranur effects were everywhere the same, and the mice all showed the same symptoms upon death.

Neither did it make any great difference whether the different groups had been kept within the bathroom of the laboratory or within the cabin 100 feet outside. Oranur had penetrated many hundreds of yards far outside the laboratory building. However, it was quite clear from the appearance of the mice, that those which had been kept continuously in the

388 WILHELM REICH

experimental hall during the Oranur work had suffered most. The common symptoms of Oranur sickness were:

Immobilization to various degrees; rough fur; cold perspiration; total body contraction; cyanotic tails, noses, lips, ear lobes; tremendous scratching and restlessness before the onset of immobilization; severe thirst, which corresponded to the findings in the biopsies—dry tissues and dehydrated blood. It seemed significant that mice offspring died faster and sooner than the adult mice. It also seemed important that originally bio-energetically weakened organisms, like the offspring of cancer mice, died at a faster rate than healthy mice. But on the whole, *all* the mice in the vicinity had suffered gravely. In some, pure OR treatment seemed to help. Also, in some human beings, OR energy application seemed to alleviate the distressing symptoms. On the other hand, most of the workers who had participated fully in Oranur work, passed through a period of disliking to use the OR accumulator.

It was striking that this intolerance extended even to such small accumulating devices as a simple metal-lined box or an 8-inch-square accumulator used to measure temperature differences.

Sunday, February 11, 1951

One assistant, who took care of the experimental mice that day, came up in the morning from the lower laboratory with some thirty mice which had died within the last twelve hours, i.e., since the last observation the day before. Among them were mice which had remained in the experimental hall all through the Oranur experiment, some leukemia mice which had been in the bathroom during that same period, many offspring of cancer mice which had been treated with OR, and several healthy mice which had been removed to the small wooden mouse cabin some 100 feet away from the students' laboratory.

This mass death gave all of us a terrible shock. These mice had doubtless died en masse in consequence of the Oranur experiment. We did not understand why so many had died that same day.

The autopsy of these mice (we worked all through that Sunday), revealed one single pathological picture, no matter whether the respective group of mice belonged to the leukemia, the Oranur or the Ca group. These symptoms, common to all of the mice, were the following:

1. Pneumonia in the hemorrhagic or organizational stage.

2. A severe fibrinous exudate covering the pleural cavity in every single mouse fully, and in some mice extending over the abdomen toward the pelvis. The pelvic subcutis and the genital, as well as the perineum, were affected in *all* mice. This type of exudate was well known to us from many previous autopsies of mice who had died from strong T-bacilli injections.

3. Postmortal, greenish T-discoloration of the subcutis.

4. Severely distended veins (V. porta and V. cava), including carotid vein. Severely distended auricles, blackish blood in the veins.

5. Purple discoloration of the genital organs, with severe distention of seminal vesicle or ovarian tubes.

6. Grayish or cyanotic, hardened, somewhat screwshaped tails in all mice.

7. Cyanotic ear lobes, toes and lips.

8. In the blood picture of all dead or freshly-killed mice, no matter of what origin, were deformed RBCs of the same shape as those found in leukemia mice during our work on leukemia in early December. In some mice, but not in all, a high incidence of white cells.

9. T-cultures, positive.

10. In some Oranur mice, a highly enlarged spleen, up to four times its normal size.

11. A striking dryness of the peritoneum, and an apparent *deficiency of fluid* in the blood system. (We all had suffered gravely from sore and dry throats during the Oranur experiment.)

I omit here other, atypical findings. It was necessary to restrict this report to the most general characterization. Detailed elaboration over a long period of time will prove crucial. However, how should we continue with these essential research efforts if the workers themselves would be endangered by the very conditions necessary for the job?

Survey on Mice Affected by Oranur—March 26, 1951

1. *Forty healthy mice* ordered in December 1950, scheduled for injection with Isotope P-32, were treated daily beforehand with (*preventive*) OR irradiation until January 5, 1951. These mice were kept within the experimental hall. Fourteen of these 40 mice died during the experiment; 26 mice were still alive but gravely ill with Oranur sickness at this date.

2. Total of experimental mice present at beginning of the Oranur experiment: 286. Fifty-seven of these 286 mice died during the Oranur experiment from Oranur sickness. Twelve in severe distress were killed for the purpose of fresh autopsy material. The remaining 217 mice have been gravely affected by Oranur sickness; all are ill to various degrees.

3. Offspring of cancer mice were especially affected by Oranur. Of 23 mice in this group, none had seemed to be affected during the first few days; however, thereafter all 23 mice died spontaneously with the symptoms of Oranur sickness.

4. *However, of 40 mice treated by Dr. S. Tropp with abundant overirradiation two to three months before the Oranur experiment, none died during or after the experiment until this date (May 1951). We had the impression that chronic overirradiation with OR energy in bearable amounts induced the organism to adjust to the higher energy level and thus, possibly, made survival possible.*

5. Of 42 leukemia mice which had been treated with OR energy, 16 died spontaneously and two were killed for autopsy shortly before death. The remaining 26 mice are ill with Oranur sickness. Of 34 *untreated* leukemia control mice, 30 were alive but ill.

Why had dozens of mice died, all with the same symptoms, on that black Sunday? We worked all day long at the autopsy table and at the microscope to find out. Let us summarize the pertinent observations which might provide an answer:

1. All the dead mice had belonged to experimental groups which had in common a *weak bio-energy* level. Conclusion: LOW BIO-ENERGY ENHANCES ORANUR DEATH.

2. High levels of Life Energy provide enough supplementary OR energy to step in when NR has depleted the available resources in the organism: PROPHYLACTIC HIGH CHARGING OF ORGANISMS WILL LESSEN THE EFFECTS OF ORANUR MUCH MORE EFFICIENTLY THAN APPLICATION *after radiation illness strikes*.

3. On February 11, there had been a very murky, foggy, though not humid (40-50% relative humidity) night and day. This had apparently lowered and thus weakened the atmospheric OR energy. There was, accordingly, *less fresh OR supply from the air;* the animals had to draw energy from their own tissue charges, and this, again, enhanced the mass death. Similarly in the common cold, bad weather will lower the atmospheric OR tension and thus, indirectly, weaken the bio-energy supply of living organisms.

4. Evasive human nature does away with important matters glibly. Why not simply explain the mass death of mice by pneumonia acquired during bad weather in a wooden cabin in sub-zero weather? I myself had thought of this. However, the facts did not permit of such an easy escape from a severe responsibility: Mice had died during the Oranur experiment, before and after the 13th of February, during sunny, warm weather. Formerly, the mice had been in that wooden cabin, heated to 60-70 degrees F. though it was 25 degrees below zero outside, *without* dying. Upon special investigation, it was established that the caretaker had taken good care of the stove that cold night. And, finally, the symptoms we found in the dead mice went far beyond a simple pneumonia. Pneumonia was among the *final* causes of death only in some mice, not in all. Besides, we all had been sick with Oranur symptoms to a certain degree on and off in the best of weather. Accordingly, there was no escape from the conclusion that weakened organisms had succumbed to an additional strain.

With the knowledge and demonstration of a concrete, measurable, usable life energy in the living organism and in the atmosphere, such superficial and evasive statements as that this or that one has died from "air germs" or "virus X," never seen, never demonstrated, never practically handled, are no longer acceptable. There *is* something in the living organism that is acted upon by "air germs" and by "virus X"; this "something" reacts to noxious influences. There *are* such things as higher production of white blood cells (wherefrom? the air?), congestion toward the diseased region (WHAT moves? ions? salts? chemicals?), shifting heat, concentration here, thinning there (WHAT IS ORGANISMIC HEAT?), convulsions, fascicular fibrillations, and (personally observed in the experiment) fibrillations in the peritoneum even after the heart had stopped beating. The "something," which congests toward a diseased part of the body, which creates heat and keeps its level constantly higher than the temperature of the environment, which shifts within the organism from place to place irrespective of any nerves and membranous boundaries, which twitches and convulses as in the orgasm, is the organismic orgone energy, the LIFE ENERGY. The factual interrelations have become too numerous and too clear to be overlooked much longer. Without the knowledge of this concrete life energy, not a single feature in the course of the Oranur processes is understandable. *With it*, on the other hand, we can follow the events intelligently and proficiently.

We were at times astonished at being witness to the logic with which old observations, disconnected functions, and even tentative assumptions fell into line and made most minute functions understandable. Thus it was when overirradiated RBCs at first appeared gleaming bright and after a few minutes became bluer; they had returned, in the process of loss of energy, to the physiological level of energy, a fact which needs must remain incomprehensible to any other than the orgonomic approach. Or, the other fact, that with a stronger degree of deterioration, the RBCs would form into shapes which were exactly like those found in leukemia mice weeks before the Oranur work began. This at once linked up comprehensibly radiation sickness and leukemia. It also made comprehensible why and how leukemia, rather than the slower process of cancerous shrinking, is so prevalent in infancy and puberty: LEUKEMIA, TOO, SEEMED TO BE ROOTED IN AN OVERCHARGE OF THE RED CELL SYSTEM. All this remained to be elaborated in detail on a rich basis of observations and experiments, yet to be harvested.

A vast vista opened up on the realm of disposition to disease. But, in the midst of it all, there was ample reason to worry. After the removal of all NR material from the observatory, only a scintilloscope for the observation of alpha particles had remained, a negligible amount which in its shielding, can safely be carried around in one's pocket. But even this tiny amount was sufficient to cause a DOR reaction in the total building, to such an extent that my wife and my son, 7 years old, developed severe symptoms of blood disintegration and had to be evacuated. The blood symptomatology deserves to be dealt with extensively and in a separate context. Here, it should only be emphasized that every single blood picture which showed enough deterioration to cause serious worry, had some features in common with blood leukemia. For years, we had been used to seeing one to three white cells in one field of blood in saline solution at a magnification of 3 to 400. In these pictures of deterioration, we saw more—four to eight white cells in one field.

In leukemia we had observed a delicate granulated structure within the RBCs in the dark field. Now, we could see in some RBCs the same granulation which, to our view, means T-degeneration, in other words, putrid decay. Some of the positive blood cultures confirmed this point of view, as they always do in advanced cancer biopathies.

In most leukemia mice we had observed as signs of orgonotic overirradiation, that *red* centers in the RBCs (instead of bright blue centers) developed long before the development of full-blown leukemia with glandular involvement. This condition was now clearly observable in the blood of all workers who had participated in the Oranur experiment.

HEALTH MEASURES AND EVACUATION
OF DISEASED WORKERS

At the peak of the Oranur effects, it seemed impossible to achieve anything useful for the protection of the personnel against the raging fury of the uncontrollable Oranur effects. Most of the workers used to leave Orgonon around five o'clock in the afternoon and did not return until the morning of the following day. They had some sixteen hours respite from the continuous effects of Oranur. Others, among them myself, my family and the caretaker who lives at Orgonon, had no chance of getting such periodic relief and intermittent recovery. It turned out that *originally strong organisms did not react severely, whereas organisms which had somehow been weakened* BEFORE *Oranur had started, developed strong reactions even if they lived away from Orgonon.* I myself never felt the need for bed rest, though I was often tired. But my boy had fallen seriously ill after he had developed a common cold due to wetting his feet while playing in the snow. In spite of the fact that I had evacuated all NR material which functioned as an irritant trigger for the Oranur reaction, the pressure in the air at the observatory continued to be high and oppressive if the windows were kept closed for as little as fifteen or thirty minutes, with the background CPM climbing to 60-70. And to keep the windows open continuously in near-zero temperature was difficult.

Complications arose when the child began to develop slight weakness in the legs, shooting pains, and an inclination to immobility even in respiration. Such symptoms were usually easily removed by use of the OR blankets which we had built in the process of preparing for an Oranur field service. But, now these same OR blankets also acted as sources of Oranur action. This we had overlooked during the first few days. The child became more ill. He was pale, at times to the point of livid discoloration; his palms were wet with cold perspiration, a sure sign of sympatheticotonic contraction; he felt malaise continuously, was uncomfortable, and there seemed to be nothing we could do about it. Since prolonged airing of the building did not remove the effects, we could not hope to cope with the situation with airing alone. He was transferred into another part of the house where the DOR effects seemed less strong; it helped some, but not enough. The blood test showed severe overirradiation of the RBCs, an increase in the number of white cells, and, to our distress, a few signs of leukemic deterioration in the blood corpuscles. Dr. Simeon J. Tropp, who lives in Rangeley, urged us to evacuate the child to his home. I had hesitated to suggest such a measure, since I was not sure at all whether an organism once affected with Oranur would not affect other organisms. The mice which had died en masse had shown clear signs of strong radiation themselves, and had a very bad odor. Also, my own palms had increased their bioenergetic activity manifoldly. Finally, I consented. The child recovered slightly after a few hours at Dr. Tropp's home, but the following day he still suffered from spells of weakness.

Also, the child's mother, Ilse Ollendorff, had developed severe Oranur sickness as evidenced by a highly suspicious blood picture. She, too, was pale and slightly livid in her face. She was evacuated from Orgonon the following day and began to recover soon thereafter. At this time, all other persons were ordered to stay away from Orgonon.

But all this was an unsatisfactory solution of our problem. The technical assistant who had stopped working already during the second week of Oranur, was still suffering from Oranur sickness, though he did not come to Orgonon any longer. The OR sickness lingered on for weeks, however. At irregular intervals, he would slump into weakness and come out of it again, slowly. His blood picture improved unequivocally. The red centers disappeared from the RBCs; the type of disintegration switched more and more toward the normal bionous picture;

he was no longer pale but became tanned. He was not readmitted to the Oranur work for reasons of health. We could not take any risks with other people's lives as long as we did not know the ultimate *outcome* of the Oranur sickness.

All through this period, we felt, on the basis of our constant, steady contact with Oranur as well as with the workers in it, *that something very crucial with respect to a future weapon of health had happened;* we waited patiently for further developments. One incident a few days later shocked us into keen awareness of the ferocity of the force we were dealing with.

A Close Call for One Physician

We slowly began to understand the *specific* reactions of the various workers to the Oranur effects, and we learned better how to read the signs as the days passed by. However, this knowledge was not rooted well enough to have enabled us to judge the danger to one special physician in advance. This physician had suffered since her puberty, due to a severe emotional upheaval she had gone through, from a *bradycardia* of around 50 pulse rate. After she had gone through psychiatric orgone treatment two years previously, the bradycardia had improved to around a pulse rate of 70 per minute. She also had suffered for many years from an inability to cry fully. "Swallowing" the emotion of crying was one of her major biopathic symptoms. I had been well aware of the possible connection between this emotional block and the bradycardia:

"Swallowing of crying" *actually* is carried through by swallowing in the esophagus; a pressure is exerted upon the organs of the chest and the diaphragm by a constant "pulling in" of the lower organs of the mouth and throat. Since the vagus nerve, acting as a "depressor" nerve on the heart, runs downward from the base of the brain, through the medulla oblongata and along the esophagus and the trachea, the constant pressure exerted upon these organs most likely affected the vagus depressor nerve indirectly, and thus had caused the chronic bradycardia. Accordingly, this physician had suffered off and on from spells of weakness (of the vagotonic type), and during her orgone therapy had on two or three occasions actually felt as if she "would stop moving entirely." This was known to me as well as to another medical orgonomist who had handled her case. But, somehow, in the rush of the Oranur work, and due to the amazing incredibility of what went on, the specific Oranur effect did not, in our minds, connect up with this physician's specific biopathic structure, and we let her, a most eager physician and research worker, go on attending the mice, working in the bacteriological department, etc. She had not shown any severe reactions up to the day when she collapsed and, nearly passed away completely. This happened in the following manner:

On February 19, 1951, at around 11h, while I was working in my library, this physician came into the room slightly wavering and very pale, with a livid discoloration around her mouth and chin. She was visibly in shock, frightened and in severe distress. She told me that she had just cleaned out one metal-lined cabinet in the laboratory. In order to get things out, she had to reach deeply into the cabinet with her arms. She "smelled" something like Oranur, and in order to make sure, had put her head into the cabinet. Thereupon it had "hit her like a wall." She was losing her balance and was brought up to the observatory by car by another physician.

I took her out onto an open porch to get fresh air. She paled more and more, and then began to complain of cessation of vision and hearing. I could see, at the same time, the change in her eyes. Her pulse was barely palpable, she continued to grow paler, the pulse rate was about 46 per minute. We put her to bed and began applying stimulants. The heartbeat slowed and weakened further, to a most dangerous degree. Her paleness did not seem to budge at first, but after some thirty minutes began to alternate with hot flushes. She was encouraged to keep talking all the time. At times, after a very strong expansion, visible in the reddening of her cheeks, a more severe contraction would set in; several times with cyanotic lips and lividity in cheeks and both arms. I kept stimulating her with cognac, strong coffee, talking to her and joking with her. Several times her eyes lost contact and seemed to "break." At this moment, a strong stimulus or repeated request to look at me would prevent the cessation of functioning. For the period of one whole hour, it was difficult to find her pulse. We kept attending her, and had to shout at her on several occasions to keep her breathing going. One could clearly see when she threatened to give up, and when she expanded again. Her arms and hands were limp and cold, as were her feet. Tactile sensations were nil or numb. A warm water bottle was put on her solaris region. I did not dare to apply OR energy, as I would surely have done otherwise. Also, all OR devices were out of the building. For two hours, we kept rubbing her cheeks, neck, heart region and arms with ice-cold towels. This seemed to help a great deal.

On one special instant, she seemed to fail to speak. There was no doubt about the involvement of the medulla oblongata and the thalamic region. The alteration between severe slowing-down and expansion of the life apparatus continued, with the latter slowly gaining the upper hand.

Finally, after some two hours, she began to recover. She regained her balance of autonomic functioning. She dictated the following protocol herself soon thereafter:

February 19, 1951; 12:30 P.M.

Protocol on ...., M.D.

I was perfectly all right on the morning of February 19, 1951. I spent twenty minutes inside the students' laboratory, aware of stuffiness there due to the many accumulators around, and I opened all the doors and windows. Then I looked for other sources of DOR or accumulators that had not been disassembled, and I found a one-fold, old accumulator in the back portion of the laboratory in which glassware had been stored. This accumulator had not been opened during the past five weeks except for a moment on one or two occasions. This accumulator stood along the wall representing the outer wall of the metal OR room. I very quickly removed all the contents onto a shelf, just putting my arms inside, and when I had finished, *I tested the accumulator with my head which is my most sensitive area. I put my head inside for a moment, and felt suddenly as if hit with a sledgehammer on my head.* I felt a heavy pressure and dizzy sensation, and I knew I had to go out immediately. There was a progressive increase of the following symptoms over the next five minutes: I began to feel more and more dizzy and my total body became weak. I felt as if I did not belong to myself, as if I could not feel whether my legs were moving or whether I had control over my legs. There was a tremendous effort to move my arms and legs. I felt as if all movements were slow, and as if I had to hold myself up against gravity. I felt very heavy. By the time we reached the observatory, I felt as though I were two people, as in anesthesia, and had to tell myself what to do, such as to take the snowshoes off, etc. I began to feel fear, which increased until it was the most severe death anxiety that I have ever experienced. This was due to the following sensations:

A sense of total stoppage, localized in my brain, bandlike around the ocular segment and in my arms. Also, weakness, and dissociation of the rest of my body. I was semi-conscious, could not see clearly, there was a buzzing in my ears, and I could not hear clearly. I found it difficult to swallow, my pulse was very weak and slow, between 45 and 48. I had a hard time breathing, and I had to support myself against the wall because I was so dizzy. At this point, my external appearance was that of incipient shock with livid skin color, expression of anxiety, especially in the eyes. I felt as if I were going to die, just simply stop. My memory is very cloudy as to the events from the time I came up to the observatory to the time I lay down in bed. I have never fainted in my life. I did not feel nausea.

I lay down in bed, the room was aired, and my head and extremities were rubbed with wet cold towels. The recovery took almost one hour and occurred in waves. Episodes of anxiety occurred about three times. First of all, the anxiety disappeared when I was reassured and I noticed that I was getting better, and I was not afraid of dying any more.

My pulse was feeble and remained between 48 and 50 for an hour. It then became fuller and stronger. The arms felt heavy, the motion was slow, skin sensation was dull and asymmetric. One recurrence gave severe head pressure and dullness down to the neck, with difficulty in breathing and dull tongue. When that passed, there remained a band-like pressure around the head. Afterward, my face began to tingle and lighten, and there were sensations of waves around the base of the brain.

Two hours later there was still slight dizziness on sitting up. The stoppage of OR function was replaced by extreme warmth, tingling and clarity. At that time, the pulse was between 60 and 64. At the age of five, I had suffered from a severe diphtheria with severe bulbar symptoms and paralysis of legs.

Four hours later, pulse was 64 and heart action was normal. What had actually happened was apparently this: When she put her head into the *unventilated* metal-lined cabinet, DOR had hit her hard at her weakest spot in a *specific* manner: It affected the vagus and respiration center in the medulla oblongata. This weak spot had been established for the first time in her life when some 21 years ago she had suffered from post-diphtherial affliction with a slight paralysis of her arms and legs, and slight impairment of her bulbar functioning. Thus, a syndrome of deadly symptoms had slumbered unnoticed for nearly two decades, only to be sought out, as it were, and reactivated by DOR in such a dangerous manner.

The OR energy had, as usual, attacked the weakest spot in a specific manner. Here, I believe, a great hope for powerful treatment of severe diseases is contained. We can safely assume that, with further detailed experimentation with Oranur, it will be possible to direct the healing power of OR energy at any weak link in the totality of organismic functioning, with the OR energy finding its way to the diseased organ or system. The dangerous character of some of these reactions should not deter us. In applying chemotherapy or shock treatment, we endanger the life of the patient to a higher degree, just as we do with anesthesia and major operations, WITHOUT being able to direct the healing agent in the organism. NOW, the specific autonomic, selective power of the OR energy, combined with a well-worked out, carefully applied dosage, would enable us to get at every spot in the organism therapeutically, and, most likely, also in every disease.

This last sentence requires careful scrutiny from the standpoint of what "BACKGROUND OF DISEASE" or "DISPOSITION" actually means or represents. There can no longer be any doubt, since we are already experienced in handling LIFE ENERGY (bio-energy), that the disposition to disease is becoming palpable in the form of certain describable and manageable orgonotic functions and dysfunctions. I shall reserve a first attempt to discuss these implications theoretically, for a future paper. The Oranur experiment has yielded *too* rich a harvest in this respect to be discussed now. It will take some time to gather the harvest from the field of operation and to bring home all that is worth preserving for future use and study.

INTERRUPTION OF THE ORANUR EXPERIMENT

During the latter part of February 1951, the workers at Orgonon lived in a suspense which became unbearable when the severe Oranur attack nearly killed the physician who had been in charge of the laboratory mice. The dilemma, with its pressure of contradictory decisions to be made right away, caused some confusion. We had to warn the health authorities of the USA of the danger which seemed to threaten all of us and possibly also large sectors of the Eastern USA if we had continued the Oranur experiment on a larger scale. We also notified them that because of the danger we had decided to interrupt the Oranur experiment.

Let me now summarize briefly the measures taken toward this end:

1. No one was permitted to work in the vicinity of the original Oranur action for periods longer than a few minutes at a time.

2. All OR accumulating devices were completely dismantled and the panels ("layers") were put away in such a manner that

no two panels ever faced each other. Parallel arrangement of two OR layers is sufficient to create a strong OR energy field.

3. The OR metal-lined room was completely disassembled. The sheet metal was torn off the walls, the ceiling and the floor, and taken out to air.

4. Since water absorbs OR, it was assumed that it would also absorb Oranur; accordingly, the walls of the hall and the accumulators were washed with water and soap, abundantly.

5. Since airing alleviates the OR effects, frequent and extensive airing were employed wherever such effects had been heavy.

6. All workers were advised to dismantle their OR accumulators in their homes for the time being, to take much fresh air and to sleep with wide open windows.

7. Several workers and one child were evacuated from the observatory building for several days and did not return until a few days after the dismantling of all OR accumulating devices.

8. All NR material was put half a mile away, enclosed in a safe with heavy four-inch walls of steel and cement; this, of course, was not done because the NR material was dangerous, but because it excited OR into Oranur action. We had to assume on the basis of many subjective as well as objective observations that the whole region of the 280 acreage at Orgonon continuously possessed a much higher level of OR than any other region, due to the continuous OR work that had been carried on there for many years. Also, the presence of many accumulating devices and the presence of a highly charged OR room had to be taken seriously.

9. Last but not least, it was decided to take a rest from all experimentation for several months. This was necessary in order to arrange the facts and observations without the impact of *new* facts, and to permit the workers to recuperate. The AEC was informed to this effect.

10. The background counts in the observatory came down from 50-80 CPM to an average of 30-40 CPM after these measures had been taken. However, the walls of the OR room were still

"glowing," even after dismantling of their metal lining, as late as during May 1951.

A test in complete darkness showed, as late as March 26, several weeks after the OR energy accumulators had been dismantled, that the visual impressions, were not blue-gray, as is usual, but red to purple, a sure sign of high-pitched OR energy activity.

Many practical issues had to be settled before the basic natural-scientific implications of Oranur could be approached. One of the most acute problems to be solved was how to explain all this to the security agencies of the USA. *Oranur had revealed a deadly quality*. This quality in the hands of unscrupulous, malignant men, would only add confusion to the already overstrained social atmosphere we are living in. On the other hand, to keep the result secret appeared no longer possible. Knowledge of the Oranur effects had gone around too far. Many among us felt that telling it all to everybody would be the surest way to safety for the world. Then, at least, there would be *serious*, responsible workers who would *work out the medical efficiency in Oranur to the good of everybody*. It was regrettable that in some cases the healing effects would only be obtained in a deadly, dangerous manner, but this could not be helped by anyone.

While this turmoil kept us busy day and night, while we tended our sick, made blood test after blood test, examined everything we could to the best of our knowledge, worrying what murderous men of politics would or could do with our labors, we began to discern bright sunlight among the dark clouds:

After a few days had passed since the deadly attack suffered by the physician mentioned before, she began to recover in a most hopeful manner. She still felt dizzy, "as if floating or losing balance"; she still felt "dulled" at the base of her brain, but her eyes were sparkling as never before; she looked better than ever before, was fully alive on a higher level of energy functioning. Another physician who had reacted severely with paleness and slight jaundice, was now tanned and looked vigorous. Another worker who used to suffer from occasional dullness in her eyes was bright and sparkling with life. The boy who had so strangely fallen ill was, after his return to the observatory building, in full, brilliant health. I myself felt more active and alive than ever. I did not need much sleep, the ideas and arrangements flew freely and fully. I felt vigorous and imbued with great zest.

Gradually it became clearer that Oranur could, in the hands of peaceful people, turn into one of the greatest healing powers humanity had ever possessed: *Properly dosaged, well applied and carefully controlled, it would drive to the surface and possibly cure even latent diseases. It may even possibly* IMMUNIZE *the population against NR effects all over the planet and thus wring from the hands of the evil-spirited ones the murder weapon they now command. These possibilities are definitely there. We know that Oranur had accomplished what atomic energy research so very eagerly had tried to reach and had so prematurely promised:* THE MEDICAL USE OF COSMIC ENERGY.

Thus, here we were, with the most powerful healing power humanity had ever known in our hands; but rendered impotent by the emotional plague in many places of society. The situation grew more and more complicated and dangerous, to people at large as well as to ourselves as the responsible workers in Oranur experimentation.

STATE OF AFFAIRS AS OF THE END OF MARCH 1951: FIFTEEN WEEKS AFTER ORANUR STARTED

1. The student's laboratory, in which the Oranur experiment was conducted, was still unusable despite dismantling of the OR energy metal room in the beginning of March. It was again put into tentative operation on March 26. It was still glowing on April 8 and work in it had to be stopped again on April 14.*

* Today (August 1951) the laboratory is still radiating, but is usable again. The health of the workers is regularly checked through bi-weekly orgonomic examinations. A separate report on Oranur biophysical reactions after April 1951 will be published in a future article.

2. All other OR accumulating devices without exception are being kept dismantled and separated from inhabited buildings. Only one new OR charger, which is located singly in the open air, is still assembled. It has never been used for Oranur production, but it houses a 20-fold Oranur-affected charger.

3. It is still impossible to reassemble any of the OR accumulators which had been in use before January 5, 1951. They are highly active and drive the background counts to two to four times the usual rate, 100 and more CPM.

4. Most workers who had participated in Oranur have returned to normal health. But occasionally, certain symptoms such as malaise, nausea, fatigue and overirradiated RBCs recur if they come in touch with devices employed in Oranur.

5. It has been noticed by some workers that their cars are "active" after having been close to *dismantled* Oranur-affected accumulators in the same garage.

6. Every second week, blood tests are done on the workers. The difference between the alive blood picture of persons affected with Oranur, and the blood of newcomers is marked. Full and proper evaluation is not yet possible. No leukemic tendencies in the blood pictures have been noticed during the last two or three weeks.

7. The buildings are still active with Oranur effects. Lack of proper ventilation drives the Geiger counts high.

8. In general, the workers are all well. Single persons complain about occasional recurrence of symptoms they had had earlier in life. This points to a *diagnostic possibility in Oranur*.

9. Repeating the Oranur experiment is out of the question at present for lack of sufficient funds and facilities. Also, the health of the workers must be taken into serious consideration. It is doubtful that they would stand another steep Oranur impact. We are forced to wait and see when and how we can get at Oranur again, next time better prepared, and equipped with more experience.

10. While, during the whole duration of Oranur, all workers developed an increased aversion against using their OR energy

accumulator, lately the need for OR irradiation has returned in many of them. Some workers who had not had a cold or other trouble for many years on account of regular use of the OR energy accumulator, now have again begun to develop slight sniffles in bad weather, and the need for OR has returned.

11. Oranur-affected shooters, which must be kept outside any inhabited building, are most effective in combating a slight cold when manifested locally in the nose and sinuses. A few minutes irradiation have helped to stop the discharge.

All these new experiences need to be retested and to be worked out on a much larger scale. This will take years and much money.

The details and the consequences of the First Oranur Experiment are, of course, still mostly unclear. It may require years and great funds to collect and arrange theoretically what has actually been set into motion by the dramatic clash between OR and NR. As mentioned before on several occasions, working with Oranur is fraught with danger to the experimenting personnel, and no protection against the deadly overirradiation exists, except careful dosage. The health protection devices which were elaborated in connection with work on atomic energy, are not applicable since OR as well as Oranur penetrates everything. This constitutes a major, at present unsurmountable obstacle in the way toward detailed elaboration of the problems involved. Since the Oranur experiment has been stopped, early in February 1951, and after Reich Blood Tests showed that all workers had slowly returned to normal functioning, several attempts were made to test the situation: Did the DOR effect disappear or not? How soon, if at all, would it vanish from the affected Oranur devices? Or would the Oranur action go on indefinitely? Nobody could tell then or can tell now.

However, we tried to test the situation by bringing back into the observatory building one or two small, one-cubic-foot sized OR "shooters" which had been affected by Oranur. We repeated this procedure several times, and every single time the background count went up to around 80 CPM and to 0.02 MR/R or more when the Oranur-affected devices were present for as short a while as only one hour. These effects disappeared again soon after the Oranur accumulator had been removed into the open air, with the background count coming down to as low as 30, and the MR/H to about 0.008.

One evening, a small shooter was brought into a bedroom in order to treat a cut in a finger. It was forgotten there, and during the night the person who slept in that room woke up with severe dryness in the throat and severe thirst; also with a feeling that oxygen was lacking in the air. The shooter was immediately removed, and the symptoms of distress disappeared.

At the time of the writing of these lines, in the middle of April 1951, the large students' laboratory where the first Oranur experiment had been conducted in the metal-lined and highly charged orgone energy room, was still unusable. This in spite of the fact that the sheet metal had been removed from the walls, the ceiling and the floor, i.e., the mechanism of accumulation having been disassembled. The cement board walls are still slightly "glowing" and some workers suffer distress when they work in the hall. Others feel comfortable while working at the restoration of the OR energy room. They are ordered to work only an hour or two at a stretch, and then to "air out." It is not at all certain whether this building will be fully restored to its original function, or, if so, when.

The physician who had nearly died when she had put her head into an Oranur-affected cabinet has recovered completely. The "flu epidemic" which raged through New England during this period, and affected nearly every single home, left Orgonon untouched. No one at Orgonon came down with anything near the degree of influenza suffered in the near-by village where it put people to bed en masse and for weeks on end.

Blood tests were carried on every second week with every single worker who had participated in the Oranur experimentation. The red centers in the RBCs, sure sign of overirradiation, had disappeared entirely. The OR energy frames of the RBCs were still "blurred," as we came to call this particular appearance, and the picture of the RBCs was still clearly distinct from the picture of the blood in people who came from New York or Philadelphia to Orgonon. These problems will be dealt with extensively elsewhere; however, they had to be mentioned briefly in this context.

XRAY EFFECTS AND ORANUR SICKNESS

It will be necessary to separate the medical aspects of Oranur from the physical effects and to devote a special paper to this all important subject. The harvest of medical experience was too rich and is still too confused to be dealt with at this point. However, it appears essential to mention a few facts concerning the effects of *Xrays* on OR energy already in this report in order to prevent unnecessary harm to people working with both.

The following incident may be well suited to highlight the point in question.

At the end of April, I was asked by one of our medical orgonomists for help in his own behalf. He lived and worked in New York, 500 miles away from Orgonon and Oranur. He had not been at Orgonon except for a brief, one day visit during December 1950. He had not been in contact with any of the devices or experimental arrangements which were used in connection with Oranur. When he arrived at Orgonon he appeared quite ill on the first impression. His face was livid, discolored in a bad way; the eyes were inflamed. He had felt nauseated for more than two months. His strength seemed to fail, and he suffered from constant fatigue, great thirst, weakness, malaise and a severe pressure in the diaphragmatic segment. Upon careful orgonomic examination, no apparent cause for the severe discomfort could be found. I knew this physician well from the training he had gone through with me several years before. I expected to find some armoring block in the diaphragmatic segment which would account for the severity of his status. I could, however, find no impairment of his bio-energetic motility. He was soft all over his body; no blocks were distinguishable. The case constituted a riddle.

During the further exploration, it turned out that he had constructed several OR energy blankets in connection with the anti-nuclear civil defense field service for which he was preparing himself and his staff in his private medical office.

These OR energy blankets had never been at Orgonon, and also, they had never come in touch with any Oranur-affected material. This only complicated the riddle. Was it possible that the OR energy blankets which were built with wire mesh instead of with sheet metal, produced a different, noxious type of OR radiation? This seemed unlikely. After further inquiry, it was found that *an operating Xray machine was located several rooms away from his office in another physician's office.* This answered the problem. *He had suffered all the time from Oranur effects.* The clinical symptoms were the same as those we had seen so dramatically at Orgonon. A blood test was performed immediately and it corroborated this conclusion: His blood showed an increase in white cells, highly overcharged RBCs and the typical picture of leukemia-like end-products of RBC disintegration.

He was advised to remove immediately upon return, all OR accumulating devices, to air his quarters abundantly, to drink much water and to take frequent, prolonged baths.

It is obvious that the Xrays had had the same effect upon the concentrated OR energy atmosphere in his office as the radium at Orgonon.

Several years ago, in the early 1940s, I had gone through, without having been aware of what was happening, a similar situation. I had had an Xray machine in my office in Forest Hills which was mainly used for study of the diaphragmatic immobilization in patients and for photography of the OR energy fields of different setups. During that time, I had felt weak, often nauseated, thirsty and generally fatigued. The Xray machine was later sold and now I understand why I had begun to feel better after its removal. The building in Forest Hills had been overcharged with OR energy for many years.

I had gone through the Oranur effects without having been aware of it, and was immunized against the effects in the Oranur experiment of 1951. I had suffered least among the workers.

We assume with some certainty that the *well-known damage inflicted upon patients by Xray treatment are true, full-fledged Oranur effects in the first stage.* I had always strenuously objected to simultaneous OR energy *and* Xray treatment in cases of cancer. This was no more than one of those guesses which are empirically right. I had often seen OR-treated cancer patients decline more rapidly when at the same time they took Xray treatments. But now this is quite clearly understandable: The OR energy treatment increases the energy charge and the reaction to Xrays is strong. Xrays always damage the blood system and cause malaise as well as general decline, also without OR. *It is the organismic* OR *energy which reacts to the Xray therapy with Oranur effects.* This conclusion is quite safe now, though it might disturb the Xray therapist. However, the orgonomist has become used over decades to disturbing many people in many ways. This is inevitable with any type of new basic knowledge.

In concluding this brief report, I would like to warn against using or living in high OR energy concentration if any kind of Xray, radium or similar radiation work is being done in the same building. It is necessary that all physicians using OR energy treatment with their patients make sure that OR and NR are not brought near each other.

The important consequences of these interconnections for the understanding of disease after atomic blasts at Hiroshima, of the peculiar radioactivity in maritime life, as it has been discovered years after the Bikini explosion, the ill effects upon people working with NR energy in the vicinity of steel wool, etc., should be regarded with care and further study should be devoted to all situations which are similar to Oranur setups.

FROM THE RECORD: APRIL 12—APRIL 30, 1951

We met with a new startling surprise on April 12, 1951; it was due to our own reluctance to accept fully, without hesitation, the theoretical consequences of basic orgonomy. As so often before, I had, while reaching out into the unknown, still anchored myself in the prevalent ideas about the particular realm of knowledge. For instance, long after the discovery of the bio-energy in energy vesicles in 1936, I still presented the emotional bio-energetic functions at the skin's surface in terms of "bio-electricity" (1937). This had to be corrected later in order to make further progress possible. In a similar manner, I adhered to the accepted notions on nuclear radiation when I separated the NR sources from the OR energy concentration. The reader may remember that I had put away the two milligrams of radium into a *safe* which was located in an empty building about 1200 feet away from the students' experimental laboratory, each milligram of Ra within its one-half inch lead container. The safe which housed the containers has a wall of steel and concrete of about *four inches thickness*. According to the nuclear theory of radiation, lead and steel plus concrete of altogether some five inches thickness should have been perfectly sufficient to shield the activity of two milligrams of radium and a few micrograms of other nuclear sources. This seemed to be the case in accordance with the accepted notion of nuclear radiation, and I no longer worried about the faraway, heavily shielded nuclear material. I should repeat again that the danger was not thought of as due to these small amounts of NR but as due to its triggering effects on concentrated OR energy. There were no OR accumulating arrangements in the summer dwelling except: THE STEEL CONCRETE SAFE ITSELF. This I had overlooked, and thus I committed a grave mistake, which under slightly different conditions could have caused much harm. *The safe itself which housed the NR source acted as an OR energy accumulator.*

This we learned on April 12, 1951, when, after the snow had

melted away on the road, we went down to the empty building
with our GM survey meter and discovered that the Oranur
experiment had actually gone on all the while since February.
The following table provides a survey of the Oranur effects as
measured that same and the following day with Tracerlab
SU-5 Beta Gamma Survey Meter.

PLACE OF MONITORING	CPM IV. 12th	MR/H	CPM IV. 13th	MR/H	DISTANCE FROM SAFE, CONTAINING NR SOURCE SHIELDED ½ INCH LEAD
At main road	60-80	0.004	70	...	600-700 feet
Road	60	....	60	...	400-500 ”
Road at turn	60-80	0.02	60-80	...	100 ”
Road close to building	100	0.02			40 ”
Main entrance			50		50 ” ????
Maid's room	800 !!		1000 !!		300 cm.
Room with safe			6000 !!		200 cm.
AT SAFE WALL		5-10 !!	10-20,000 !	3-4 !	1 cm. from wall, 30 cm. from source inside
Safe			600		100 cm.
Safe			100		1000 cm. outside building

This result was shocking. The counts at the caretaker's cabin
700 feet away were around 40 CPM, i.e., normal for Orgonon.

It was not comprehensible why the count at the road, 100
to 700 feet away, was so much higher than the count at the
main entrance, only 30 feet away. However, 20,000 CPM at the
wall of the steel concrete safe seemed quite exorbitant.

One physician, who was with me, and I myself felt the
Oranur effects right away, strongly: malaise, pressure, etc. The
physician did not look well on the second day. We were afraid
to open the safe, since we had experienced the accident with
the physician who had put her head into an Oranur device. To
simply dump the whole safe into the lake did not seem advisable, since the Oranur activity would most likely have affected
the lake. To bury it in the ground seemed equally impossible

since the OR energy from the soil would, to our notion, have continued to react. The building itself seemed to have become unusable for the summer. We could not carry the responsibility all alone. It was imperative to get help from the administration in Washington and Augusta, Me. Later, our caretaker told us that he felt pain in his chest when four weeks ago he had gone to get some foodstuff from the freezer which was located in that building 30 feet away from the shielded source.

On April 13, we had put several mice of different types (Ca, Lk, healthy mice and newborn ones) into the room which harbored the safe. The mice were kept close to the safe. These mice were reported to be well on April 14. The following day, April 15, a Sunday, another careful check was carried out in the region. Here are the results of the monitoring:

MONITORING OF SAFE CONTAINING TWO MILLIGRAMS OF RADIUM, SHIELDED, AT LOWER HOUSE ON APRIL 15, 1951

		CPM	MR/H
1. AT SAFE:	1 cm.	*20,000 at bottom, 5,000 at top*	10-20
	100 cm.	1000	0.4
	1000 cm.	150-200	0.04
	5000 cm.	60-80, 400 CPM, GM tube without shielding	0.16
2. Adjoining maid's room:		200	0.02
3. ROAD:	200 feet		0.016
	240 feet		0.02 (near H_2O)
4. AT BADGER ROAD:		60	0.012
	30 meters	60-80	0.02
	40 meters	60-80	0.018
	50 meters	*400*, GM tube without shielding!!	0.016
	60 meters		"
	70 meters		"
	80 meters		"
	100 meters		"

Between 50 meters and toward cabin: 60-80 CPM.
Without shield at 30 meters from cabin: 200 CPM.
Mouse box monitored afterward in students' lab: 40-50 CPM.

20,000 CPM and 10-20 MR/H at the outside wall of the safe, steel and concrete four inches thick, from a source some 30 to

50 cm. away inside the safe and two milligrams of radium, each shielded with ½ inch lead, seemed quite enormous. Also, 400 CPM 50 meters or 150 feet away in the open air, measured with the tube taken out from its shielding, seemed enormous.

It was only the fact that the mice had remained healthy after 56 hours close to this safe which made us stop and think. WERE WE HERE DEALING WITH NR ACTIVITY AT ALL? HAD OR ENERGY PERHAPS DONE ITS JOB OF KILLING THE NR COMPLETELY? How otherwise could the good health status of the mice be explained?

The thought that we had possibly reached our original goal of Oranur experimentation, went like an illumination through our minds. Perhaps . . . Possibly . . . If this would withstand the most severe tests in the future, we were obviously dealing with several phases in the Oranur process:

FIRST PHASE:

NR affects OR at first in a most damaging manner. The organismic and atmospheric OR energy reacts to sudden, unexpected NR action with prostration, decline, helplessness, as it were, psychologically speaking.

SECOND PHASE:

OR energy, after the first blow by NR has been suffered, and if it was overcome, FIGHTS BACK *ferociously. It goes mad, runs berserk, as it were. It becomes a killer itself, attempting to kill the irritating NR. In this struggle it itself deteriorates into a killer of the organism which it governs:* RADIATION SICKNESS, *followed by death or some chronic destructive ailment, as for instance leukemia. The blood system is the most sensitive part of the organism in this respect.*

THIRD PHASE:

IF OR ENERGY HAS THE OPPORTUNITY TO KEEP FIGHTING THE NR IRRADIATION; IF IT CAN OBTAIN FURTHER SUPPLY AND REPLACEMENT OF FRESH ATMOSPHERIC OR ENERGY SUFFICIENT ENOUGH TO KEEP THE UPPER HAND, IT WILL FINALLY SUCCEED IN RENDERING NR RADIATION HARMLESS. *It will replace the noxious* SECONDARY

ACTIVITY OF THE NR BY PENETRATION OF THE NR MATTER, AND WILL PUT IT AT ITS OWN SERVICE. WHAT WE ARE DEALING WITH HERE IN THIS THIRD PHASE IS NO LONGER NR BUT OR ENERGY WITHIN THE FORMERLY NOXIOUS MATERIAL. IN THIS FORM, THE PROPERTIES OF THE CHANGED NR MATERIAL WILL SHOW ALL SIGNS OF OR ENERGY: PENETRATION OF ALL WALLS NO MATTER OF WHAT KIND OR THICKNESS, HIGH COUNTS, BUT NO ILL EFFECTS UPON ORGANISMS.

This is, apparently, what we had been dealing with all through the years when small samples of NR sources were first irritating the OR energy and finally were changed into innocent though highly active material which had lost the power of "ionization" and of harming living tissues.

It was in this third phase that we felt quite well, even in the vicinity of an activity of 10 MR/H; that the mice were untouched, and that we felt Oranur only very slightly. On April 23, 1951, twelve days after they were put to the test, all mice were still all right.

But such IMMUNITY *to Oranur, most likely required having gone through and suffered the life-dangerous phases One and Two.* The organism is a highly adjustable functional unit. If it is not knocked out right away during the first two phases; if it is given a chance, time and fresh OR supply, to adapt its own OR reactions to NR activity, it will fight back vigorously in the end and not suffer any longer from NR or secondary radiation.

This now appeared as a solid basis for further procedures toward the *original* goal of the Oranur project, i.e., *immunization against atomic bomb effects.* The concrete practical accomplishment of this task appears still far away; however, the way toward it was clearly designed and marked. The main pioneering job had been done; the main danger signals had been recognized: Oranur phase One and Two; the main symptoms in these intermediary steps were in the open. Behind phase One and Two, there was clearly outlined *phase Three*, the impotence of NR and the victory of OR energy.

The job was basically done. The rest of it was now up to the people and their representatives, the health agencies, the AEC, the national administration, the UN, the medical and physical sciences.

Let us consider carefully what had happened, by comparing a few results which, taken each separately do not make sense, but put together like pieces in a puzzle, reveal the secret behind it all:

The measurement of the activity near the closed safe was high, more than 10 MR/H and 20,000 to 30,000 CPM, coming *apparently* from a source of only two lead-shielded radium needles of one milligram each, and a few micrograms of other nuclear material, through four inches of heavy steel and concrete. On the basis of this finding, one should have expected that the source itself, measured *naked, without any shielding, at only one centimeter distance with an approximately ten times more sensitive counter tube* would yield a correspondingly much higher count.

I opened the safe myself, using a wet mask over my mouth and nose, and a long-handling tongs in removing the source from the safe. Before actually taking out the radium, I measured the activity in the inner space of about 40 x 40 x 50 centimeters. The counts were so high that the GM survey meter needle raced toward the highest scale and beyond it. There were far more than 20 MR/H and far above 100,000 CPM at a distance of about 40 to 50 cm. from the shielded source *within* the safe. I removed the NR material to the outside several meters away and measured again inside. The activity sank nearly immediately to approximately 50% above the normal count of 30-50 CPM. Any doubting physicist, being present at this performance could certainly have triumphantly said, "I told you so. Your Oranur is just so much of a hoax. NR cannot possibly be changed by anything. Give up. . . . The reason for the high activity outside the safe was the NR source . . ."

To all common sense he would have appeared to be right. The high count on the *inside* actually disappeared soon after the removal of the NR source. Still, he could not have answered the question as to how it was possible that through ½ inch lead and 4 inches of concrete and steel, the counts were still as high as they were, in MR/H only half of what they were within the safe, 40 cm. away from the shielded *ONE mg. of radium.*

All the following will teach us is that common sense alone is not good enough; that one cannot judge such a basic function from the standpoint of the atomic theory; that one has finally to start thinking in *cosmic* terms if one wants to comprehend Oranur.

We raced the NR material by car up to the observatory on the hill. It was removed from its shielding and measured immediately with the large 4096 Tracerlab Autoscaler, at 1200 volts and with a counter tube of a mica window thickness of 2.3 mg./cm.² as against the SU-5 Survey Meter and a tube of 30 mg./cm.² wall thickness. Here are the results, synoptically:

		COUNTS	
SHIELDING	MR/H		CPM
1. SHIELDED: ½" lead, 4" concrete and steel			
DISTANCE: approx. 40 cm. out-safe			
GM TUBE: wall thickness 30 mg./cm.²	10+		20,000++
2. SHIELDED: ½" lead			
DISTANCE: 30-40 cm.			
WITHIN safe			
GM TUBE: wall thickness 30 mg./cm.²	20+++		100,000+++
3. SHIELDING: NONE. NEEDLE NAKED	DISTANCE		
TUBE THICKNESS (MICA WINDOW),			
2.3 mg./cm.²	ONE CM		30,000 to 35,000
4096 Autoscaler (Tracerlab)	100 cm.		approx. 3,000

Thus, to the amazement of everybody present and to the detriment of all well-set theories about NR radiation, THE SAME NR SOURCE WHICH ALLEGEDLY COULD MAKE THE GM COUNTER RACE UPWARD THROUGH LEAD SHIELDING AND AT FORTY CENTIMETERS

DISTANCE, TO A HUNDRED THOUSAND PLUS CPM WAS NOT CAPABLE
OF YIELDING MORE THAN AROUND THIRTY THOUSAND CPM NAKED AT
A FORTIETH OF THE DISTANCE AND WITH A TUBE AT LEAST TEN
TIMES MORE SENSITIVE.

WE HAD ACHIEVED OUR RESULT: THE RESULT WAS THERE.

The problem was what it was, then, if it was NOT the NR
source, that had made the GM counter race so high outside and
inside the safe. It could not be anything else than the ATMOS-
PHERIC OR ENERGY WHICH SURROUNDED THE SHIELDED SOURCE AND
THE SAFE AS WELL AS THE BUILDING HOUSING THE SAFE AS FAR AS
600 FEET UP TOWARD THE ROAD.

I put all the NR material into the great charger and into the
20x OR accumulator. There it remained until the following day
late in the afternoon when I had to take it out again because
of a new severe reaction.

Several days later the two milligrams of radium in their
shielding were taken up to the Orgone Energy Observatory,
where they were measured, both naked and with shielding at
the GM Autoscaler. The results are summarized in the chart
on the facing page.

Before proceeding further, let us again review the facts in
their interrelations, AND *not* SINGLY:

FIRST: *The naked NR material gave a much lower count* (ONE
TENTH) *than the same material enclosed in heavy lead shielding.*

SECOND: *The ten times higher counts in the atmosphere
around the shielded NR material is a function of the OR energy
fighting against NR.*

THIRD: *As soon as the interaction between OR and NR is
stopped, the high OR activity vanishes and sinks down to the
normal atmospheric level.*

FOURTH: *OR energy alone does not react severely unless irritated by NR.*

The Oranur reaction was again severe immediately after the
NR material was put into the big charger *without the safe*. The
counts were as high as 2000 CPM on the outside of the charger.
The air became heavy again and we felt the typical Oranur

MEASUREMENTS OF TWO NEEDLES OF ORANUR RADIUM (one mg. each), IN
SHIELDING AND NAKED, AT GM AUTOSCALER, APRIL 28, 1951, 3 P.M.

All measurements at one cm. distance. Each measurement average of several measurements.

Material	Scale	With Shielding	Naked	Time in sec.	CPM
1. Ra 1 (one mg. untreated)	4096	+	..	0.8	307,200
2. Ra 2 (one mg. OR-treated)	4096	+	..	1.05	245,760
3. Ra 2	256	..	+	0.4	38,400
4. Ra 2	4096	..	+	2.8	81,920
5. Ra 1	4096	..	+	8.3	28,877
6. Ra 1	4096	+	..	0.8	307,200
7. Ra 2	4096	+	..		307,200
8. Ra 2	4096	..	+	3.0	81,920
9. Shielding alone	64			3.15	1,280
10. Microgram Ra—OR-treated 5 yrs.	4096			0.8	307,200
11. Watch, one month owned	4096			10.0 / 10.0	24,576 / 24,576
12. Watch, 2 yrs. owned	4096				
13. Calibration after measurements	256			4.25	60 cycles per sec.

symptoms (malaise, nausea, pressure) which we had NOT FELT
so severely previously near the safe. This gave us another clue
for further procedures, thus:

Apparently, *when the NR material was within the heavy steel
and concrete safe, the OR energy which can penetrate everything could easily get* INTO *the safe whereas the NR activity
could* NOT *get* OUT *of the safe.* Thus the chances in the fight of
OR against NR were shifted to the advantage of OR *against*
NR. On the other hand, when NR material was not sufficiently
shielded, it had an even chance to irritate and to trigger OR
energy into DOR action. This was the reason why we had not
felt malaise of a severe nature in the vicinity of the safe,
whereas we felt it right away severely in the vicinity of the
charger. Now it seemed clear that in order to reduce the DOR

effect, one had to put the NR material into heavy shielding and thus confined, into the charger. OR would get at NR, but not NR at OR. We decided right away to build a housing for the safe to put the NR material into the safe again and to put the safe, containing NR, in the vicinity of the charger. This would secure the Oranur effect without the DOR element IF we were on the right track of reasoning.

The further elaboration of this problem must wait until the *second* Oranur series of experimentation can be carried out.

In the end a control experiment with a peculiar result deserves to be mentioned:

We ordered a third mg. of radium from New York. We had it tested before it was brought up to Orgonon. The results of the measurements taken in a radiation laboratory in New York were for this one mg. of radium:

Naked . . . Ca. 16,000 CPM

Within ½ inch lead shielding . . . ca. 7,000 CPM

We measured the same source in thick lead shielding *immediately* upon its arrival at Orgonon: The result was ca. 300,000 CPM with the Gm Autoscaler and ca. 100,000 CPM with the SU-5 Survey Meter. Does the Oranur effect act instantly raising the counts five- to twenty-fold? Only further work will answer this problem.

However, the conclusion appears safe: *It is the OR energy in the atmosphere, surrounding the NR material, which reacts at the GM counter. It is the organismic OR energy within living bodies which continues to react to NR material for months and even years* (bio-energetic radioactivity; "radiation sickness").

OUTLOOK

We all felt that we had gone through some awful, deadly dangerous experience which we could not quite fully grasp, which had thrown us into some great depth, a heretofore well-hidden domain of cosmic functioning. In spite of the many clear-cut physical manifestations, observed and measured with exact instruments, and in spite of our deep disinclination toward any kind of metaphysical thinking, we could not help being impressed by the *psychological* implications of these experiences. It is much too early to go into detail here. However, we wish to convey some degree of realization of the fact that the first Oranur experiment not only had confirmed the basic antithesis of OR and NR, as I had predicted many years ago; it had brought into sharper focus many seemingly insignificant assumptions regarding cosmic orgone energy functions such as, for example, its "meaningful" behavior, which distinguished it from any kind of purely mechanical functioning such as electricity or magnetism. We are fully aware of the danger of mystical misinterpretation entering the scene at this point. Yet, if millions of people have developed and lived in metaphysical beliefs for millennia, had believed in a "Prana" and such, there must be something in it. And this truth seemed urgently to want to reveal itself to us:

IF MYSTICISM AND METAPHYSICS ARE BASED ON AN IRRATIONAL APPREHENSION OF THE COSMIC ENERGY WITHIN AND WITHOUT THE ORGANISM, IT SHOULD BE EXPECTED THAT THIS ENERGY IN ITS *truly physical* MANIFESTATIONS WOULD SHOW FUNCTIONS WHICH ARE AKIN TO OR THE VERY BASIS OF ALL FUNCTIONS ALLIED WITH *life* AND *emotions*.

This fact was not new to us. We had observed the performative stages of psychic functions in the realm of merely physical OR functions for many years, and though quite logically fitting into the framework of our work on Life Energy, these similarities had kept amazing us. For instance, the contraction of the OR energy in freezing bion water; a freezing animal behaves exactly the same way. Or, the fluid, *functional*, non-mechanical type of behavior of all, but all, OR functions such as the spontaneous discharge of OR-charged electroscopes, or the fluctuating, yet lawful behavior of the orgonotic temperature difference in connection with the equally fluid, non-mechanical, yet lawful weather changes; or the fusion of primitive bions, which so clearly demonstrated the physical nature and basis of the fusion in copulation; or the lifelike, "meaningful," "playful" movements of small energy vesicles to be seen under high magnification, and many other similar phenomena which have but one thing in common: They are qualitatively akin to higher functions of the living and the mind.

It is clear why an observer of these basic functions of nature, who is not properly trained in the knowledge of the bio-energetic emotions, would surely miss the point and would not understand what he is seeing. On the other hand, the bio-energetically well-trained observer, who by his professional daily activities is used to seeing and judging emotional movements and bio-energetic expressions and to reading their meaning without a word spoken on the part of the patient, will readily, and often even before understanding the physical functions, grasp the "meaning" of these microscopic orgonotic phenomena. In the mechanistic technician of physics, the observation of the physical functions of nature split off from the emotional manifestations as "physics" *here* and "mysticism" or "religiousness" *there*. On the other hand, in the well-trained orgonomic observer, these two modes of experiencing nature, otherwise so much opposed to each other, are united into one single picture. Here the *physical* does not exclude or contradict the *meaningful*, nor the quantitative the qualitative. We are aware that these matters are of a deep natural-philosophic significance. *The sharp boundary lines between physics and what is called "metaphysics" have broken down.* The metaphysical intuition has a physical basis: "GOD" and "ETHER" are ONE. When a theoretically well-trained orgonomist, i.e., trained *physically* as well as bio-energetically, which is rare indeed, reads of the many attempts at a reconciliation between the *physical* world picture which governs thought in *Western* Civilization, and the *mystical*, "aesthetic" world picture which governs the *Eastern* world; when he follows the attempts to reconcile the Objective in Western science and the Subjective in Eastern religious philosophy, he must, inevitably, see before his eyes the behavior of bions, of an electroscopic charge, of a frozen bion water preparation with its contracted yellow core from which later living plasmatic flakes will derive, and he will be awed by the unity of *physical action* and *emotional meaningfulness* in the Oranur effects.

Newton and Goethe are, with their respective physical world pictures, no longer as much antipodes as they used to be. Their points of view can and will be reconciled. The *scientist* and the *artist* are no longer keepers of two disparate, unmixable worlds, as they still seem to be. Intellect and intuition are no longer irreconcilable opposites in scientific work. As a matter of fact, they have never been so in basic natural research.

The reader understands well what we are driving at here: ALL BOUNDARIES BETWEEN SCIENCE AND RELIGION, SCIENCE AND ART, OBJECTIVE AND SUBJECTIVE, QUANTITY AND QUALITY, PHYSICS AND PSYCHOLOGY, ASTRONOMY AND RELIGION, GOD AND ETHER, ARE IRREVOCABLY BREAKING DOWN, BEING REPLACED BY A CONCEPTION OF THE BASIC UNITY, A BASIC CFP OF ALL NATURE WHICH BRANCHES OUT INTO THE VARIOUS KINDS OF HUMAN EXPERIENCE.

This does not mean, of course, that the distinctions entirely cease to exist. On the contrary, in the light of the functional identity between *man* and *animal, orgastic* longing and *cosmic* longing, God and Ether, etc., the specific *differences* emerge the more sharply, and to the good of rational discrimination.

We learned more dealing with this basic change in the modes of thinking: ORGONOMY IS NOT MERELY A BRANCH OF NATURAL SCIENCE, NOR IS IT A MERE ARTISTIC PROCEDURE, NOR PSYCHOLOGY ALONE, NOR BIOLOGY ALONE. IT IS, TRULY, IN FULL ACCORDANCE WITH ITS OBJECT OF INQUIRY, *a body of knowledge which deals with the basic law of nature*.

From the cosmic OR energy ocean all other functions emerge through variation. This makes *identity* and *variability* compatible with each other. With the breakdown of all sharp, mechanical distinctions, of necessity a new view upon our cosmic existence emerges. This is already true, although we may still not know exactly how to go about it all.

To return: Also, NR radiation, as a *secondary* natural function, once emerged through differentiation, from OR energy functions. Now, we experienced not only the antithesis between OR and NR; we also experienced, in a deadly manner, that OR itself can go wild with "rage" as we are accustomed to calling it. We all had the impression during that period, that we "had somehow provoked the otherwise benign OR energy and turned it into a wild beast."

A Frank Discussion

This conclusion is a very serious one, involving matters pertaining to the very health and security of people in general. Therefore, blunt language and avoidance of any circumlocation are imperative.

Before entering the subject in question, I would like to alleviate some of the possible hesitancies which might obstruct a frank discussion of this work. My sharp theoretical and practical formulations on biopsychiatric aspects of public health should not stand in the way, since they are already at least partially incorporated in present-day teachings all over the world. My past affiliations with the revolutionary movement in Europe of some twenty years ago should not stand in the way since for more than eighteen years I have had no political affiliations whatsoever. I have never been active in the POLITICAL sense of the word, but I have kept myself well-informed on every feature of the plague of dictatorship, black as well as red. I have fought dictatorship of any and every kind factually since the very early beginning of my career; and I have particularly fought every sneaking evildoer, no matter in what party, as early as 1931, with all my vigor and knowledge, long before anyone really knew what it was all about; also long before the recognition of the USSR government by the USA. I have not the slightest intention of forcing any of my scientific beliefs upon any nation or any part of it; and I believe myself to be the only one today who *really knows* where the dangers connected with orgonomic teachings are to be watched out for. My belief, based on rich experience, is that if there is any hope of ever emerging from the present-day social chaos into the bright light of peaceful social living—and to my mind there *is* great hope—its factual, powerful roots are harbored by the alive, forward-looking forces that are at work everywhere in the world. Only a very few responsible people are fully aware today that an old, tired, bound-up world is breaking down, and that a new, hopeful, young world is slowly and painfully being born. The current *biosexual revolution,* now in progress over the past thirty years, constitutes its core.

Hoping to have eliminated this obstacle to a free exchange of opinion, I proceed to the main point: The Oranur experiment has, without or even against our intentions, reached proportions which threaten not only to get out of control here at Orgonon (at present, May 1951), but which particularly endanger the security of the USA in case its government should further delay to take these affairs seriously and to direct them to the benefit of the country. To sum up: The Oranur experiment has so far revealed grave implications; their scope and revolutionary character are nobody's fault or intent. The factual evidence and the theoretical framework of the results are much too involved to be brought forth at this point. I have, for security reasons, not published anything about the immediate practical and theoretical background of Oranur for many years, since about 1947; I had sensed that what might happen was what actually did happen.

[*Note inserted in galley proof, Sept. 12, 1951:* The following summary reflects in its pessimistic aspects the severe situation as of about April 1951, when the Oranur Experiment was still exerting its frightening influence upon the workers of Orgonon. The frightening events were partially due to the fact that we went into this experiment entirely unprepared for its scope and danger, a disadvantage which from now on is not operative.

I would like to mitigate greatly the pessimistic impression that especially points 1, 6, 7 and 8 in the following may make on the reader. It is also necessary to eliminate the fear that a new murder weapon has been created by a scientist and that the deadliness of Oranur far outweighs its positive life-serving functions. During the five months following the conclusion of this first report, much of the pessimistic outlook was far over-shadowed by new observations which left no doubt as to the *life-positive* medical and biological results of Oranur. These results appear tremendous at present and will require a long period of time for careful scrutiny. I feel justified in stating that under the condition of proper handling of Oranur all the dangers mentioned below can be eliminated, and that the life-positive effects on man, animals, and vegetation seem secured. The reason why I leave the original text as of April 1951 unchanged is to render a completely true picture of our emotional and biological reactions to the first run of the Experiment, reactions which doubtlessly will occur in nearly everyone who attempts to experiment with Oranur for the first time. A second, additional report about the outweighing positive effects of Oranur is already in preparation.]

1. By putting only one milligram of radioactive nuclear material into a highly concentrated OR energy atmosphere (in a twenty-fold OR energy charger or a room charged through years of work with OR energy), a change takes place in the atmospheric energy which beyond any doubt has the qualities of a *slow* but *enduring chain reaction*. This reaction of OR energy to nuclear energy is dangerous to life if it transcends certain limits of intensity or duration.

2. *There is no protection whatsoever against OR energy running wild when irritated by NR radiation, since OR energy penetrates everything, including lead and brick or stone walls of any thickness.* The present-day safety measures, as employed by the Atomic Energy project, are not effective against Oranur.

3. Once the Oranur effects take place, they travel through the air as if infesting, chainlike, one area after another. Here at Orgonon, such infestation has been found as far away as two miles from the place of the original effect. Only 1 mg. of NR

within a 20x OR charger has been used. The possible effects of 1 gram NR in a 500x OR charger are unpredictable and would, I am afraid, be disastrous.

4. It is most likely, and even imperative to assume that quite ordinary materials such as rock, metal, and especially material arrangements which have the faculty of accumulating OR energy, continue to be active long after the originally triggering NR material has been removed. This *resembles induced* radioactivity. It is at present hard to tell whether or not the rock actually disintegrates. But it undoubtedly is active and continues to be so. This effect developed quite unexpectedly and unintentionally when we started to test the influence of OR energy (five to ten times concentration) upon one mg. of radium. This activity is merely a sharp increase of normal, natural activities.

5. Structures which are capable of accumulating atmospheric OR energy, such as steel wool, metal filing cabinets or simple metal-lined boxes, become active even if they have not been directly influenced by NR radiation; it is sufficient that they come into contact with a directly affected orgone energy accumulator.

6. A criminal hater of mankind, or a political enemy, if he knew about this, and *if the USA did NOT know about or did NOT study these effects*, could easily drop activated Oranur devices, looking like simple metal-lined boxes; these could infest a whole region, if not a whole continent.

7. According to what we have learned over a period of only four months' observation and experimentation, people would fall sick due to the Oranur-infested atmosphere. Each person falling ill would react according to his or her specific disease or disposition to disease. This effect is due to the *selective* bioenergetic effect of OR energy which attacks specifically the diseased part in the organism, at first driving the symptoms to higher acuity and then:

8. CURING THEM IF PROPERLY AND CONSCIENTIOUSLY APPLIED. However, uncontrolled, unsupervised, and especially if used

with malignant intent, such infestation of the atmosphere would surely kill or at least immobolize many people. If as little as one microgram of radioactive nuclear material were left continuously in a 50- or even a 20-fold orgone energy charger, the result could be disastrous.

9. In order to illustrate the intensity and extensity of the Oranur effects: Buildings which have been freed of any kind of radioactive material, and in addition, from which every single OR energy accumulating device has been removed, still drive the background counts as high as 80 or 100 CPM if regular ventilation is neglected for only half-a-day. On the other hand, fresh air removes the effects and reduces the activity to a normal of around 25 to 40 CPM.

10. There can be little doubt as to the fact that atmospheric OR energy plays a major if not a decisive role in the dynamics of an atomic pile reaction, to judge from what has so far been disclosed in the unrestricted literature. A careful experimental study of these dynamics appears now to be of crucial, if not life-securing importance in the present state of social affairs.

11. *I did not work with fission* and *I did not produce fission during the Oranur experimentation.* It is not sure that fission actually takes place in infested material, but this might possibly be the case. Therefore, I prefer, in the interest of the great medical potentialities of OR energy research, in the interest of the people and for my personal security to report these things, and to urge emphatically that all red tape be cut through in order to look into these processes on a scale appropriate to their scope, dangers and hopes. Fullest clarity and having the cards in the open, above the table, are now crucial obligations: *IF* FISSION OF ORDINARY MATERIAL OCCURS, ITS DISCLOSURE WAS INCIDENTAL TO AN EXPERIMENT WHICH STARTED WITH AN ENTIRELY DIFFERENT GOAL IN MIND.

12. The gravity of the situation is further increased by the fact that the Oranur functions most probably are apt to overthrow many cherished beliefs of today's nuclear physics. Most

of this is still in the dark, but the outlines are already clearly visible. I shall mention only a very few of the consequences:

a. *The atomic "particle" theory of the basic structure of the universe no longer holds water.* The primordial OR energy ocean (formerly called "ether") *exists* and is *mass-free.* Inert as well as heavy mass arise from mass-free energy through certain functional processes already known to orgonomic research in some detail.

b. Exactly at the point where the atomic theory dips into the PRE-atomic functions of nature, into the realm of so-called "material waves" (a wrong, misleading expression), into the realm of the "wave particles" (again misleading), into the realm of electrons consisting of waves only, into the impossibility of determining at the same time position and momentum of an electron, the "law of merely statistical probability," etc., etc., the functional theory of orgonomy sets in. These primordial, *pre*-atomic problems are impregnable to methods of mechanistic or materialistic thinking. They divulge logical intelligibility only if approached *functionally*, i.e., orgonomically. The facts, observations and theoretical deductions have kept piling up for many years in a clear enough fashion to warrant the assumption that the whole electronic theory *as far as it pertains to cosmic,* PRIMORDIAL *functions,* will be replaced by a *functional theory of the basic functions of the universe.* These matters are naturally very serious and require intelligent unprejudiced, open-minded, courageous efforts to clear the field of misconceptions, inertia in thinking, wrongly applied theories, etc. In addition, many reputations are at stake and personal feelings will be hurt.

c. For several years now, OR energy has yielded up to 25,000 impulses per SECOND in tubes evacuated and freed of any kind of gas down to 0.5 micron pressure. Thus, the ionization theory, which is based upon the assumption that it is the "ionization effect" exerted upon the "*gas*" particles in the counter tubes by the impinging radiation "particles" has become undermined. NO GAS-FILLING IS NEEDED TO OBTAIN ORGO-

NOTIC GEIGER EFFECTS. OR energy luminates and acts in a clear-cut quantum manner in high vacuum. It depends only on atmospheric weather changes and such cosmic influences as, for instance, sunspot cycles. The greater the *frequency* in the orgonotic quantum action, the more does *continuity* or *linear* action replace the former.

13. OUTLOOK ON MEDICAL POSSIBILITIES: Medical Oranur effects are *powerful* as well as *dangerous*. *They attack and bring to the foreground the specific disease characteristic of the individual.* In this process, if tampered with ignorantly, the sick may die prematurely. However, the fact itself, that a medically active agent has been found which *searches out the specific syndrome and its organismic location,* is highly promising. The application of Oranur would be not by injections or other mechanical devices, but simply by *exposing the sick organism gradually and cautiously to the necessary dose of Oranur.*

14. Since NR activates OR and changes it to Oranur, Oranur continues, chainlike, to affect other OR devices; an initial trigger effect would be sufficient to start a chain of Oranur activity, as said before. We would have, then, to distinguish OR accumulators which had *not* been triggered by NR; they would be applied as heretofore, for total, regular, preventive irradiation, treatment of wounds, burns, etc. However, Oranur devices could not be kept in any inhabited building and would have to be handled with the greatest of care, since they, in contradistinction to simple OR accumulators, are potentially dangerous. Apart from individual treatments with Oranur, the new possibility offers itself, *to affect whole regions simply by powerful Oranur arrangements and thus to fight epidemics, mass diseases, and possibly NR radiation sickness* EN MASSE *in a preventive manner*. The latter possibility will, of course, require much detailed elaboration and strict legal precautions. This task is far beyond our financial scope and our obligation.

Thus the short-range importance of Oranur. However, from a long-range view, the effects of Oranur upon human *emotional* reactions are of infinitely greater importance. Here, as things look at present, we may well be prepared for great events.

A government of nations, bent on abolishing the threat of atomic warfare, on securing peace in the world and bringing health and happiness to people EVERYWHERE, could do untold good. Cosmic energy could finally serve useful purposes, since *slowness* of chain reaction and *medical efficiency* have been found in *the cosmic primordial forces*. Such humane efforts would command respect and secure the deep confidence of people in our endeavors everywhere. No single man or organization could accomplish this end; only allied social institutions could do it—from the nursery school to the institute of higher learning, from the professional organization to the military Pentagon in every land.

VII. COSMIC ORGONE ENGINEERING

1. DOR REMOVAL AND CLOUD-BUSTING

Preliminary Communication

THE "DOR-CLOUDS"

It has become possible to *apply the principle of the orgonomic potential to the dissolution and formation of clouds*. This technical application of the orgonomic potential was forced upon this institution during the emergency which shook Orgonon from about March 21, 1952, till the present date, September, 1952. It was a matter of survival in this region to find a way to remove the "DOR-clouds," as we came to call the nauseating concentrations of DOR over ORGONON.

Let me first explain what these DOR-clouds are, how they look, what they do and what can be done about them. DOR-clouds were observed and comprehended for the first time during the early days of May, 1952. The main characteristics of these DOR-clouds, as they appear at various intervals over Orgonon, coming in mostly from the west, are the following:

1. "Stillness" and "Bleakness"

A "stillness" and "bleakness" spread over the landscape, rather well delineated against unaffected surrounding regions. The stillness is expressed in a real cessation of life expressions in the atmosphere. The birds stop singing; the frogs stop croaking. There is no sound of life anywhere. The birds fly low or

---

From the *Orgone Energy Bulletin*, vol. 4, no. 4, October, 1952.

hide in the trees. Animals crawl over the ground with greatly reduced motility. The leaves of the trees and the needles of the evergreens look very "sad"; they droop, lose turgor and erectility. Every bit of sparkle or luster disappears from the lakes and the air. The trees look black, as though dying. The impression is actually that of *blackness*, or better, *bleakness*. It is not something that "came *into* the landscape." *It is, rather, the sparkle of Life that* WENT OUT *of the landscape.*

2. Vanishing of Luster and Sparkle

The vanishing of luster and sparkle from the sunny landscape had been independently confirmed by several observers who have grown up on farms. Trees, rocks, telegraph poles, mountainsides, and houses appear "black" although it is not really blackness. It is, rather, like the *absence of light.* To the orgonomic observer, it appears to be the result of thinning or a failing of the OR energy substratum that usually luminates into brilliant daylight, with sparkle and luster. It should be carefully noticed that DOR-clouds appear while the sun keeps on shining. The green color of trees and meadows disappears from the mountain ranges. Everything seems to go black or *"dull."* One cannot help but feel this to be DEATH, "BLEAK DEATH," as some call it. This bleak blackness hovers especially over landscapes without any vegetation, and over swampy regions. Swamps have a peculiar bearing on DOR effects. Swamps are basically accumulations of stagnant water which enhance decay processes and are the opposite of fresh running brook or river water which counteracts decay. They are distinguished by the absence or, respectively, presence of orgonotic metabolism. Everything still remains to be carefully investigated in this realm. We are only breaking trail for a first over-all orientation.

The lack of luster can be understood in terms of some *reduction of orgonotic pulsation and metabolism in plants and animals.* This seems to be confirmed by the fact that at the lake surfaces orgonotic pulsation also ceases; the water becomes calm and motionless.

A DOR-cloud is usually surrounded by normal atmospheric OR activity, such as *blueness* of the mountain ranges, sparkling of the sunny atmosphere, greenness of the trees. One cannot help but feel that natural cosmic OR energy retracts from the "evil," "bleak," "black," "lifeless" DOR-cloud and lets it pass. Observations made at night show luminous OR surrounding and fighting the lusterless DOR-clouds. In daytime the mountains appear *black* while losing the normal blue-gray orgone energy color. The emotional impression here again is "sadness." The color of the mountain ranges is now somehow "dirty," or blackish with a *purple* tint. After the passing of the DOR-cloud, the intense *blue-gray "haze"* returns. We learned to realize exactly when normal OR activity replaces again the nauseating DOR blackness.

3. Bio-energetic Distress in Human Beings

People react to the DOR-clouds with rather grave distress. Many do not know or cannot explain what happens to them. They call it "heat," or "some atom dust," or just "bad air." Some are biologically insensitive to a degree which puzzles the orgonomist. There are others who *know* the deadly quality of these clouds, not intellectually, but rather with their *First, Orgonotic Sense.* "There is something wrong in the air," one hears them say, or, "Something is going on somewhere," a statement expressing awareness together with suspicion. "I cannot get any air," or, "It hits me like a brick when I enter my shop in the morning," etc. In some cases one must persist in asking the same question over and over until the answer creeps to the surface from a frightened or bewildered mind: "Yes, if you want to know, I feel it sometimes like something closing in on my face, like a wall, but I cannot really feel it, you know; and then I get that bad headache of mine," or, "My sinuses are going bad . . . ," etc. etc.

If they are not completely dead emotionally, i.e., far below the normal bioenergetic level of functioning, people are usually aware of the *"changing in the weather,"* too; in vegetation and in the "general *feel*" of things. In the early spring, already in the middle of April, 1952, the buds were coming out in the Rangeley region. People did not quite dare to admit such an astonishing fact, since buds are not expected there before the end of May. Remarks in the beginning of June about the peculiar "black" clouds that were coming from the west and for some peculiar reason remained "stuck," as it were, over Orgonon, were frequent. Also, the lushness of the vegetation was duly acknowledged and generally appreciated.

4. Geiger Counter Reactions

The reactions of the Geiger counter to the DOR-clouds deserves special attention. At this point, only a few basic phenomena should be mentioned:

During the passage of DOR-clouds over a certain region, the GM counter will act in peculiar, extraordinary ways. When these reactions were seen for the first time during the early spring of 1951, they were dismissed as "only" or "nothing but" failure of the batteries. Since then, we learned to respect these "failures" and to read their meaning to a sufficient degree to form reliable opinions about the atmospheric OR conditions before, during and after the passage of DOR-clouds. It is advisable to distinguish the "disorders" of the GM counter as follows:

a. *"JAMMING":* The portable GM counter (SU-5, Tracerlab) will *"race"* to the limit of 100,000 CPM or 20 MR/H.

b. *"FAILING"* or *"FADING":* The counts will drop again rapidly until they will sink beneath the normal background count of 30-40 CPM. The needle will remain at 5 or 10 CPM or it will point to Zero with the range 100 CPM turned on. This will happen in an extremely highly charged atmosphere.

c. *"JAMMING"* as well as *"FADING"* may occur each by itself in a very high OR atmosphere. Sometimes the fading is preceded by jamming. One also sees rather frequently the GM set in with the normal background reaction of 30 to 50 CPM, and then, after a minute or two, start racing toward the higher or even the highest possible counts, which would cause alarm in any atomic plant. The details of these functions are as yet unknown. But it would appear reasonable to assume that *Fading, Jamming* and *Racing* are all variants of one and the same basic disorder: OVERCHARGE of the GM counter tube. To repeat: The pointer will not move at all: FAILING; or it may fail after an initial normal count: FADING. It may rush to abnormally high values: RACING, instantly or after a brief period of normal reaction. It may race to the highest possible count and beyond and then get stuck there with or without subsequent fading, i.e., JAMMING.

These distinctions are naturally subject to corrections and to further detailed interpretation.

d. *The "ERRATIC" GM Counter:* During the passage of DOR-clouds, one can, furthermore, observe a type of behavior on the portable GM as if, psychologically speaking, the GM counter had become "nervous" and could not make up its mind, as it were, whether to race, to fade or to jam. In such cases, one sees the needle start in with the normal 30 to 40 CPM; then it races, say, to 500 CPM, drops thereafter slowly, in the fading manner, to 100 and further to 70, only to start racing again to 10,000 or even 30,000 CPM; eventually this is followed by still higher "*erratic*" oscillations back and forth between 10,000 and 100,000; it may end in jamming or complete fading.

These few distinctions in the disorderly behavior of the GM portable counter may suffice. It should be noticed, however, that GM counters which are enclosed in *plastic* material will most likely only fade or fail; this is so, to judge from only one single observation with a new plastic-covered GM counter, because plastic material absorbs OR avidly without reflecting the OR energy. This observation requires further elaboration and confirmation.

In the beginning, during March and April, 1952, we were

under the impression that the DOR-clouds coming from the west, originated from atomic blasts in the western United States. However, it was later ascertained that there were no atomic detonations in the USA in March, 1952. Thus, the origin of the DOR-clouds remains a mystery to this date. The onset of the disaster at Orgonon soon after the tornado struck in the West, March 21, 1952, centered our attention on the possibility that we were dealing with some very obscure *cosmic events.*

The DOR emergency at Orgonon worsened quickly during April. Emotional and physical distress became unbearable, and it was now a matter of survival to remove the black DOR accumulations that hovered ever more frequently over Orgonon. An inconspicuous, long-neglected observation came to the rescue:

Far back in 1940, when the atmospheric OR energy had been seen for the first time at Mooselookmeguntic Lake in the Rangeley region through long metal pipes, casual pointing of some pipes at the surface of the lake seemed to affect the movement of the waves. This appeared quite incredible at that early period of OR research; the matter was abandoned and soon forgotten. However, the incredible effect of metal pipes upon energy motion such as waves, seemed to have lingered on in my mind over all these dozen years. When the suffering from DOR became unbearable at Orgonon late in April, a few metal pipes, 9 to 12 feet long and 1½ inch in diameter, were directed toward the black DOR concentrations overhead, and connected through BX cables to a deep well.

The effect was instantaneous: The black DOR-clouds began to shrink. And when the pipes were pointed *against* the OR energy flow, i.e., toward the west, a breeze west to east would set in after a few minutes "DRAW," as we came to call this operation; fresh, blue-gray OR energy moved in where the nauseating DOR-clouds had been a short while before. Soon we learned that rain clouds, too, could be influenced, increased and diminished as well as moved, by operating these pipes in certain well-defined ways.

From the first hesitating attempts to end the emergency at Orgonon, more systematic experiments in the creation and destruction of clouds, as well as rain-making and stopping of rain began to develop successfully over several months, till the first two C.OR.E. "CLOUDBUSTER" units were finally constructed at Portland, Maine, in September-October, 1952, for more elaborate CORE operations.

In the following pages only the basic principles of "CLOUD-BUSTING" will be presented. A detailed presentation of the technical aspects will follow in a broader context of Cosmic Orgone Engineering (*C.OR.E.*).

THE PRINCIPLES OF "CLOUD-BUSTING"

1. "Cloud-Busting"

The term "Cloud-Busting," as used in this paper, shall denote all engineering techniques which deal with the destruction as well as the *formation* of clouds of water vapor in the atmosphere and of orgone energy concentrations of all kinds including gravity; briefly, with all phenomena which are related to or derive from atmospheric changes of climate including weather, humidity, amount of rainfall per unit of time, storms, hurricanes, "DOR-clouds," Oranur functions in the atmosphere, atmospheric OR energy changes of all kinds, the origin of deserts as well as of areas of green vegetation, and all similar functions which depend on the presence or absence, on the scarcity or plentifulness of OR energy, oxygen, water vapor, rain, sun and wind and their interaction.

2. Technological Use of the "Orgonomic Potential"

The "orgonomic potential" denotes all functions in nature which depend on the flow of cosmic energy, or potential, from LOW TO HIGH or from WEAKER TO STRONGER SYSTEMS. Thus the orgonomic potential is the basis of and functions contrary to the mechanical potential, heat, electromagnetic energy, mechanical potential of position, etc. The orgonomic potential is most clearly expressed in the maintenance in most animals on this planet of a temperature higher than that of the environment, and in the function of *gravitational attraction*. In both cases, the stronger energy system draws energy from or attracts a weaker system nearby; in both cases the *potential is directed from low to high*, or from *weak to strong*. Gravitation obviously functions on this basis.

The technique of cloud-busting is to a very large extent, if not wholly, based on the technological use of the orgonomic potential as it governs the OR energy functions of the atmosphere.

The technological use of the orgonomic potential can be divided, basically, into two major groups:

A. *INCREASE of the OR potential:*

In this case we *concentrate* OR energy and *build up* a steeper or stronger OR potential. This will have entirely different effects than

B. *DECREASE of the OR potential:*

In this case we *disperse* or *dissipate* OR energy; we *lower* the potential difference and create a tendency toward more or less equal distribution of the OR energy in the atmospheric OR energy envelop of the planet. We act in the direction of the mechanical potential.

Rain clouds, thunder clouds, hurricanes and tornadoes are, seen from the viewpoint of orgonomy, different expressions of basically one and the same function, i.e., *combinations of concentrated OR energy streams and water vapors*. On the intensity, direction, location and similar conditions related to the combination of water and OR energy ($H_2O \leftrightarrow OR$) many atmospheric conditions depend; most of these conditions still await detailed study and logical comprehension.

However, the two basic principles of cloud-busting, *increase* and *decrease* of the OR potential, suffice at the moment to make their technological use comprehensible.

If we wish to *destroy* clouds we must use the orgonomic potential in such a manner that the potential *decreases*.

If we wish to create clouds or to increase the power of existing clouds, we must use the OR potential in such a manner that the potential between clouds and their immediate environment *increases*.

In order to execute these two basic principles in a satisfactory manner, we must, logically, construct and use a device which is capable of adding OR energy to the atmospheric OR energy envelope; or, we must construct a device which will DRAW ENERGY FROM THE OR ENVELOPE in such a manner that the affected region *loses* certain amounts of energy to other regions, thus changing the atmospheric energy concentrations.

Since at present, adding energy to the atmosphere is not yet possible, we must use the other principle, that of DRAWING ENERGY FROM THE ATMOSPHERE.

3. *Drawing Off Atmospheric OR Energy*

In order to draw off atmospheric OR energy, we must accomplish two tasks: a) we must use a device which *draws* OR energy; b) we must know into what place to draw this energy.

This is accomplished by changing, basically, the principle of the functioning of the LIGHTNING ROD:

The lightning rod, too, functions according to OR energy principles, since "lightning" is atmospheric OR energy discharge in a very narrow space. The pointed rod, reaching into the atmosphere, attracts the lightning discharge and conducts it through heavy wires into the ground. This lightning rod system functions according to *orgonomic*, and not according to electrical principles: In the lightning rod system, the atmospheric charge is drawn *from* the atmosphere *toward* the point of the rod and further toward the earth's crust. It is, thus, the *orgonomic* potential *from weak to strong* which is operative also in the case of the lightning rod. If the electrical potential from high to low were operative in the lightning rod system, the direction of flow would necessarily be the reverse, from the earth's crust toward the atmosphere; the energy would stream off and *away* from the point of the lightning rod.

Cloud-busting operates in *agreement* with the functioning of the lightning rod, only if we put *both* functions, cloud-busting and lightning rod, on the common functional basis of the OR potential.

Cloud-busting *deviates* from the lightning rod principle in four ways: (1) Its purpose is not to draw and to ground bolts of lightning, but *to draw OR energy charges* out of atmosphere and clouds. In doing so, it deals with the same kind of force as in the lightning, with one important difference: *The cloud-buster draws the charges slowly, in small amounts at a time, dispersed,* as it were, in time as well as in concentration, and not in the form of sudden lightning. It does so by way (2) of long, *hollow pipes,* and not of solid steel rods.

The pipes, any number of them, and any length beyond a minimum of about 4 meters or 10 feet used in our first cloud-busting experiments, have the function (3) *of triggering the atmospheric OR energy flow into certain directions.* The function of the pipes is fulfilled with this triggering of directional flow. Once the OR energy flow is directed at will, it continues to flow in the same direction, until another natural or artificial stimulus changes it again. The lightning rod, on the other hand, is not intended to direct OR energy flow. It only functions as a conductor toward the ground IN CASE *concentrated* OR energy discharge, i.e., lightning, happens to come its way.

(4) *The OR charges are drawn* (not into the ground but) *into* WATER, preferably into *flowing* water of brooks, flowing lakes and rivers. We draw into water since the attraction is greater between water and OR energy than between other elements and OR energy. Water not only attracts OR speedily but it also holds it, as especially in clouds. We thus have the following picture in the process of cloud-busting:

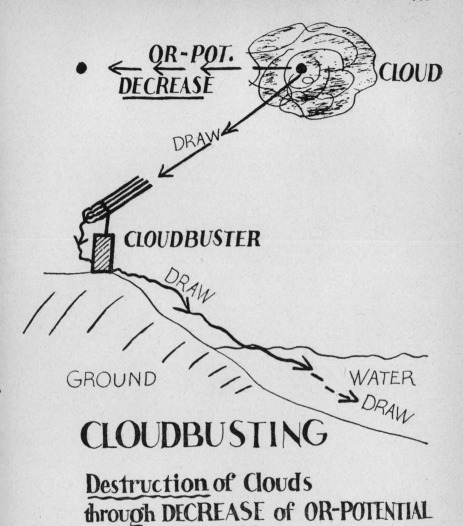

CLOUDBUSTING

Destruction of Clouds through DECREASE of OR-POTENTIAL

This sketch depicts the *principle* of cloud destruction only. It does not suffice to enable the technician to destroy all existent types of clouds. This remains a task of future experimentation in cosmic engineering, to be solved in many ways, in various regions of the globe, with various models of cloud-busters (various as to number, length and width of pipes, direction of draw, size of clouds, maturity of our experience, etc.). The principle, however, may be described as basically complete:

ONE DISSIPATES CLOUDS OF WATER VAPOR BY WITHDRAWING, ACCORDING TO THE ORGONOMIC POTENTIAL, ATMOSPHERIC (COSMIC) OR ENERGY FROM THE CENTER OF THE CLOUD. THIS WEAKENS THE COHESIVE POWER OF THE CLOUD: THERE WILL BE *LESS* ENERGY TO CARRY THE WATER VAPORS, AND THE CLOUDS NECESSARILY MUST DISSIPATE. THE ORGONOMIC POTENTIAL BETWEEN CLOUD AND ITS ENVIRONMENT IS LOWERED.

4. The Creation of Clouds

The principle used in the *creation* of clouds is the same as that in the destruction of clouds: the orgonomic potential from low to high. However, while in the destruction of clouds we draw off energy from the cloud proper, we draw ENERGY FROM THE CLOSE VICINITY OF THE CLOUD IF WE WISH TO ENLARGE EXISTENT CLOUDS AND TO PROCEED TOWARD RAIN-MAKING. The chart on page 445 depicts the process.

The technological experiment bears out the theoretical assumption: Clouds *dissipate* when the cloud-buster pipes are aimed at the *center;* they *grow* when we aim at the close vicinity in the *cloud-free sky.*

One may create clouds in the cloud-free sky in a certain manner, by *disturbing the evenness in the distribution of the atmospheric OR energy;* thus clouds appear upon drawing energy from the air. The more clouds that are present and the heavier the clouds, the easier it is to induce growth of clouds and finally rain. The fewer clouds, the more difficult it is and the longer it takes until the clouds give up their water. Practically, a rather sharp distinction exists between rain-making in a *cloudy* as against a cloud-*free* sky.

No matter what the variations, the principle remains the same as described: Drawing from an existent cloud destroys the cloud. Drawing from its vicinity makes it grow.

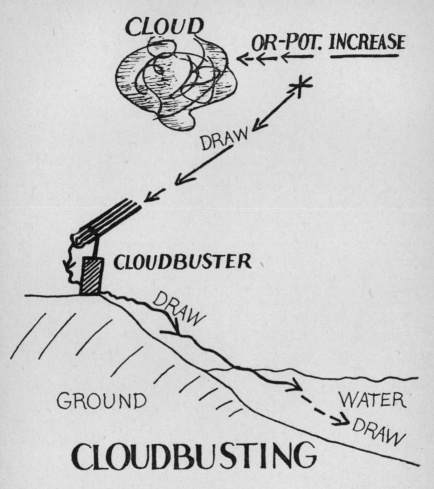

CLOUDBUSTING

Making of Clouds through INCREASE of OR-POTENTIAL

It is necessary to stop at this point. Strong reactions to cloud-busting in Rangeley, Maine, have been observed in distant regions (Boston); such influence on far-away regions is due to the continuity of the OR envelope; the details will require extensive and careful study. We have always been cautious not to overdo while cloud-busting, since small twisters and rapid changes of winds have been observed beyond any reasonable doubt. Also, on one occasion, heavy, prolonged rain occurred upon faulty operation.

Cloud-busting as a task of *Cosmic OR Engineering* will by far transcend the facilities and potentialities of any single institution and even state or country. Cloud-busting is truly an international affair with no regard for national borders. There are neither passport controls nor custom officers in the sky where the weather is being made. This is good and as it should be in *Cosmic OR Engineering* (C.OR.E.).

LAWFUL REGULATION OF CLOUD-BUSTING WILL PROVE INDISPENSABLE IF CHAOS IS TO BE AVOIDED.

(April till August, 1952.)

2. THE EMOTIONAL DESERT

INTRODUCTION

Attempts at a natural scientific formulation of medical and psychiatric functions must be based upon reliable criteria of judgment. Such a statement would have sounded banal only half a century ago. However, with the beneficial effects of what may be termed democratization of science and medicine, went unpermissible abuse of clean method in thinking and experiment. In the realm of psychiatry, two opposite directions had

From *CORE*, vol. VII, nos. 3-4, December, 1955. This article was originally Part One of "The Medical DOR-Buster (1942-1955)."

developed from the old dichotomy between the "*meaning*" and the "*energy functions*" of disease. To many psychologists and psychotherapists it seems to be unclear that an "opinion" or an "idea" about a symptom or a disease picture is in no way a scientific statement. "Scientific" here has nothing to do with a self-centered scholasticism. It means integration of various criteria for the security of our judgments against error and against uncontrollable opining. Let us, while taking the development of character analysis from 1924 to 1955 as an adequate object of such judgment, summarize briefly a few of the indispensable criteria of sound judgment. This will be necessary since the final changes in medicine will be quite radical.

The first requirement is full orientation about the realm under investigation. A flier must know first of all whether he is piloting a piper cub or a jet plane. A chemist, if he claims the distinction of being "scientific," must know that his realm is confined to the analysis of dead matter. He would inevitably go wrong and cause much damage, if in a position of authority, were he unwise enough to judge matters of psychiatry of the insane. In this volume, the red thread of our inquiry was not oriented according to the ideas in disease but exclusively according to the energy functions. The first groping attempts to come to grips with the "character" of a person were methodically clear as to the moral approach. In putting aside ethical judgment of what is considered "good" or "bad," an entirely different measure of orientation was substituted: *the energy functions active in the organism* under all circumstances. Variations of these energy functions, the economy of energy charge and discharge, the "energy equilibrium" and the pathological "energy household" were centered around the assumption that there existed a concrete biological energy, the Life Energy. This energy was at first hypothetically assumed to govern both functions of the soma and of the mind in the common functioning principle of the bio-energetic CORE of the organism. With this functional innovation in our approach to disease, we escaped the fateful pitfalls of both mechanistic rigidities of thinking as well as the mystical, merely psychological, baseless ideas about what is healthy and what is not. *"Character"* thus became a term of *bio-energetics*. It comprised both the somatic, mechanical as well as the realm of ideas. "Emotional," too, was no longer something "psychic." It is the *motion* of energy potentials in the organism. "Libido stasis," always conceived as the physiological element in mental disease, came more and more to mean *stagnant, immobilized* bio-energy. The technique of character analysis aimed basically at mobilizing the stagnant energy contained in the armor in the "middle layer" of the character structure. The *"principle of energy withdrawal"* governed the total effect of cure. By withdrawing energy from the disease symptoms, at first only of the psychic ones, it was possible to achieve dissolution of the ideas which constituted the compulsive idea or the phobic structure. *"Withdrawal of energy"* meant loss of energy in one place, but it also meant increase of the energy level in other places or functions of the living organism. The better the result in the withdrawal of energy from rigidities, muscular armor, symptoms, the more alive and mobile became the organism, until the *"contact anxiety,"* in the genital sphere, *"orgasm anxiety,"* emerged as the last major obstacle to the establishment of the equilibrium in the organismic energy household.

The Principle of Energy Withdrawal with the Cloudbuster (1952)

The principle of "energy withdrawal" was first established around 1924, slowly replacing the method of destroying symptoms by way of association. In 1952, 28 years later, several of the old familiar functions of character analysis turned up, quite unexpectedly, but logically on firm ground during the great DOR emergency at Orgonon. For more than two years during the Oranur experiment, beginning in January, 1951, our survival at Orgonon depended upon *"drawing off the* DOR *clouds,"* which gathered and hovered over Orgonon, into a well

or a lake. We met again with the principle of energy withdrawal, this time not in the realm of bio-energetics but in the
realm of non-living nature.

DOR energy soon was recognized as immobilized, or stalemated atmospheric Life Energy. Early in 1952, several persons
at Orgonon observed an excitation of the natural, bluish OR
energy surrounding the blackish, nauseating, depressing DOR
clouds. It was obvious that unaffected OR energy became somehow highly excited by the presence of the DOR clouds; also it
seemed to encircle the deadly DOR.

When pipes, connected with a well or the lake, (see DOR
Removal and Cloud-Busting) were pointed toward the DOR
cloud, it began slowly to shrink from the periphery toward the
center, the normal blue extended further toward the formerly
blackish realm, until the DOR clouds vanished completely.
Thereupon, the high excitation of blue OR energy seemed to
abate. The symptoms of nausea and oppression, too, vanished
in the observer.

The observation was in agreement with the fact that in the
Oranur reaction it was the surrounding atmospheric energy, and
not the nuclear material, which sent the Geiger Counter soar-
ing to 100,000 counts per minute and more.

In both cases, *the natural, well-functioning Life Energy
reacted with severe excitation to the presence of immobilized,
stale, deadly Life Energy.* However, *immobilized* energy is *not
inactive* energy. When an organism dies, i.e., ceases to function
as an integrated unit, it begins to decay, i.e., it loses its energy
level; the energetic system disintegrates into smaller functional
units down to rot bacteria and the ultimate T-bacilli.

This activity of the immobilized energy unit going stale is
the factor that irritates the main normally-functioning energetic
system. The first response on the part of the total organism to
this type of irritation is what we must, in a broader sense, call
the SEQUESTRATION of the diseased part; "disease" here means
the isolation or exclusion of the diseased part from the inte-

grated whole. The sequestration is the visible result of this basic isolation of the diseased part or organ.

OR versus DOR in Medical Pathology

Let us now summarize a few typical examples from well-known medical pathology which demonstrate the sequestration of disease on the part of the well-functioning whole:

Rise in temperature in infectious disease is the immediate expression of an excitation of the orgonotic energy system, its activation for sequestration on a higher level of functioning.

Local inflammation is basically the same kind of process, no matter what kind of irritating stimulus is involved: the intrusion of a splinter, an acute local infection, an injury of whatever mechanical kind, etc. We know that the reactive fever is a sign of the life force fighting the disease. Functional fever is, too, a reaction of the organismic life energy to a disturbance of its integrity.

There are two well-known borderlines which must not be overstepped lest the organism as a whole perish: one is the over-excitation beyond a certain measurable temperature level, varying with the species, the other is a too weak reaction which permits the invader to spread its deleterious effects even till death of the whole. In the first case the organism perishes from its own excessive reaction. In the second case it perishes from being overwhelmed by the noxious agents, no matter whether in the form of sepsis, gangrene, cancer dissemination ("cancerosis") or similar processes. The common denominator is failing sequestration with subsequent disintegration of the unity of organs.

The function of cure thus seems to depend entirely upon a balance in the struggle between the noxious invader and the reacting sequestration. Too much sequestration, in other words using all of the body's energy reserves in the combat of the invader, will deplete the organism of energy necessary for its own use. Too weak, too little or incomplete sequestration will permit the invader to immobilize the organism piece by piece. We shall later realize how this functioning is applicable to the combat of the Emotional Plague.

In the process of *inflammation* white blood cells multiply rapidly and poured into the diseased region, surrounding and permeating completely the sequestered part. In the process of *immunity* the organism has been forewarned by a mild attack, still innocuous, of the true nature of the invader. The Life Energy has become "used" or "accustomed" to the danger. In case of a repeat attack it would know much better how to sequester the invader.

In all these cases and in many others of a similar nature the living organism perpetuated its totality and integration organs by exclusion of the dissenting part which was not strong enough or was unfortunate to succumb to the first steps toward death. Death is at first locally confined, but in every case potentially capable and directed to destroy the total organism.

We may with good reason assume that wherever a disease afflicts an organ before it afflicts the total organism, the pertinent part of OR energy has changed into a certain amount of immobilized, stalemated energy. The unity, totality of the organism, has been punctured, as it were. The *edema* which so typically accompanies inflammation of the liver, an inflamed tooth, a cancerous tumor of the stomach or even puffiness after too much drinking are vivid expressions and direct witnesses to the immobilization of life energy in the diseased part. Edema comes about by cessation of circulation of fluid; this cessation is the direct result of immobilization of the moving force, the organismic orgone energy.* Thus, the movement of the Life Energy in the organism appears as the common denominator of the mechanical movement of organ and fluids, of the integration of the organs into the functional totality of what we call organism.

We shall now take a step further into this interesting terri-

---

* There is also another approach to understanding edema, ascites, etc.

tory of functional medicine. We must ask how immobilized life energy, called DOR, appears to our eyes when examining the diseased organism directly, not only by mere influence from such functions as inflammation or immunization or edema. These are secondary manifestations. There must be primary ones.

Let us first distinguish DOR as the massfree energy form of stalemated Life Energy from MELANOR as the *material*, substantial form of immobilized life energy.

In order to comprehend well-known phenomena in the microscope and in clinical examination in terms of these functions of primary life, we must remind ourselves of what we already know about MELANOR and DOR from atmospheric OR energy research.

The functional interrelation of atmosphere and organism is obvious. The living organism depends on the atmosphere for oxygen, water vapor, water, for the elimination of carbon dioxide; it depends first of all on the presence of Life Energy (the problem of life in the desert is a special one). Finally the basic constituents of life as well as of atmosphere are, it cannot be repeated often enough, the same; O, H, C and N. There can therefore be little hesitation to link up the living organism with the atmosphere and the outer crust of the earth much more closely than merely chemically-oriented medicine was capable of doing heretofore.

To the free-moving, pulsating, luminating Life Energy in both the organism and in outer nature we must attribute the crucial role of maintaining life. Water and rain in the desert are useless unless there is OR energy active to make the soil absorb and *hold* the fluid, just as water and oxygen are useless for an organism which has lost OR energy in a sinking OR energy potential sufficient to make it impossible to hold water, to continue the metabolism of O_2–CO_2. Thus the functional view supersedes the mechanical view in medicine on mere observational grounds.

SEQUESTRATION OF DOR IN LIVING
AND NON-LIVING NATURE:

We shall not be surprised to learn that the same principle of sequestration of the invading disturber of the integrity of the organism holds true in non-living nature, too, in the formation of "dustdevils," tornadoes and similar disturbances of the atmosphere. DOR clouds are encircled by highly excited OR energy. When drawing fresh OR energy from the west or southwest, whirling air currents develop, similar to the "dustdevils" in deserts and in regions developing into desert. The atmospheric Geiger reaction may reach 100,000 and more counts per minute, as a sure sign of high excitation in the atmospheric energy. *It is as if the atmosphere were feverish.* Strong winds usually in the form of sudden gusts develop, driving blackish, dirty-looking clouds ahead of themselves. These whirlwinds stir up dust; therefrom stems the term *"dust"* devil. But this has really little to do with "dust." It is the reaction of an excited atmospheric energy to the deadly, stale DOR that kills life. The whirl may develop into a true dust storm or into a veritable tornado. The reasons for the different consequences in strength and form are still obscure. But the common principle is clear: *sequestration* and *elimination of the stale intruder* into an integral system. It makes no difference whether the intruder is coming from outside or has become a foreign body by decay or by separation from the totality of the system.

It would be dangerous now to draw the conclusion that *any* "disturbing" element, in social affairs, too, should be "lawfully" sequestered and expelled. We are still suffering from the ugly misinterpretation of the Darwinian principle of the "struggle for survival" as a biological excuse for predatory social behavior. However, it is clear that what is meant here as "intruder" is only a *life negative, deadly* element which threatens the safe existence of the total organism. The appearance of the reproductive cells is not life negative, although these cells are certainly intruders in adolescence, disturbing the peace and quiet of the home or the community if disregarded as crucial development.

It is a basic characteristic of life-positive functions which develop anew within a well-balanced organism that they are being integrated organically into the total organism. This is true for the embryonic development where the integrating orgone function of the organism keeps its unity together in the orderliness and functional lawfulness of the sequence and extensiveness of the events. Any fallout in this phase will create a freak which will destroy the integrating powers of the organism and will either be sequestered or it will destroy the whole biological environment, including the mother organism. Cancer is here a point in fact. In Raynaud's disease the first member of a digit will slowly die off; it will blacken due to Melanor, which is dead OR energy, and it will be either sequestered and fall off or destroy the rest of the hand and arm through a spreading gangrene. Gangrenous tissue is black and green due to Melanor and T-bacilli development. Many questions remain unanswered. But the basic outline is clearly drawn.

The mummification of dead matter, the appearance of black Melanor on dying trees, mildew, Melanor on rye and wheat, and others belong here.

The functional problems emerging from these identities are grouped around the fact that Melanor and Orite are functions at the very roots of life. It is advisable not to delve further into these problems at this moment, to avoid speculation and to await the results of careful observation and experimentation in the primordial realm of the Living. This includes the bions, the T-bacilli, the massfree OR energy functions, the processes in the soil and in desert development and direct work with Melanor, Orite, Orene and atmospheric energy.

Let us now return to safer territory.

CHARACTEROLOGICAL ARMOR IS
SEQUESTERED DOR ENERGY:

Developments over decades, as demonstrated by the red thread that connects the first formulations about the character armor thirty years ago with the problems of desert development, are in themselves proof of the validity of the method employed in this development. There cannot be any development of consistent thought unless the method of research is sound.

The term "armor" already includes the physiological, energetic viewpoint. The armor is neither psychological nor static but a *dynamic blocking*. Life Energy is blocked, i.e., prevented from moving in the armored domain. It is the total organism with the still mobile energy that does the blocking. Let us now fill in this picture of the character structure by way of the newer and deeper insights.

We are, thus, slowly reaching firm ground in the depth of the organism, beyond the confines of mechanical as well as psychological functions, in the antagonism of the life energy functions themselves; in the contradiction between a fully functioning and a stalemated or immobilized life energy. To illustrate again by way of our functional abstraction

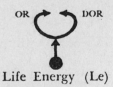

Life Energy (Le)

This abstraction, of course, means no more than a visual, handy presentation of a most complex reality; it does not tell anything without this reality which is constituted of innumerable mobile, ever-changing functions. From the infinite variety of functions at the very base of living existence we are capable of crystallizing, among a few others, one crucial all-pervading principle: the priority of the Le (Life Energy) functions in the interrelations of organic chemistry, in water and oxygen metabolism, in respiration and energy metabolism, including the orgastic function.

These primal Le functions (Life Energy functions) pervade every part of the organism, every cell, the organic fluids, the nervous system as one total highly excitable and responsive function. Its immediate mechanical tool is the autonomic nervous system, which to some histologists and physiologists represents a "syncytium," in other words a network of nerves without terminals. Orgonomic observations of autonomic fibers in worms add the *contractile, pulsatory* nature of the autonomic and perhaps of all nerves. The syncytial, autonomic nerve system is preceded by nerve-free protoplasm in the ameba realm of the living. And it represents in its organized nervous form the amebal, primitive form of living in the most complicated and developed metazoal system. Thus, with life energy in its massfree energy form and in its organized, mobile nerve structure, the lowest and the highest formations of life are integrated in living organisms. The swelling and erection of sexual organs in the process of excitation preserve and demonstrate the most primitive life functions as existent and powerfully active in coordination with the highest intellectual functions.

Among those basic functions of life we have found the protective function of *sequestration* of functions which are foreign to the system and cannot be assimilated. This is true both ways, for the fully functioning as well as for the crippled, secondary, emergency functions of life. It is also true that the basic foundation of sequestration of the unassimilable, foreign intruder governs both the realm of fully functioning life and the crippled, armored or otherwise handicapped life, from the desert plants on to highly developed social conflicts.

It is so very characteristic of orgonomic research and functionalism in general, that wherever basic functions are encountered we are forced to deal with such generalizations and simplifications as:

both cloud and ameba are identical with regard to the orgono-mic potential;

both the animal tissue and the social organism demonstrate the sequestration of foreign bodies;

both the nerveless ameba and the autonomic nervous system in highly developed animals, are governed by slow expansion and contraction in the processes of pleasure and anxiety;

both the secondary plant growth and animals in desert life as well as the armored human being show the "prickly" attitude in their outer reactivity.

In the same vein, armored life exerts its power of sequestra-tion of unarmored life just as unarmored living functioning exerts its function of sequestration of intruding, unassimilable foreign bodies. To present a well-known example from the social realm:

The life positive manifestations of natural genitality in ado-lescence are functions of love for love's sake; to armored life, subdued and governed by the secondary laws of the emotional desert life, these natural primary manifestations of basic life are "intruders," foreign, dangerous to existence. Armored life lives only, and can only live, on the basis of a strict negation of bodily natural love. Therefore, whenever and wherever ar-mored life meets with natural love, especially with the most outstanding function in this realm, the natural genitality of children, adolescents, men and women, it will exert the pressure of "social ostracism," of a negative, threatening public opinion, of slander, gossip and defamation or, worse, injunction. Armored life will thus still try to sequester and eliminate the menace to its existence on the basis of a primordial function of the living, in defense of its organismic integrity and persist-ence. The growth of cancer cells destroys the natural structure of normal cells; the growth of cholla and similar plants in the desert destroys the natural growth of trees and prairie grass; the growth of neurotic ideals and ideas destroy the natural, true, primary manifestations of life. Spreading of DOR clouds in the atmosphere reverses the life process downward again, toward absence of water, reduction of oxygen, toward dehydration and reduction of the chemistry of living things in general.

Briefly, OR and DOR are mutually exclusive, although both use the principle of sequestration for the preservation of their existence.

Since, now, all social life has over the past few thousand years, for very good reasons, been a secondary type of life, armored, happiness-negating life, it has eliminated, destroyed by the stake and by the sword, by slander and degradation all primal life dangerous to its existence. It somehow, we do not know how, knew well that it would collapse and cease to exist in case primal life would again enter the biosocial scene. It knew, somehow, that the secondary vegetation in the desert dies out when the natural green prairie grass returns, when the soil regains its capacity to hold OR and thus to hold water.

How did armored life "know" the danger that threatened its continued existence? We do not know. However, this question is of a similar order to the old biological problem: how does the newborn offspring "know" how to find the nipple of the mother with such certainty? How does life "know" all the many and marvelous things it so beautifully performs?

I believe that the problem is not so much how does life "know" as how is it possible that man has so successfully avoided knowing how life functions. As we proceed toward the common roots of variable and contradictory manifestations of nature, things appear simple, matter-of-fact. One should, at the surface of things, not easily expect that the atmospheric life energy would act in a manner analogous to the manner in which the character structure acts. Yet it does.

At the very beginning of character-analytic research in the 1920's, the structure of the human character presented itself as if it were composed of three distinct layers: the *outer*, socially adjusted layer; the middle layer, which contained all the *armor* blocks, "repressed impulses"; and the *core* which functioned as the highly excitable, responsive and mobile autonomous plasmatic life system, including the organized autonomic nerve system which seemed to be governed only by primordial charge-discharge functions in balancing the energy system.

It is now not surprising to find the corresponding human reactions to the discovery of the Life Energy also active on the social scene. To take the example of my own scientific and social career: the first ten years, up till about 1930, were characterized not only by most amicable relations with my colleagues in the profession of depth psychiatry; my early work on the problems of genitality and character structure brought me soon into the foreground of psychiatric pioneering. Much was expected, as the documents show, from my further researches into the realm of the physiological background of the psychic structure. The world of psychiatry seemed enchanted and delighted. This attitude of admiration for my accomplishments in such publications as *The Impulsive Character* (1925), *The Function of the Orgasm* (1927) and my publications on the character resistance beginning 1928 was clearly replaced by fear mixed with awe in the early thirties as my work on the human character structure brought me ever closer to the full recognition of what today is a matter of fact everywhere: the sensations of *streamings* in the organism in every single case where the dissolution of the armor, the "middle layer" of the personality, was successful. It was obvious at the very beginning of these experiences that the streamings were manifestations of physical, deeply-rooted bio-energetic functions. This finding not only brought forth anxieties in the average psychiatrist, it infuriated him to an extent which made it incomprehensible how the formerly friendly, enthusiastic men and women could have changed so suddenly and so furiously into the exact opposite.

The consequences of this deep fear and hatred toward my discovery of the later so-called "orgonotic streamings" harrassed my existence and further development for nearly two decades, from approximately 1934 to 1954. Rumors about my alleged

psychosis and my having been interned were rampant. Defamation of every sort, from moral to medical, from social to professional, came my way. I trained myself to ignore the rumors,
the silent malignancy, the anxieties, etc. I had the distinct
impression, where acute dangers did not immediately blur my
vision, that here I had met with the average human character
structure, with its armored middle layer in my friends, colleagues, and even some of my former most enthusiastic students.
It was obvious that this hatred was designed to make my
work impossible, to stop me by all means and worse. The
greater the mystical admiration had been before, the more
fanatic seemed the following hatred, as if the haters had decided that I had frustrated or, worse, cheated them out of a
promise of some paradisiacal fulfillment. The obstacle was, of
course, *in them* and not in me. I had done my very best, to my
knowledge, to guide the early friends along the rich but dangerous and treacherous path into the bio-energetic depth of human
nature. The danger and the treachery always seemed to come
from what had been known to me and the profession for a long
time as "pre-orgastic anxiety," in other words as the well-known
fear of *involuntary* experiences, especially during the acme of
the genital embrace. Orgonomy has never lost the view of this
crucial disturbance in armored man. On the contrary, this view
has been sharpened as the decades passed by in careful study
of man's so-called "second" nature.

Only in 1955, when I witnessed in the southwestern U.S.A.
the secondary desert vegetation withering away under the continued removal of the stale DOR energy and the consequent re-
emergence of moisture in the atmosphere and prairie grass on
formerly rocky, parched ground, did it dawn upon me why I
had met with such deadly dangerous hatred on the part of so
many former friends at the discovery of the plasmatic streaming in the core of the organism. Not only a paralyzing anxiety
had been mobilized, the orgasm anxiety; *the very existence,
the very ability to continue one's armored life had been chal-
lenged.* Did they sense that with the return of the primal

functions of life in the organism, with the natural self-regulation of primitive functions, with the disappearance of sadistic hatred, of the peculiar neurotic, perverted, confused, hidden entanglements, death would be near or would actually overcome them? We do not exactly know, but the kind and magnitude of the battle waged by neurotic organisms upon an unsuspecting new discipline concerning the Living made it, often too late, very likely that this was so. In the first place, the admiration had been merely a reflection of the deep hope for delivery from the secondary nature, from the confusion and inner emotional desert functions. But when the middle layer actually began to melt away, when the alive force of the plasmatic streaming threatened to take hold of the total organism, and thus to change all functions, emotional, social, ethical, the organism must have felt like perishing under the strain of such basic change.

THE EMOTIONAL DESERT:

When a desert begins to develop, when the natural, original vegetation gradually falls prey to and perishes under the strain of drought, lack of dew in the morning, progressive parching of the land under a burning sun, and particularly under the constant pressure of DOR energy, the deadly blackish, dehydrating and oxygen-reducing stale life energy, life still fights on. A *new type* of life, *a secondary vegetation*, adapting itself to the harsh conditions of existence in the desert, arises. It is an ugly, poorly-equipped life. The stems of the chollas or cactus or palo verdes are not solid as the stem of an oak or birch. The stem consists of single, narrow strings which are and remain brittle, and have no connection, show no fusion with each other. The whole plant is covered with bristles, reminding us in analogy of the prickly outer behavior of human beings who are empty and desert-like inside. This is not a mere analogy. The simile goes very far, indeed. The desert plants grow either leathery, prickly leaves as does the cactus plant, or as in the cholla, the chlorophyl-bearing structure is restricted to the utmost ends of the branches. It is so very characteristic of desert life that even animals have a bristly, prickly surface or sharply-pointed organs to kill: the scorpion, the rattlesnake, the Gila monster.

Desert vegetation is adapted to the DOR atmosphere, to the minimal amounts of available water, to the parching, burning heat, a heat which is due to sun radiation which has to pass through the DOR layer that covers the land. This vegetation slowly replaces the last remnants of the primal vegetation, until, with the progress of desert development to the last stage, the Sahara sands desert, the secondary vegetation, too, dies out, and nothing remains but sand dunes.

With the spreading of the global desert, civilizations go under, life perishes completely in the affected realm, man either tries to escape or he adjusts, too, to the life in the desert on rare spots of green, called "oases."

The continuous presence of death (DOR atmosphere) and the ever-present dull awareness of the inevitable end is characteristic of both life in the desert and life in armored man. The desolation of emotion, the dehydration of tissues alternating with puffy swelling, fatty flabbiness or inclination to edema or disease which causes edema, alcoholism which serves the stimulation of what is left over from an original sense of life, crime and psychosis and last convulsions of a thwarted, frustrated, badly maltreated life are only a few of the consequences of the emotional desert.

The bitter hatred and the readiness to kill primary life on the part of desert life is not merely an expression of frustration. It is in a deep sense, as shown before, a struggle for survival and prevailing in the face of natural, healthy life. Therefore, the bitter, well-organized fight against the forces of life. Therefore, the perfect organization in the execution or degradation of anything that has to do with living life.

We still remember the compulsive feeding schedules of the Viennese pediatrician, Pirquet, expressly designed to kill any self-regulatory move in the infants; it has created a whole generation of orally and otherwise frustrated neurotics, who in their turn ruined another generation of infants by way of their own distortions and emotional emptiness.

We remember the pathological prescriptions of neurotic physicians and gynecologists to the effect that babies must be separated from their mothers and be frustrated by withholding the nipple.

We remember the devastation exerted upon the whole population of this globe for ages in the prohibition of anything connected with genital functioning that did not agree with the conditions set for life by emotional desert souls. Who has ever or will ever count the number of the victims of this butchery alone, of the victims that have rotted away in the lunatic asylums, in the slums, in the penitentiaries, innocent victims of an organized, heavily-guarded malignant ignorance?

Making more and more laws will not accomplish anything. It will make things worse. It is like trying to save a ship with a leak in mid-ocean by removing the water pouring in with thousands of coffee cups instead of plugging the leak. The more laws that are made in the attempt to cope with ever more complicated and numerous transgressions of penal and moral codes, the more severe is the entanglement of the social machinery. The civil population knows less and less about the rules of government, since even the lawyers cannot follow any longer the details in laws made by anxious or ambitious lawmakers in confused assemblies. This may go on until a large, formerly clear-thinking, powerful nation finds itself enmeshed in paperwork as if bound up with ropes self-administered, ready to be toppled by any little quirk of a nuisance political scoundrel.

The remedy is to plug the holes in the social system; to remove old, obsolete laws so that no pathological lawyer or judge may have an easy excuse for his personal abuse of innocent victims of the tangle; to restrict making new laws to the necessary minimum to cope with basically new issues, such as adolescent genitality, the emergence of a new type of locomotive device, world air traffic, the existence of a cosmic energy, etc., etc.

The religious Indian or Jewish believer tries to get rid of his "sins" by dipping into the river or the lake. His organism somehow knows that water relieves one of DOR.

The common root of paradoxical behavior, such as *"Do Not Ever Touch The Plague"* appears to be *the fear to perish oneself* from one's own deadly sequestered, carefully-blocked DOR-armor layer. Speaking up for the victim, standing upright in the face of defilement, smearing the dirty mess right back into the face of the pestilent smearer, requires being free of having to guard one's own messy, sequestered middle layer.

We are translating old, well-known psychological and bio-energetic terms into more fundamental physical terms. The function of genitality had been taken out of the psychological realm at the very beginning of character research, having been recognized as a bio-energetic function beneath and beyond psychology. We must be prepared to encounter the deeper, physical functions in other familiar psychiatric and medical realms as orgonomy proceeds toward the common roots of both biological and physical existence. We may approach the riddle of the *"latent negative transference"* and *"negative therapeutic reaction"* equipped with the understanding that the *armor energy is true, physical* DOR energy.

Investigation of a more recent date revealed the fact that people in general are aware not only of their being blocked emotionally, but that, in the form of "HIDING," they are more or less dimly aware of *what* they are hiding: DOR energy. Armored people are aware of the potential expressions of the armor: its blocked emotions are felt as "shameful," "intolerable," "unclean" or outright "dirty." This kind of self-awareness seems to be the very essence of the typical withdrawnness, bashfulness, embarrassment of people, especially of the reluctance to understand oneself. They have not only sequestered off the dead, stale bio-energy in their organism; they have not only put up *"defenses"* (*psychologically* speaking), "armor blocks" (*bio-energetically* speaking) against the DOR-energy and its expressions in their organisms, they are aware of the situation and hide as best they can even in the best of psychiatric treatment. The "negative therapeutic reaction," in other words, the getting worse upon successful treatment can now be easily understood as a manifestation of a sharpening of the awareness of the organismic ugliness, of the ill smell, as it were, of what threatens to come forth with a final improvement of things. There is no other way to get to health than through the complete revelation and experience of the ill smelling, blocked off, sequestered realm of the self. And to do so, to have to face this humiliation, one gets worse instead of better on the approach to health. This is comparable to the "crisis" in diseases characterized by high temperature, such as sepsis, pneumonia, etc.

The getting worse when one should get better is no more paradoxical than the well-known function of the *"latent negative transference"* which character analysis has shown to be the most essential behavior to be treated in the beginning of the psychiatric treatment. This well-hidden hatred of anyone who does point out the existence of a deadly, ill-smelling DOR energy; the "resistance" to revealing one's true being, even in front of the very physician who is to provide the cure; the general attitude of *"hiding"* anything that has to do with genitality, the system of energy discharge, the general evasiveness of human second nature, the "Do-Not-Ever-Touch-It," "It" meaning the crucial, the essential, the point in question; the hatred of truth; the killing of truth seekers, the worship of the masters of perfect evasion; the great hatred that persecutes living life . . . all these are so many varied expressions of one and the same basic fact: the hiding, the sequestering off and keeping off the dead, stale energy in one's organism. From here several elucidations of man's roots in nature emerge.

We should not be surprised to find identical functions or sequences of natural functions wherever we meet with the basic relationship of fully functioning life energy to stalemated, dead and deadly DOR energy.

In the human character structure, the healthy life functions surround and shut off from activity the DOR functions in the armor.

On the social scene, we experience the three layers of the human armored character structure in the relationship to orgonomy as intense enthusiasm at first, as bitter, murderous hatred following the enthusiasm, second, and finally, after long and bitter struggles with oneself and with the development toward better self-knowledge, slow, carefully executed adaptation to the realities of the natural in man: his love organs; his rational hatreds and their expression; his relation to truth and truthful living; his abandoning of hiding, conniving, circumventing indirectness, evasiveness of the crucial in life.

In atmospheric physics we encounter the Oranur reactions which show three distinct phases. When the normal, natural OR energy in the atmosphere is suddenly attacked by the nuclear explosion or similar noxious happenings, it acts as if prostrated, helpless, submitting to the deadly blow, near perishing. What is left of the OR energy after the paralyzing blow, turns powerfully "mad," hitting back, raving with a healthy, good, honest rage. The third phase is characterized by a calm superiority, a majestic conquest of DOR by OR energy, as if what *is* dead should be *declared* dead and be eliminated from the process of living, seething life.

There is much good reason to assume at this basic level of understanding that the hurricane, the tornado, the dustdevil in the desert and similar natural upheavals are functionally identical with attempts at self-cure in the catatonic seizure, the epileptic attack, the septic fever, the simplest inflammation of tissue: OR energy surrounding, sequestering, expelling the DOR energy.

VIII. THE EMOTIONAL PLAGUE

1. THE TRAP

"Man is born free, and everywhere he is in chains. One thinks himself the master of others, and still remains a greater slave than they. How did this change come about? I do not know."

Jean Jacques Rousseau asked this question in the very beginning of his "Social Contract" some two hundred years ago. Unless the answer is found to this basic question, there is little use in setting up new social contracts. *There has for many ages been something at work within human society that rendered impotent any and every single attempt to get at the solution of the great riddle,* well known to all great leaders of humanity during the past several thousands of years: *Man is born free, yet he goes through life as slave.*

No answer has been found till now. There must be something at work in human society that obstructs the asking of the correct question to reach the right answer. All human philosophy is riddled with the nightmare of searching in vain.

Something, well hidden, is at work, that does not permit posing the right question. There is, accordingly, something in operation that continuously and successfully *diverts attention* from the carefully camouflaged access to where attention should be focused. The tool used by the well-camouflaged something to divert attention from the cardinal riddle itself, is human EVASIVENESS with regard to living Life. The hidden something is THE EMOTIONAL PLAGUE OF MAN.

From *The Murder of Christ*, 1953. (The reader is referred to the Decree of Injunction, reprinted in the Appendix of this volume.)

467

On the correct formulation of the riddle will depend the proper focusing of attention, and on this in turn will depend the eventual finding of the correct answer as to how it is possible that man is born free everywhere and yet finds himself in slavery everywhere.

Certainly, social contracts, if honestly designed to maintain life in human society, are crucial tasks. But no kind of social contract will ever solve the problem of human agony. The social contract, at best, is no more than a makeshift to maintain life. It has heretofore not been able to remove the agony of life.

These are the constituents of the great riddle:

Man is born equal, but he does not grow equal.

Man has created great teachings, yet each simple teaching has served his oppression.

Man is the "Son of God," created in His image; yet man is "sinful," a prey of the "Devil." How can the Devil and Sin be, if God alone is the creator of all being?

Humanity has failed to answer the question as to how there can be EVIL if a perfect GOD has created and governs the world and man.

Humanity has failed in establishing a moral life in accordance with its creator.

Humanity has been ravaged by war and murder of all sorts ever since the inception of written history. No attempt to remove this plague has ever succeeded.

Humanity has developed many kinds of religions. Every single kind of religion turned into another way of suppression and misery.

Humanity has devised many systems of thought to cope with Nature. Yet nature, functional and not mechanical, as it really is, has slipped through its fingers.

Humanity has run after very bit of hope and knowledge. Yet, after three thousand years of search and worry and heartbreak and murder for heresy and persecution of seeming error, it has arrived at little more than a few comforts for a small sector of humanity, at automobiles and airplanes and refrigerators and radios.

After thousands of years of concentration upon the riddle of the nature of man, humanity finds itself exactly where it started: with the confession of utter ignorance. The mother is still helpless in the face of a nightmare which harrasses her child. And the physician is still helpless in the face of such a small thing as a running nose.

It is commonly agreed that science reveals no permanent truth. Newton's mechanical universe does not fit the real universe which is not mechanical but functional. Copernicus' world picture of "perfect" circles is wrong. Kepler's elliptical paths of the planets are nonexistent. Mathematics did not turn out to be what it so confidently promised to be. Space is not empty; and nobody has ever seen atoms or the airgerms of amebas. It is *not* true that chemistry can approach the problem of living matter, and the hormones did not keep their promises either. The repressed unconscious, supposedly the last word in psychology, turns out to be an artifact of a brief period of civilization of a mechano-mystical type. Mind and body, functioning in one and the same organism, are still separated in man's thinking. Perfectly exact physics is not so very exact, just as holy men are not so very holy. Finding more stars or comets or galaxies won't do it. Neither will more mathematical formulas accomplish it. Philosophizing about the meaning of Life is useless as long as one does not know *what Life is*. And, since *"God" is Life*, which is certain, immediate knowledge common to all men, there is little use in searching or serving God if one does not know what one serves.

Everything seems to point to one single fact: *There is something basically and crucially wrong in the whole setup of man's procedure of learning to know himself.* The mechano-rationalistic view has completely broken down.

Locke and Hume and Kant and Hegel and Marx and Spencer and Spengler and Freud and all the others were truly great thinkers, but somehow it left the world empty after all and the mass of mankind remained untouched by all the philosophical digging. Modesty in proclaiming truth won't do it, either. It is often no more than a subterfuge for hiding one's evasion of the crucial point. Aristotle, who governed thinking for many centuries, turned out to be wrong, and little can be done with Plato's or Socrates' wisdom. Epicurus did not succeed and neither did a single saint.

The temptation to join the Catholic point of view is great after the deleterious experience of the latest great effort of humanity, made in Russia, to come to grips with its fate. The devastating effect of such attempts has revealed itself too drastically. Wherever we turn we find man running around in circles as if trapped and searching the exit in vain and in desperation.

It IS possible to get out of a trap. However, in order to break out of a prison, one first must confess to *being in a prison. The trap is man's emotional structure, his character structure.* There is little use in devising systems of thought about the nature of the trap if the only thing to do in order to get out of the trap is to know the trap and to find the exit. Everything else is utterly useless: Singing hymns about the suffering in the trap, as the enslaved Negro does; or making poems about the beauty of freedom *outside* of the trap, dreamed of *within* the trap; or promising a life outside the trap after death, as Catholicism promises its congregations; or confessing a *semper ignorabimus* as do the resigned philosophers; or building a philosophic system around the despair of life within the trap, as did Schopenhauer; or dreaming up a superman who would be so much different from the man in the trap, as Nietzsche did, until, trapped in a lunatic asylum, he wrote, finally, the full truth about himself—too late. . . .

The first thing to do is to find the exit out of the trap.

The nature of the trap has no interest whatsoever beyond this one crucial point: WHERE IS THE EXIT OUT OF THE TRAP?

One can decorate a trap to make life more comfortable in it.

This is done by the Michelangelos and the Shakespeares and the Goethes. One can invent makeshift contraptions to secure longer life in the trap. This is done by the great scientists and physicians, the Meyers and the Pasteurs and the Flemings. One can devise great art in healing broken bones when one falls into the trap.

The crucial point still is and remains: to find the exit out of the trap. WHERE IS THE EXIT INTO THE ENDLESS OPEN SPACE?

The exit remains hidden. It is the greatest riddle of all. The most ridiculous as well as tragic thing is this:

THE EXIT IS CLEARLY VISIBLE TO ALL TRAPPED IN THE HOLE. YET NOBODY SEEMS TO SEE IT. EVERYBODY KNOWS WHERE THE EXIT IS. YET NOBODY SEEMS TO MAKE A MOVE TOWARD IT. MORE: WHO-EVER MOVES TOWARD THE EXIT, OR WHOEVER POINTS TOWARD IT IS DECLARED CRAZY OR A CRIMINAL OR A SINNER TO BURN IN HELL.

It turns out that the trouble is not with the trap or even with finding the exit. The trouble is WITHIN THE TRAPPED ONES.

All this is, seen from outside the trap, incomprehensible to a simple mind. It is even somehow insane. *Why don't they see and move toward the clearly visible exit?* As soon as they get close to the exit they start screaming and run away from it. As soon as anyone among them tries to get out, they kill him. Only a very few slip out of the trap in the dark night when every-body is asleep.

This is the situation in which Jesus Christ finds himself. And this is the behaviour of the victims in the trap when they will kill him.

The functioning of living Life is all around us, within us, in our senses, before our noses, clearly visible in every single animal or tree or flower. We feel it in our bodies and in our blood. Yet it remained for the trapped ones the greatest, most inaccessible riddle of all.

However, Life was not the riddle. The riddle is how it could have remained unsolved for such a long period of time. The great problem of biogenesis and bio-energetics is easily acces-sible by direct observation. The great problem of Life and the origin of Life is a *psychiatric* one; it is a problem of the character structure of Man who succeeded so long in evading its solution. The cancer scourge is not the big problem it seems to be. The problem is the character structure of the cancer pathologists who in so masterly a way have obfuscated it.

It is the BASIC EVASION OF THE ESSENTIAL which is the problem of man. This evasion and evasiveness is a part of the deep structure of man. The running away from the exit out of the trap is the result of this structure of man. Man fears and hates the exit from the trap. He guards cruelly against any attempt at finding the exit. This is the great riddle.

All this certainly sounds crazy to the living beings in the trap. It would mean certain death for the speaker of such crazy things if he were within the trap together with them; if he were a member of a scientific academy which spends much time and money on studying the details of the walls of the trap. Or, if he were a member of a church congregation which prays, in resignation or hope, to get out of the trap. Or if he were the provider for a family whose only concern is not to starve in the trap. Or if he were an employee of an industrial concern which does its best to make life in the trap as comfortable as possible. It would mean death in one form or another: by ostracism, or by being jailed for the violation of some law, or, under appropriate conditions, the electric chair. Criminals are people who find the exit from the trap and rush toward it, with violence toward the fellow man in the trap. Lunatics who rot away in institutions and are made to twitch, like witches in the middle ages, by way of electric shock, are also trapped men who saw the exit but could not overcome the common horror of approaching it.

Outside the trap, right close by, is living Life, all around one, in everything the eye can see and the ear can hear and the nose can smell. To the victims within the trap it is eternal agony, a temptation as for Tantalus. You see it, you feel it, you smell it, you eternally long for it, yet you can never, never get through the exit out of the trap. To get out of the trap simply has become an impossibility. It can only be had in dreams and in poems and in great music and paintings, but it is no longer in your motility. The keys to the exit are cemented into your own character armor and into the mechanical rigidity of your body and soul.

This is the great tragedy. And Christ happened to know it.

If you live in a dark cellar too long, you will hate the sunshine. You may even have lost the power of the eye to tolerate light. From this comes hate toward sunlight.

The living beings in the trap, in order to adjust their offspring to the life in the trap, develop elaborate techniques to keep life going on a tight, low level. There is not space enough in the trap for great swings of thought or action. Every move is restricted on all sides. This has, in the long run of time, had the effect of crippling the very organs of living Life. The sense of a full life itself has gone from the creatures in the trap.

Still, a deep longing for happiness in life and a memory of a happy Life long past, before the entrapment, has remained. But longing and memory cannot be lived in real life. Therefore, *hatred of Life* has grown from this tightness.

Let us subsume all manifestations of this hatred against the Living under the heading "MURDER OF CHRIST." Jesus Christ had fallen prey to the *Hatred of the Living* on the part of his contemporaries. His tragic fate offers itself as a lesson in what our future generations will encounter when they will reestablish the laws of Life. Their fundamental task will be coping with human malignancy ("Sin"). As we search along this trail, trying to get a glimpse of future possibilities, good and bad, Christ's story acquires a tragic significance.

The secret of why Jesus Christ had to die still stands unsolved. We shall experience this tragedy of two thousand years ago, which had such tremendous effects upon the destiny of mankind, as a logical *necessity* within the domain of armored man. The true issue of the murder of Christ has remained untouched over a period of two thousand years, in spite of the countless books, studies, examinations and investigations of this murder. The riddle of the murder of Christ has remained hidden within a domain entirely removed from the vision and thought of many diligent men and women; and this very fact is a part of the secret. The murder of Christ represents a riddle which harrassed human existence at least over the whole period of written history. It is THE problem of the *armored* human character structure, and not of Christ alone. Christ became a victim of this human character structure because he had developed the qualities and manners of conduct which act upon the armored character structure like red color upon the emotional system of a wild bull. Thus, we may say that *Christ presents the principle of Life* per se. The form was determined by the epoch of Jewish culture under Roman rule. It is of little importance whether the murder of Christ occurred in 3,000 B.C. or 2,000 A.D. Christ would certainly have been murdered at any time and in any culture if the conditions of the clash between the *life principle* (OR) and the *emotional plague* (EP) had been socially given in a manner similar to what they were in the old Palestine of Christ's time.

It is a basic characteristic of *the murder of the Living by the human armored animal*, that it is camouflaged in many ways and forms. The superstructure of human social existence, such as economics, warfare, irrational political movements and social organizations which serve the suppression of Life, are drowning out the basic tragedy that besets the human animal, in a flood of what we may call rationalizations, cover-ups, evasions of the true issue; in addition to all this, it can rely on a perfectly logical and coherent rationality which is valid only *within* the framework of law versus crime, state versus people, morals versus sex, civilization versus nature, police versus criminal and so forth all along and down the line of human misery. There is no chance whatsoever to ever penetrate through this mire unless one has put oneself outside the holocaust and has made oneself inaccessible to the big noise. We are hurrying to assure the reader that we do not consider this noise and empty busyness as merely irrational, as nothing but aimless and senseless activity. It is a crucial characteristic of the tragedy that this nonsense is valid, *meaningful* and *necessary*, though only within its own realm and under certain given conditions of human conduct. But here the plague irrationality rests on sound rock bottom. Even the silence which engulfed the orgasm function, the life function, the murder of Christ and similar crucial issues of human existence for millennia makes good sense to the prudent student of human behaviour.

The human race would meet with the worst, most devastating disaster if it obtained full knowledge of the Life function, of the orgasm function or of the secret of the murder of Christ with one stroke as a whole. There is very good reason and a sound rationality in the fact that the human race has refused to acknowledge the depth and the true dynamics of its chronic misery. Such a sudden breaking-in of knowledge would incapacitate and destroy everything that still somehow keeps human society going in spite of wars, famine, emotional mass killing, infant misery, etc.

It would amount to insanity to initiate such major projects as *"Children of the Future"* or *"World Citizenship"* without comprehending how it was possible that all this misery went on for millennia unabated, unrecognized, unchallenged; that not a single one of the many brilliant attempts at clarification and relief was successful; that with every step toward the fulfillment of the great dream, the misery only deepened and got worse; that not a single religious creed succeeded in realizing its objectives in spite of the best of intentions; that every single great deed turned into a menace to humanity, as for instance, socialism and brotherhood which became statism and oppression of man of the worst sort. In short, to consider such serious projects without first looking around and learning what murdered humanity for ages, would be criminal. It would only add more misery to the existent one. At present, thorough investigation of the murder of Christ is far more important than the most beautiful children we may be able to raise. Every hope of ever breaking through the mire of educational misery would be lost forever, irretrievably, if this new and so hopeful attempt at a new type of raising infants would bog down and turn into its very opposite, as have all former hopeful tasks ever set up by human souls. And let there be no mistake about it: *The reshaping of the human character structure through a radical change in the total aspect and practice of raising children, deals with Life itself.* The deepest emotions the human animal can ever reach far outdistance any other function of existence in scope, depth and fatefulness. Also, the ensuing misery would be correspondingly deeper and greater if this crucial attempt would fail and degenerate. There is nothing more devastating than Life which was irritated and thwarted by frustrated hope. Let us never forget this.

We cannot possibly try to work out this problem in a perfect, academic, detailed fashion. We can do no more than scan the territory to see where treasures are hidden for possible future use, where wild animals are roaming the countryside, where hidden traps are set to kill the invader, and how it all works. We do not wish to get bogged down in our own impatience, in our own daily routine, or even in interests which have nothing whatsoever to do with the problem of education. At a meeting of orgonomic educators several years ago, the fact was mentioned that education is a problem for the next few centuries. It appeared most likely that the first few generations of Children of the Future will not be able to withstand the manifold impacts of the emotional plague. They would certainly have to yield here and there; we do not know exactly in what way. But there *is* hope that slowly a general awareness of Life would develop in these newtype children and would spread over the whole human community. The educator who makes a profitable business out of education would not be interested in education if he believed this were so. Let us beware of this type of educator.

The educator of the future will do systematically (not mechanically) what every good, true educator does today: He will *feel* the qualities of living Life in the child, he will *recognize* its specific qualities and *promote* their development to the fullest. As long as the social trend remains what it is to such an overpowering extent today, i.e., directed *against* these inborn qualities of living emotional expression, the true educator will have a double task: He will have to know the natural emotional expressions as they vary with each child, and he will have to learn how to handle the close and the remote social environment as it steps up against these alive qualities. Only in some distant future, when such conscious upbringing of children will have straightened out the severe contradiction of culture and nature, when man's bio-energetic and social living will no longer oppose each other, but will support, supplement, and enhance each other—only then will this task lose its dangerousness. We must be prepared that this process will be slow, painful, and that it will require much sacrifice. Many victims will be lost to the emotional plague.

Our next task is to outline the basic, typical characteristics of the clash between the inborn, highly variable emotional expressions of the infant and those qualities in the mechanized, armored human structure which will generally and specifically hate and fight these qualities.

Regardless of the innumerable variations in human conduct, character analysis has so far succeeded in outlining basic patterns and lawful sequences in human reactions. It has done so extensively with regard to the neuroses and psychoses. We shall not attempt to do the same with regard to the typical dynamics of the *emotional plague*. Specific descriptions of the individual plague reactions will have to be done amply in order to equip the educator and physician with the necessary detailed knowledge.

In the Christian world and the cultures directly or indirectly influenced by Christianity, a contradiction between "sinful man" and his "God" is sharply pronounced. Man was born in the "likeness of God!" He is encouraged to become "godlike."

Yet, he is "sinful." How is it possible that "sin" came into this world if it was created by "God?" In his actual behaviour, man comprises both the godlike and the sinful. The "godlike" was there first, then "sin" broke into his existence. The conflict between the ideal of God and the reality of sin derives from a catastrophe which turned the godly into the devilish. This is true for his past social history as well as for the development of every single child ever since a mechano-mystical civilization has begun to drown out the "godlike" qualities in man. Man derives from paradise and he keeps longing for paradise. Man has somehow emerged from the universe and he yearns to return to it. These are factual realities if we learn to read the language of his emotional expressions. Man is basically good, but he is also a brute. The change from good to "brutish" actually happens in every single child. God is, therefore, INSIDE man, and not to be sought for outside alone. The Kingdom of Heaven is the Kingdom of the inner grace and goodness, and not the mystical "beyond" with angels and devils into which the brute in the human animal has turned its lost paradise.

The cruel persecutor and murderer of Christ, Saul of Tarsus, had clearly, but in vain, distinguished between the "BODY," which was god-given and good, and the "FLESH," which was devil-ridden and bad, to be burned at the stake one thousand years later when he turned Paul, the church builder, himself. In the distinction between the *"body"* and the *"flesh"* in early Christianity, our present orgonomic distinction between the *"primary,"* naturally inborn drives ("God"), and the "secondary," perverted, evil drives ("Devil," "Sin") was anticipated. Thus mankind was always somehow aware of its crucial biological plight, of its natural endowment as well as of its biological degeneration. In the Christian ideology, the sharp antithesis of "GOD" (spiritualized body) and "DEVIL" (body degenerated to flesh), this tragedy is plainly known and expressed. In real man, the "god-given" genital embrace has turned into the pornographic 4-lettering male-female intercourse.

ORIGINAL SIN—A MYSTERY

Life is plastic; it adjusts to every condition of its existence with or without protests, with or without deformation, with or without revolt. This plasticity of living Life, one of its greatest assets, will be one of its slave chains when the Emotional Plague will learn to misuse the plasticity of Life to its own ends. One and the same Life is different at the bottom of the deep sea, and different on a high mountain ridge. It is different in the dark cave and different again within the blood vessel. It was different in the Garden of Eden, and different in the trap that caught humanity. Life knows nothing of traps in the Garden of Eden; it just lives paradise, innocently, gayly, without an inkling of a different kind of life. It would refuse to listen to an account of life in the trap; and, if it listened, it would comprehend it with its "brain" only, not with its heart. Life in paradise is fully adapted to the conditions in paradise.

Within the trap, Life lives the life of souls caught in a trap. It adjusts quickly and completely to the Life in a trap. This adjustment goes so far that nothing will remain beyond a faint memory of Life in paradise, once Life has been caught in a trap. Restlessness, hurry, nervousness, a dim longing, a dream long past—yet, still around somehow—will be taken for granted. No trace of an inkling that these are signs of a dim memory of Life in paradise long past will disturb the peace of soul of the captives. The adjustment is complete. It reaches proportions beyond the limits of reason.

The Life in the trap will soon become completely self-absorbed as Life in a prison is supposed to be. Certain character types will develop which will belong to Life in the trap, and would not make sense where Life walks the world freely. These characters, molded by bearing Life in prison, will greatly vary among themselves. They will disagree and fight each other. They will, each in his own manner, proclaim the absolute truth. Only ONE characteristic will they all have in common: *They will join together and kill in unison whoever will dare to*

ask the basic question: "HOW IN THE NAME OF A MERCIFUL GOD
DID WE EVER MANAGE TO GET INTO THE UGLY PREDICAMENT OF
THIS NIGHTMARE OF A TRAP???"

WHY DID MAN LOSE PARADISE? and

WHAT DID HE ACTUALLY LOSE WHEN HE FELL VICTIM TO SIN?

Man in the trap has, over the millennia, created a great book:
the BIBLE. This book is the story of his fights and anguishes
and glories and hopes and longings and sufferings and sin-
nings in the entrapment. It has been thought and written in
many languages by many different people. Some of its basic
features can be found in places far apart, in the written and
unwritten memory of man. That things had, once upon a time
long past, been quite different, that somehow man once had
fallen to the devil, to sin and ugliness, is common to all
accounts of the distant past.

The bibles of the world are the accounts of man's fight
against man's sin.

There is so much the Bible tells about the life in the trap,
and *so little about how men got into the trap.* It is obvious that
the exit out of the trap is exactly the same as the entrance
into the trap, through which they were driven from paradise.
Now, why does nobody say anything about it except in a very
few paragraphs which are as one to a million to the rest of the
Bible, and in a veiled language which is meant to conceal the
meaning of the words?

The downfall of Adam and Eve is obviously, beyond any
doubt due to something they did against the Laws of God in a
genital way:

"And they were both naked, the man and his wife, and were not
ashamed."   (Genesis 2: 25)

From this it follows that in paradise man and woman were
not aware or ashamed of nakedness, and this was *God's* will,
and the way of Life. Now, what happened? The Bible says
(*Genesis* 3: 1-24):

Now the serpent was more subtil than any beast of the field which the Lord God hath made. And he said unto the woman, Yea, hath God said, Ye shall not eat of every tree of the garden?

And the woman said unto the serpent, We may eat of the fruit of the trees of the garden;

But of the fruit of the tree which is in the midst of the garden, God hath said, Ye shall not eat of it, neither shall ye touch it, lest ye die.

And the serpent said unto the woman, Ye shall not surely die:

For God doth know that in the day ye eat thereof, then your eyes shall be opened, and ye shall be as gods, knowing good and evil.

And when the woman saw that the tree was good for food, and that it was pleasant to the eyes, and a tree to be desired to make one wise, she took of the fruit thereof, and did eat, and gave also unto her husband with her; and he did eat.

And the eyes of them both were opened, and they knew that they were naked; and sewed fig leaves together, and made themselves aprons.

And they heard the voice of the Lord God walking in the garden in the cool of the day: and Adam and his wife hid themselves from the presence of the Lord God amongst the trees of the garden.

And the Lord God called unto Adam, and said unto him, Where art thou?

And he said, I heard thy voice in the garden, and I was afraid, because I was naked; and I hid myself.

And he said, Who told thee that thou wast naked? Hast thou eaten of the tree, whereof I commanded thee that thou shouldest not eat?

And the man said, The woman whom thou gavest to be with me, she gave me of the tree, and I did eat.

And the Lord God said unto the woman, What is that that thou hast done? And the woman said, The serpent beguiled me, and I did eat.

And the Lord God said unto the serpent, Because thou hast done this, thou art cursed above all cattle, and above every beast of the field; upon thy belly shalt thou go, and dust shalt thou eat all the days of thy life:

And I will put enmity between thee and the woman, and between they seed and her seed; it shall bruise thy head, and thou shalt bruise his heel.

Unto the woman he said, I will greatly multiply thy sorrow and thy conception; in sorrow thou shalt bring forth children; and thy desire shall be to thy husband, and he shall rule over thee.

And unto Adam he said, Because thou hast hearkened unto the voice of thy wife, and hast eaten of the tree, of which I commanded thee, saying, Thou shalt not eat of it: cursed is the ground for thy sake; in sorrow shalt thou eat of it all the days of thy life;

Thorns also and thistles shall it bring forth to thee; and thou shalt eat the herb of the field;

In the sweat of thy face shalt thou eat bread, till thou return unto the ground; for out of it wast thou taken: for dust thou art, and unto dust shalt thou return.

And Adam called his wife's name Eve; because she was the mother of all living.

Unto Adam also and to his wife did the Lord God make coats of skins, and clothed them.

And the Lord God said, Behold, the man is become as one of us, to know good and evil: and now, lest he put forth his hand, and take also of the tree of life, and eat, and live for ever:

Therefore the Lord God sent him forth from the garden of Eden, to till the ground from whence he was taken.

So he drove out the man; and he placed at the east of the garden of Eden Cherubims, and a flaming sword which turned every way, to keep the way of the tree of life.

There was a serpent in paradise "more subtil than any beast of the field which the Lord God had made." To the Christian commentator, the serpent, in his Edenic form, is not to be thought of as a writhing reptile. The serpent originally was "the most beautiful and subtle of creatures." Traces of that beauty remain despite the (later) curse. Every movement of the serpent is graceful, and many species are beautifully colored. In the serpent, Satan first appeared as an angel of light. The serpent, thus, is a symbol of Life itself and the male phallus.

Then, somehow, out of nowhere as it were, disaster strikes.

Nobody knows or has ever known or ever will find out how and why it happened: The most beautiful serpent, the "Angel of Light," the "most subtle of creatures," "less than man," is cursed and becomes "God's illustration in nature of the effect of sin": it changes from "the most beautiful and subtle of creatures to a loathsome reptile."

And, as if a special counsel had met to veil the most dramatic, the most devilish, the most disastrous happening in the history of the human race, and to remove it forever and ever from any grasp by intellect or heart, this catastrophe becomes mysterious and untouchable; it becomes a part of the great mystery of the entrapment of man; it doubtless contains the solution to the riddle as to why man in the trap refuses to simply walk out of the trap using the exit through which he had come into the trap. The Biblical interpreter himself says at this point: "The deepest mystery of the atonement is intimated here," i.e., in the change of the serpent from the "most beautiful and subtle of creatures to a loathsome reptile."

Why all this? Let's hear.

There was a peculiar tree in the Garden of Eden, and God had said to man in paradise: "Ye shall not eat of every tree of the garden."

And the woman said unto the serpent, We may eat of the fruit of the trees of the garden;

But of the fruit of the tree which is in the midst of the garden, God hath said, Ye shall not eat of it, neither shall ye touch it, lest ye die. (Genesis 3: 2,3)

Did anyone ever in the course of six thousand years explain that tree? No one ever did so. Why? The mystery of this tree is a part of the mystery of man's entrapment. A solution of the mystery of the tree could possibly answer the predicament why man is in the trap. The solution of the mystery of the forbidden tree would certainly point to the entrance to the trap, which, used the other way around, would become an exit *out* of the trap. Accordingly, no one ever thought of solving the riddle of the forbidden tree, and everybody in the trap was busy for millenia to scholasticize, talmudize and exorcise the predicament of being within the trap, using millions of books and myriads of words, with one single goal in mind: *To prevent the solution of the riddle of the forbidden tree.*

The serpent, still beautiful and subtle, knew better. "And the serpent said unto the woman, Ye shall not surely die: For God doth know that in the day ye eat therof, then your eyes shall be opened, and ye shall be as gods, knowing good and evil."

Now, since the beautiful serpent thus brought about man's downfall, what in the name of sanity does all this mean:

If man in paradise, living happily the ways of God, eats from a certain tree, then he will be like God, his eyes will be opened, and he will "know good and evil." *How does such a devilish tree manage to get into God's garden in the first place?*

And if you eat from such a tree which bears the fruit of *knowledge* and you become like God himself, why then do you *lose* paradise? The Bible, to my knowledge, doesn't tell. And it is to be doubted that anyone ever asked such a question. The legend doesn't seem to make sense: If the tree is a tree of knowledge, to know the difference between good and evil, what's bad, then, in eating of its fruits? If you eat of its fruits, then you certainly can follow God's ways *better*, and not worse. Again, it doesn't make sense.

Or is it forbidden to know God and to be like God, which means to *live* God's ways, even in paradise?

Or is all this the cooked-up fantasy of man in the trap, regarding a faint memory of a past life outside the trap? It doesn't make sense. Man is haunted all through the ages by the request to know God, to follow God's Ways, to live God's love and life; and when he starts seriously to do so by eating from the tree of knowledge, he is punished, expelled from paradise, and condemned to eternal misery. It simply does not make sense, and we fear that no representative of God on earth has ever asked this question, or even dared to think in its direction.

*And when the woman saw that the tree was good for food, and
that it was pleasant to the eyes, and a tree to be desired to make one
wise, she took of the fruit thereof, and did eat, and gave also unto
her husband with her; and he did eat.*

*And the eyes of them both were opened, and they knew that they
were naked; and they sewed fig leaves together, and made themselves aprons.* (*Genesis* 3: 6,7)

When man thus was first trapped, confusion beclouded his
mind. He did not understand why he got into the trap. He felt
he must have done something wrong, but he knew not *what*
wrong he had done. He had not felt ashamed being naked, and
then, suddenly, he felt ashamed of his genital organs. He had
eaten from the tree of forbidden "knowledge," which, in Biblical
language means, he *"knew"* Eve, he *embraced her genitally.*
For this now he has been expelled from the Garden of Eden.
God's own most beautiful serpent had seduced them; the symbol of wavy, living Life and of the male sexual organ had
seduced them.

From here to the life in the trap there is a wide, deep gap in
comprehension. In its adjustment to the life in the trap, Life
developed new forms and means of existence; forms and
means which were unnecessary in the Garden of Eden, but
were crucial for life in the trap.

A silent and suffering and dreaming and toiling mass of
humanity, cut off from God's Life, provided the broad foundation on which grew priests, and the prophets against the priests;
the kings, and the rebels against the kings; the great healers of
man's misery within the trap, and with them the great quacks
and the medical "authorities," the traumaturgists and the oc-
cultists. With the emperors there came about the freedom
peddlers, and with the great organizers of man in the trap were
born the political prostitutes, the Barabbases and the sneaking
vermin of bandwagon riders; Sin and Crime against the law,
and the judges of Sin and Crime and their executioners; the
suppression of liberties unlivable in a trap, and the Unions for
Civil Liberties within the trap. Also, from the mire grew great

political bodies called "parties," designed either to keep up what they called the "status quo" within the trap, the so-called "conservatives" (since they tried to preserve the law and order which had been established to keep life in the trap going), and, opposing them, the so-called "progressives" who fought and suffered and died at the gallows for advocating more freedom within the trap. Here and there such progressives conquered power over the conservatives and began to establish "Freedom in the Trap" or "BREAD AND FREEDOM in the Trap." But, since there was no one who could "*give*" the broad herd of men bread and freedom, since they had to *work for it*, the progressives soon became conservatives themselves, for they had to maintain law and order just as their eternal enemies, the conservatives, had done before. Later, a new party arose which thought that the *masses* of suffering humanity in the trap should rule Life in the trap, and not the priests or kings or dukes. They tried hard to get the mass of people on their legs and into action; but apart from a few murders and the destruction of the homes of some rich men in the trap, little happened. The broad mass of humanity just repeated what it had heard and seen from above for millenia, and nothing changed; only the misery became greater when a very clever party was formed which promised to humanity a *"PEOPLE'S FREEDOM IN THE TRAP"* and brought about hell here and there by using all the old and outworn slogans formerly used by the kings and the dukes and the tyrants. The *people's* freedom parties had, to begin with, until their designs were found out, great success. Their slogan of a "PEOPLE'S" freedom in the trap, as distinguished from other freedoms in the trap, and the use of the old methods of the old kings, worked, since the leaders of this party had come, as little freedom peddlers, from among the herd of entrapped men themselves, and when they obtained power over a little area they were stunned to find how easy it is to push buttons and to see police, armies, diplomats, judges, academic scientists and representatives of foreign powers act according to brief, sharp pulls and pushes on neat buttons. The little freedom peddlers liked that game of push-button-power so much, that they forgot all about "PEOPLE'S FREEDOM IN THE TRAP" and just enjoyed themselves pushing buttons whenever they could in the palaces of the old rulers whom they had murdered. They just went power drunk with joy of pushing buttons on the tables of power machines. But they did not last long and were soon replaced by good, old, decent power-button-pushers, the good, old conservatives who had retained some decency and bearing in their souls as a fading memory from the days of paradise.

They all fought and quarreled with each other, pushed each other here and there, killed their adversaries with or without the law; briefly, they gave a true picture of man's Sin and the fulfillment of the curse in the Garden of Eden. The mass of entrapped humanity did not really partake in this holocaust of plague-ridden Life in the Trap. From among two billion human souls, no more than a few thousand partook in the turmoil. The rest just suffered, dreamed and waited . . . for WHAT? The redeemer, or for something unheard of to happen to free them; for delivery of their souls from the trap called the body; for reunification with the great world soul or for hell. But dreaming, toiling and waiting were the main occupations of the broad herd of humanity far removed from the political turmoil. There was also great dying in the great wars within the trap, with enemies changing from year to year like people cashing money at a banking counter. It did not matter much, though it hurt. The mass of suffering humanity was waiting for delivery from this sinful life, anyhow, and the few noisemakers did not really amount to much, seen in the perspective of Life or "God" in the Universe.

And God's Life was born in billions of infants everywhere in the trap, but it was killed right away by the people in the trap who either did not recognize God's Life in their infants, or were frightened to death at the sight of living, moving, decent, simple Life. And so it came about that man perpetuated his entrapment. These infants, if left to themselves as God had created them, would certainly have found the exit from the trap. But this was not allowed to happen. It was particularly forbidden during the reign of "THE PEOPLE'S" freedom in the trap. All loyalty had to be for the *trap*, and not for the babies, under punishment of death by the "Great Leader and Friend of All the Entrapped Ones."

2. MOCENIGO

THE MURDER OF CHRIST IN GIORDANO BRUNO

There are empty souls which thirst for excitement of some kind to fill their desert minds. They will, accordingly, hatch evil. Not all of them, true, but a few will do it, and their victims will most likely be a Giordano Bruno. And Giordano Bruno is chosen as a victim because he rediscovered Christ in the Universe, i.e., the love of God in terms of astrophysics.

Bruno had, in the sixteenth century, by mere thought, anticipated the factual discovery of the cosmic orgone energy in the twentieth century. He had discovered and captured in a system of thought, the interrelations between the body and the mind, the single organism and its environment, the basic unity and multiplicity of the universe, an infinite universe embracing infinitely numerous worlds. Everything exists for itself, and yet it is an integral part of a whole. Therefore, the individual unit or soul exists for itself and, at the same time, is a part of the whole which is infinite, one and multiple at the same time. Bruno believed in a universal soul which animated the world; this soul to him was identical with God. Bruno was basically a functionalist. He knew about the simultaneous functional identity and antithesis, even if only in an abstract manner. He moved within the general stream that carried human thought

From *The Murder of Christ*, 1953.

to the concrete formulation of functional orgonometric equations four hundred years later. He described, according to his orgonotic sense, many qualities of the atmospheric orgone energy which the discoverer of the Life Energy in the twentieth century made visible, manageable and usable in a practical, bio-energetic way. To Bruno, the universe and all its parts had qualities identical with life. In his system there was no unbridgable contradiction between individualism and universalism, since the individual was an integral part of an all-encompassing whole, and not a mere number to a part in a sum of parts, as in mechanical mathematics. The "World Soul" was in everything, acting as an *individual* soul and, *at the same time*, as an integral part of the *universal* soul. These views are, in spite of astrophysical formulation, in accord with modern orgonomic functionalism.

Bruno had discovered the road that leads to knowing God, and therefore he had to die. And die he did, indeed, a death of nine long years, from 1591 till 1600, when on February 16th in the early morning he was led, with prayers, by the heirs of Jesus Christ, to the stake and given over to the flames, all in the name of love of the Creator.

Though the Catholic church, due to the great power it exerted over millions of human souls, had developed the cruel techniques of empire builders; though it developed them into a great art, among them the burning at the stake of dangerous searchers of the realities of Christ's world, it would be wrong to attribute these ways of the devil to the church only. The church is no more responsible for the creation and maintenance of the methods of the emotional plague than was Nero or Caligula or Genghis Khan or, in modern times, the Hitlers and the Stalins. The plague has developed its rampant malignancy wherever leaders had to face the grave task of holding sick, deadened, cruel multitudes together in unity and cooperation.

Bruno's teachings, in the right direction as they were, carried with them too much force, too much power to change the order which kept the still-slumbering mass of human animals together—a mass which within the next three centuries would develop its dreams into upheavals that were destined to shake the world of man to its very foundations. To permit the discovery of God and his Kingdom to become a practical reality, to let men grasp with their minds and hearts and their practical lives what the church had transformed into a mystery, removed far away into unreachable heavens, would have amounted to precipitation of an early general disaster. This is the tragedy of all knowledge which emerges at the wrong time into an unprepared world. Therefore, Bruno the Nolan, had to die.

It is rarely the inquisitors in high places, the attorney generals, the high pontiffs of established beliefs, who start the trouble. It is not the multitude of passive, suffering and dreaming mankind which takes the Bruno's before the tribunal of inquisitors, condemned in advance to die, and thereupon delivered to the stake to burn. Neither inquisitor nor sleeping mass of mankind are or feel responsible for the death of a knower. The sleeping men are entirely unaware of what is perpetrated in their behalf, and the inquisitor only follows the set rules of certain laws, mechanically, in a wooden manner, like a robot, without mercy or freedom to act otherwise.

The true killer who starts the ugly show, is usually an inconspicuous, "upright" citizen who has nothing to do with either the problem of the sleeping and dreaming herd of men or with the grave administrative responsibilities of the inquisitors and judges. The true killer is the bloodhound who stirs up the escaped prisoner, not because he hates the prisoner or because he is out to restore justice or because he knows anything at all what it is all about. *The true killer is an accidental nuisance*, a mishap that strikes the victim without rhyme or reason, like a stray bullet from the gun of a hunter who misses a deer and kills a casually by-passing game warden.

The true killer does not intend to kill this specific person or any other individual. The victim becomes the prey of the pestilent killer for reasons which have nothing whatsoever to do with his true life or with his beliefs or his relationship to the killer. The victim only happened to cross the way of the killer at a certain moment; a moment which bears importance to the life of the *killer*, but not to the life of the victim. An executioner who is paid for his job of killing, does not hate his victim, he does not choose it or wish it evil. The executioner kills because he chose the profession of killing, no matter who happens to be under his ax or guillotine blade or in the electric chair. The killer, on the other hand, kills because he *must kill*. The victim happens to be a victim only because he happened to be around at a certain opportune moment.

The killer of Giordano Bruno happened to be a Venetian nobleman by the utterly unimportant name of *Giovanni Mocenigo*. This name has no rational meaning whatsoever. Nobody had heard of it before the killing, and nobody even cared to remember it after the killing. His name could have just as well been Cocenigo or Martenigo. It wouldn't matter at all. Mocenigo is a nonentity of some proportion. He knows nothing, does nothing, loves nothing, cares for nothing except his complete nothingness. He sits around or walks around, not necessarily always in a palace, habitually breeding evil. He produces dreams of evil like a hen lays eggs, one every once in a while. He is too smart to just do evil like a simple, daring, foolhardy criminal, such as robbing a bank to get money the easy way, or attacking a girl on the street at night out of sex-starvation. The pestilent killer does not even produce a sound reason for his evil deed. Since there is no sound reason within himself to commit a crime, he must search in someone else for a reason to kill. His own barrenness of soul and emptiness of mind is no good reason to kill; why should he kill somebody else if he himself is empty like a desert? Therefore, the pestilent character will hatch out a most elaborate reason to kill somebody, no matter whom. The victim must only have one characteristic to provide the good reason to be murdered: He must in some way be at variance with the ways of the sleeping or sitting crowd, preferably a soul like Christ who knows the smell of eternity.

The pestilent killer will, in contradistinction to the reasonable killer who goes after money or rape, gain nothing from the murder. He murders his victim simply because he cannot stand the existence of such souls as Bruno's or Christ's or Ghandi's or Lincoln's. He may be anybody in any government or commercial office, in a bacteriological university institute or in a cancer society. He may be young or old, a man or a woman. What matters is only one thing: *He breeds evil out of frustrated, cruelly perverted genital desire, and hates the Love of God which he is resolved to kill in the name of God or Christ or national honor.*

Accordingly, Mocenigo, the en..ₜ ᵗv do-nothing nobleman from Venice, writes two letters to Bruno, who at that time lived in Frankfurt, inviting the scholar to teach him the "art of memory and invention." That means: Mocenigo knows Bruno is very rich in a quite different manner than he himself, and he plans to suck dry his future victim. Bruno believes in the power of love which binds all together in all and is the urge to all good. Therefore, he is scheduled to be killed by Mocenigo. Believing firmly in the great love in the universe which binds all men together into one and creates the great good in man, just as Jesus Christ believed in the power of Love as the great force in the Kingdom of God, Bruno agrees to move into the home of his murderer.

Bruno is expected to impart his knowledge of the great art of thinking to his murderer, Mocenigo. He is not supposed to give this knowledge to anybody else. When Bruno expresses his desire to return to Frankfurt to get some works printed, Mocenigo objects and threatens Bruno with the holy office. Mocenigo, of course, as every similar killer, has his connections with the inquisition. He is going to use them to the detriment of the rich giver should the latter not be willing to convey upon the killer his great art of thinking and memory. Mocenigo is firmly set to get what he wants, even at the price of murder. Of course, Mocenigo does not care for knowledge. He would not know what to do with it, how to handle it, how to let it grow or how to apply it.

He is only capable of sitting and breeding evil out of dead genitals. He does not care in the least for knowledge for the sake of knowing or learning or finding or solving riddles. He just wants knowledge as you want a nice car or a juke box to play gay tunes, or a rowboat or a girl from a certain bar, or just a dish of fish to fill your belly. *It is the getting*, the getting it from somebody else who has worked and toiled hard for it, *that matters*. Mocenigo must be filled up with knowledge which he can neither produce nor digest himself when he gets it. He cannot stand anybody else having knowledge or the skill of obtaining wisdom. He cannot bear seeing somebody, even a thousand miles away, enjoying the belief in love and a universal soul which, possibly, sometime in an uncertain future, could or even factually would bind men together in peace. Whether you call them Mocenigo or Caiaphas or Judas or Saul of Tarsus or Stalin, it is and remains always the same old story. They just cannot stand it; it makes them green with envy; it fills them with unbearable desire for something they are utterly incapable of possessing, and therefore, they will deliver Christ to the cross and Bruno to the stake or scientific sociology to the dogs. The closer the future victim is to the Kingdom of God with his knowledge, the surer will he be chosen to be murdered by the pestilent character.

All this goes on with not a single soul, not even the murderer himself being aware of what is happening. When Bruno insists on departure, perhaps sensing the malignancy of his murderer, Mocenigo seizes him at night from his bed with the help of an "arm of the Law." From here onward the machinery of the organized emotional plague of all ages takes over like a robot grindstone, never to stop until the victim is squeezed to pulp. The envy and evil plotting of Mocenigo does not count and does not even appear among the arguments in the protocols. The true motive of the murder is not mentioned or even admitted to court at any time, neither in 1592 nor in 1952; neither in

Italy nor in the USA nor in the USSR. The true motive of the cowardly killer is banned from inquiry all over this planet, except where simple routine murders are concerned, never in cases of the Murder of Christ. The Bar Associations of all lands do not tolerate even the discussion of the motivation of such killing. The judges who sentence and the executioners go free, no matter how innocent the victim. If, occasionally, after decades, the error can no longer be kept hidden, the victim, if alive, must say, "Thank you very much," or, if dead, somebody kneels in prayer at his grave. But nobody dares to attack the true killer.

From now onward, it is of no importance whatsoever what fills the protocols, whether it is forbidden to have the Earth circle around the sun or to believe in a Soul of the Universe or in Universal Love or whether one has lectured here or lectured there, whether one has been decent all his life and committed only the blunder of meeting accidentally a pestilent sniper shooting from ambush. Nothing matters, since the true motive is the murder of Christ who could actually accomplish the dreaded realization of the Kingdom of God on Earth. It does not matter whether Jesus actually proclaimed himself as the King of the Jews or not. It is merely a pretext, and everybody is aware of this; therefore, nobody mentions it or does anything about it. The established law is geared to eternal *seeking* of the Kingdom of God, but not to the *finding* of the Kingdom of Heaven, not to the ways of Christ who knows the ways of the Kingdom of God. Only formalities count. Every appearance of fairness and precaution *not* to commit a judicial murder will be carefully guarded in order to commit the murder in the "proper, legal" ways. No one should ever be accused of injustice. The record of honor must remain clean. Everybody knows what has been done, and nobody moves a finger.

Much later, when the victim will have been long dead, when his screams to heaven in the evocation of God will have been silenced forever, when the myth of "justice done" will have evaporated, historians will dig out the facts, when all is fairly safe; and it might happen that a Pope kneels at the grave of one of the victims to restore his posthumous honor. Thank you, Sir! we hear the victim whisper. And God once more turns away from his Godlike creation, Man, and continues to send his prophets to preach in vast, empty deserts. Mocenigo is forgotten. Nobody investigated him, nobody even thought him guilty, though a few may despise him. More, there will be many who will tell you that Christ has been justly crucified, for he has acted as a common rebel against established government, that he had unnecessarily provoked the scribes, that he would better have sat still and quiet and left the souls of men alone in peace to sit it out forever and ever after. And books will be written and read by the multitude, books that tell you how to escape the truth about the Murder of Christ, how to obtain peace of mind. Don't touch it, ever!

3. THE BIO-ENERGETIC MEANING OF TRUTH

Truth is full, immediate contact between the Living that perceives and Life that is perceived. The truthful experience is the fuller the better the contact. Truth is the more comprehensive the better coordinated are the functions of living perception. And the living perception is coordinated exactly to the extent of the coordination of the motion of the living protoplasm. *Thus truth is a natural function in the interplay between the Living and that which is lived.*

Truth, basically, is not, as many believe, an ethical ideal. It became an ethical ideal when it was lost with the loss of "paradise," i.e., the loss of the full functioning of the Living in Man. Then truth was suppressed and the ideal mirror image of truth seeking appeared. Neither is truth something to be striven for.

From *The Murder of Christ*, 1953.

You do not strive to make your heart beat or your legs move, and you do not, by the same token, "strive" for or seek truth. Truth is in you and works in you just as your heart or your eyes work, well or badly, according to the condition of your organism.

The Living, in its constant interplay with its environment, *lives* truth fully to the degree in which it is in contact with its own needs or, which means the same, with the influencing of the environment to satisfy the natural needs. The cave man, in order to survive, had to know the ways of the wild animals, i.e., he had to know the truth about their manner of living and acting. The modern flier, in order to arrive safely at his destination, must be in full contact with and fully reactive to every gust of wind, to the slightest change in the balance of his plane, to the clarity of his own senses and to the movements of his body. He flies truthfully. The slightest blurring of his sensory reaction to his inner and outer environment would kill him. Thus he lives truthfully when he manages the elements and survives. Yet, he does not "search" or "strive" for truth while flying.

Truth, therefore, is a natural function, just as is walking or running or hunting the bear by the Eskimo or finding the tracks of the enemy by the Indian. It is, within the framework of the totality of natural functioning, an integral part of the organism and it depends on the integrity as well as integration of all the senses. *The first,* ORGONOTIC *sense must be intact.* Truth, no matter in what realm of life or whatever its scope, is thus a tool of the Living, in line with all other tools that are given or shaped by the senses and the organismic motility. The use of the weapon of truth is, therefore, the use of the fullest possible contact with all situations of life, the sensing, the knowing, the contacting and the influencing of everything within and without. Therefore, truth is a function most akin to growth, since development is reaction of expansion and variation to various outer and inner stimuli. Only the truthful organism can grow experientially, and the organism that cannot grow is not truthful, i.e., not in accord with its own bio-energetic necessities. It remains sitting on the spot.

There are certain truths which are *a priori* given by one's senses and movements. That Life, Living, is constant MOTION, is such a self-evident truth itself. That Love is the merger of two organisms, is another such truth, self-evident from the sense of longing for merger, actual merging and loosing one's circumscribed individual identity during the embrace. That there exists something very alive and emotionally enlivening and vibrating and life-giving in the atmosphere around us, is another such self-evident truth, no matter whether it is called God or the Universal Spirit or the Great Father or the Kingdom of Heaven or Orgone Energy. This experience is common to all men and indelible. It is far older and more persistent than any any other, less comprehensive perception of one's being. Watch a cocker-spaniel deliver and care for its puppies, and you know what is meant here, *what naturally given truth is.* Truth is not something to be learned or imparted to the organism. It is born as a crucial function within the organism and it develops as long as the organism maintains its unitary functioning which means full orgonotic sensing.

With the loss of paradise, that is, with the loss of living Life, with the exclusion of crucial functions from man's senses, such as the genital embrace according to natural needs, the "TRUTH SEEKER" broke into this world of a ravaged humanity. What is called "Sin" by the Christian world, "Sabotage" by the Red Fascists, "Ignorance" by the scientist is the expression of the loss of the full orgonotic contact with one's life; accordingly, *substitute, false, inadequate contacts* had to develop to maintain life, as if on crutches. (About *"contactlessness"* see *Character Analysis,* 3rd ed., 1948.) And this is the plague at its inception. With the sin the prophet came about, with sickness, the medicine man. And among them there was rarely, very rarely, a Christ who dared to touch upon reality fully, without restriction, still here and there being bound down by the apron-strings of his time, his culture or his people's customs.

It is so very significant for the understanding of the emotional plague that the searching for truth becomes the more artificial and futile the closer what it searches for is to the genital emotions of mankind. Because Christ had touched exactly upon man's loss of living Life within himself, which is, ultimately, the loss of his genital functioning replaced by the dry, empty, frustrating 4-lettering, pushing desperately toward the lost paradise, his truth was deep, of cosmic dimensions, and it won a great part of the world—and was distorted *worst* of all, the distortion centering upon the "Sin of the Flesh." With the seeking of the truth, instead of the living of the truth, the EVASION OF TRUTH became the inseparable companion of truth-seeking. Evasion of truth, not truth-seeking has prevailed so far.

This is easily understandable. Truth, as a manifestation of Life's fullest contact with itself and its environment, is inextricably bound up with Life's energy economy. Truth, accordingly, if lived fully, stirs up the deepest emotions, and with the deepest emotions it stirs to high activity the urge for the genital embrace. *Since, now, the core of the energy release of the Living has been excluded and ostracized by men for ages, truth needs must be evaded, too.* Every movement toward truth inevitably brought man closer to the lost function. It is, therefore, no wonder that every truth-seeker was accused of "immorality" at all times and in all cultures built on genital suppression, and that the reactionary mind always fought truth as the way of the devil toward "immorality."

The more genitality is excluded from man's senses and activities, the harder the fight against the truth, the more complete is the transformation of a *biological* truth into a *mystical* "truth." The Christian religion is a *mystified* religion of the Living, directed against the very reality of what it represents and adores as an ideal. All lost *actual* virtues of nature reappear as *ideal* virtues, to be striven after. With this the dichotomy between the devil, who is a perverted God, and the realm of ethics is ever being born.

The EVASION OF THE TRUTH, so characteristic of man who lost paradise, i.e., who lost the feeling of God in his body, has, accordingly, its well justified *raison d'etre*. Truth, under the conditions of the full suppression of the laws of Life, stirs exactly those emotions which would upset the orderly way of life which became crucial to *armored* man's existence. Truth, penetrating to the core of man's misery, would *impede* the joys he learned to obtain in his substitute life: the little, secret love affairs, the little two weeks vacation, the little joy in listening to the radio, the little squanderance. It would disturb severely his *necessary* adjustments to the hard way of life under given structural and work conditions. Let an American Indian or a northern Eskimo or even a Chinese peasant live in full use of the most advanced technical acquisitions of civilization, and they would be rendered helpless in their usual way of life. These are banal things. What is meant here, essentially, is that the crooked character structure of present-day man has its *rational* meaning and function which cannot be lightly discarded as the freedom peddlers of all nations would advocate doing. They are ignorant of what "adjustment" means. They could not manage a single nervous breakdown due to inability to function actually according to the dreams.

Even the dream of paradise, no matter in what form it appears, is rational and necessary. It fills the heart with a remainder of the old glow of Life within a dreary actuality, as a pin-up girl adds strength to the soldier's guts in the firing line. The pin-up girl acts as a continuous torture, true, but it also helps to maintain the dream of life.

All this tells us that, though crucial and the only weapon capable of disarming the plague as the truth is, it cannot possibly be commanded or injected or taught or forced upon anybody who has not grown it in his organism from the very beginning. TRUTH IS BEING EVADED BECAUSE IT IS UNBEARABLE AND DANGEROUS TO THE ORGANISM WHICH IS INCAPABLE OF USING IT.

Truth means full contact with oneself as well as with the environment. Truth means knowing one's own ways as distinct from the ways of others. To force upon the fellow man truth which he cannot live, means stirring up emotions impossible for him to carry; it means endangering his existence; it means kicking off balance a well-set, even if disastrous, way of life.

Truth is not what the Russian political prostitute thinks it ought to be: a tool of power, to be changed at will. One cannot change the truth, as one cannot change one's basic character structure.

This must be constantly borne in mind as a protection against the prophets who, it is true, see the light but do not know how to enable their fellow men to take it in peace and full enjoyment. This, now, amounts to advocating the devil.

There is, however, an irrational rationale in the persecution of the truth, which cannot be overlooked if truthful living is eventually to prevail. Truth turns critically toward itself, as it were. If it has been persecuted through the ages, it reasons truthfully, there must be a good reason for it. There was a good reason in the rise of fascism of both the black and the red variety: *Fascism has awakened a sleeping world to the realities of the irrational, mystical character structure of the people of the world*. The rationale of the evil influence of fascism in the twentieth century upon the Asiatic masses is a serious reminder of what harm the mystical transformation of living Life has done to billions of human beings over the ages. Such rational functions within the ugly irrational are a part of living Life, and the truthful organism will acknowledge it. If we do not exactly agree with the command to love one's enemy, we can readily agree that "Love Your Enemy" had the meaning of "*Understand the motives of your Enemy.*" Not a single leading politician in Germany before Hitler's ascent to the reign of terror had really studied Hitler's gospel. So they kept babbling about his being a "bought servant of the bourgeoisie." *To know the rational in the deeply irrational is the mark of truthful living*, that is, of fully alive perception of the conditions of one's life. Only the stupid self-righteousness within the empty bag of a freedom-peddler manages to believe itself fully perfect and the enemy fully bad. There is a rational motive in the most evil happenings. The grave situation in which adolescent youth finds itself today, the so-called juvenile delinquency, which means in six out of ten cases simply the performing of the natural embrace under the most devastating circumstances, inner as well as outer—this situation is truly a reminder, directed toward a sitting world, of the laws of living Life within a maturing organism. And this voice will not stop screaming until the world stops sitting and starts moving onward.

The evasion of the truth in matters of adolescents' plight is *rational* on the part of the educational and medical bodies carrying grave responsibiliti.. ; they *would not know how* to start doing, *what* to do, *where* to proceed in a single case of adolescent misery. They have, d.. .. to the chronic evasion and the continuous misrepresentation o.. 'he issue, lost the ability to learn and to know how to act. The ..ld laws do not fit. They never did. The police is not the prope.. agency to deal with juvenile misery, except in cases of full c.. ..e against life and safety. The physicians brought up in mea. al schools which either eschew the subject completely ("DO NO.. EVER TOUCH IT") or adhere to old, wrong, outworn concepts giv.. n by old, outworn, dried-out lifeless parents and educators, c..nnot possibly take responsibility or do anything. The educators are in a similar situation. Therefore, the plague maintains itself. Evasion of the issue becomes rational in a very bad way. And proclaiming the full truth about the plague without preparation for its successful extermination would be equally criminal. What could millions of adolescents without parents who understand their plight, without public support, without help of any kind, and in addition, with a frustrated structure and with sick minds, do with the full truth about their lives?

The knower of the misery of adolescence keeps off the way of the freedom peddler. The peddler peddles "freedom of sex" for adolescents as he used to peddle "bread and freedom," not having the slightest whiff of an idea as to how bread and freedom are to be had; so he would, as he actually *did* for a while until he was stopped, peddle "freedom of sex for youth" in a most dangerous manner. No solution of any major social problem is possible without the full support of the public and without full knowledge of what is entailed. We must, by all means, nip in the bud the flourishing of a new brand of social nuisance, the *Truth Peddler*. He will do more harm than any lie has ever done.

The solution of the problem of adolescence and with it of juvenile delinquency requires:

A complete turn in matters of extramarital living together of boys and girls, secured by law.

Full cooperation of the parents based on rational, medical understanding of adolescence.

An upbringing of children *from infancy onward* which would insure a character structure which could take the sever jolts of a rich life and would be capable of full adaptation to the laws of bio-energy.

Full support on the part of the social administration.

Housing of the population which would take into account the need for privacy for adolescents.

Sufficient numbers of educators and physicians, *healthy themselves*, who would stand by in emergencies. This would require full public recognition of the evasion of truth on the part of psychoanalysts who today help to form public opinion on mental health.

A thorough revision of our ancient laws concerning rape and seduction of minors, to distinguish between *love in adolescence* and true criminal *seduction*.

Full endorsement of the subject of human biology (in the *orgonomic* sense) in the schools.

Adequate protection against the emotional plague which could and certainly would wreak havoc among the young ones who live happily.

And many other grave matters which would turn up in due time.

All this is unknown, and if known, it is inaccessible to the *freedom peddler.* It will be equally inaccessible to the *truth peddler.* Their only interest is to get youth into their organizations by way of political exploitation of the sexual misery of youth. The freedom peddler will in the future, as he so often has done in the past, start youth movements and later betray the very core of the life of adolescents by becoming more reactionary than the old, good conservative, since he had promised more than he could possibly fulfill. Beware of the freedom peddler in matters of love and Life. He does not mean what he says. He does not know anything about Life and the obstacles in its way. He transforms all realities into formalities and all practical problems of living Life into ideas about a future paradise of humanity. Actually, in this very manner, he lands himself and, if brought to power by gullible masses of people, he lands the whole population too in utter misery.

The freedom peddler makes out of matters of truth a bait to lure people into a trap. Truth to him is an "ideal" and not a daily *way* of doing things. He believes that he defends the truth if he is righteous. The conservative, who, out of an instinctive knowledge of the great difficulties connected with the pursuit of truth, defends the *status quo* in social living, is by far more honest. He has, at least, a chance of remaining decent. The freedom peddler *must,* if he wishes to get along, sign his soul over to the devil.

Truth should be used cautiously against the *fear* of truth *which is justified* by actual conditions. Truth cannot be used as a tool without the infliction of pain, often severe pain; but neither can it be used like a medical drug. It is an integral part of the way of life of the future and *has to grow organically within the senses and primal movements in our children from the very beginning* in infancy. And this requires social and legal protection which no freedom or truth peddler is ready or able to give.

All truth as *a way of living* requires an opportunity to express itself freely. It then will grow by its own devices. All it needs is an equal chance with the lie and the gossip and the maligning and the killing of Life.

Is this too much to ask for?

Truth can be used as a weapon against the Murder of Christ only if it has grown straight like a tree and is branching out like an oak in the forest.

A body that lies by way of its very movement, a soul which lies in the way it expresses itself, not being able to help it, cannot have truth implanted or injected into its veins. Truth in such containers would turn into a far worse lie than the simple lie that had been developed for the protection of the remainder of one's Self. Such truth, injected and turned into a lie, would be a horrible killer. It would have to prove continuously that it is NOT a lie, that it is TRUTH *per se*, that *not* to believe that it is the very essence of truth is sacrilege versus the holy smoke of the church or the state or the patron or the matron or the ruler or the nation or the this or that. Listen to the proclamation of "true bolshevist truths" and you will know right away what truth injected into crooked bodies and turned into lies looks like and what it does.

Therefore, beware of the freedom peddler who peddles truths like shoestrings in the market place. He is worse than a horse thief. The horse thief does not promise heaven on earth; he just steals a horse. The horse thief is strung up by the neck with a rope from the tree, but the freedom peddler goes free.

The freedom peddler refuses to learn why there has been lying in the world for so long a time and in so many people.

Learn how to recognize the freedom peddler by his righteousness, by his stalwart uprightness, by his erect forefinger kept up high in the air like a teacher's rod; learn to know him by his cruelly glowing eyes and his rasping voice, by his rigid mouth and his inhuman absoluteness in his quest for the impossible.

The truth which grew organically in a truthful body is a truth that combats the fake truth grown in rigid minds which deny the reality of nature and its manifestations. The sap of life has gone from their blood. They believe that truth is what follows logically from a given premise. The truth is what reveals to you first of all why truth is so rare and so difficult to obtain, and why there exist impostors of truth who disclaim the reality of our existence.

The system of a lunatic is not truthful though it follows logically from its premises. However, there is *some* kernel of truth in everything proclaimed by men.

People avoid the truth because the first bit of truth uttered and lived would draw more truth into action and so on indefinitely, and this would rip most people right off the customary tracks of their lives. But people, basically, know what is true and what is not, even if they so often render help to the lie. They support the lie because the lie has become a crutch without which life would not be possible. Therefore, in common human intercourse, the truth, and not the lie, is suspected of being phony.

From the lie in daily living has developed a technique to know the lie and be reconciled to it, to live with it, as it were. To use the truth against this lie would set the crusader beyond the pale of the human community.

It is not a matter of "proclaiming truth" but of *living truth ahead of one's fellow man.* And this *is* possible, but only if the truth is a *true* truth, and not a made-up, cooked-up, proposed or propagated truth. The truth must be a piece of your Self as is your leg or your brain or your liver. Otherwise, do not try to live a truth which is not akin to your whole being. It will turn into a lie in no time, and into a worse one to boot, than the lie which has grown organically in the makeshifts of social living.

And this is the true difficulty in getting across the truth one lives. You are in danger of being a voice in the desert if you preach the truth. *Don't preach truth.* Show people by example how to find the way to *their own* resources of truthful living. Let people live *their own* truths, *not* your truth. What is organic truth to one is no truth at all to another man or woman. There is no absolute truth just as there are no two faces alike. And yet there are basic functions in nature which are common to all truth. But the individual expression varies from body to body, from soul to soul. It is true that all trees have roots in the soil. But the concrete tree A could not use the roots of the concrete tree B to draw nourishment from the soil since they are not his. To maintain the special in the common, the variation in the rule is the essence of wisdom. The variation, divorced from the common, the differentness, is the way of the freedom peddler in his youth. The way of the common and the dictatorial rule for all is the way of the freedom peddler *when his youth has gone out of him.*

The world is split up between the one and the other. It is called "individualism" and "statism" at present, and will be called many other names before it will vanish from the surface of the earth. The children have not been born yet who will live the laws of Life as they are in the trees of a forest or in the birds or in the corn in the fields.

Freedom peddling robs the truth of its opportunity to prove itself, to sharpen its tools, to structuralize its conduct, to know its enemy, to cope with trouble, to persist in danger, to learn where it can turn into a lie worse than the native lie. Therefore, no rules can be given as to how to use the weapon of truth, as many a reader may have expected from these pages. It is again a sign of the mystification of Christ that rules of conduct common to *all* are expected from *another* prophet. This is to escape the trouble of finding your own special truth within your own special Self as it fits *you*, and not somebody else.

There is only *one* common rule valid in finding the special truth valid for you. That is to learn to listen patiently into yourself, to give yourself a chance to find your own way which is yours and nobody else's way. This leads not into chaos and wild anarchism but ultimately into the realm where the *common truth for all* is rooted. The ways of approach are manifold and none alike. The source from where the sap of truth is streaming is common to all living beings, far beyond the animal man. This must be so because all truth is a function of living Life, and living Life is basically the same in everything that moves by way of pulsation. Therefore, the basic truth in all teachings of mankind are alike and amount to only one common thing: *To find your way to the thing you feel when you love dearly, or when you create, or when you build your home, or when you give birth to your children or when you look at the stars at night.*

Accordingly, common to all sages who knew the truth or were searching for truth, was the expression in their eyes and the meaning of the alive movement in their faces. It is sad but true that the great clown in the circus carries this expression behind his mask. He has touched upon great truths. It is the exact opposite of the howling of a mob throwing stones into windows. It is far from the giggle of a coquettish girl who lures men to find out again and again how dangerous a man could be to her. It is contrary to the looks of an executioner or the expression in the face of a dried-up, cruel, cunning, sneaking, hiding, ruthless, unscrupulous liberator of peoples. *Know the faces of the fake liberators.* Learn to see them wherever they turn up, potential ones and mature ones. Learn to know the clever bandwagon rider who cannot look straight into your eyes. And you will know, by contrast, what the truth looks like.

Truth knows no party lines, nor national boundaries, nor the difference of the sexes or of ages or of language. It is a way of being common to all, and potentially ready to act in all. This is the great hope.

But truth is only *potentially* there; it is not ready to act as yet, like the seed in the field is only potentially there to yield the bread in the fruit. Draught and freezing cold can stop it where it is and prevent it from bearing fruit.

The emotional plague is the freezing cold and the draught that keeps the seed of truth from yielding the fruit. The plague reigns where it is not possible for the truth to live. The eye, therefore, should be centered primarily on the plague and not on the truth, on the prevention of draught and freezing rather than on what the seedling will or might do. The seedling will know its ways toward the Life-giving sun. It is the plague that kills the movement of the stem and it, therefore, requires all our attention. It is not the learning to walk in the infant, but the rock or the precipice in its way that is to be watched. It is a part of the tragedy of man that he did not see the precipice and believed in a perfect, readymade walking of the infant, instead of removing the obstacle in the way of the growing truth.

This is how truth should be used.

4. HIDEOUS DISTORTIONS OF ORGONOMIC TRUTH

In the twentieth century, society went through the frightful experience of what a system of thought, distorted by armored man, can do. No leader conscious of his importance and responsibility will ever dare forego the lessons from the mass murder that followed the distortion of sociological teachings in the heads of men in power who were forced to keep society together. And the leaders who will be responsible for the new Life processes which will emerge from the discovery of the Life Energy, will be forced to be more careful a hundred fold. *A teaching of living Life, taken over and distorted by armored man, will spell final disaster to the whole of mankind and its institutions.* There should be no mistake about this.

A brief survey will easily show in what direction such distortions of a teaching based on Life Energy will act.

By far the most likely result of the principle of "orgastic potency" will be a pernicious philosophy of 4-lettering all over the place everywhere. Like an arrow released from the restrain-

---

From *The Murder of Christ*, 1953.

ing, tightly tensed spring, the search for quick, easy and dele-terious genital pleasure will devastate the human community.

The constant, patient struggle for improvement of *health*, based on carefully drawn experiences, will be replaced by the idea of a "perfect," readymade "health" as an absolute ideal with new social stratification in "healthy" and in "neurotic" people.

Physicians and philosophers, to judge from past distortions, will probably establish a new virtue, the perfect ideal of *"freedom of emotion"* which will harass human interrelations. Rage will have no reason nor rational direction. It will rage for rage's sake only, to be *"emotionally free."*

Self-regulation, instead of being the easy, spontaneous flow of events with up's and down's, to follow and to guard, will become a "principle" to be applied to life, to be taught, to be exercised, to be imposed upon people, possibly with prison or death penalties, no matter whether it be called "sabotage of the holy living principle of self-regulation" or "crime against the freedom of Life and Liberty." And those revolted by the sight of the evil doings will most likely blame an innocent, distorted, misinterpreted orgonomy for the actions of living beings bare of any sense of proportion.

The function of *work democratic interrelations among working people* will most likely drown in the verbiage of what work-democracy *should* be like (not of what it actually *is*), and new political ideas will emerge to depict and secure the new hope of mankind: *"work democracy."*

Orgastically impotent physicians in the realm of medical orgonomy will mess up the medical techniques to establish the orgonotic streaming in sick organisms or will forget them alto-gether and start quibbling about whether the jaw or the shoul-der muscles should be attacked first, for centuries to come.

They will form one end of a line at the other end of which they will be opposed by the 4-letterers who will demand *"freedom of love"* and the right to live life according to the *"principles of orgonomy."*

Self-regulation in the upbringing of newborn infants will not work in hands which will not know what a *spontaneous* decision or action is, and the enemies of children and even the friends will rave about the evil consequences of that cockeyed idea of self-regulatory upbringing in infancy.

We can imagine all these developments and many more very easily, and there will be those wisecrackers who will tell everybody that nothing can be done anyhow, that it always has been that way and always will be . . . . . until some new Living Christ will walk upon this earth in the midst of the nightmare and will preach the principles of Life only to be nailed to the cross again by the high priests of the "Science of Living Life."

All this will actually happen unless man will find the exit from the scarred battlefield of the human emotional plague, the entrapment of poor souls.

The prostitute in politics, the glib freedom peddler, the mystical liberator are not to be blamed for the great misery. They are to be blamed for *obstructing the access* to the realization of their own ideals and the removal of the misery they created. They are not to be blamed for peddling "freedom" and "bread" and "democracy" and "peace" and the "will of the people" and all the rest of the register. They are to be blamed for persecuting everybody who clarifies what freedom is and what *obstacles* are in the way of self-government and what *obstructs* peace. They are not to be blamed for promising land to poor, starving peasants. They are to be punished for *obstructing* the access to making the peasant capable of tilling his land *freely* and *efficiently* so that the mass murder of peasants in the process of compulsory collectivization as in 1932 becomes impossible in the future. They are not to be blamed for holding out hopes for heaven on earth, but for betraying and obstructing every single step in the direction of true betterment of human conditions. They are not to be blamed for having ideals but for having *emptied all ideals from any content whatsoever,* for having put human high ideals into the mirror and for killing everyone who *lives* an ideal or tries to bring reality somewhat closer to the ideal; in short, they are to be blamed for being characterological scoundrels. They are not to be blamed for having theories or for feeling themselves the "sole" liberators and the "only" possessors of the holy truth, but for killing millions for not believing in their alleged truths and for torturing those who do not think that they liberate anything. They are not to be blamed for speaking about the liberation of those in low social standing but *for doing exactly the opposite* of what they are talking about, for depriving the lowly ones of all and every opportunity to get on their feet because it does not fit the ghastly corps of a theory.

The Catholic hierarchy is not to be blamed for preaching Christ's teachings, but for obstructing these very same teachings by the mystification and disembodiment of the living, true, original Christ. They are not to be blamed for being ignorant of the identity of Life and God and sweetness in the genital embrace, but for hating and killing everything that even remotely reminds one of Christ's true living existence, and for keeping from mankind the knowledge of Christ's relations to the love of the body. They are guilty of ossification of a living creed and of murdering Christ in the bodies of countless infants and children and adolescents, thus creating the very Sin they later punish with fire in hell. We accuse them of obstruction to learning and development and improvement and recognition of obvious, simple, clear facts of Life. They are guilty of not joining, with their great power those who have looked a bit deeper into the darkness of human existence and who have thrown some, if ever so dim a light upon what is meant by the word "God." They are to be blamed for having remained sitting since the fourth century A.D.

A kneeling and praying humanity, two and a half billion strong, feels Life in their frozen bodies when they pray, though they call it by different names. They fight holy wars over the kind of name to be given to what they have *in common*. And the high priests have abandoned their sacred duty to lead these kneeling and bowing and praying multitudes toward exactly

what they have in common when they feel
blood what they call "God." And here no
since Christ cursed the Pharisees at the t
Nothing! The priests have not learned an
worse, they obstruct and fight tooth and
trying to learn. This is what they are guilty

An ossified humanity has put ossified prie
and the ossified priests maintain the ossifica
born ge eration. That is what religion is gu
nal tr e teachings of Buddha and Christ ar
all s ove toward the same goal. Ossified h
un erstand or accept these teachings, and t
ght kind of priest to keep the teaching f
n the mirror. This is the great tragedy: *Th*
penetration of the fog, not the fog itself; th
realization of religious beliefs and goals a
religious, original moral teachings.

Not the freedom of speech and its advoca
but the abuse of the freedom of speech b
and gossipers and maligners and undergro
stroy the foundations of liberty because t
stand liberty. To be blamed is not the ignor
the *gossiping* psychiatrist who maligns the
ery of frustrated love.

It is true: *If anyone had the guts and p*
freedom and self-regulation be established
est disaster in the history of mankind woul
our lives like a flood. If revolution by force
Constitution of the USA as a right of the
government, would and could do the job o
sane mind would hesitate to be all out *for i*
of the downfall of all freedom movements
that freedom can *not* be established by dec
fear of freedom *is in the peoples themselve*
fear the streaming of living Life in their b
truth and avoid it by all means.

somewhat closer to the ideal; in short, they are to be blamed for being characterological scoundrels. They are not to be blamed for having theories or for feeling themselves the "sole" liberators and the "only" possessors of the holy truth, but for killing millions for not believing in their alleged truths and for torturing those who do not think that they liberate anything. They are not to be blamed for speaking about the liberation of those in low social standing but *for doing exactly the opposite* of what they are talking about, for depriving the lowly ones of all and every opportunity to get on their feet because it does not fit the ghastly corps of a theory.

The Catholic hierarchy is not to be blamed for preaching Christ's teachings, but for obstructing these very same teachings by the mystification and disembodiment of the living, true, original Christ. They are not to be blamed for being ignora of the identity of Life and God and sweetness in the genital embrace, but for hating and killing everything that even remotely reminds one of Christ's true living existence, and for keeping from mankind the knowledge of Christ's relations to the love of the body. They are guilty of ossification of a living creed and of murdering Christ in the bodies of countless infants and children and adolescents, thus creating the very Sin they later punish with fire in hell. We accuse them of obstruction to learning and development and improvement and recognition of obvious, simple, clear facts of Life. They are guilty of not joining, with their great power those who have looked a bit deeper into the darkness of human existence and who have thrown some, if ever so dim a light upon what is meant by the word "God." They are to be blamed for having remained sitting since the fourth century A.D.

A kneeling and praying humanity, two and a half billion strong, feels Life in their frozen bodies when they pray, though they call it by different names. They fight holy wars over the kind of name to be given to what they have *in common.* And the high priests have abandoned their sacred duty to lead these kneeling and bowing and praying multitudes toward exactly what they have in common when they feel in their streaming blood what they call "God." And here nothing has changed since Christ cursed the Pharisees at the temple of the Jews. Nothing! The priests have not learned anything at all, and, worse, they obstruct and fight tooth and nail those who are trying to learn. This is what they are guilty of.

An ossified humanity has put ossified priests into its temples, and the ossified priests maintain the ossification in every new-born generation. That is what religion is guilty of, not its original true teachings of Buddha and Christ and Confucius. They all strove toward the same goal. Ossified humanity could not understand or accept these teachings, and they established the right kind of priest to keep the teaching frozen, unreachable, in the mirror. This is the great tragedy: *The obstruction of the penetration of the fog*, not the fog itself; the *threat against the realization of religious beliefs and goals and morals*, not the religious, original moral teachings.

Not the freedom of speech and its advocates are to be blamed but the abuse of the freedom of speech by liars and cheaters and gossipers and maligners and underground moles who destroy the foundations of liberty because they cannot live or stand liberty. To be blamed is not the ignorant psychiatrist but the *gossiping* psychiatrist who maligns the revealer of the misery of frustrated love.

It is true: *If anyone had the guts and power to decree that freedom and self-regulation be established overnight, the greatest disaster in the history of mankind would inevitably swamp our lives like a flood.* If revolution by force, guaranteed in the Constitution of the USA as a right of the people against *evil* government, would and could do the job of true liberation, no sane mind would hesitate to be all out *for* it. It was the essence of the downfall of all freedom movements based on such belief, that freedom can *not* be established by decree or force, because fear of freedom *is in the peoples themselves*. As long as people fear the streaming of living Life in their bodies, they will fear truth and avoid it by all means.

TO TOUCH THE TRUTH IS THE SAME AS TO TOUCH THE GENITALS.
Therefrom stems the *"Touch-It-Not"* of anything serious, cru-
cial, life-saving, of anything leading toward true self-reliance.
This explains the great taboo "TOUCH-IT-NOT" against genitals as
well as against truth. This is the subversive power of the plague.
*To turn mass attention away from the conferences of the politi-
cal windbags toward these crucial facts will be the primary job.*
From this job, once done, other developments will follow.
Therefore, the current Biological Revolution which has gripped
humanity over the past thirty years, is of such tremendous
importance. It opens the gates toward the truth by making
mankind aware of the great taboo: "DON'T TOUCH IT," and, by
making people aware of it, it brings them closer to their genitals
as well as to their inner truth. This means the reversal of a
situation of some ten thousand years' standing. To be aware of
the scope of this penetrating process means to be aware of a
huge sweep of history over the following two to three thousand
years. No freedom peddler and no political prostitute will
accept this. They will talk, gossip, malign, fight, slander and lie
it away wherever they meet it. *To the same extent to which the
problems of human genitality become accessible to multitudes,
will truth be wanted and no longer avoided or killed.* And then
things will run their own logical course.

Catholicism, which denies the love in the body, can survive
this revolution in our lives only if it returns to Christ's true,
original meaning which was so badly and thoroughly transformed into the exact opposite. Should it happen that Christen-
dom will not, swimming in the general stream of life, revert to
the original meaning of Christ, more, much more blood, innocent blood will be spilled, and still Life will remain stronger and
the church will slowly vanish from the surface of this earth.
Otherwise, it will survive as a great institution which, in spite
of the terror and darkness it has spread over the ages, had done
so much to keep a miserably despondent humanity somehow
going. It is those who feel Life in the body's streaming and
want the sweetness of true love who know better than the rep-

resentatives of a distorted Christ that the perversion of Christ's true meaning was, in the face of the sexual misery of mankind, *absolutely necessary.*

St. Paul is not to be blamed for having introduced the most cruel system of sexual starvation mankind has ever known. He *had to* if he was to build up the Christian church. *He had to build strong dams against the pornographic, filthy, sick mind of man in sexual matters, even at the price of killing the true Christ.* But he would in the person of his representatives be guilty of treason against mankind if he were to obstruct the *way back* to the true Christ, by fire and sword, by a knifing-in-the-back of the new leaders who will arise in this struggle, and by conniving in secret conferences to *kill* Life. It won't work any longer; it will only cost innocent blood. And this blood, spilled for no good reason, will be on the consciences of the obstructors of the truth of Christ.

The safeguarding of a healthy, natural, life-saving love life in the newborn generations is the task of the new type of physician and psychiatrist. It is *their* domain; here the truth of Life was born and protected against evil attacks. The church is the domain of the priests. Let each domain have its own rights, equal and honest. Just as no psychiatrist or physician will try to interfere with the *inner* affairs of the church, no church should be permitted to extend its influence and power beyond its own domain. Let us keep to our own domains and not interfere with what is none of our business. This is *mutually* valid.

Life surpasses by its very nature all boundaries, all little frontiers, all custom barriers, all national restrictions, all racial biases; it is truly supreme in the cosmic sense, just as the Christian thinks the Lord supreme in the cosmic sense. But Life only lives its way, it does not *force* anyone anywhere to live its way. It does not interfere with what is none of its business. This is its greatness. Once discovered and understood, it is bound to come to govern all that derives from it. It is in no disagreement with either the true original meaning of God or of Christianity, nor with the true, original meaning of socialism, nor with any other true striving toward human life, liberty and happiness. The yearning and striving for Life, Liberty and Happiness is the common denominator of *all* factions of human political organizations which today are at each other's throats. It is and always has been the emotional plague which split the basically identical human strivings apart and drove them against each other. Therefore, the enemy is not a particular belief but the work of the plague in man.

Red Fascism is the sum total of *organized* techniques to split into pieces and apart the common roots of Life in all people. It has shut every single entrance to the knowledge of living Life. It has banned the laws of the unconscious human mind, the laws of infant and childhood genitality, the knowledge of repression and armoring and secondary drives and natural self-regulation from its schools and its books. Thus it will never reach anything positive in human affairs. And this will, ultimately, be its downfall. The mechanistic mind cannot possibly, in the long run, win out against the cosmic point of view in man.

IX. CONCLUSION

THE ROOTING OF REASON IN NATURE

THE YEARNING FOR KNOWLEDGE

We have finished our surveying flight over the new territory flaming with new knowledge, yet to be harvested. We are turning homeward again, back into well-charted, familiar terrain. While we go over in our thoughts what we have seen unfolding beneath us, it may be well-advised to ponder about the greatest riddle of all: *The ability of man to think*, and by mere thinking to *know* what nature is and how it works. This ability is generally taken for granted. Yet, it remains the greatest unsolved riddle so far. And on the solution of this riddle most probably depends the solution of the next-greatest riddle, the riddle of the existence and perpetuation of the tremendous human misery for ages into ages. Men of knowledge do not feel called on to solve these riddles on order, as it were. They can only keep aloof as best they can from the maze and entanglements of daily routine and *ad hoc* public opinion, and pursue their well-reasoned trains of search and thought.

There can be no doubt that rational thought, and not political maneuvering, that hard, straightforward work on problems of existence, and not mere voting, will open up the vastness of future human potentialities. It thus appears appropriate to ask ourselves at the end of our flight what place the human function of *knowing* may occupy in the scheme of natural events. We do not propose to enter into a complicated philosophical

From *Cosmic Superimposition*, 1951.

517

debate. We simply want to know what KNOWING itself does to man. So far it seems to have done rather little to improve his lot. On the contrary, the more he learned to know up till now, the worse became the mass killing which has become one of the most horrible routines of daily life.

In pessimistic moods of hopelessness one is prone to ask what use there is in saving people from death by cancer if babies are being killed emotionally before and soon after birth by the million in nearly every single home all over the planet with the consent and help of their parents, their nurses, their doctors; when, furthermore, these emotionally flat-ironed human babies later on as grownups carry any and every misdeed of cranks, politicians, dictators, emperors and whatnot to evil power over men.

"SO WHAT?" From a biological and cosmic point of view it does not seem to matter at all; so goes one type of reasoning. Man has been maimed and killed by the billion over millennia. Whole species of living things have arisen and perished. Civilizations have grown and vanished again. Religions have come and gone. Mighty empires which shook man's existence for centuries have crumbled with no trace left, except a few ruins left over as witnesses of decay. So WHAT, it sounds into our searching minds again and again.

The cosmic orgone ocean, which has been surveyed in some detail in this paper, pursues its eternal course whether we know it or not, whether we understand the cancer scourge or not, whether the human race exists or not. It does not seem to matter. One understands well the mood of the retired and praying monk who lives only to return to God. Knowing about the cosmic orgone ocean one has a better understanding of and feeling for the essentially ascetic nature of all major religious systems. Nothing matters. . . .

Yet, there lives and thrives in us a quest for knowledge which is stronger than any philosophical thought, be it life-positive or life-negative. This burning yearning for knowing can be felt like a stretching out of our senses beyond the material framework of our body; we understand the rational in the metaphysical view of existence.

While we yearn to know and to know better and safer all the time, to pick up what those before us have learned, and to transmit it with our own little insights to the next and the following generations, we feel, in spite of all the so WHATS and IT-DOES-NOT-MATTERS, that we could not stop yearning for knowledge. We feel as tools of this yearning to know, like babies and puppies most likely feel as tools of their plasmatic movements no matter whether there is sense and meaning in these movements or not. Seen from the bio-energetic standpoint, the human yearning for knowledge obtains concrete meaning with regard to cosmic events.

The quest for knowledge expresses desperate attempts, at times, on the part of the orgone energy WITHIN *the living organism to comprehend* ITSELF, *to become* CONSCIOUS *of itself. And in understanding its own ways and means of being, it learns to understand the cosmic orgone energy ocean which surrounds the surging and searching emotions.*

Here we touch upon the greatest riddle of life, the function of SELF-PERCEPTION and SELF-AWARENESS.* This riddle is shrouded with awe; at times it results in frightening amazement up to complete confusion and disintegration of the searching ego, as in schizophrenia. All striving for perfection appears, in this light, as striving for fullest integration of one's emotions and intellect; in other words, it is striving for the fullest measure of bio-energy flow without blockings and deterring splitting of self-perception. Therefore, the full emotional merger in the sexual embrace (pornography excluded) with full swinging of bio-energy is most longed for and gratifying, as well as most beautiful in the aesthetic sense.

In this sense, and only in this, striving for perfecting knowledge has *cosmic* meaning. In penetrating to the deepest depth and the fullest extent of emotional integration of the Self, we

---

* *Cf. Character Analysis,* "The Schizophrenic Split," 1949, pp. 398-510.

not only experience and feel, we also learn to *understand*, if only dimly, the meaning and working of the cosmic orgone ocean of which we are a tiny part.

This full self-awareness is, seen from a deeper angle, since the "SELF" is only a bit of organized cosmic orgone energy, a step in the functional development of the cosmic orgone energy itself. Life energy has been defined as cosmic orgone energy, streaming and swinging within a membranous system. From this basic functioning all other and "higher" functions of the living system, including the intellect and the faculty of reasoning, emerge. Basically, the function of reasoning is not opposed or contradictory to the bio-energetic streaming. There is ample evidence in the biographies of great explorers, philosophers and religious pioneers that their original reasoning grew out from their experiencing of their own life functions as cosmic events. And justly so.

Thus, in an ultimate sense, in self-awareness and in the striving for the perfection of knowledge and full integration of one's bio-functions, *the cosmic orgone energy becomes aware of itself*. In this becoming aware of ITSELF, knowing about itself, growing into consciousness of itself, what is called "Human Destiny" is taken out of the realm of mysticism and metaphysics; it becomes a reality of cosmic dimensions; it merges *understandably* with all great philosophies and religions of and about living man, as conscious design of one's life.

No great poet or writer, no great thinker or artist has ever escaped from this deep and ultimate awareness of being somehow and somewhere rooted in nature at large. And in true religion this was always felt, though never realized in its factual concreteness. Up till the discovery of the cosmic orgone energy, this experience of one's own roots in nature was either mystified in the form of transpersonal, spiritual images, or ascribed to an unknowable, forever closed realm beyond man's reach. This is what has always turned the quest for knowledge into mystical, irrational, metaphysical, superstitious beliefs. Thus, again "everybody is right in some way, only he does not know in what way he is correct." The discovery of the cosmic orgone ocean, its realities and concrete physical manifestations such as the streaming of life energy in living organisms, puts an end to the compulsion of turning deeper searching into unreal, mystical experiences. The human animal will slowly get used to the fact that *he has discovered his God* and can now begin to learn the ways of "God" in a very practical manner. The human animal might well continue fighting his own full self-awareness for centuries to come; he might well continue to murder one way or another those who threaten his self-imposed blindness by orgonomic disclosures. He will most probably, as a mechanist or chemist, defame this truly physical insight as a return to the phlogiston theory or to alchemy, and as a religious fanatic he may well feel inclined to regard such a quest for extension of knowledge as a challenge to the greatness of the idea of an unknowable God, as criminal blasphemy. However this may be, the events cannot be reversed any longer. The discovery of the cosmic orgone ocean and its bio-energetic functioning is here to stay.

OBJECTIVE, FUNCTIONAL LOGIC AND MAN'S REASONING

The chain of events which unfolds during basic natural research depicts the *logic* of connections between various natural phenomena. The young research scientist experiences the unfolding of the logical chain of events as if there existed such a thing as "reason" in the universe. This is especially the case when *mathematical* logic enters into the chain of sequences. It is most likely that the first ideas about an absolute "world spirit," no matter what you name it, in other words, the beginning of religious thought, emerged from man's capacity to observe and to reason about nature in such a fashion that *consistent, objective* logic emerged from this activity. We also have good reason to assume that once in the historic past the human animal was flabbergasted at this ability to reach logical chains of events which were beyond himself, so to speak. What we are used to calling "objective natural science" is the summation of such chains of logical connections *beyond* ourselves.

Now this sounds like mysticism of the first order. The practical, technical business mind and the glibly brilliant intellectual are wont to sneer at such statements. However, they would fail completely in comprehending the fact that abstract mathematical reasoning is able to predict objective natural events. The deep-going processes of basic scientific thought are foreign to them. So are the connections between deep intuition and crystal-clear intellectual elaborations of first intuitive contacts with natural functions. So are, furthermore, such bio-energetic functions as the perfect care of mothers for their offspring in the animal kingdom; the rational, logical activities of organs; most of the rational (objectively logical) processes in the growth of plants; the production of a true musician or painter. To refer to these functions as the doings of an unconscious mind means nothing here. To identify the "unconscious" with "irrational" is nonsense. The next question is unescapably: WHENCE STEMS THE UNCONSCIOUS MIND? And, if all functions below the conscious intellect are "irrational," how is it possible that life functioned well long before the development of reason? There can be no doubt: *Natural, objective functions are rational, to begin with.*

The objective logic which leads from superimposition in the genital embrace to superimposition in the microcosmic (creation of matter) and in the macrocosmic realms (creation of the ring of the aurora, of hurricanes and galaxies) has stunned the discoverer and shaken his emotions to their innermost depth. He has rejected these results for years and refused to believe that the conclusions from these results could possibly be true. He balked at admitting that true religion could, in spite of all its mystical distortions, be so very rational; that there could be such a thing as a *rational* core of all religious beliefs in an objective rational power governing the universe. He did not change his natural-scientific position; he did not now believe that a personified or absolute "spirit" governed the world. On the contrary: More than ever his conviction was confirmed that there exists and acts a *physical* power in the universe at the roots of all being; a power, or whatever you may call it, which finally has become accessible to being handled, directed, measured, put to useful purposes by man-made tools such as thermometer, electroscope, telescope, Geiger counter, etc. The discovery of the cosmic orgone energy, the primordial creative force in the universe, soared to new triumphant heights. This was not the main reason for the shake-up of the discoverer's emotions. What shook him to the very roots of his total emotional and intellectual existence, was the tremendous impact of the workings of an *objective* functional logic in the natural functions beyond his personal being. He understood, in the midst of his emotional upheaval, the absolute necessity of the emergence of the idea of "GOD" all over this planet among all peoples no matter what their race or the kind of their primitive awareness of this logic in nature may have been. It did not matter then that the rational, logical chains of happenings in the universe had been so badly mystified and personified; or that religious feelings and thought had so often and so cruelly been misused in the interest of secondary drives such as wars, exploitation of human helplessness and misery, and the like. "GOD," at this point, *appeared to be the perfectly logical result of man's awareness of the existence of an objective functional logic in the universe.* Furthermore, it now appeared quite logical that man had again and again realized, in spite of all distortion and confusion, that somehow this same logic of nature was functioning *within himself.* Otherwise, how could man possibly have become aware of the logic outside in nature? How could he, furthermore, fail to become aware that he played a double role in the stream of nature: *First*, in realizing his ability to become actively aware of the logic in nature beyond his own Self; and *second*, in spite of this ability, being so badly and helplessly *subjected* to the powerful logic beyond himself, in birth and death, in growth and love, and, above all, in his insuperable drive toward the genital embrace. He must have felt right from the beginning that his genital drive made him "lose control" and reduced him to a bit of streaming, convulsing nature. Here, the now well-known human *orgasm anxiety* may well have originated. It is no wonder, then, that most religions which tended toward monotheistic thought condemned the genital embrace through complete denial of all pleasure, as in the Buddhist religion, and through defamation of the genital embrace as "lust" as in the later Catholic religion. It is safe to assume that the impelling drive to overcome the basic natural function of the orgastic convulsion which rendered man helpless, was later on confirmed and justified by the development of ugly, secondary, perverse, sadistic cruel drives in man. Against these later *distortions* of nature, the first fight of the founders of many religions was quite obviously and sharply directed. Since no distinction between natural genital and secondary, perverted, cruel, lascivious drives was as yet possible, the most essential root of man in nature, his orgastic convulsion, fell prey to suppression, physiological blocking and finally to severe condemnation together with the secondary antisocial drives from which the primary drives were not distinguished.

In this manner, man "*lost his paradise*" (orgastic root in nature) and fell prey to "*sin*" (sexual perversion). He lost contact with one of his most crucial roots in nature, and thus with nature itself, not only in the sensory and emotional, but also in the intellectual realm. From here onward, nature could neither be contacted nor understood, except in devious, mystical or abstract reasoning ways. In higher mathematics a few human animals retained a bit of natural contact with logic in objective nature, and they stood out as particular and prominent minds, separated from the rest of mankind which had lost its sense of natural functions within and without. From here onward, furthermore, Life, God, Genitality remained as if forever tabooed, inaccessible, unreachable whether they were glorified into heaven or condemned into hell. The ambiguity of hell and heaven, God and Devil, their mutual interdependence and exchangeability remained a basic characteristic of all moral theology. This sharp antithesis was reflected in many other dichotomies over the millennia such as nature versus culture, love versus work, etc.

Let us not further follow this line of sequences. It has been dealt with on many occasions, in many different contexts of human pathology, sociology, ethnology, in early orgonomy as well as in many other branches of human knowledge. The only additional piece of insight to be secured in this treatise is the basic identity between objective logic in nature, as it meets man's senses, and the power of reasoning itself *within* man. To express the same thing in terms of our orgonometric, functional language:

$$\text{Natural processes} \left\{ \begin{array}{l} \text{objective functional logic of orgone energy} \\ \text{subjective functional, logical reasoning, on} \\ \text{the basis of } \textit{orgonotic self-perception} \end{array} \right.$$

To repeat: The discoverer of the primordial orgone energy, which functions *within* man *(bio-energy)* and *without* man *(cosmic primordial energy)*, found himself confronted with this functional identity of objective and subjective natural logic. He felt himself as a tool of this logic, as a very active and faithful tool. He followed it with awe and a deep sense of responsibility as well as humility, wherever it would lead him. The functional identity of biological and cosmic superimposition was the result of this symphony of outer and inner natural logic.

What basic function, then, in the flow of natural development has the discovery of the cosmic orgone energy?

It is not empty speculation to determine one's place in the stream of natural events. What is specifically meant here is not the fact that man as an animal grew out of the cosmic evolution; the question here is what the *process of the discovery of the orgone energy flow within and without man entails for his place in and his handling of nature.* Man is not only rooted in nature; he also perceives, tries to comprehend and to *use* nature.

The undoing of the *mystification* of nature will be a necessary consequence of the discovery of the primordial dynamics of nature. Is it then too much to say:

The discovery of the cosmic orgone functions within the human animal may well represent a major evolutionary step forward in the direction of a FUNCTIONAL UNITY *of the cosmic and the intellectual flow of developments, free of contradiction.*

Human history leaves little doubt that until this discovery, man's intellectual activities functioned mainly in a direction *opposite* to the cosmic energy. Partially this opposition expressed itself in mystification and personification of the primordial mover and creator; in other respects it expressed itself in the form of rigid, mechanistic interpretations of nature. This was especially true for the last three centuries. The mechanistic, atomic, chemical view grew in opposition to the mystical distortion of nature. In ETHER, GOD AND DEVIL, an attempt has been made to show that the primitive animistic view was closer to the natural functioning than the mystical and the mechanistic. The first was overcome by the latter; however, mysticism never lost its hold on the minds of the majority of mankind. Both mysticism and mechanism have failed as systems of thought. Mechanism had to abdicate during the first half of this century, beginning with the discovery of nuclear radiation and Planck's demonstration of the quantum action at the basis of the universe. The *animistic* view, and not the mystical, was a forerunner of functional thinking, as expressed most clearly in Kepler's *"vis animalis"* that moves the heavens.

Orgonomy, first without being aware of it, had picked up the thread which led in a hidden manner from the most primitive perception of ancient man (animism) toward the establishment of the perfect functional identity between the life energy (organismic orgone energy) and the cosmic orgone energy.

This identity of the two forms of existence, naturally, is a late development. Before man could ponder about nature, he had to exist as an organized tiny part of the cosmic orgone energy; and before he could exist he had to develop out of a long series of predecessors: these predecessors, whether they pondered about their origin or not, again had to develop from most primitive plasmatic, orgonotic living beings which doubtless already possessed the ability to perceive and to react to the surrounding orgone energy ocean. This is merely a survey in order to reach a firmer hold on our basic problems:

1. *Why did man as the only living animal species develop an armor?*

2. *Was the armoring of the organism, which clearly is responsible for the mystification as well as mechanization of nature, a "mistake" of nature, as it were?*

The problem of why man as the only animal species did develop an armor around his living core, bothers the orgonomic educator and physician in his daily tasks. He has to remove the armor in sick people, and he has to prevent the armoring in children. In this difficult task he not only experiences the terror which strikes man or child when the armor is dissolved; he also suffers from all kinds of dangerous attacks upon his work and very existence on the part of people everywhere in his environment. If now, there is nothing in existence beyond the confines of natural processes, why then does the armoring of the human species exist at all, since it *contradicts* nature in man on every single step and destroys his natural, rich potentialities? This does not seem to make sense. Why did nature make this "mistake"? Why only in the human species? Why not also in the deer or in the chipmunk? Why just in man? His "higher destination" is, clearly, not the answer. The armor has destroyed man's natural decency and his faculties, and has thus precluded "higher" developments; the 20th century is witness to this fact.

Or is the process of armoring in man no mistake of nature at all? Is it possible that the armor came about in some understandable, rational manner notwithstanding its irrational essence and consequences?

We know that it is mostly socio-economic influences (family structure, cultural ideas on nature versus culture, civilization requirements, mystical religion, etc.) which reproduce the armor in each generation of newborn infants. These infants will as grownups force their own children to armor, unless the chain is to be broken somewhere, sometime. The present-day social and cultural compulsion of the armor does not imply that at the very onset of the armor in the far away past of the development of man, it was also socio-economic influences which set the armoring process into motion. It seems rather the other way around: The process of armoring, most likely, was there first, and the socio-economic processes which today and throughout written history have *reproduced* armored man, were already the first important *results* of the biological aberration of man. The emergence of the mystical and mechanistic way of life from the armoring of the human animal are too clearly expressed and too well-studied to be overlooked or neglected any longer. With the breakdown of the armor the total outlook of the human being changes in such a basic and total manner, in the direction of contact and identification with his natural functioning, that there can be no longer any doubt as to the relationsh p between armor and mysticism as well as mechanism.

Still the question of how the armoring of the human a mal as the only animal species came about remains with , unsolved, overshadowing every theoretical and practica step in education, medicine, sociology, natural science, etc. N attempt is made here to solve this problem. It is too involved The concrete facts which possibly could provide an answer are buried in a much too distant past. Concrete reconstruction of this past is no longer possible.

What follows now is more than empty speculation, since it is based on present-day and abundant clinical experience. It is less than a practicable theory since it does not provide any better hold on the problem. However, it is interesting to follow a certain line of thought, to see where it is going to lead, and, finally, to reflect upon one's own relation to one's *ability to think* and to reason out such things as the reality of two cosmic orgone energy streams which by superimposition produce hurricanes which spin counterclockwise north and clockwise south of the equator. Thus, our curiosity is well justified.

The development of orgonomy was guided throughout by the logical integration of natural functioning:

First: It was functional reasoning about the layering of human character structure which led toward the deepest emotions confined in the armor.

Second: From the logical, functional peeling off of the armor layers, resulted the discovery of the deeply hidden orgastic anxiety and the orgastic convulsion.

Third: It was reasoning about the *trans*personal and *trans*-psychological nature of the orgasm function which disclosed its *bio-energetic* nature and the well-known fourbeat of the Life Formula: Tension—Charge—Discharge—Relaxation.

Fourth: It was functional reasoning again, more and more closely mirroring natural objective functions, which led from the Life Formula to the bions or energy vesicles and from here to the discovery of radiating bions: i.e., BIO-ENERGY.

Fifth: The same red thread of functional thinking led from the energy *within* living organisms to the same kind of energy *outside* in the atmosphere and from here further into the universe at large: COSMIC ORGONE ENERGY.

Sixth: Finally, it was again the orgasm function, abstracted into a generally valid natural principle, *superimposition*, which led toward the understanding of the ring of the aurora and from there to the characteristic spin of multi-armed hurricanes and galactic nebulae.

The reader may well be aware of the fact that such sequence could not possibly have been thought out arbitrarily. No human brain and no keen human phantasy could match this factual logic in abundance of phenomena and interconnections which yielded their secret to the natural observer who did the functional reasoning.

This consistency of thought with the chain of the increasingly numerous natural functions which revealed themselves, was no less amazing and at times even frightening to the

WILHELM REICH

observer who reasoned, than it must be to the reader of orgonomic literature covering a period of some thirty years. As the
process of functional reasoning unfolded more and more, the
observer not only worked out the method of this kind of functional reasoning, but he also *experienced most vividly his own
amazement at his own power of reasoning which was in such
perfect harmony with the natural events thus disclosed. The
function of reasoning itself*, as part of natural functioning, *came
to be a major problem.* And here are some of the thoughts about
the faculty of reasoning itself:

Before there was any life, there was the streaming of cosmic
orgone energy. When climatic conditions were sufficiently developed on the planet, life began to appear, most likely in the
form of primitive plasmatic flakes as reproduced in Experiment
XX. From these flakes, single-cell organisms developed over the
aeons. Now, the cosmic orgone energy not only was flowing in
the vast galactic spaces, but also in tiny bits of membranous
matter, caught within membranes and therefore flowing, still
in a spiraling fashion, within these membranes, following a
closed system of flow. We cannot assume that this little bit of
streaming protoplasm already had developed the faculty of
perceiving itself, though it already possessed the faculty of
reacting to outer and inner stimuli. It was excitable, in agreement with the excitability of the orgone energy which flows
without the confines of membranes.

*The confinement of a bit of cosmic orgone energy by and
within membranes was the first clear differentiation of life from
nonlife, of organismic from nonliving orgone energy.* This much
seems clear, even if it is as yet impossible to say much about
the Hows and Whys of this genetic differentiation.

A large number of years, unimaginable to human thinking,
must have passed, before this orgone energy, flowing within
membranes in closed paths like the blood in higher animals,
began to develop the faculty of perceiving its own flow, excitation, expansion in "pleasure," contraction in "anxiety." Thus,
the first beginnings of *self-perception* most likely ensued, fol-

lowing after a long evolutional interval the objective streaming of a physical energy within membranes.

We already have here *three* orgonotic streamings, integrated with each other, emerging from one another: The *cosmic flow*, the *confined flow within membranes*, and the *first perception of the flowing itself:* ORGONOTIC SENSATION. A worm or snail might well represent the stage of development where sensation was added to objective plasma streaming. This orgonotic sensation is most clearly expressed in the drive to superimposition in the sexual process. Convulsion and discharge of surplus energy are already formed. This state of affairs must have lasted again over an immense period of time until it reached the stage of the higher animals. In a deer or an elephant, objective streaming of energy and sensation of streaming are still united; there is probably as yet no contradiction, no blocking, no wonderment; only pleasure, anxiety and rage govern the bio-energetic scene.

Then man developed. At first, over long stretches of time, he was little more than an animal which already had instinctual judgment, with the FIRST ORGONOTIC SENSE of orientation in full swing. But there did not exist yet what we are used to calling *reasoned thinking*. This type of natural functioning must at some time have slowly developed from the exact, sure contact between nature *within* and nature *without* the orgonotic system. Whether or not the brain has anything to do with reasoned thinking, we do not know. The purposeful behavior of animals without a developed brain tells us that life does not require a fully developed brain to function properly. It is probable that reasoned thinking, in contradistinction to primitive, orgonotic reasoning as in all animals, somehow developed with stronger gyration of the brain; we must ask *what kind* of functioning forced the animal brain into a higher or more complicated form of existence. We generally assume that *functioning precedes and induces structural developments of organs*, and not the other way around. Whatever the answer to this riddle may turn out to be: Man slowly began to reason *beyond* his strong orgonotic contact and harmony with nature which heretofore had been entirely sufficient to keep him alive and to develop him further, even into a reasoning being. We know nothing and cannot know anything about those distant times when man began to think.

It is, however, obviously wrong to assume that thinking is a sharply distinguishing mark between animal and man. The transitions, to judge from natural processes in general, are always and everywhere slow, evolutionary, stretched over immense periods of time. In the process of this development, man must have begun to *reason about his own feelings of streamings,* about his *ability to perceive himself and to perceive at all.* To judge from the studies of the theories of knowledge, nothing can compare with man's amazement at his capacity to feel, to reason, to perceive himself, to think about himself and nature around him.

In thinking about his own being and functioning, man turned involuntarily against himself; not in a destructive fashion, but in a manner which may well have been the point of origin of his armoring, in the following way:

We know well from schizophrenic processes that an overstrained *perception of self-perception* necessarily induces a split in the unity of the organism. One part of the organism turns against the rest, as it were. The split may be slight and easily vanish again. It also may be strong and persistent. In the process of this *"depersonalization"* man perceives his streamings as an OBJECT OF ATTENTION and not quite as his own. The sensation of bodily streamings then appears, even if only in a passing manner, as alien, as coming somehow from beyond. Can we dare to see in this sharp experience of the Self the first step toward mystical, transcendental thinking? We cannot tell exactly, but the thought deserves consideration.

There is much good reason to assume that in such experiences of the Self *man somehow became frightened and for the first time in the history of his species began to armor against the inner fright and amazement.* Just as in the well-known fable, the milliped could not move a leg and became paralyzed when he was asked and started thinking about *which* leg he puts first and *which* second, it is quite possible that the *turning of reasoning toward itself induced the first emotional blocking in man.* It is impossible to say what perpetuated this blocking of emotions and with it the loss of organismic unity and "paradise." We know well the consequences of the blocking of emotional, involuntary activity: It immobilizes the organism and disturbs the integration of all biological functions. These consequences may well have been the same when man first turned his attention upon himself. From here onward everything follows by its own inner logic of life-*negative* design. (*Cf.* fig. 1.)

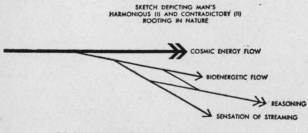

SKETCH DEPICTING MAN'S
HARMONIOUS (I) AND CONTRADICTORY (II)
ROOTING IN NATURE

COSMIC ENERGY FLOW

BIOENERGETIC FLOW

REASONING

SENSATION OF STREAMING

(I) MAN—ROOTED IN NATURE; CULTURE IN HARMONY WITH NATURE

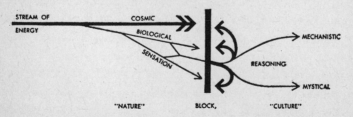

STREAM OF
ENERGY

COSMIC

BIOLOGICAL

SENSATION

MECHANISTIC

REASONING

MYSTICAL

"NATURE"   BLOCK,   "CULTURE"

(II) MAN—DEVIATING FROM NATURE "CULTURE" VERSUS "NATURE"

FIG. 1. SKETCH DEPICTING MAN'S HARMONIOUS (I) AND CONTRADICTORY (II) ROOTING IN NATURE

The conclusion following from these thoughts is clear: While turning against his own streaming in an attempt to understand it and himself, MAN FIRST BEGAN TO ARMOR AND THUS TO DEVIATE FROM NATURE. The first split into a *mystical* alienation from himself, i.e., his core, a mechanical order of existence instead of the organic, involuntary bio-energetic self-regulation followed with compulsive force. In the brief sentence, "Cogito, ergo sum," *(I think, therefore I am)* the conclusion of one's personal existence follows from the statement of the ability to think. The fright which overcomes man still in our time when he thinks about himself; the general reluctance to think at all; the whole function of repression of emotional functions of the Self; the powerful force with which man resists knowledge about himself; the fact that for millennia he investigated the stars but not the inside of his own organism; the panic that grips the witness of orgonomic investigations at the core of man's existence; the fervent ardor with which every religion defends the unreachability and unknowability of God, which clearly represents nature *within* man, and many other facts speak a clear language regarding the terror which is connected with the deep experience of the Self. To stand aside, entirely logical and drily "intellectual," and observe your own inner functioning amounts to a splitting of the unitary system which only a very few seem to bear without deep upset. And the few who, far from being frightened, enjoy the submerging in their own Selfs are the great artists, poets, scientists, and philosophers. Are they, now, exceptions from the rule or the original rule itself?

There are, at present, only very few who, far from being frightened, submerge in their innermost Selfs and create from the depth of their free-flowing contact with nature within and without; in higher, abstract mathematics no less than in poetry or music.

Are now these creative workers, artists, inventors, discoverers, composers, engineers, philosophers, social reformers, etc., exceptions from the rule of the average; or is the majority of the human species the exception in the sense that it deviated from the oneness with the natural orgone energy flow, whereas the few did not. On the answer of this question—this is perfectly clear—depends the basic answer to the misery of man. For, if the multitude represents the rule of the nature of things, and the few are the exceptions from the "normal," as so many want us to believe, then there is no hope of ever overcoming the split in the cultural setup, the wars which emerge from this split, the splitting of character structures, the hate and universal murder. Then, thus runs the conclusion, all the misery is a natural manifestation of the given, unalterable order of things.

If, on the other hand, *the majority is the exception from the general run of things*, and the few creators are in agreement with this general rule, then things would look better. It would become possible, by the most strenuous effort ever made in the history of man, to adjust the majority to the flow of natural processes. Then, if our exposition of the armoring blocking is correct, man could return home to nature; and what appears today as exceptional in a very few could become the rule for all.

It will be exactly those who suffered most from the deviation who will most strenuously object to the second possibility.

Here we encounter the possible effect of the discovery of the cosmic orgone energy upon further human development in its fullest consequence. The discovery of the bio-energy is, as said before, here to stay. It will be opposed, most severely, by exactly those who lost contact with nature to the greatest extent. They will object, malign the discovery of life energy in the future as they have done for years in the past; they will defame the discoverer and the workers in the field of orgonomy; they will not shy away from any measure to kill the discovery, no matter how devilish the means of killing may be; they will shy away only from *one* thing: from looking into microscopes or from doing any kind of observation which confirms the existence of an all-pervading cosmic energy and its variant, the bio-energy.

In this process of fighting the discovery of the cosmic orgone energy, a slow, but most effective process of *softening up* of the rigidities in the armored character structures will inevitably take place. The hardest, the toughest and most cruel character structure will be forced to *make contact with the basic problem of the existence of a Life Energy*, and, thus, for the first time in the history of man, the rigidity in the human structure will begin to crack, to soften, to yield, to cry, to worry, to free life, even if, to begin with, in a hostile, murderous manner. The need for medical help by medical orgonomists will do its share in the softening-up process.

It is to be expected, furthermore, that as the public discussions of the orgone energy functions will spread over ever-widening areas of the globe, other human problems of existence will come into flux, too; they will be subjected to a new type of scrutiny, and many gaps in understanding things will be filled by what is already known about the basic cosmic force. The Catholic will have to revise his attitude toward the natural genitality of children and grownups; he will learn to distinguish pornography ("lust") from the natural embrace ("happiness," "body"); he already has begun to change his viewpoint with regard to the sexuality of children. Government officials will learn through sharp experiences in dangerous situations that man is far more than a *zoon politician*, that he is an animal with emotions which determine the course of history, with *irrational* emotions to boot, which messed up the world in the 20th century. One could even imagine that such rigid politicians as the Russian dictators would feel "weakness" toward human affairs creep up in their frozen bodies. Religion will most probably revise its basic foundations as to the sharp antithesis of man and nature, and it will rediscover the real truth which had been proclaimed with little factual knowledge or effect by most founders of religion all down the line of history. WORK will enter the social scene as the toughest and most efficient combatant of political irrationalism. Man will learn *to work for his life* and love and children and friends, and not merely babble about the politics of the day, forced upon him by non-working parasites of society.

In this manner, the blocking of natural contacts with the Self and the surrounding world will slowly, maybe as long as over several centuries, diminish and finally, as the prevention of the armoring in the newborn generations succeeds, will completely vanish from the surface of this earth.

This is no prophecy. Man, and not fate, is burdened with the full responsibility for the outcome of this process.

APPENDIX

1. RESPONSE

February 25th, 1954

The Hon. Judge Clifford
Federal Court House
Portland, Maine
Dear Judge Clifford:

I am taking the liberty of transmitting to you my "Response" to the complaint filed by the Food and Drug Administration regarding the Orgone Energy Accumulator. My "Response" summarizes my standpoint as a natural scientist who deals wi' matters of basic natural law. It is not in my hands to judge ..e legal aspects of the matter.

My factual position in the case as well as in the world of science of today does not permit me to enter the case against the Food and Drug Administration, since such action would, in my mind, imply admission of the authority of this special branch of the government to pass judgment on primordial, pre-atomic cosmic orgone energy.

I, therefore, rest the case in full confidence in your hands.

Sincerely yours,

/s/ Wilhelm Reich, M.D.
Wilhelm Reich, M.D.

From *History of the Discovery of the Life Energy*, Documentary Supplement No. 3, A-XII-EP, 1954.

Regarding the Request of the Food and Drug Administration (FDA) to Enjoin the Natural Scientific Activities of Wilhelm Reich, M.D.

In order to clarify the *factual* as well as the *legal* situation concerning the complaint, we must, from the very beginning, distinguish concrete *facts* from *legal procedure* to do justice to the facts.

Technically, legally the US Government has filed suit against the natural scientific work of Wilhelm Reich.

Factually, the FDA is NOT "The US Government." It is merely one of its administrative agencies dealing with Foods, Drugs and Cosmetics. It is not empowered to deal with *Basic Natural Law*.

ORGONOMY (see "Bibliography on the History of Orgonomy") is a branch of BASIC NATURAL SCIENCE. Its central object of research is elucidation of the Basic Natural Law.

Now, in order to bring into line the legal procedure with the above-mentioned facts, the following is submitted:

The common law structure of the United States rests originally on Natural Law. This Natural Law has heretofore been interpreted in various ways of thinking, metaphysically, religiously, mechanistically. It has never concretely and scientifically, been subjected to natural scientific inquiry based upon a discovery which encompasses the very roots of existence.

The concept of Natural Law as the foundation of a secure way of life, must firmly rest upon the practical concrete functions of LIFE itself. In consequence, a correct life-positive interpretation of Natural Law, the basis of common law, depends on the *factual* elucidation of what Life actually is, how it works, what are its basic functional manifestations. From this basic premise derive the claims of natural scientists to a free, unmolested, unimpeded, natural scientific activity in general and in the exploration of the Life Energy in particular.

The complaint of the FDA is factually intimately interconnected with a basic social issue which, at present, is reverberating in the lives of all of us here and abroad.

Abraham Lincoln once said: "What I do say is that no man is good enough to govern another man without that other's consent. I say this is a leading principle, the sheet anchor of American republicanism."

At this point, I could easily declare "I refuse to be governed in my basic natural research activities by the Food and Drug Administration." But exactly here, in this constitutional right of mine, the basic confusion in the interpretation of Natural and Common Law becomes apparent.

There are conspirators around whose aim it is to destroy human happiness and self-government. Is now the right of the conspirator to ravage humanity the same as my right to free, unimpeded inquiry?

It obviously is NOT THE SAME THING. I shall not try to answer this basic dilemma of American society at the present. I shall only open an approach to this legal and factual dilemma. It has a lot to do with the position of the complainant, trying to enjoin the experimental and theoretical functions of Life in its emotional, educational, social, economic, intellectual and medical implications.

According to natural, and in consequence, American Common Law, no one, no matter who he is, has the power or legal right to enjoin:

The study and observation of natural phenomena including Life within and without man;

The communication to others of knowledge of these natural phenomena so rich in the manifestations of an existent, concrete, cosmic Life Energy;

The stir to mate in all living beings, including our maturing adolescents;

The emergence of abstractions and final mathematical formulae concerning the natural life force in the universe, and the right to their dissemination among one's fellow men;

The handling, use and distribution of instruments of basic research in any field, medical, educational, preventive, physical, biological, and in fields which emerge from such basic activities and which, resting on such principles, must by all means remain free.

Attempts such as branding activities and instruments of such kind as "adulterated," in other words as fraud, only characterizes the narrowness of the horizon of the complaint.

No man-made law ever, no matter whether derived from the past or projected into a distant, unforeseeable future, can or should ever be empowered to claim that it is greater than the Natural Law from which it stems and to which it must inevitably return in the eternal rhythm of creation and decline of all things natural. This is valid, no matter whether we speak in terms such as "God," "Natural Law," "Cosmic Primordial Force," "Ether" or "Cosmic Orgone Energy."

The present critical state of international human affairs requires security and safety from nuisance interferences with efforts toward full, honest, determined clarification of man's relationship to nature within and without himself; in other words, his relationship to the Law of Nature. It is not permissible, either morally, legally or factually to force a natural scientist to expose his scientific results and methods of basic research in court. This point is accentuated in a world crisis where biopathic men hold in their hands power over ruined, destitute multitudes.

To appear in court as a *"defendant"* in matters of basic natural research would in itself appear, to say the least, extraordinary. It would require disclosure of evidence in support of the position of the discovery of the Life Energy. Such disclosure, however, would invoke untold complications, and *possibly national disaster*.

Proof of this can be submitted at any time only to a duly *authorized* personality of the US Government in a high, responsible position.

Scientific matters cannot possibly ever be decided upon in court. They can only be clarified by prolonged, faithful bona fide observations in friendly exchange of opinion, never by litigation. The sole purpose of the complainant is to entangle orgonomic basic research in endless, costly legal procedures a la Panmunjon, which will accomplish exactly NOTHING rational or useful to human society.

Inquiry in the realm of Basic Natural Law is *outside the judicial domain*, of this, or ANY OTHER KIND OF SOCIAL ADMINISTRATION ANYWHERE ON THIS GLOBE, IN ANY LAND, NATION OR REGION.

Man's right to know, to learn, to inquire, to make bona fide errors, to investigate human emotions must, by all means, be safe, if the word FREEDOM should ever be more than an empty political slogan.

If painstakingly elaborated and published scientific findings over a period of 30 years could not convince this administration, or will not be able to convince any other social administration of the true nature of the discovery of the Life Energy, no litigation in any court anywhere will ever help to do so.

I, therefore, submit, in the name of truth and justice, that I shall not appear in court as the "defendant" against a plaintiff who by his mere complaint already has shown his ignorance in matters of natural science. I do so at the risk of being, by mistake, fully enjoined in all my activities. Such an injunction would mean practically exactly nothing at all. My discovery of the Life Energy is today widely known nearly all over the globe, in hundreds of institutions, whether acclaimed or cursed. It can no longer be stopped by anyone, no matter what happens to me.

Orgone Energy Accumulators, the *"devices"* designed to concentrate cosmic Orgone Energy, and thus to make it available to further research in medicine, biology and physics, are being built today in many lands, without my knowledge and consent, and even without any royalty payments.

On the basis of these considerations, I submit that the case against Orgonomy be taken out of court completely.

WILHELM REICH, *M.D.*
Chairman of Basic Research
OF THE WILHELM REICH FOUNDATION

Date: February 22, 1954

2. DECREE OF INJUNCTION

CIVIL ACTION No. 1056

Plaintiff having filed a Complaint for Injunction herein to enjoin the defendants and others from further alleged violations of the Federal Food, Drug, and Cosmetic Act; and each defendant having been duly served, on February 10, 1954, with a summons and copy of the Complaint; and no defendant having appeared or answered in person or by representative, although the time therefore has expired; and each defendant having been duly served, on February 26, 1954, with a copy of Requests for Admissions; and no defendant having served any answer to said Requests, although the time therefor has expired; and the default of each defendant having been entered herein; and it appearing that the defendants, unless enjoined therefrom, will continue to introduce or cause to be introduced or delivered, or cause to be delivered into interstate commerce orgone energy accumulators, devices within the meaning of the Federal Food, Drug, and Cosmetic Act, 21 U. S. C. 301 et seq, which are misbranded and adulterated, and in violation of 21 U. S. C. 331 (a) and (k); and the Court having been fully advised in the premises;

IT IS HEREBY ORDERED, ADJUDGED, AND DE-CREED that the defendants, THE WILHELM REICH

From the court record, U.S. Court of Appeals for the First Circuit, *Wilhelm Reich, et. al., v. U.S.A.*

FOUNDATION, WILHELM REICH, and ILSE OLLEN-DORFF and each and all of their officers, agents, servants, employees, attorneys, all corporations, associations, and organizations, and all persons in active concert or participation with them or any of them, be, and they hereby are, perpetually enjoined and restrained from doing any of the following acts, directly or indirectly, in violation of Sections 301(a) or 301(k) of the Federal Food, Drug, and Cosmetic Act (21 U. S. C. C. 331(a) or (k)) with respect to any orgone energy accumulator device, in any style or model, any and all accessories, components or parts thereof, or any similar device, in any style or model, and any device purported or represented to collect and accumulate the alleged orgone energy:

(1) Introducing or causing to be introduced or delivering or causing to be delivered for introduction into interstate commerce any such article of device which is:

(a) Misbranded within the meaning of Section 502(a) of the Act (21 U. S. C. 352(a)) by reason of any representation or suggestion in its labeling which conveys the impression that such article, in any style or model, is an outstanding therapeutic agent, is a preventive of and beneficial for use in any disease or disease condition, is effective in the cure, mitigation, treatment, and prevention of any disease, symptom, or condition; or

(b) Misbranded within the meaning of Section 502 (2) of the Act (21 U. S. C. 352(a)) by reason of any representation or suggestion in its labeling which conveys the impression that the alleged orgone energy exists; or

(c) Misbranded within the meaning of Section 502(a) of the Act (21 U. S. C. 352(a)) by reason of any photographic representation or suggestion with a caption, or otherwise, which conveys the impression that such is an actual photograph depicting the alleged orgone energy or an alleged excited orgone energy field; or

(d) Misbranded within the meaning of Section 502(a) of the Act (21 U. S. C. 352(a)) by reason of any other false or misleading representation or suggestion; or

(e) Adulterated within the meaning of Section 501(c) of the Act (21 U. S. C. 351(c)) in that (1) its strength differs from or its quality falls below that which it purports or is represented to possess or (2) it purports to collect from the atmosphere and accumulate in said device the alleged orgone energy; or

(2) Doing any act or causing any act to be done with respect to any orgone energy accumulator device while such device is held for sale (including rental, or any other disposition) after shipment in interstate commerce which results in said device becoming misbranded or adulterated in any respect; and

IT IS FURTHER ORDERED:

(1) That all orgone energy accumulator devices, and their labeling, which were shipped in interstate commerce and which (a) are on a rental basis, or (b) otherwise owned or controlled by any one of the defendants, or by the defendants, be recalled by the defendants to their place of business at Rangeley, Maine; and

(2) That the devices referred to in (1) immediately above, and their parts, be destroyed by the defendants or, they may be dismantled and the materials from which they were made salvaged after dismantling; and

(3) That the labeling referred to in paragraph (1), just above, except those items for which a specific purchase price was paid by their owners, be destroyed by the defendants; and

(4) That all parts or portions of orgone accumulator devices shipped in interstate commerce and returned to Rangeley, Maine, or elsewhere, and awaiting repair or reshipment be destroyed by the defendants, or, they may be dismantled and the materials from which they were made salvaged after dismantling; and

(5) That all copies of the following items of written, printed, or graphic matter, and their covers, if any, which items have constituted labeling of the article of device, and which contain statements and representations pertaining to the existence of orgone energy, its collection by, and accumulation in, orgone energy accumulators, and the use of such alleged orgone energy by employing said accumulators in the cure, mitigation, treatment, and prevention of disease, symptoms and conditions:

The Discovery of the Orgone by Wilhelm Reich
    Vol I—The Function of the Orgasm
    Vol II—The Cancer Biopathy
The Sexual Revolution by Wilhelm Reich
Ether, God and Devil by Wilhelm Reich
Cosmic Superimposition by Wilhelm Reich
Listen, Little Man by Wilhelm Reich
The Mass Psychology of Fascism by Wilhelm Reich
Character Analysis by Wilhelm Reich
The Murder of Christ by Wilhelm Reich
People in Trouble by Wilhelm Reich

shall be withheld by the defendants and not again employed as labeling; in the event, however, such statements and representations, and any other allied material, are deleted, such publications may be used by the defendants; and

(6) That all written, printed, and graphic matter containing instructions for the use of any orgone energy accumulator device, instructions for the assembly thereof, all printed, and other announcements and order blanks for the items listed in the paragraph immediately above, all documents, bulletins, pamphlets, journals, and booklets entitled in part, as follows: CATALOGUE SHEET, PHYSICIAN'S REPORT, APPLICATION FOR THE USE OF THE ORGONE ENERGY ACCUMULATOR, ADDITIONAL INFORMATION REGARDING SOFT ORGONE IRRADIATION, ORGONE ENERGY ACCUMULATOR ITS SCIENTIFIC AND MEDICAL USE, ORGONE ENERGY BULLETIN, ORGONE ENERGY EMERGENCY BULLETIN, INTERNATIONAL JOURNAL OF SEX-ECONOMY AND ORGONE RESEARCH, INTERNATIONALE ZEITSCHRUFT FUR ORGONOMIE, EMOTIONAL PLAGUE VERSUS ORGONE BIOPHYSICS, ANNALS OF THE ORGONE INSTITUTE, and ORANUR EXPERIMENT, but not limited to those enumerated, shall be destroyed; and

(7) That the directives and provisions contained in paragraphs (1) to (6) inclusive, above, shall be performed under the supervision of employees of the Food and Drug Administration, authorized representatives of the Secretary of Health, Education and Welfare; and

(8) That for the purposes of supervision and securing com-

pliance with this decree the defendants shall permit said employees of the Food and Drug Administration, at reasonable times, to have access to and to copy from, all books, ledgers, accounts, correspondence, memoranda, and other records and documents in the possession or under the control of said defendants, including all affiliated persons, corporations, associations, and organizations, at Rangeley, Maine, or elsewhere, relating to any matters contained in this decree. Any such authorized representative of the Secretary shall be permitted to interview officers or employees of any defendant, or any affiliate, regarding any such matters subject to the reasonable convenience of any of said officers or employees of said defendants, or affiliates, but without restraint or interference from any one of said defendants; and

(9) That the defendants refrain from, either directly or indirectly, in violation of said Act, disseminating information pertaining to the assembly, construction, or composition of orgone energy accumulator devices to be employed for therapeutic or prophylactic uses by man or for other animals.

/s/ John D. Clifford, Jr.
United States District Judge
for the District of Maine.

March 19, 1954.
2:45 P.M.

A true copy of original filed at 2:45 P.M. on March 19, 1954.
ATTEST:

/s/ Morris Cox
Clerk, United States District Court

[The works of Wilhelm Reich listed above in paragraph 5 have been withheld from the general public. The material listed in paragraph 6, including his books and other publications, was burned under the supervision of agents of the Food and Drug Administration: This occurred on August 23, 1956, and, again, as recently as March 17, 1960. Ed.]

3. BIBLIOGRAPHY

(This Bibliography, with slight changes, is reprinted from *Bibliography on Orgonomy*, Orgone Institute Press, Rangeley, Maine, 1953.)

BOOKS BY WILHELM REICH

1. DER TRIEBHAFTE CHARAKTER, Internationaler Psychoanalytischer Verlag, 1925.
2. DIE FUNKTION DES ORGASMUS, Internationaler Psychoanalytischer Verlag, 1927. English excerpts appeared in *International Journal of Psychoanalysis*, 1930.
3. DIALEKTISCHER MATERIALISMUS UND PSYCHOANALYSE, 1st ed., "Unter dem banner des Marxismus," German and Russian, 1929. 2nd ed., Sexpol Verlag, 1934. Trans. Serbian.
4. SEXUALERREGUNG UND SEXUALBEFRIEDIGUNG, Muenster Verlag, Vienna, 1929. Three editions (10,000 copies). Trans. Hungarian, 1930.
5. GESCHLECHTSREIFE, ENTHALTSAMKEIT, EHEMORAL, Muenster Verlag, Vienna, 1930.
6a. DIE SEXUALITAET IM KULTURKAMPF, Sexpol Verlag, 1936.
6b. LA CRISE SEXUALLE, Editions sociales internationales, Paris, 1934.
6c. SEXUALITEIT EN NIEUWE KULTUR, Uitgeverij voor Sociale Psychologie, Rotterdam, 1939.
6d. THE SEXUAL REVOLUTION, Orgone Institute Press, 1945. Three editions. Peter Nevill, Vision Press, London, 1952. Trans. by Theodore P. Wolfe, M.D.
7a. DER SEXUALLE KAMPF DER JUGEND,† Verlag fuer Sexualpolitik, Berlin, 1932.
7b. SEXUALNI BOJ MLÀDĚZE, Knihovna leve fronty, Prague, 1933. Trans. Hungarian.

---

† Political aspects outdated and surpassed, therefore invalid. The clinical and theoretical formulations remained valid.

7c. Der Sexuelle Kampf der Jugend (1948), Freiheitlich-So-zialistische Schriftenreihe, Zuerich-Amsterdam, 52 pp. (mimeo., 1948.) Published for mere political reasons without any mental hygiene precautions. Publishers were rebuffed by WR.

8. Der Einbruch der Sexualmoral, Verlag fuer Sexualpolitik, Berlin, 1932. 2nd ed., Sexpol Verlag, Oslo, 1935. English in manuscript.

9a. Charakteranalyse, 1st ed., Sexpol Verlag, 1933. Trans. Spanish, mimeo. edition.

9b. Character Analysis, 2nd ed., Orgone Institute Press, 1945. 3rd ed., enlarged, Orgone Institute Press, 1949. 4th ed., Nevill, Vision, London, 1950. 5th ed., Vision, London, 1958.* All editions trans. by Theodore P. Wolfe, M.D.

9c. Analisis del Caracter, Editorial Paidos, Buenos Aires, 1957.*

10a. Massenpsychologie des Faschismus, 1st ed., Sexpol Verlag, 1933. 2nd ed., Sexpol Verlag, 1934.

10b. Mass Psychology of Fascism, 3rd ed., Orgone Institute Press, 1946. Trans. by Theodore P. Wolfe, M.D. Extensive Excerpts in "Les Primaires," France.

11. Psychischer Kontakt und Vegetative Stroemung, Sexpol Verlag, 1937. (DO. I.)

12. Experimentelle Ergebnisse Ueber die Elektrische Funktion von Sexualitaet und Angst, Sexpol Verlag, 1937. English in manuscript.

13. Orgasmusreflex, Muskelhaltung und Koerperausdruck, Sexpol Verlag, 1937. (DO. I.)

14. Die Bione, Sexpol Verlag, 1938.

15a. Bion Experiments on the Cancer Problem, Sexpol Verlag, 1939.

15b. Drei Versuche am Statischen Elektroskop, Sexpol Verlag, 1939. *OEB*, III, 3 (English).

16a. The Discovery of the Orgone: Vol. I, The Function of the Orgasm, 1st. ed., Orgone Institute Press, New York, 1942. 2nd ed., Orgone Institute Press, 1948. Trans. by Theodore P. Wolfe, M.D.

---

* Works known to be available at this time.

16b. DET LEVENDE, Seksualoekonomiske Meddelelser, No. 3, Copen-
    hagen, 1942.

16c. LA FONCTION DE L'ORGASME, L'Arche, Paris, 1952. (German in
    original manuscript.)*

16d. LA FUNCION DEL ORGASMO, Editorial Paidos, Buenos Aires,
    1955.*

17. THE DISCOVERY OF THE ORGONE: Vol. II, THE CANCER BIO-
    PATHY, Orgone Institute Press, New York, 1948. Trans. by
    Theodore P. Wolfe, M.D.

18. LISTEN, LITTLE MAN! Orgone Institute Press, New York, 1948.
    Trans. by Theodore P. Wolfe, M.D.

19. ETHER, GOD AND DEVIL, Orgone Institute Press, Rangeley,
    Maine, 1951. Chaps. I-IV trans. by Myron R. Sharaf.

20. THE ORGONE ENERGY ACCUMULATOR, Orgone Institute Press,
    Rangeley, Maine, 1951.

21. COSMIC SUPERIMPOSITION, Orgone Institute Press, Rangeley,
    Maine, 1951.

22. THE ORANUR EXPERIMENT, First Report (1947-1951), Orgone
    Institute Press, Rangeley, Maine, 1951.

23. ARBEITSDEMOKRATIE, Sexpol Verlag, 1937. Politisch-Psychol.
    Schriftenreihe, No. 4.

24. WEITERE PROBLEME DER ARBEITSDEMOKRATIE, Sexpol Verlag,
    1941. Politisch-Psychol. Schriftenreihe, No. 5.

25. THE EMOTIONAL PLAGUE OF MANKIND: Vol. I, THE MURDER OF
    CHRIST; Vol. II, PEOPLE IN TROUBLE, Orgone Institute Press,
    Rangeley, Maine, 1953.

26. CONTACT WITH SPACE, Oranur Second Report (1951-1956),
    Core Pilot Press, New York, 1957.

ARTICLES ON ORGONOMY

by WILHELM REICH

A list of abbreviations appears at the end of the bibliography.

1.	"Ueber einen Fall von Durchbruch der Inzestschranke"	ZSW, 1920, VII.
2.	"Triebbegriffe von Forel bis Jung"	ZSW, 1921.
3.	"Der Koitus und die Geschlechter"	ZSW, 1921.
4.	"Ueber Spezifitaet der Onanieformen"	IZP, VIII, 1922.

5. "Zur Triebenergetik" — ZSW, 1923. English in manuscript.

6. "Kindliche Tagtraeume einer spaeteren Zwangsneurose" — IZP, 1923 (?).

7. "Ueber Genitalitaet" — IZP, IX, 1923.

8. "Der Tic als Onanieequivalent" — ZSW, 1924.

9. "Die therapeutische Bedeutung der Genitallibido" — IZP, X, 1924.

10. "Die Rolle der Genitalitaet in der Neurosentherapie" — ZAP, I, 1925.

11a. "Eine hysterische Psychose in statu nascendi" — IZP, XI, 1925.

11b. "Hysterical psychosis in statu nascendi" — IZP (London), VIII, 1927 (pp. 159-173).

12. "Weitere Bemerkungen ueber die therapeutische Bedeutung der Genitallibido" — IZP, XI, 1925.

13a. "Ueber die Quellen der neurotischen Angst" — IZP, XII, 1926.

13b. "The sources of neurotic anxiety" — IZP (London), VII, 1926. Published in honor of Freud's birthday.

14. "Ueber die chronische hypochondrische Neurasthenie mit genitaler Asthenie" — IZP, XII, 1926.

15. "Eltern als Erzieher" — ZPP, Heft 3, 1926.
"Eltern als Erzieher," continued — ZPP, Heft 7, 8, 9, 1927.

16. "Zur Technik der Deutung und der Widerstandsanalyse" — IZP, XIII, 1927, (CA)

17a. "Ueber Charakteranalyse" — IZP, XIV, 1928 (CA).

17b. "On the Technique of Character Analysis" — PR, 1948.

18a. "Onanie im Kindesalter" — ZPP, Heft 4, 5, 6, 1928.

18b. "About genital selfsatisfaction in children" — OEB, II, 2, 1950.

19. "Wohin fuehrt die Nackterziehung" — ZPP, Heft 2, 3, 1928 (SR).

20a. "Der genitale und der neurotische Charakter" — IZP, XV, 1929 (CA).

20b. "The Genital Character and the Neurotic Character" — PR, 1948.

21a. "Ueber kindliche Phobie und Charakterbildung" — IZP, XVI, 1930 (CA).

21b. "Infantile Phobia and Character Formation" — PR, 1948.

22. "Sexualnot und Sexualreform"   Verhandlung der *WLSR*,
                                                  IV, Congress, Vienna,
                                                  1930.

23. "Ueber den epileptischen Anfall"   *IZP*, XVII, 1931.
                                                  IZP, London, 1932 (?).
                                                  Spanish in manuscript.

24. "Die charakterologische Ueberwindung   *IZP*, XVII, 1931, (CA).
     des Oedipuskomplexes"

25a. "Der masochistische Charakter"   *IZP*, XVIII, 1932 (CA).

25b. "The masochistic Character"   *IJSO*, III, 1944.

26. "Der Orgasmus als elektrophysiologische   *ZPS*, I, 1934 (29-43).
     Entladung"

27. "Der Urgegensatz des vegetativen Lebens"   *ZPS*, I, 1934
                                                  (125-142, 207-225).
                                                  English in manuscript.

28. "Zur Anwendung der Psychoanalyse in der   *ZPS*, I, 1934 (4-16).
     Geschichtsforschung"

29. "Ein Widerspruch der Freud'schen Ver-   *ZPS*, I, 1934 (115-125).
     draengungslehre"

30. "Roheim's 'Psychoanalyse primitiver Kul-   *ZPS*, I, 1934 (169-195).
     turen' "

31. "Was ist Klassenbewusstsein?"   *ZPS*, I, 1934 (16-29)
                                                  (90-107, 226-255).

32. "Ueberblick ueber das Forschungsgebiet   *ZPS*, II, 1935 (5-13).
     der Sexualoekonomie"

33. "Zur massenpsychologischen Wirkung des   *ZPS*, II, 1935 (26-31).
     Kriegsfilms"

34. "Die Funktion der 'objektiven Wertwelt' "   *ZPS*, II, 1935 (32-43).

35. "Unterschiede zwischen liberalistischer   *ZPS*, II, 1935 (99-103).
     Sexualreform und revolutionaerer Sex-
     ualpolitik"

36. "Wie wirkt Streicher's sadistische Porno-   *ZPS*, II, 1935 (129-133).
     graphie?"

37. "Die Bremsung der Sexualrevolution in der   *ZPS*, II, 1935 (145-166).
     USSR"   (SR).

38. "Der Kulturpolitische Standpunkt der Sex-   *ZPS*, III, 1936
     pol"   (1-7), (SR).

39. "Ein Briefwechsel ueber Dialektischen   *ZPS*, III, 1936 (8-22).
     Materialismus"

40. "Die Sexpol als Organisation der dia-   *ZPS*, III, 1936 (22-24).
     lektisch-materialistischen Psychologie"

41. "Fortpflanzung—eine Funktion der Sex-   *ZPS*, III, 1936 (24-31).
     ualitaet"

42. "Au secours de la famille" — ZPS, III, 1936 (38-43).

43a. "Gespraech mit einer vernuenftigen Mutter" — ZPS, III, 1936 (52-61).

43b. "A Talk with a sensible Mother" — IJSO, I, 1942 (11-17).

44a. "Charakter und Gesellschaft" — ZPS, III, 1936.

44b. "Character and Society" — IJSO, I, 1942.

45. "Der Film 'The Shape of Things to come'" — ZPS, IV, 1937 (12-19).

46. "Einige aktuelle Fragen der zweiten Front" — ZPS, IV, 1937 (1-12).

47a. "Der Orgasmusreflex" — ZPS, IV, 1937 (76-88) (DO I).

47b. "The Orgasm Reflex" — IJSO, I, 1942.

48. "Der dialektische Materialismus in der Lebensforschung. Bericht ueber die Bion Versuche" — ZPS, IV, 1937 (137-148).

49. "Dialektisch-materialistische Facharbeiter contra geistige Irrlichter der sozialistischen Bewegung" — ZPS, IV, 1937 (149-161).

50. "Communication to the French Academie des Sciences on Bion Experiment VI" — January 1937, incl. in Die Bione, Chap. IV, 1938.

51. "Die drei Grundelemente des religioesen Gefuehls" — ZPS, V, 1938 (7-13) (MPF).

52. "About the History and the Activities of our Institute" — IJSO, I, 1942.

53. "Biophysical Functionalism and Mechanistic Natural Science" — IJSO, I, 1942.

54a. "The Discovery of the Orgone" — IJSO, I, 1942 (DO II).

54b. "Die Entdeckung des Orgons" — IZO, 1/2, April 1951. IZO, 1/3, Febr. 1952.

55a. "The Carcinomatous Shrinking Biopathy" — IJSO, I, 1942 (DO II).

55b. "Die Krebsschrumpfungs-Biopathie" — IZO, 1/3, Febr. 1952.

56. "The Natural Organization of Protozoa from Orgone Energy Vesicles" — IJSO, I, 1942, (DO II).

57. "Experimental Orgone Therapy of the Cancer Biopathy" — IJSO, II, 1943 (DO II).

58. "Give Responsibility to Vitally Necessary Work" — IJSO, II, 1943, (MPF).

59. "The Biological Miscalculation in the Human Struggle for Freedom" — IJSO, II, 1943, (MPF).

60. "Work Democracy versus Politics" — IJSO, II, 1943, (MPF).

61. "Thermical and Electroscopical Orgo-   *IJSO*, III, 1944 (DO II).
     nometry"

62. "Orgonotic Pulsation. Talks with an Elec-   *IJSO*, III, 1944.
     tro Physicist"

63. "The 'Living Productive Power, Working   *IJSO*, III, 1944.
     Power' of Marx"   Incl. in *People in Trouble*.

64. "Anorgonia in the Carcinomatous Shrink-   *IJSO*, IV, 1945 (DO II).
     ing Biopathy"

65. "Some Mechanisms of the Emotional   IJSO, IV, 1945
     Plague"   (CA, 1949).

66. "Orgone Biophysics, Mechanistic Science,   *IJSO*, IV, 1945.
     and 'Atomic Energy'"

67. "Experimental Demonstration of the Prac-   *IJSO*, IV, 1945 (DO II).
     tical Orgone Energy"

68. "The Development of the Authoritarian   *IJSO*, IV, 1945 (MPF).
     State Apparatus from Rational Social
     Relationships"

69. "Work Democracy in Action"   *AOI*, I, 1947.

70. "Searchlight Phenomena in the Orgone   *OEB*, I, 1949.
     Energy Envelope of the Earth"

71a. "A Motor Force in Orgone Energy"   *OEB*, I, 1949.

71b. "Eine motorische Kraft in der Orgon En-   *IZO*, I/1, April 1950.
     ergie"

72. "An X-Ray Photograph of the Excited   *OEB*, I, 2, 1949
     Orgone Energy Field of the Palms"

73. "Further Physical Characteristics of Vacor   *OEB*, I, 3, 1949.
     Lumination"

74. "Public Responsibility in the Early Diag-   *OEB*, I, 3, 1949.
     nosis of Cancer"

75. "A Dilemma in Social Self-Government"   *OEB*, I, 3, 1949.

76. "Cosmic Orgone Energy and 'Ether'"   *OEB*, I, 4, 1949. (EGD)

77a. "Orgonomic Functionalism" Part II   *OEB*, II, 1, 1950.

77b. "Orgonomic Functionalism" continued   *OEB*, II, 2, 1950.

77c. "Orgonomic Functionalism" continued   *OEB*, II, 3, 1950.

78. "Orgonomic and Chemical Cancer Re-   *OEB*, II, 3, 1950.
     search"

79. "Orgonomy 1935-1950 (I)"   *OEB*, II, 3, 1950.

80. "Orgonometric Equations"

80a. I. General Form   *OEB*, II, 4, 1950.

80b. II. Complete Orgonometric Equations   *OEB*, III, 1, 1951.

81. "Meteorological Functions in Orgone Charged Vacuum Tubes" *OEB*, II, 4, 1950.

82. "Children of the Future"—First Report on the Orgonomic Infant Research Center *OEB*, II, 4, 1950.

83. "The Orgone Energy Observatory (1948)" *OEB*, II, 4, 1950.

84. "A 'Control' of Reich's Cancert Experiments" *OEB*, II, 4, 1950.

85. "The Orgonomic Anti-Nuclear Radiation Project (ORANUR)" *OEEB*, No. 1, Dec. 1950.

86. " 'Cancer Cells' in Experiment XX" *OEB*, III, 1, 1951.

87. "The Storm of November 25th and 26th, 1950" *OEB*, III, 2, 1951.

88. "The Leukemia Problem: Approach" *OEB*, III, 2, 1951.

89. "Armoring in a Newborn Infant" *OEB*, III, 3, 1951.

90. "Dowsing as an Object of Orgonomic Research" *OEB*, III, 3, 1951.

91. "Wilhelm Reich on the Road to Biogenesis" (1935-1939) *OEB*, III, 3, 1951.

92. "Orgonomic Thinking in Medicine" *OEB*, IV, 1, 1952.

93. "An Experiment in Social Administration" *OEB*, IV, 3, 1952.

94. "Truth Versus Modju" *OEB*, IV, 3, 1952.

95. "DOR Removal and Cloud-Busting" *OEB*, IV, 4, 1952.

96. "Orgonomic Functionalism, Part II" continued *OEB*, IV, 4, 1952.

ABBREVIATIONS

AOI   Annals of the Orgone Institute

CA   Included in *Character-Analysis*

DO I   Included in *The Function of the Orgasm*

DO II   Included in *The Cancer Biopathy*

EGD   Included in *Ether, God and Devil*

IJSO   International Journal for Sex-Economy and Orgone-Research

IZP   Internationale Zeitschrift fuer Psychoanalyse (International Journal for Psychoanalysis)

OEB   Orgone Energy Bulletin

OEEB   Orgone Energy Emergency Bulletin

PR   *Psychoanalytic Reader,* by Robert Fliess

SR   Included in *The Sexual Revolution*

WLSR   World League for Sexual Reform

ZAP   Zeitschrift fuer Aerztliche Psychotherapie (Journal for Medical Psychotherapy)

ZPP   Zeitschrift fuer Psychoanalytische Paedagogik (Journal for Psychoanalytic Pedagogy)

ZSW   Zeitschrift fuer Sexualwissenschaft (Journal for Sexology)